Primary Source Collections in the Pacific Northwest

Primary Source Collections in the Pacific Northwest

AN HISTORICAL RESEARCHER'S GUIDE

Nancy A. Bunker

LIBRARIES
UNLIMITED
A Member of the Greenwood Publishing Group

Westport, Connecticut • London

Library of Congress Cataloging-in-Publication Data

Bunker, Nancy A.
   Primary source collections in the Pacific Northwest: an historical researcher's
guide / Nancy A. Bunker.
        p. cm.
   Includes bibliographical references and indexes.
   ISBN 1–59158–127–3 (alk. paper)
   1. Special libraries—Northwest, Pacific—Directories. 2. Library resources—
Northwest, Pacific—Directories. 3. Archival resources—Northwest,
Pacific—Directories. 4. Northwest, Pacific—History,
Local—Sources—Directories. I. Title.
Z732.N95B86 2005
026′.00025′795—dc22   2005019162

British Library Cataloguing in Publication Data is available.

Library of Congress Catalog Card Number: 2005019162
ISBN: 1–59158–127–3

First published in 2005

Libraries Unlimited, 88 Post Road West, Westport, CT 06881
A Member of the Greenwood Publishing Group, Inc.
www.lu.com

Printed in the United States of America

The paper used in this book complies with the
Permanent Paper Standard issued by the National
Information Standards Organization (Z39.48–1984).

10   9   8   7   6   5   4   3   2   1

Contents

Preface

History is a fascinating study of the past. It is the reinterpretation of past events through fresh eyes and hindsight experience. It is also interpreted through the known pieces of information that have survived. But for every known historical information tidbit there are hundreds of thousands that will never be uncovered. True historical research requires the researcher to review original records and accounts, to go back to the source to look for new questions as well as to find answers.

This project was undertaken because of a difficulty in locating historical information, particularly primary source documents, on a specific region of the country. I have been involved in historical research for 20-plus years as a collection curator, a researcher, and a reference librarian.

For seven years I managed a local history collection in Englewood, Colorado (a suburb of Denver). Located in a medium-sized public library, the research materials were constantly overlooked by the research community. The researchers went to Denver Public Library or the Colorado State Historical Society or the University of Colorado, all of which have great research collections. Their research was published using the same tired images that had appeared in numerous other books and articles. They did not use the collection I was managing because they did not know it existed and they didn't have the time or inclination to look further. No matter how much time I spent processing the collection, how much indexing was done to the collection, the collection was under-utilized. The fresh historic images and information that the collection held were not being located and accessed.

After returning to the Pacific Northwest, I became a faculty member in an academic library, where I noticed the access problem from another angle. Faculty members and other researchers approached me with their topics of interest looking for facilities that held the primary source documents, photographs, and maps that they needed to complete their research. These requests included finding the average Norwegian woman's experience in the Pacific Northwest, where religious materials were located, or how to locate letters from Japanese-Americans in the World War II period. Even with all my familiarity with the research collections of the area from doing my own research, those questions were difficult to answer, and I could not provide much more than incomplete assistance. The institutions housing the materials needed were out there, but I had no way of knowing where. The problem of connecting researchers with materials in the small institutions was now obvious from the other direction.

Like many other reference librarians, I was reduced to sending my researchers to the big institutions where I knew that they had a good chance of finding some sources of interest. These big institutional historical research collections, including those at the major universities and state historical societies, are essential but are only a small piece of the historical materials available in the region. The big guys are overrun with researchers trying to find the information. Meanwhile, the general historical community is ignoring many of the small institutions that are doing a wonderful job collecting, processing, and indexing their materials and making their collections available. This is not because of a lack of quality of the primary source materials nor because of the lack of accessibility of the documents, but simply for the lack of knowledge that these collections even exist. This book is designed to remedy some of the problems that both the institutions and the researchers face in locating each other.

This book is designed for the researcher. I have written the book that I, as a historical researcher, would like. I have included the information that I would like before I walk into an institution to spend the day doing research. This book is geared to the individual who is willing to travel to the remote locations to find the information that has not yet been mined in order to recover those pieces of the history that have been buried in the institutions of the Pacific Northwest.

The book is also designed for the reference librarian. I have included the information to assist researchers to find the best historical information for their project, but the book is also intended to aid librarians in identifying the best institutions to steer their researchers toward for locating those needed primary source materials.

This project was spread over a three-year period and took countless hours in research, travel, and writing. I would like to acknowledge the many people at Whitworth College who allowed me to have sabbatical time and far more to do the research and writing of this work. Thanks are owed to the library staff and faculty for putting up with my grumbling and distraction and to my student assistants who did data entry and Web searches. Special heartfelt thanks to Judy Dehle for her limitless help and advice throughout the project. I would also like to thank my wonderful family for their patience and support from beginning to end. To Richard for keeping everything together when I was traveling, to Ray and Megan who waited patiently and visited far more historical museums and libraries than they ever wanted to, and to my parents who read over the drafts; I owe this book.

1

Introduction and Methodology

METHODOLOGY

Selection of Institutions

Locating institutions to include in this project was the first hurdle faced in compiling this book. In the beginning I examined three separate and distinct lists for help in identifying institutions that would qualify for inclusion in this particular project. I used the *American Library Directory* (American Library Association, 2000–2001), *The Official Museum Directory* (American Museum Association, 2000), and *The Directory of Historical Organizations in the United States and Canada* (American Association of State and Local History, 2002) to compile a master list of institutions from Idaho, Oregon, and Washington. Information on selected institutions was added to a database and surveys were sent to the institutions asking specific questions about their holdings in regard to primary source documents. Surveys included questions regarding whether they hold historical research collections and the availability of such collections to researchers. Each institution was also asked where historical documents and photographs from their area could be found outside of their institution. Some institutions not listed in any of the three sources came to light in the responses of their neighboring institutions. The final survey list was 715 institutions from all three states.

I was looking for institutions that had primary source documents and/or photographs on the history of the Pacific Northwest. I excluded from the survey art museums, natural history museums, science museums, zoological parks, and historical sites not having archives on the premises. Privately held collections are also not included. I realize that many of these institutions have archives, but their focus is not primarily the life and history of the three-state region.

Some institutions received multiple surveys sent first by email and then by snail mail. Return of the survey was not conditional on whether the institution was included in this project. The responses to the survey were used in evaluating an individual institution for inclusion in this particular project. The return rate for the survey was 55 percent.

Analysis of individual Web sites provided some additional information on institutions. The Web sites were viewed to help determine what types of collections, as well as the size of collections, an individual institution may have. Lack of a Web site or lack of information on a Web site did not immediately eliminate/disqualify an institution; however, lack of information on a detailed Web site would indicate a low priority of a given institution for promoting and maintaining its historical collections.

Institutions were contacted individually for more information. It became obvious that the three reference sources used were wholly inadequate in identifying institutions. Numerous institutions not only did not appear on any of the three lists but were not listed in any published source. More institutions kept appearing as I compiled my data on neighboring institutions. Some of those institutions were able to be integrated into the project and others were not.

After the fact, I am sure that there will be a number of institutions or communities that will question their absence from this work. There are as many reasons an institution was not included as there are institutions. Some were missed because of lack of information about their existence. Others were not judged to have sufficient unique materials because of my lack of information about them. Some institutions were staffed by individuals unknowledgeable or uncaring of the contents of the collection.

The few institutions that requested not to be included in the publication had varying reasons, but I have no way of knowing whether that was a widespread policy of the institution or the personal preference of the individual involved. Institutions with too small a collection or no regular open hours have not been included. Also not covered are those which habitually did not return phone calls or emails. If the institution would not respond to me as a researcher, I assume that you as a researcher would experience similar difficulty.

Research and Site Visits

Those institutions meeting the requirements of size of holdings and research availability had a personal research visit. Two hundred and seven visits were conducted over a 25-month period. Most visits were conducted during regular scheduled research hours by appointment.

The first institutions visited were mostly in Idaho. Because a large percentage of the institutions holding primary source materials in Idaho are small, the inclusion rate of small institutions is greatest in that state. The state of Washington not only had more institutions than Idaho (or Oregon), but the average size of the institution was much larger. Institutions in the large metropolitan areas needed to have larger research collections to be included than those in the rural areas.

Seattle and King County have more than 100 historical associations, only a quarter of which are covered here. The complete listing is available in chapter 7, "Digital Sources of Pacific Northwest History." All do not have archives of course, but many more do than those included here. There was no way that the project could encompass the scope of all these institutions. Rural collections were judged to be more significant (for inclusion) because of the originality of the materials and the difficulty in finding information about those particular collections. This selection criterion is unfortunate, but unavoidable, for this publication to meet the constraints of deadlines and budget.

Research visits were arranged by areas to minimize travel time and difficulty. Numerous institutions were kind enough to open their doors to me on days or months off in order to accommodate this project. I owe them a debt of gratitude. The Pacific Northwest is an immense geographic region that covers all types of terrain and encompasses 245,288 square miles. The difficulty in scheduling the site visits was based sometimes more on geographical constraints than anything else.

A small number of institutions have been profiled and are included in the book without having a review visit. One institution completed a new building in fall 2004, after being closed for an extended period of time, so a visit could not be scheduled. Several others were federal or municipal archive facilities. Another was not visited because of scheduling conflicts but was an institution where I have researched previous projects. These institutions have profiles that were written from information provided by the institutions and are noted as having not been visited.

Profile Updates

In November 2004, 179 qualifying institutions, with qualifying research collections, were sent copies of their profiles in order to update, clarify, and add to the content before it was sent to the publisher. Most institutions responded promptly with minor updates of phone numbers, contact people, and email addresses. At least five had dropped their post office boxes recently. Several institutions had significantly remodeled their research areas and one had changed its name. Changes big and small were incorporated into the profiles. One hundred sixty institutions returned their profiles and four were dropped from the final list for publication. The remaining institutions may not have returned the profiles because of lack of corrections or changes needed. Last-minute drops included an institution that is currently closed to the public, several that had incomplete information, and one that had been consistently unresponsive during my requests for information.

Institutions that updated their profiles are indicated at the bottom of their description. The entire profile, including the reviews of facilities and collections, was sent to the institutions and many gave feedback on facts and details. Each response was evaluated, but the reviews remain my opinion of the institution. Institutions were not allowed to rewrite their reviews, although several tried. Rankings are based on the facilities and staffing of the institution. Institutions were not sent the ranking. See the next chapter for details on each section of the profiles.

Historical Snapshot

Hopefully, I have written a useful book to bridge the information needs of someone doing primary source research. The book is a beginning and not an end to the quest for primary source document information. The collections descriptions and subject headings given in the profiles are only a starting place. The profile is not meant to be a complete guide to any institution's holdings. The institutions surveyed are constantly in a state of flux. New collections are donated, old collections are processed, and research gems are discovered under the attic eaves. The institutions build new buildings, hire new personnel, and merge with other facilities. Their email addresses change faster than their funding levels.

The finished product is far from perfect and I am aware that some information will be out-of-date long before the book sees the first printing press. That is the nature of published materials. But the book should be a snapshot into the current state of historical primary source collections in Idaho, Oregon, and Washington.

2

⤸

Archival Research

Historical research in primary source document collections and archives is for many people a new and very different experience. If you have been successfully researching in archives for years, this chapter may only be a review. If you are new to archival research this chapter can start you on a successful and profitable research quest in the dusty documents of previous generations.

ARCHIVES ARE NOT LIBRARIES

From childhood most of us are brought up with the idea of libraries, where we are not only allowed, but encouraged, to check out the materials, and for free. It might be a school library, a public library, or even the academic library, but users are encouraged to remove the materials from the library, peruse them at their leisure, and after a specified amount of time return them. Interlibrary loan and universal borrowing systems allow users to borrow books from other libraries in the area or even from across the country. This system of free exchange of information is one of the main problems that archives face. Some users simply do not understand that there is, or should be, a difference with archival or special collection material.

The fundamental difference between libraries and archives is the purpose for their existence; the library to make information available, and the archives to preserve the information for future generations.

Materials are Different

Libraries collect published materials from a variety of sources and a wider variety of topics. Most are secondary sources that can be obtained from multiple libraries and other institutions. Archives may hold books and other published materials but they tend to be hard to locate materials on very narrow subjects that pertain to the remainder of the collecting areas. The bulk of an archival collection is primary source documents and materials. Those one-of-a-kind pieces of the past are the mainstay of the archive. Because of the uniqueness of the material, extra care is taken to ensure that not only the information contained on the document is maintained but also the document itself.

Preservation is Paramount

In an archival setting, preservation of the materials is more important than their use. Therefore, use of materials may be severely restricted and monitored. Most institutions maintain strict protocols to protect the materials from damage or loss. Although some of the institutions profiled in this book have more stratified use policies than others, all have the same goal: to preserve the photographs, documents, and other materials in their care. Rules of who can use the materials, how, where, and for how long they may be used should be an expected part of all archival research.

LOCATING PRIMARY SOURCE DOCUMENTS

Finding out who has the types of materials needed can be one of the most challenging parts of any research project. Since you are reading this book, some of the preliminary research has been done for you. The subject indexes can help you find which institutions may have materials of your interest and the profiles can give you more information about the size, type, and layout of the facility, but these are still only the beginning steps in your preparation.

Narrowing down which institutions have the information you need goes much further than this book can possibly answer. An institution may be listed as having items on the history of Japanese Americans, but there is no way of determining whether they are nineteenth-century letters or World War II photographs. Contact with the institution will help you determine if the subject you are researching is available in sufficient quantity or quality to necessitate a visit.

Planning is Essential

Unlike most libraries with scheduled open hours and flexibility to access materials, most archives require a planned visit. Make an appointment. Many of the institutions allow access to the collection by appointment only while others have scheduled opened hours and technically will take walk-ins. The most successful research trip will be the one with prior arrangements made. Walk-in visits make the researcher vulnerable to long waits, lack of table space on which to work, and the possibility of materials not being available for viewing. If you are unsure of whether a particular collection will have what you need, ask.

When making your appointment, describe the nature of your research; the more specific you can be, the more successfully the archivist (or volunteer) can locate the best sources for you to examine. This is often harder than it would appear. Without knowing what an institution has to offer, it can be hard to know what you hope to find. A starting place and a well-thought-out research topic will make both your task, and the job of the staff member or volunteer assisting you, easier. Reviewing the existing secondary source material on your topic beforehand will familiarize you on the pertinent dates, names, and locations that may appear in the documents you study. Without prior knowledge of the topic, it is easy to overlook possible important historical information. As you are looking through the materials, you may find other questions appear, and new directions for your research to take.

Research Is Not Free

This book has attempted to record which institutions require fees when doing research at the facility. The fees schedules are all subject to change. Many institutions do not charge researchers, but that does not mean that research is free. All research has a cost to someone. Maintaining a research facility, whether large or small, is costly in supplies, staffing, and physical overhead. It is becoming more common to pass on some of the costs to the researchers. Staff assistance may have fees associated with it, even if the staff is a volunteer one. Often they will allow half an hour of staff time per researcher before additional fees are charged. The more time you demand from the staff the more it will cost. Being prepared and self-sufficient will eliminate many of the time demands your research will place on the staff. In many institutions the fee schedules are at the discretion of the staff. Reasonable, friendly, and appreciative people get charged less (and receive better service) than demanding, obnoxious ones.

Doing research remotely will have a greater cost. Remote research may be by telephone, fax, snail mail, or email. You are asking that the staff spend time looking through the collection for you, so expect to pay for the privilege. Send a self-addressed stamped envelope on all mail inquiries, or a mailing label and stamp. Acknowledge that you understand they are doing you a favor. Indicate a willingness to pay not only the photocopy costs but research costs as well. An experienced researcher (or one who appears to be) will usually get better assistance.

THE RESEARCH VISIT

When visiting the archives remember to use common courtesies. Call if you will be delayed or need to cancel. And remember that emergencies happen at their end as well. When making your appointment leave a way for them to contact you, if necessary, by cell phone or by leaving a message at the hotel where you are staying. Pipes break, people become ill, cars break down. Every reason you can think of that may delay or cancel your visit can happen from the other end as well. Larger institutions may have staffing adequate to handle individual absences, but many smaller institutions may have only one or two individuals who are knowledgeable about the collection.

Most good facilities will require that you register as a user. This is a security issue as well as a statistical one. Many will ask that you provide picture identification, so make sure you have it with you. If you have made an appointment, some of your personal information may already be available to them, but you may need to fill out a card or form upon entering. Some institutions will hold the registration for a period of time (often a year), making second visits easier.

Be prepared to abide by the rules of the institution. Many facilities require that you not take personal items into the research room. Some provide secure storage for personal items left outside and others do not. If you don't want a staff member putting your briefcase or purse behind their desk, leave it in the car. The same is true for your laptop case. Carry only your identification, some cash for fees or copies, notepaper, and several pencils into the room. A less encumbered visit allows you to concentrate on your research and not on the security of your personal belongings. If you have a cell phone, mute it or leave it outside—there is nothing more annoying than listening to someone else talk on the phone while you are trying to concentrate.

Pencils only are the rule at many institutions and those who don't have this rule should. Sometimes pencils are limited to only number two pencils. Laptops are being allowed in most facilities, but many do not have electrical outlets available in a convenient place. Notepaper is usually allowed for your note- taking, but notebooks and binders are not. The staff needs to see what you bring into the room and what you take out. Your research visit will go smoother if you respect basic archival research principles.

Using the Materials

After you have checked in to use the facility, you will need to speak to a staff member about your research needs. In the library world this is called the reference interview, and it helps the researcher and the staff member to understand the needs and possibilities of research. Since you contacted the institution in advance of your visit, identified possible areas to start, and have an appointment, this stage should be fairly painless. They may have already pulled the materials for your use.

In most institutions the materials will be brought to you. You may not browse the collection. In some smaller institutions the materials may be stored in the research room, but that does not give you permission to open any boxes not specified by the staff. Books are often available for browsing, but many file cabinets are not. If you don't know what you can look at, ask. Inquire in a way that will indicate which of the materials in general are browse able and which are not so you don't have to ask each time you see another item you wish to view.

Materials should be viewed in small quantities. Many institutions will only allow a limited number of items on a research table at one time. This minimizes the chance of materials being refiled in the wrong box or folder. Even if multiple boxes are brought out, only one should be opened and used at a time.

Historical documents are fragile or eventually will be. Every care needs to be undertaken to ensure that the materials are left in as good a condition as they were found. This may mean not leaning on items, stacking them too high, rearranging the order, or setting your notes on top of the items when you are writing. Cotton gloves may need to be worn when handling certain materials. If gloves are required, the institution will provide them.

Note-taking is a lost art but still the best option when dealing with primary source documents and materials. Plan on taking notes during your research visit and plan on using pencil. Most institutions will not allow pens of any type to be used while using historical materials. The chance of stray marks on the documents is too great. If you think it won't happen, you haven't done much research with documents in hand. Stray pencil marks can be carefully erased (by a staff member).

Adhesive material on things such as "sticky notes" can also damage materials by leaving residue that will later attract dirt and permanently damage the materials. If you need to mark your place in the documents you are reviewing ask for some scraps of paper to slip between the pages, and remove them when you are done.

Reproduction of Materials

Light damages paper. It is an unfortunate fact but one that is faced by preservationists everywhere. Because of this, photocopying of materials may be strictly curtailed if not totally forbidden at many institutions. Sometimes, only the staff is allowed to photocopy materials, and service is not on demand. You may not be able to walk out the door with your photocopies but instead may have to wait until you return home and they are mailed to you, after you have paid for the copies and the postage.

Scanners also use light and damage paper. I have heard people say, if I can't photocopy it I will just scan it. No, no, and no. Scanners are every bit as damaging to the paper materials as are photocopies. Even the newer lower density light scanners can harm the materials. Many institutions prohibit the use of hand-held scanners. Some research reports that the scanning and photocopying of photographs actually degrades the original image on a permanent basis. Preservation of the images and documents is paramount to the institutions' function, so a researcher needs to be cognizant of the problems of asking for photocopies of materials.

To obtain photographic reproductions there are more options than ever before. However, there is a limit on what is and is not possible for photographic reproductions. You are asking for a service and will be expected to pay, with very little control over it. Photographs can not be checked out and taken to the nearest copy shop to get the best price. Even if they are being sent to the photographer next door, it will be handled by a staff member. And you will need to wait.

If you are paying to have a traditional photographic copy made (emulsion process), you may need to pay for the cost of having a negative made, as well as the cost of the print. The negatives that you purchased will remain the property of the institution and you will just have the print. Photos will need to be picked up sometimes weeks later or you will need to pay for shipping in addition to the cost of the photographic prints.

More and more institutions are relying on digital prints to provide photographs to their researchers. Some small-town institutions do not have photographic processing labs nearby and so they cannot easily get photographs printed in a traditional form. Reliance on digital prints is problematic. Digital prints are only as good as the ink and paper used. Although a digital print may look as good as or even better than the original, the longevity of the image is in question. For short-term projects the savings of obtaining a digital print over a photographic print may be advisable. But for long-term storage of images, the old photographic processes are still preferred. If you want the image to be viewed by your great- grandchildren, many forms of digital prints may not be a viable option.

Some institutions will allow you to have a digital copy of the photograph either through email or on CD. Having the image in electronic form does not allow you any more rights to the image than a print does. Use of any photographic image requires that you credit the institution from which it originated. (ask the institution for their preferred wording for the source credit statement). If the image is to be used in any publication, presentation, film, or in any other public manner, user fees will be owed the institution. The fees are usually dependent upon the type of use, number of copies, and for what purpose the images are used. Even the smallest institution is entitled to decide their fees for using their images. Be prepared to pay for the rights.

Citing Materials

It is important that you record what materials you used, and at what institution. This is essential if you are publishing the research, but just as important if you are not. Notes that don't specify where or when the materials were viewed will be useless later if you can't verify the source. Include the name of the institution; the collection, box, or file numbers; and a description of the items. If you are unable to finish with a collection, note what was searched and at what point you left off. Relying on memory is not usually a good idea for most people. Finding specific pieces of information again in a large collection can seem an impossible task.

For a project that will be published, a writing style manual will need to be consulted to determine how to cite the primary source materials. *The Chicago Manual of Style* (University of Chicago Press), now in its 15th edition, presents the source documentation formats most often used in the historical community. This manual provides more detail on citing primary source documents by type than any of the other common style manuals available. Citation details may be located on the internet for basic material formats such as books or newspapers, but they often do not cover such things as unpublished diaries or photographs. If you have a short-term need for the manual check it out from your local library. Becoming familiar with the citation needs for various types of documents beforehand will ensure that the necessary information is recorded during the research process.

NOTES OF ADVICE AND CAUTION

Even if you have carefully researched which institution to visit, made an appointment, and viewed the materials you have identified, you are not guaranteed a successful search for the information you seek.

Plan to Be Surprised

When you are researching in a primary source document collection, you can plan on a certain amount of surprise. Items that you had no idea existed will surface in the most unusual places. Unique and interesting items can sidetrack you from your goals. Make a note of them and go back if you have time or make another visit to view them. Research gems uncovered in small institutions may have remained buried forever in a large collection.

Plan to Be Frustrated

Research into primary source documents seldom goes as smoothly as we imagine it will. Finding the materials that are needed, at the time they are needed, can be difficult. Knowing what a collection has, and what information it will reveal, is impossible from surface research. Even governmental and organizational archives that are required to keep certain types of documents may find that the one issue you are looking for is missing.

Most primary source collections are dependent upon donation of materials. Donors can give as much or as little as they want of the business records and family papers. Families may want Grandpa be seen in a favorable light, so the documents regarding his bankruptcy hearing are missing from the "complete" collection of his papers. Donors (and even archivists) weed out important historical materials because they cannot comprehend why anyone would be interested in the information. A new research plan may have to develop, if the materials being sought do not exist.

Plan to Be Flexible

Successful research into primary source documents can be a fascinating experience but it is a process. Research takes time and a great deal of patience. The fast-food generation sometimes cannot slow down long enough to do thorough, detailed historical research. Take the time to do it right. The documents were not created in a day, so cannot be absorbed and analyzed in an hour. Allow time for sidetracks, interesting conversations, and unexpected discoveries. Allow time to absorb as well as analyze.

Historical research can also be a great deal of fun. Planning well, being responsible, being thorough, and being flexible will allow for a successful and enjoyable research experience.

3

Profile Explanations

PROFILES OF INSTITUTIONS

Institutions are arranged by state and alphabetically by city name. List of institutions by name and by county are available among the indexes in the back of this book. Some institutions will not have information in all categories. All institutions have a photocopy machine on the premises. If institutions have multiple special collections, the ones on Pacific Northwest history are the ones described.

PROFILES: GENERAL INFORMATION AND FACILITIES

Name: Institution name

County: County where institution is located

Mailing Address: Mailing address, including city, state, and zip codes

Street Address: Street address or physical location (may be the same as the mailing address)

Institution Email: Institutional or general address email

Telephone and Fax Number: Contact numbers for the archive

Contact Name: Name of individual who is contact person for the archive

Contact Email: Contact person's email address

Institution Type: Primary function of the institution where the archive is located including: Academic Library; Public Library; Archives; Historical Society; Local Museum; Regional Museum; or Historical Site. Historical Societies are listed as such if the research facility is physically separate from the museum. Most but not all historical societies also have a museum.

Affiliation: Organization institution is associated with may be government or funding agency.

Web site URL: Web site of the institution or may link directly to archives

Hours: Hours the research collection is available, which may be different from rest of institution

Staff in Archives: Number of full-time employees, part-time employees, and volunteers working directly with the archival materials (for example, 1f, 1p, 5v = 1 full-time paid, 1 part-time paid, 5 volunteers)

Archives Are Handicapped Accessible: If shown as "yes," it is reasonable to assume that a wheelchair can easily enter the research room. This does not speak to table height, doors that may require assistance, or restrooms.

Access Description: Description of the possible barriers found at an institution and advice to circumvent barriers to access

Cost for Researcher—In-house: Fees charged by the archives for a researcher viewing materials in the research room of the institution. Some museums require museum admission be paid and others do not. Some have flat fees. Some facilities have fees for staff assistance only.

Cost for Researcher—Remote: Institutional charges for queries or research done for individuals through telephone, fax, email, or mail requests. On most profiles it is listed as Fee Schedule, since costs may vary by type of assistance and length of time spent. Average charge is $10 to $30 per hour, often with the first half hour free.

List of Researchers Available: If "yes," the archives maintain a list of people available to do research locally for out-of-area historians. Fees are negotiated with the local researcher.

Review of Facilities: Descriptive and subjective review of the physical layout of the facilities, including where the archive is located and what a researcher can expect to find in the research room/library. May include description of storage facilities of collections in the research room or describe storage facilities that are separate and removed from the public research area.

PROFILES: COLLECTIONS

Vertical Files: Vertical file materials are miscellaneous materials usually in file folders with a subject arrangement, although some may be filed by accession number. They may include clippings, ephemera, originals or copies of documents, and assorted paper materials. Some collections have researcher open access while others require staff-mediated access.

Vertical Files in Cubic Feet: The volume of materials in these types of collections estimated in cubic feet

Vertical File Description and Subjects: Listing or description of the types of materials included in the Vertical file collections

Manuscripts: Manuscript materials may include papers, records, scrapbooks, ledgers, letters, and other materials produced by individuals or groups in the course of their life, activities, or business.

Manuscripts Volume in Cubic Feet: The volume of the manuscript collections is estimated in cubic feet. Some institutions' numbers may be in linear feet, but the figure translates fairly equitably. Many institutions had little idea of the size of their manuscript materials.

Manuscript Types: The kind of records held in the collection. Includes:

Archives—Official records of the organization housing the records such as the university or government agency or records of the museum itself

Business records—Papers, records, and ephemera of business and manufacturing concerns of all types

Family papers—Significant groupings of papers of multiple members of a family or about the family in general

Government records—Can be county, city, or special districts such as fire or water; these records were originally produced by a governmental entity.

Land records—Includes property and land records, abstracts of title, and related records

Legal records—May include probate records, courts records, wills, or vital records

Organizational records—Papers, records, and ephemera of clubs, civic, fraternal, social, religious, or business groups

Personal papers—Papers or writings of individuals in the community may include significant documents from all areas of the person's life, such as the organizations, business, or other areas in which they were involved.

School records—Documents dealing with the K–12 schools in the area. Documents may pertain to one school or many and may include business records of the school or written history materials.

Diaries, ledgers, and scrapbooks—These are often listed separately, although many records of this type are included in personal papers, organizational records, or business records as well. In these cases, this format may be the only records of the type and not part of larger varied-format collections.

All manuscript types—Large institutions with multiple collection types will be listed with this designation since they probably include most if not all types in their holdings.

Manuscript Subjects: Description of the materials in the manuscript collections. Some institutions provided detailed summaries of collections, others are more general.

Photographs: Photographic images in the collection may include prints, negatives, slides, daguerreotypes, tintypes, postcards, stereopticon slides, glass-plate negatives, panoramic photographs, and other formats.

Number of Photographs: The number of images in the photographic collection including all types listed above. Some institutions only list those parts of the collection that are accessible to researchers.

Storage of Photographs: General description of how the photos are stored: file cabinets, document boxes, or digitally. Also notes the availability of photos in a browsing collection—that is, whether the collection offers photocopies, a computer database, copy-photos, or other formats.

Photograph Subjects: Description of the subject areas that are the main focus of the collection. Most collections have general subjects as well as some of the specialized ones listed.

Photo Reproductions Are Available: Indicates if it is possible to order reproductions of images: Photographic Prints (emulsion based photographic prints) Digital Prints, or Digital images on CD. Costs of reproductions were not tracked, as each institution has fee schedules, which vary by type and size of reproduction ordered.

Books: Published and semipublished materials usually on limited subject areas that are housed in the archive/research collections

Number of Books in Collection: Books listed are only those volumes that are in the archive/research room collection. Public and Academic Library holdings list only the books that are considered part of the special research collection. Other institutions will list those books held for use by researchers.

Description of Books: General subjects such as local history, regional history, annuals, telephone books, and city directories are listed. Special subjects of interest are also noted. "Professional collection" relates to books of interest to curators or librarians on maintaining the museum or library, pricing guides of historical objects, identification guides and preservation manuals. "Old books" is a category that refers to non-subject-related books of indeterminate value often held to be used in museum exhibits.

Newspapers: General circulation–type newspapers from a city, county, or community; this does not include newsletters or other publications of organizations or businesses.

Newspapers in Paper Format: Institution has holdings in loose or bound paper copies of original newspapers.

Papers and Dates: Profile may list individual titles or ranges of years for multiple local titles.

Newspapers on Microfilm: Institution has holdings of microfilmed local and regional newspapers. Unless stated, the institution has a microfilm reader/printer available on premises.

Microfilm and Dates: Profile may list individual titles or ranges of years for multiple local titles

Oral Histories: Oral history interviews usually done of local area residents on audio tape or video recording.

Oral Histories Number: The number of interviews held at an institution

Oral Histories Description: The description will list specific subjects of the interviews if known, the dates the interviews were done, and the format in which they are stored. Formats may include audiocassette (most common), videocassette, reel-to-reel tapes, or paper transcriptions. If transcriptions are available of recorded interviews, it should be listed as well. Older or even newer interviews may be illegible because of deterioration of the magnetic media and paper transcriptions may be the only remnants of the interview. Some institutions were unclear on numbers and whether they had transcriptions of the recordings in their collections.

Maps and Drawings: General category including all types of maps, architectural drawings, large-scale aerial photographs.

Estimated Number of Maps and Drawings: Estimated number of maps, drawings, and other items in this category

Description of Maps and Drawings: Description of maps and drawings in collection, including years, if provided. Lists some commercially produced atlases or map sets (such as Sanborn, Metskers, or Kroll) if appropriate.

Genealogy Sources: indicates presence of genealogy materials

Genealogy Sources Description: Items that are of particular interest to genealogists, including family histories, biography files, birth records, death records, marriage records, cemetery records, or other vital records either original or compiled.

Special Collections: The presence of special collections that may be of particular interest to the researcher is noted here. These collections may fall into any of the above listed areas of manuscript, photographs, books, maps, or genealogy.

Special Collections Description: A description of the special collection is provided.

Indexes: Indexes cover a wide range of types. Common indexes are on 3 × 5 cards or the newer computer databases that replace them. Some institutions have multiple card files that cover an individual format of materials. Others have large general subject indexes that index multiple material formats. Indexes may also include lists of materials or computer printouts of databases.

Manuscript Finding Aids: Manuscript finding aids come in a variety of formats. Institutions with finding aids to their manuscript collections may have them on a computer system, in binders, in file cabinets, or listed on the internet. The finding aids may be at the collection level, the box level, or a folder level. Seldom do institutions have the resources to process a manuscript collection to the item level. Finding aids are a basic resource and vary greatly with the institution.

Online Sources: The online sources are those which are available free through the internet.

Published Guides: Directories, guides, finding aid listings, and other descriptions of the collection which have been published for researchers to use are described in this category.

Review of Collections: The holdings and collections of an institution are reviewed here. Important details and interesting highlights of the collections are noted.

OTHER INFORMATION

Museum on Premises: Indicates whether there is a museum at the same location as the archives. Many institutions have museums in adjacent or nearby buildings, and others are miles away. This will only list those with museums in the same or directly adjacent buildings.

Museum Hours: Hours that the museum is open. These usually differ from the hours of the archives/research rooms listed earlier in the profile.

Cost of Entry to Museum: Museum admission fees, if known

Museum is Handicapped Accessible: If the museum is handicapped accessible, it will be listed. This may differ from the accessibility of the archives/research room.

Description of Museum: A brief description is given on some of the museums. Many were not visited by the reviewer and most are not reviews but general impressions.

Parking: Parking availability and list of possible places to park. If a fee for parking is required, it is noted. Fees and parking are subject to change in municipal areas and university campuses; it would be advisable to check with the institution beforehand for current information.

Lunch: Description of possible lunch venues nearby. Local restaurants refer to non-chain restaurants that may range from top to lesser quality. Tourist restaurants refer to the clientele that the facility is trying to reach and may be listed as upscale. Ethnic restaurants include a variety of specialized cuisines, often Chinese or Mexican but also from all parts of the globe. Restaurants may change faster than anything else in the book besides email addresses. These are suggestions only as restaurants were not reviewed.

Lodging: Lodging options are given with Web sites of local tourist centers or chambers of commerce. Because of the variety of levels of lodging, no attempt was made to classify or rate the individual properties. Other possible places to look include AAA or the state sites listed in the Travel Sources section (chapter 8).

Nearest Commercial Airport: Airport name (City where airport located) (Airport Code) [distance to airport from institution]. Note: these only include airports that have commercial flights available. Most towns have airstrips that will accept private or charter flights; for details look the "Air Travel" section of chapter 8, Travel Sources.

Date of Reviewer's Visit: Date the institution was visited by the reviewer

Profile Updated by Institution: The date the institution updated its profile

GUIDE TO RANKINGS OF INSTITUTIONS

✹✹✹✹✹   Five-star research collections are maintained to the highest archival standards by a professionally trained or certified archivist. There is a research room dedicated to the collection. Finding aids and indexing are available for most manuscript collections. Indexing is available for other parts of the collection. Regularly scheduled hours are available to researchers.

✸✸✸✸ Four-star research collections are maintained by a librarian (that is, a person holding a master's degree in library science), a museum curator, or a professional trained in archival work. Finding aids and indexing are available for most parts of the collection. Four-star institutions have a dedicated research area, the chief function of which is the research of archival and primary source collections.

✸✸✸ In three-star institutions, the research collection is maintained by a paid employee or highly skilled volunteer. Care has been given to maintain and classify the collection in an archival manner. A separate room or area is devoted to the research collections but may be utilized by other parts of the institution.

✸✸ A two-star collection is maintained by either a curator or by an employee for whom this task is a minor part of the job, or by volunteers. A separate research area may be maintained but usually shares space with other institutional functions.

✸ A one-star collection is maintained by volunteers who are trying really hard. An attempt is being made to organize and classify the collection. Money and/or institutional support are limited in the processing and maintenance of this collection.

No Stars: Little or no institutional support is given to maintain this collection. It may be unorganized or improperly cared for. Institutions with no stars have not been included in this resource.

4

Idaho Profiles

Population (2003 estimate): 1,366,332
Land area: 82,747 square miles
Persons per square mile (2000 estimate): 15.6

BOISE

Name: Basque Museum and Cultural Center, Inc.   **County:** Ada

Mailing Address: 611 Grove St.

City: Boise   **State:** ID   **Postal Code:** 83702-0000

Street Address: 611 Grove St.

Institution Email: bmccinfo@basquemuseum.com

Telephone Number: (208) 343-6959   **Fax Number:** (208) 336-4801

Contact Name: Jeffrey Johns   **Contact Email:** basq_curator@hotmail.com

Institution Type: Regional Museum

Web site URL: http://www.basquemuseum.org

Hours: Tu–F 10–4, Sa 11–3

Staff in Archives: 1f 1p 7v

Archives Are Handicapped Accessible: Yes

Review of Facilities: The Basque Museum and Cultural Center is located in the refurbished area known as "Old Boise." The museum shares the block with sidewalk cafes and upscale shops. The building is a single-story contemporary storefront. The research rooms are in the staff quarters of the museum. The library collection is housed in a room devoted to bookshelves. Books are in English, Spanish, and French as well as in Basque. Manuscript materials are housed in a set of storage rooms near the back of the building. Researchers will be put to work at tables or desks in the staff area between these two collections. A dedicated research area would be a plus to this institution.

Vertical Files: Yes   **Vertical Files in Cubic Feet:** 40

Vertical File Description and Subjects: Whaling, fishing, sheepherding, boardinghouses, immigration, nationalism, blood type studies. Some of the collection is digitized in a database.

Manuscripts: Yes   **Manuscripts Volume in Cubic Feet:** 50

Manuscript Types: Scrapbooks, family papers

Manuscript Subjects: The Juanita Uberuaga Hormaechea Collection of 101 scrapbooks on the life and history of the Basques of Boise collected by one woman. Also extensive collection of the Cyrus Jacobs family (a non-Basque family whose home later became a Basque boardinghouse), including personal, legal, and business documents as well as photographs and artifacts.

Photographs: Yes   **Number of Photographs:** 10,000

Photograph Subjects: Basque life in Boise and Southern Idaho

Photograph Reproductions Are Available: Yes

Photographic Prints: Yes   **Digital Prints:** Yes

Books: Yes   **Number of Books in Collection:** 5,000

Description of Books: Extensive collection of Basque books. Large collection of books in Basque, French, Spanish, and English.

Newspapers: No

Oral Histories: Yes   **Oral Histories Number:** 400

Oral Histories Description: The Oroitzapenak Basque Oral History Project consists of a variety of oral history interviews on the Basque-American experience taken from individuals in Idaho, Oregon, California, and Nevada.

Maps and Drawings: Yes   **Estimated Number of Maps and Drawings:** 200

Description of Maps and Drawings: BLM and Forest Service, sheep grazing maps, Basque area of settlement

Genealogy Sources: Yes

Genealogy Sources Description: Marriage and death certificates, extensive obituary resources

Special Collections: Yes

Special Collections Description: Music archive of Basque folk, choral and instrumental music.

Indexes: No

Review of Collections: The cornerstone of the collections at the Basque Museum is the extensive oral history interviews. Four hundred interviews of individuals of Basque descent were collected from various oral history projects from Idaho, Oregon, California, and Nevada. These have been gathered together at the Basque Museum and Cultural Center in Boise and the Basque Studies Library at the University of Nevada, Reno. The interviews are being transferred to the Web site, where an index by name is available. Another notable collection is the Juanita Uberuaga Hormaechea Collection of scrapbooks, which chronicle the life and activities of the Basques in Boise in the twentieth century; this collection is not cataloged and is in a fragile state. There is also a music archives of Basque folk, choral, and instrumental music on records and tapes; unfortunately, the collection is not cataloged and not very accessible. The Basque Museum collection is strong in social history of the Basque people of the American West.

Museum on Premises: Yes

Museum Hours: Tu–F 10–4, Sa 11–3

Museum Is Handicapped Accessible: Yes

Description of Museum: Moderate-sized museum focusing on the life and history of the Basques in the west

Parking: Free on-street parallel parking and pay lots nearby

Lunch: Variety of sidewalk cafes in the same block

Lodging: http://www.boise.org

Nearest Commercial Airport: Boise Air Terminal/Gowen Field (BOI) [5 miles]

Subjects

Historical Periods: 1865–1900; 1900–1940; 1940–present

Eras: Spanish American War; World War I

Natural Resources: Dams; Fishing; Whaling; Logging

Mining: Gold; Silver; Copper

Transportation: Railroads

Agriculture: Ranching/Livestock; Orchards; Dry Land Farming

Business: Retail

Manufacturing: Sawmills

Organizations: Schools; Nonreligious Organizations; Civic and Fraternal; Women's

Ethnic Groups: Basque; French; Spanish

Religious Sites and Organizations: Catholic

Date of Reviewer's Visit: 10/17/2003

Profile Updated by Institution: 11/8/2004

Name: Boise State University Albertsons Library   **County:** Ada

Mailing Address: 1910 University Dr.

  City: Boise   **State:** ID   **Postal Code:** 83725-1430

Street Address: 1865 Campus Lane

Institution Email: none

Telephone Number: (208) 426-4321   **Fax Number:** (208) 426-1885

Contact Name: Alan Virta   **Contact Email:** avirta@boisestate.edu

Institution Type: Academic Library

Web site URL: http://library.boisestate.edu/special

Hours: M–F 8–5; appt. recommended

Staff in Archives: 3f

Archives Are Handicapped Accessible: Yes

Access Description: Building is ADA compliant

Cost for Researcher—Remote: Photocopying $5 plus copies; research limited to one hour

Review of Facilities: The archives and special collections at Boise State University are housed in well-planned quarters on the second floor of the Albertsons Library. The reading room has four large worktables that are well lit. The tables, each with a chair, are the only objects that occupy the room. It is functional, if a bit stark. Pencils and writing paper is all that can be taken into the reading room. The facility offers shelves on which to place belongings, but no secure storage for personal items. The book and manuscript storage areas are staff use only and are beautifully kept. Special collection books are in one room while the remainder of the collections is housed in an adjacent climate-controlled storage space. At the present, they have adequate space and do not have to rely on a secondary storage area. This makes the collection easy for the staff to access. Check the Web site and their online catalog before you go, as they don't have public access computers in the research room.

Vertical Files: No

Manuscripts: Yes   **Manuscripts Volume in Cubic Feet:** 5,500

  Manuscript Types: All manuscript types

  Manuscript Subjects: 20th-century political, environmental, and literary history of Idaho. Boise State University Archives. There are more than 100 separate manuscript collections ranging from 1/4 cu. ft. to over 100 cu. ft.

Photographs: Yes   **Number of Photographs:** 1,000,000

Storage of Photographs: Photographs are stored within the manuscript collections in file folders in boxes

Photograph Subjects: Negative collection from the *Idaho Statesman* newspaper from 1950s onward.

Photograph Reproductions Are Available: Yes

> **Photographic Prints:** Yes   **Digital Prints:** Yes

Books: Yes   **Number of Books in Collection:** 100,000

Description of Books: Idaho history and related topics

Newspapers: No

Papers and Dates: Newspapers are housed in periodicals department of the library

Oral Histories: Yes   **Oral Histories Number:** 50

> **Oral Histories Description:** Most are interviews done for the university's 50th anniversary and deal primarily with its history. Some of these have transcripts. There are a few assorted interviews done by students for other research projects.

Maps and Drawings: No

Genealogy Sources: No

Special Collections: Yes

> **Special Collections Description:** U.S. Senator Frank Church's papers; Governor Cecil D. Andrus's papers; archives of the Episcopal Diocese of Idaho

Indexes: Yes

> **Manuscript Finding Aids:** Most of the manuscript collections have inventories or finding aids, though few list at the folder level

> **Published Guides:** There are a few published finding aids to the largest collections.

> **Online Sources:** There are some finding aids online at the Web site. Most of the collections are listed in the library's online catalog.

Review of Collections: The special collections and archives at the Boise State University are professionally housed. The major areas of the collection are public affairs, religious affairs, organizations and businesses, regional interest, Boise State University, and the Idaho Writers Archive. Public policy on the environment, particularly as this deals with the state of Idaho, is well represented. Much of the collection is of national interest. The majority of the collection deals with twentieth-century topics. Although there are some nineteenth-century materials, Boise State is not attempting to collect pioneer or early settlement history. Their Web site lists their major collections and provides finding aids to some of them.

Museum on Premises: No

Parking: Attended pay lot is adjacent to the administration building off University Dr. $10 per day max. 1/2-hr. and 1-hr. meters in lot adjacent to library.

Lunch: The Student Union building has both a cafeteria and a food court. Numerous restaurants are on the perimeter of the campus but are either a sizable walking or driving distance.

Lodging: http://www.boise.org

Nearest Commercial Airport: Boise Air Terminal/Gowen Field (BOI) [5 miles]

Subjects

>   **Historical Periods:** 1865–1900; 1900–1940; 1940–present
>
>   **Eras:** Vietnam War
>
>   **Natural Resources:** Water; Irrigation; Fishing; Hunting; Logging
>
>   **Government:** State; Federal
>
>   **Organizations:** Nonreligious Organizations; Women's
>
>   **Ethnic Groups:** Native American; Latin American; Japanese
>
>   **Religious Sites and Organizations:** Protestant

Date of Reviewer's Visit: 10/16/2003

Profile Updated by Institution: 11/8/2004

✲✲✲

Name: Idaho Military Historical Society/Museum　　　　**County:** Ada

Mailing Address: 4040 W. Guard St

　　City: Boise　　　　　　**State:** ID　　　　　　**Postal Code:** 83705-0000

Street Address: 4748 Lindbergh St. Bldg 924, Gowen Field

Institution Email: None

Telephone Number: (208) 422-4841　　　**Fax Number:** (208) 422-4837

Contact Name: Gary Keith　　**Contact Email:** Gary.Keith@id.ngb.army.mil

Institution Type: Regional Museum

Web site URL: http://inghro.state.id.us/museum/

Hours: Tu–Su 12–4, and by special appt.

Staff in Archives: 1f, 30v

Archives Are Handicapped Accessible: No

Access Description: Archives located upstairs with low ceiling beams. Library is accessible on main floor and accommodation could be made to bring archival materials downstairs for research use.

Review of Facilities: The Idaho Military Historical Museum is located on the edge of Gowen Field. Entrance is outside of base, so visitors do not have to pass through secured area to access museum. The library is located on the main floor of the museum, where the books and periodicals are housed. The archival materials are housed on the second floor, which is accessed by a staircase. The upper floor has low-hanging beams to dodge. The main archival storage room on the second floor has a small worktable. The documents and files are housed in cabinets and boxes in this room. There are additional files stored in a room across the hall. The room is set up as an archival staff work area, but researchers can use the materials at this location.

Vertical Files: Yes   **Vertical Files in Cubic Feet:** 6

Vertical File Description and Subjects: Miscellaneous and military unit histories

Manuscripts: Yes   **Manuscripts Volume in Cubic Feet:** 20

Manuscript Types: Personal papers, military records, scrapbooks, ledgers, ephemera

Manuscript Subjects: Idaho National Guard or Adjutant General of State of Idaho records; muster rolls from the Spanish American War; pay records 1903–1917 (incomplete), Selective Service records for Idaho in World War II, cemetery records; enlistment and service records for World War I and World War II (various types)

Photographs: Yes   **Number of Photographs:** 10,000

Storage of Photographs: Photos are stored in file folders, slides are stored in plastic sleeves in binders arranged by date

Photograph Subjects: Aerial photos of Gowen Field, National Guard, armed services

Photograph Reproductions Are Available: Yes

Photographic Prints: Yes   **Digital Prints:** Yes

Books: Yes   **Number of Books in Collection:** 2,500

Description of Books: Tech manuals from World War I onward, all services, nonfiction books of various wars, biographies, reference books

Newspapers: No

Oral Histories: No

Maps and Drawings: No

Genealogy Sources: No

Special Collections: Yes

Special Collections Description: Extensive collection of medals, insignia, and patches from all services

Indexes: Staff has subject access to accession records in paper files.

Manuscript Finding Aids: Some of the drawers have finding lists.

Review of Collections: The Idaho Military Museum offers an interesting collection of historical military records, photographs, maps, and ephemera. The focus of the collection is the state of Idaho, but all military services and national guard units are represented. The materials are primarily from the Spanish American War and later. A large portion of the collection deals with Gowen Field and its history. Some of the military records are on loan and others are owned by the museum. They also collect histories, in both published and unpublished forms, of military units that had Idaho residents. Although the collection illustrates Idaho military experiences, it is also an important collection to consider for someone researching other aspects of twentieth-century military history (with some materials for late nineteenth century).

Museum on Premises: Yes

Museum Hours: F–W 12–4

Cost of Entry to Museum: $2 donation suggested

Museum Is Handicapped Accessible: Yes

Description of Museum: The military museum is about 7 years old and contains interesting artifacts and displays from 20th-century wars.

Parking: Free parking lot in front

Lunch: There are numerous restaurants available off the intersection of Orchard and Overland 3 miles away.

Lodging: http://www.boise.org

Nearest Commercial Airport: Boise Air Terminal/Gowen Field (BOI) [1 mile]

Subjects

Historical Periods: 1865–1900; 1900–1940; 1940–present;

Eras: Civil War; Spanish American War; World War I; World War II; Korean War, Vietnam War, Gulf War;

Transportation: Ships and Shipping; Aviation

Date of Reviewer's Visit: 10/15/2003

Profile Updated by Institution: 11/19/2004

✹✹✹✹✹

Name: Idaho State Historical Society Library and Archives   **County:** Ada

Mailing Address: 450 N. Fourth St.

City: Boise   **State:** ID   **Postal Code:** 83702-0000

Street Address: 450 N. Fourth St.

Institution Email: None

Telephone Number: (208) 334-3356   **Fax Number:** (208) 334-3198

Contact Name: Linda Morton-Keithley, Administration

Contact Email: lindamk@ishs.state.id.us

Institution Type: Historical Society Archives

Affiliation: State of Idaho

Web site URL: http://www.idahohistory.net/library_archives.html

Hours: W–Sa 9–5

Staff in Archives: 11f, 2p, 25v

Archives Are Handicapped Accessible: Yes

Cost for Researcher—Remote: $15 hr after first half hr

List of Researchers Available: Yes

Review of Facilities: The Idaho State Historical Society Library is located in a building with the Idaho State Library. The research room requires sign-in and use of pencils and paper only. Lockers are available for a returnable quarter. There are eight large well lit tables for researchers use. A group of computer stations allows public access to the computerized indexes. Microfilm machines are located in a darkened research area in one corner of the large research area. Large banks of file cabinets cover another area and the bookshelves a third. The research room has a high volume of use and is the point of service for the Idaho State Archives as well as the historical and genealogy records of the state. The Idaho State Archives are actually housed in a separate building, so in-depth research in the area would require another appointment. The manuscript collection of the historical society is mostly housed in a storage facility off site, so there is a delay in viewing any of those materials. Finding aids to most collections are available at the reference desk, as well as a number of highly skilled reference librarians to help with searching the collections. They are planning a move to a new facility within a year or two.

Vertical Files: Yes   **Vertical Files in Cubic Feet:** 90

   Vertical File Description and Subjects: Newspaper clippings, magazine articles, and ephemera dealing with Idaho history

Manuscripts: Yes   **Manuscripts Volume in Cubic Feet:** 10,000

   Manuscript Types: All manuscript types

   Manuscript Subjects: All aspects of Idaho history

Photographs: Yes   **Number of Photographs:** 300,000

   Storage of Photographs: Photographs are mounted on cardboard and filed in cabinets in the research room. There is both general and specific subject arrangement to the files. Some photos are housed with the manuscript collections, others are stored off site.

Photograph Reproductions Are Available: Yes

Photographic Prints: Yes   **Digital Prints:** Yes

Books: Yes   **Number of Books in Collection:** 25,000

Description of Books: Idaho and regional history; city directories, telephone books, family histories, and national genealogical sources

Newspapers: Yes

Newspapers in Paper Format: Yes

Papers and Dates: Various newspaper holdings from throughout the state. Some out-of-state papers.

Newspapers on Microfilm: Yes

Microfilm and Dates: Holdings list is available on Web site

Oral Histories: Yes   **Oral Histories Number:** 3,000

Oral Histories Description: The Idaho Oral History Center has reminiscences from all over Idaho covering everything from early settlement to modern life. A detailed list is available on the Web site. There are transcriptions for most of the interviews. Nontranscribed interviews have been indexed.

Maps and Drawings: Yes   **Estimated Number of Maps and Drawings:** 20,000

Description of Maps and Drawings: Originals and copies of maps representing Idaho's preterritorial, territorial, and statehood days

Genealogy Sources: Yes

Genealogy Sources Description: Large genealogy collection, including census and other microfilm genealogical series and family histories published and unpublished

Special Collections: No

Indexes: Card files for general information, biography, manuscripts, oral histories, and Idaho legislature. These files are closed. Information is being entered on the computerized catalog available in house.

Manuscript Finding Aids: Some manuscript collections have detailed finding aids, most have inventories. Large amount of unprocessed materials.

Online Sources: Some collections are listed on WorldCat others are not. Web site gives greater detail.

Review of Collections: The Idaho State Historical Society Library is made up of several distinct collections. The historical library, the genealogical library, and the state archives now share a research room. Books, photographs, vertical files, card files, microfilm, and oral histories are all available in the research room. There are 1,400 small manuscript collections housed at the reference desk in folders in cabinets. There are another 700 larger manuscript collections each from one to one hundred boxes in size. Most manuscript collections are stored off site. Manuscripts and archives can be brought to the research room on special request. Allow two to three days for transfer of files.

Museum on Premises: No

Parking: Small visitors' free parking lot adjacent or on-street metered or free parallel parking

Lunch: Driving distance to large variety of restaurants

Lodging: http://www.boise.org

Nearest Commercial Airport: Boise Air Terminal/Gowen Field (BOI) [4 miles]

Subjects

> **Historical Periods:** 1800–1865; 1865–1900; 1900–1940; 1940–present
>
> **Eras:** Civil War; Indian Wars; Spanish American War; World War I; CCC; World War II
>
> **Natural Resources:** Water; Dams; Irrigation; Fishing; Hunting; Logging
>
> **Mining:** Gold; Silver; Copper; Placer Mining; Tunnel Mining
>
> **Transportation:** Railroads; Stagecoach/Freight; Aviation
>
> **Agriculture:** Dairy; Ranching/Livestock; Vegetable/ Truck Crops; Grains; Orchards; Vineyard; Dry Land Farming
>
> **Business:** Banking; Retail; Legal/Medical Services; Entertainment/Theaters
>
> **Government:** City; County; State
>
> **Organizations:** Schools; Charities; Nonreligious Organizations
>
> **Ethnic Groups:** Native American; Latin American; Chinese; Basque

Date of Reviewer's Visit: 10/15/2003

Profile Updated by Institution: 11/9/2004

BURLEY

Name: Cassia County Historical Society   **County:** Cassia

Mailing Address: PO Box 331

  City: Burley   **State:** ID   **Postal Code:** 83318-0000

Street Address: Hiland and Main St.

Institution Email: None

Telephone Number: (208) 678-7172

Contact Name: Valerie Bowen and Joy Tracy

Institution Type: Local Museum

Affiliation: Cassia County

Web site URL: http://www.cassiacounty.org/historical-society/museum.htm

Hours: Tu–Sa 10–5, Apr 1 to Nov 1, and by appt

Staff in Archives: 2f, 1p

Archives Are Handicapped Accessible: Yes

Review of Facilities: The Cassia County Museum is set on a large parcel of land with numerous outbuildings of living history type–displays. The research area has more space than most small historical societies. There are several large well lit tables available for research. The collections are spread out through several rooms. One has a huge photo negative collection. Another has books and scrapbooks. Main room has books of photographs, vertical file materials and oral histories in file cabinets.

Vertical Files: Yes   **Vertical Files in Cubic Feet:** 8

  Vertical File Description and Subjects: 32 loose-leaf notebooks of newspaper clippings

Manuscripts: Yes   **Manuscripts Volume in Cubic Feet:** 40

  Manuscript Types: County records, school records

  Manuscript Subjects: County tax and assessment records, all pre-1918; automobile ownership records for the county,1915–1918; school district records, 1905–1919; Register of Dealers in Meats, 1930–1968; Farm Name Registry, 1911–1914; saloon license records 1891–1911; and similar records

Photographs: Yes   **Number of Photographs:** 2,000

  Storage of Photographs: Photographs stored in 3-ring subject binders with plastic sleeves

  Photograph Subjects: Images of Cassia County, 1900 onward. Negative collection from the professional photography studios in the county

  Photograph Reproductions Are Available: Yes

    Photographic Prints: Yes

Books: Yes

  Description of Books: Local history, yearbooks, and professional collection

Newspapers: No

Oral Histories: Yes   **Oral Histories Number:** 200

Oral Histories Description: Interviews of local area residents done after 1972. Few have transcriptions.

Maps and Drawings: Yes

Description of Maps and Drawings: Assorted local area maps

Genealogy Sources: Yes

Special Collections: No

Indexes: No indexing to the collection

Review of Collections: This collection is adequately housed with inadequate indexing. The staff was very helpful. Subjects dealt with in the collection include all parts of Cassia County, but particularly Albion and Burley. There are some early materials on the Oregon Trail and California trail periods, but the majority begins with the incorporation of Burley in the early twentieth century. The early county records are interesting, although probably not unique, and are of the type that never made a permanent retention plan in most state archives.

Museum on Premises: Yes

Museum Hours: Tu–Sa 10–5, Apr 1 to Oct 31

Cost of Entry to Museum: $5

Museum Is Handicapped Accessible: Yes

Description of Museum: Museum has main display building and numerous outbuildings including a schoolhouse, settlers' cabin, and mercantile

Parking: Free gravel parking lot adjacent

Lunch: Driving distance to local eateries and fast food chains

Lodging: http://www.minicassiachamber.org

Nearest Commercial Airport: Joslin Field–Magic Valley Regional (Twin Falls) (TWF) [39 miles]; Pocatello Regional (PIH) [81 miles]

Subjects

Historical Periods: 1800–1865; 1865–1900; 1900–1940; 1940–present

Natural Resources: Dams; Irrigation

Mining: Gold; Placer Mining; Tunnel Mining

Agriculture: Ranching/Livestock; Vegetable/ Truck Crops; Grains

Government: City; County

Organizations: Schools

Religious Sites and Organizations: Protestant; LDS (Mormon)

Date of Reviewer's Visit: 5/29/2003

Profile Updated by Institution: None

COEUR D'ALENE

Name: Museum of North Idaho   **County:** Kootenai

Mailing Address: PO Box 812

   City: Coeur d'Alene   **State:** ID   **Postal Code:** 83816-0812

Street Address: 115 NW Blvd.

Institution Email: None

Telephone Number: (208) 664-3448

Contact Name: Dorothy Dahlgren   **Contact Email:** dd@museumni.org

Institution Type: Local Museum

Web site URL: http://www.museumni.org

Hours: Tu–Sa 11–5, Apr–Oct

Staff in Archives: 1f, 5v

Archives Are Handicapped Accessible: Yes

Review of Facilities: The Museum of North Idaho is located on the edge of Coeur d'Alene City Park, a short distance from the lake. The building is a single-story structure that was converted to a museum in the 1970s. The research area is located off the main entrance to the museum. There is a very narrow workroom but it is pleasant and well lit. There is little workspace available as the tables are small. Collections are housed primarily in the room. A computer station with access to the on-site searchable database is available in an adjacent staff area.

Vertical Files: No

Manuscripts: Yes   **Manuscripts Volume in Cubic Feet:** 60

   Manuscript Types: Land records, government records, school records

   Manuscript Subjects: Homestead patents; probate records; forest service records relating to the St. Joe, Coeur d'Alene, and Kaniksu National Forests; school census; teacher certificates

Photographs: Yes   **Number of Photographs:** 25,000

   Storage of Photographs: Images are stored as photographs in file folders, as slides, and in electronic form on the database.

   Photograph Subjects: Coeur d'Alene region; U.S. Forest Service; Fort Sherman; Kootenai, Benewah, and Shoshone Counties; St. Joe, Coeur d'Alene, and Kaniksu National Forests

   Photograph Reproductions Are Available: Yes

     Photographic Prints: Yes   **Digital Prints:** Yes

     Digital Images on CD or Electronically: Yes

Books: Yes   **Number of Books in Collection:** 300

    Description of Books: Local history, city directories, yearbooks, phone books

Newspapers: Yes

    Newspapers in Paper Format: Yes

    Papers and Dates: Selected *Coeur d'Alene Press,* 1894–1925

Oral Histories: Yes

    Oral Histories Description: Collection of oral history tapes about labor history in the lumbering industry

Maps and Drawings: Yes   **Estimated Number of Maps and Drawings:** 240

    Description of Maps and Drawings: Metsker, Sanborn, plats, forest service, transportation, topographic, city

Genealogy Sources: Yes

    Genealogy Sources Description: Family histories, cemetery records, marriage records

Special Collections: No

Indexes: Computerized Photograph collections in-house.

Review of Collections: The collections at the Museum of North Idaho are varied and well cataloged. Although a small institution, it has a professional managing the archival collections. The collections serve a regional focus. The majority of photographs have been scanned and are searchable on an in-house computer by staff and researchers. Military history is represented in such diverse subjects as Fort Sherman and the Farragut Naval Training Station. Forest history and management, railroads, steamboats, and early road systems are also available. All these subjects and others represent the greater Coeur d'Alene area.

Museum on Premises: Yes

    Museum Hours: Tu–Sa 11–5, Apr–Oct

    Cost of Entry to Museum: $2

    Museum Is Handicapped Accessible: Yes

    Description of Museum: Small but professionally managed and displayed collection of North Idaho history, particularly of the Coeur d'Alene region

Parking: Pay parking lot adjacent

Lunch: Various restaurants within blocks

Lodging: Numerous hotels in surrounding area; http://www.coeurdalene.org

Nearest Commercial Airport: Spokane International (Spokane, WA) (GEG) [39 miles]

Subjects

    Historical Periods: 1865–1900; 1900–1940; 1940–present

Eras: World War I; WPA; CCC; World War II

Natural Resources: Water; Dams; Irrigation; Fishing; Hunting; Logging

Transportation: Railroads; Aviation

Agriculture: Dairy; Ranching/Livestock; Vegetable/Truck Crops; Grains; Orchards;

Business: Banking; Retail; Legal/Medical Services; Hotels/Restaurants; Entertainment/Theaters

Manufacturing: Cannery; Brewery; Grist/Flour Mills; Creamery; Boatbuilding/Shipyard; Sawmills; Wood Products

Government: County

Organizations: Schools; Colleges/Universities; Hospitals/Medical Facilities; Charities; Nonreligious Organizations; Civic and Fraternal; Women's; Business; Children's; Labor and Union

Ethnic Groups: Native American; Norwegian; Swedish

Religious Sites and Organizations: Protestant; Catholic

Date of Reviewer's Visit: 4/05/2003

Profile Updated by Institution: 12/21/2004

COTTONWOOD

Name: Historical Museum at St. Gertrude   **County:** Idaho

Mailing Address: HC 3 Box 121

  City: Cottonwood   **State:** ID   **Postal Code:** 83522-0000

Street Address: Keuterville Rd.

Institution Email: museum@connectwireless.us

Telephone Number: (208) 962-7123   **Fax Number:** (208) 962-8647

Contact Name: Mary Cay Henry   **Contact Email:** curator@connectwireless.us

Institution Type: Local Museum

Affiliation: Idaho Corporation of Benedictine Sisters

Web site URL: http://www.historicalmuseumatstgertrude.com

Hours: Tu–Sat 9:30–4:30; also Sun 1:30–4:30, May–Sept.

Staff in Archives: 3f, 10v

Archives Are Handicapped Accessible: Yes

Review of Facilities: The museum is in a newer building on the grounds of the St. Gertrudes Monastery. The research collections are in the main museum staff area and an adjacent research room. There is a small table in the staff office area at the side of the museum where researchers can work. The research room has a long work table in the center of the room, with bookshelves and cupboards along the wall. The space was filled at the time of the visit, but has since been reorganized.

Vertical Files: Yes   **Vertical Files in Cubic Feet:** 7,800

> **Vertical File Description and Subjects:** North central Idaho history, towns, mining, transportation, Chinese

Manuscripts: Yes   **Manuscripts Volume in Cubic Feet:** 1,800

> **Manuscript Types:** Scrapbooks, ledgers

> **Manuscript Subjects:** North central Idaho history

Photographs: Yes   **Number of Photographs:** 1,500

> **Storage of Photographs:** Photos stored by subject in Mylar sleeves in photo albums

> **Photograph Subjects:** North central Idaho

> **Photograph Reproductions Are Available:** Yes

>> **Photographic Prints:** Yes

Books: Yes   **Number of Books in Collection:** 300

> **Description of Books:** Idaho history, professional collection

Newspapers: Yes

> **Newspapers in Paper Format:** No

> **Papers and Dates:** Local papers available at the offices of *Cottonwood Chronicle* (Cottonwood, ID) and *Idaho County Free Press* (Grangeville, ID)

Oral Histories: Yes   **Oral Histories Number:** 4

> **Oral Histories Description:** Idaho pioneers, business, other general north central Idaho history

Maps and Drawings: Yes   **Estimated Number of Maps and Drawings:** 100

> **Description of Maps and Drawings:** Mining, geology, Nez Perce Reservation, National Forest, ranger districts, railroad, counties, town plat

Genealogy Sources: Yes

> **Genealogy Sources Description:** Published family histories, obituaries

Special Collections: No

Indexes: No

Review of Collections: Photos are arranged in photo albums by subject. The historic collections are on the settlement of north central Idaho only. Monastery records and history are housed separately elsewhere on the property and were not available for viewing when reviewer visited.

Museum on Premises: Yes

Museum Hours: Tu–Sat 9:30–4:30; also Sun 1:30–4:30, May–Sept.

Cost of Entry to Museum: $4

Museum Is Handicapped Accessible: Yes

Description of Museum: The museum is divided into two parts. The front section is devoted to the local history of the area. A large room in the back houses the Rhoades-Emmanuel Memorial Collection of Asian and European antiquities and artifacts.

Parking: Free gravel parking lot adjacent to building

Lunch: Variety of cafes in Cottonwood

Lodging: http://www.northcentralidaho.info/cottonwood.htm; lodging in Grangeville, 16 miles

Nearest Commercial Airport: Lewiston-Nez Perce County (LWS) [51 miles]

Subjects

Historical Periods: 1865–1900; 1900–1940; 1940–present

Eras: Fur Trade; Indian Wars; World War I; CCC; World War II

Natural Resources: Water; Dams; Fishing; Hunting; Logging

Mining: Gold; Silver; Copper; Placer Mining; Surface Mining; Tunnel Mining; Agate; Quartz

Transportation: Railroads; Stagecoach/Freight

Agriculture: Dairy; Ranching/Livestock; Grains; Dry Land Farming

Business: Banking; Retail; Legal/Medical Services; Hotels/Restaurants; Entertainment/Theaters

Manufacturing: Brewery; Grist/Flour Mills; Creamery; Brick Making; Technology/Computers; Sawmills; Wood Products

Government: City

Organizations: Schools; Hospitals/Medical Facilities; Nonreligious Organizations

Ethnic Groups: Native American; Chinese; German

Religious Sites and Organizations: Protestant; Catholic

Date of Reviewer's Visit: 9/11/2003

Profile Updated by Institution: 11/3/2004

COUNCIL

Name: Council Valley Museum   **County:** Adams
Mailing Address: PO Box 252

City: Council   **State:** ID   **Postal Code:** 83612-0000

Street Address: 100 S Galena St.

Institution Email: None

Telephone Number: (208) 253-6499

Contact Name: Dale Fisk   **Contact Email:** dafisk@ctcweb.net

Institution Type: Local Museum

Affiliation: Council

Web site URL: http://www.ctc.net/~jcpeart/history.htm

Hours: Tu–Sa 10–4, Su 1–4, June–Aug; off season call (208) 253-4582

Staff in Archives: 5v

Archives Are Handicapped Accessible: Yes

Access Description: some limitations

Cost for Researcher—In-house: Donation

Cost for Researcher—Remote: Donation

Review of Facilities: The Council Valley Museum is located one block south of downtown. The research room is upstairs in the Council Valley Museum. Ramps are available to the research room. There is a small, multipurpose workroom that is still evolving with plans to provide more research table space. This is a typical small museum research room. Most of the materials stored in the research area are on shelves or in file cabinets.

Vertical Files: No

Manuscripts: Yes   **Manuscripts Volume in Cubic Feet:** 2

  Manuscript Types: Legal records, court records, business records, family papers, scrapbooks

  Manuscript Subjects: Adams County, homesteads, mining, fruit industry, warrant, deeds

Photographs: Yes   **Number of Photographs:** 2,500

  Storage of Photographs: 800+ photographs have been digitized. The original photographs are stored in file folders.

  Photograph Subjects: Council Valley area

  Photograph Reproductions Are Available: Yes

    Photographic Prints: Yes   **Digital Prints:** Yes

    Digital Images on CD or Electronically: Yes

Books: Yes   **Number of Books in Collection:** 2

  Description of Books: "Landmarks—A General History of the Council, Idaho Area" and "The P. & I. N." The latter is a history of the railroad from Weiser to New Meadows.

Newspapers: Yes

  Newspapers in Paper Format: Yes

  Papers and Dates: *Adams County Leader,* 1909–present; *Adams County Record*

Oral Histories: No

Maps and Drawings: Yes   **Estimated Number of Maps and Drawings:** 30

  Description of Maps and Drawings: Highway blueprints, town plats

Genealogy Sources: Yes

  Genealogy Sources Description: Biographical index, cemetery index, obituary file by last name at public library

Special Collections: Yes

Indexes: There are several in-house computer indexes

  Online Sources: Adams County Cemetery Records available from the Web site. Newspaper articles related to the Council Valley area have been extracted for the years 1877 to 1950 and are available from the Web site

Review of Collections: The Council Valley area includes the communities of Council, Mesa, Indian Valley, New Meadows, and other surrounding areas, both existing and extinct. There is a wide variety of types of records in this collection: legal records, business records, homestead information, and family papers. Collection is being managed by PastPerfect software, and the continuation of computerization is in the long-term plan. The photographs are representative of the region's diverse life. The photographs are being digitized.

Museum on Premises: Yes

  Museum Hours: Summer Tu–Sa

  Cost of Entry to Museum: Donation

  Museum Is Handicapped Accessible: Yes

  Description of Museum: Small local area museum displaying history of the Council Valley

Parking: Free parking lot adjacent

Lunch: Local restaurants

Lodging: http://www.councilidaho.net; motels in New Meadows, 25 miles; McCall, 37 miles; or Ontario, OR, 69 miles

Nearest Commercial Airport: Lewiston-Nez Perce County (LWS) [176 miles]; Boise Air Terminal/Gowen Field (BOI) [126 miles]

Subjects

  Historical Periods: Pre-1800; 1800–1865; 1865–1900; 1900–1940; 1940–present

  Eras: World War I; CCC; World War II

Natural Resources: Water; Dams; Irrigation; Logging

Mining: Gold; Copper; Placer Mining; Tunnel Mining

Agriculture: Ranching/Livestock; Grains; Orchards; Dry Land Farming

Manufacturing: Sawmills

Organizations: Schools

Ethnic Groups: Native American

Date of Reviewer's Visit: 7/30/2002

Profile Updated by Institution: 11/12/2004

CRAIGMONT

Name: Ilo Vollmer Historical Society   **County:** Lewis

Mailing Address: PO Box 61

  City: Craigmont   **State:** ID   **Postal Code:** 83523-0000

Street Address: 109 E. Main

Institution Email: None

Telephone Number: (208) 924-5474

Contact Name: Shelley Kuther   **Contact Email:** skuther@camasnet.com

Institution Type: Historical Society Archives

Web site URL: None

Hours: W 1:30–4:30

Staff in Archives: 14v

Archives Are Handicapped Accessible: Yes

Access Description: Oversize door jamb

Cost for Researcher—In-house: Donation

Cost for Researcher—Remote: Donation

Review of Facilities: The Ilo-Vollmer Historical Society is named for the two towns that merged to form Craigmont. This historical society does not have a museum, so all the efforts of the dedicated volunteers are toward researching and maintaining the documentary records of Lewis County. The historical society has several rooms on the lower floor of the Craigmont city hall in the back of the building. The entrance is ground level from the parking lot. The research room is well lit with several long tables for workspace. The arrangement is not self-service, although most materials are stored in an adjoining room.

Vertical Files: Yes   **Vertical Files in Cubic Feet:** 18

Vertical File Description and Subjects: General subject files

Manuscripts: No

Photographs: Yes   **Number of Photographs:** 1,000

  Storage of Photographs: In Mylar sleeves in binders.

  Photograph Subjects: Arranged by subject: buildings in town, recreation, and businesses

  Photograph Reproductions Are Available: Yes

    Photographic Prints: No   **Digital Prints:** Yes

Books: Yes   **Number of Books in Collection:** 100

  Description of Books: Local interest, family histories, annuals

Newspapers: No

  Microfilm and Dates: Local newspapers are on microfilm at University of Idaho

Oral Histories: Yes   **Oral Histories Number:** 80

  Oral Histories Description: Interviews with local residents, various years, 1980s to present. Most are transcribed and on the computer.

Maps and Drawings: Yes   **Estimated Number of Maps and Drawings:** 100

  Description of Maps and Drawings: Local aerial maps, railroad maps, old roads and trails of the region, land and topographic maps of the region.

Genealogy Sources: Yes

  Genealogy Sources Description: Biography files (5 cu. ft.); birth and marriage records; obituary and death records in county; death certificates; funeral home records; cemetery records for Lewis and some surrounding counties.

Special Collections: No

Indexes: Photographs being listed in staff computer (incomplete). Indexes to the genealogy records also listed on the staff computer.

Review of Collections: The collections at this small institution are impressive for the research hours behind many of them. They have gathered an impressive collection of most, if not all, the cemetery, death, and obituary records from all of Lewis County from 1911 onward. Beginning in 1911 the marriage records have been compiled as well. These records are mostly copies of the original records from Boise, University of Idaho, and other places. They are notable because of the time and attention placed on gathering a complete run of each type of record.

Museum on Premises: No

Parking: Free gravel parking lot adjacent

Lunch: Several local restaurants

Lodging: http://www.northcentralidaho.info/craigmont.htm

Nearest Commercial Airport: Lewiston-Nez Perce County (LWS) [51 miles]

Subjects

    Historical Periods: 1865–1900; 1900–1940; 1940–present

    Natural Resources: Logging

    Transportation: Railroads

    Agriculture: Grains; Dry Land Farming

    Business: Retail; Legal/Medical Services; Hotels/Restaurants

    Manufacturing: Sawmills

    Government: City; County

    Organizations: Schools; Charities; Nonreligious Organizations; Civic and Fraternal

    Religious Sites and Organizations: Protestant

Date of Reviewer's Visit: 9/11/2003

Profile Updated by Institution: 11/15/2004

DONNELLY

Name: Valley County Historical Society and Museum   **County:** Valley

Mailing Address: PO Box 444

    City: Donnelly   **State:** ID   **Postal Code:** 83615-0000

Street Address: 13131 Farm to Market Rd., Roseberry

Institution Email: wisdomgr@ctcweb.net

Telephone Number: (208) 325-8628

Contact Name: Bev Ingraham, Eileen and Juan Duarte

Institution Type: Local Museum

Affiliation: Long Valley Preservation Society, Valley County

Web site URL: None

Hours: Tu 9–12 or by appt.; off season call 208-325-5000

Staff in Archives: 1p 3v

Archives Are Handicapped Accessible: No

Access Description: not accessible when reviewed

Review of Facilities: The Valley County Museum is a collection of old local buildings moved on site to form a small town. Most are in beginning stages of restoration. When reviewed, the archival collection was stored upstairs in an old building. They have since moved to a single-story accessible building across the street. The Nelle Tobias Research Center is now in operation but was not visited by the reviewer.

Vertical Files: Yes   **Vertical Files in Cubic Feet:** 6

Vertical File Description and Subjects: Biography of local residents including oral history transcripts

Manuscripts: Yes

Manuscript Types: Personal papers, organizational records

Manuscript Subjects: Valley County history, Finnish Americans

Photographs: Yes   **Number of Photographs:** 1,500

Storage of Photographs: Photographs stored in files cabinets by photo accession number. There is a subject index in a card file.

Photograph Subjects: Valley County history, farming, ranching, lumbering, mining, Finnish Americans

Photograph Reproductions: Yes

Photograph Prints: Yes

Books: Yes

Description of Books: Local history, numerous Finnish-language books

Newspapers: Yes

Newspapers in Paper Format: Yes

Papers and Dates: *Star News* and *Payette Lake Star* (early 1900s; not a full run for either paper)

Oral Histories: Yes   **Oral Histories Number:** 70

Oral Histories Description: Oral history interviews with local area residents available with transcriptions only. Audiocassettes are available at the Idaho State Historical Society.

Maps and Drawings: Yes   **Estimated Number of Maps and Drawings:** Unknown

Description of Maps and Drawings: Idaho, Valley County history, roads, railroads

Genealogy Sources: Yes

Genealogy Sources Description: Family and biography files

Special Collections: No

Indexes: Subject index to the photographs is in a card file.

Review of Collections: The Valley County Museum collection is maintained by a group of dedicated volunteers. Although there is little or no budget for the archival collections, the pride in the collection was obvious. They are very receptive to researchers. Collection includes 70+ oral history transcripts of local people (tapes are at the Idaho State Historical Society). There are business records and ledgers and a collection of maps. In 1905, 40 percent of the residents of the area were Finnish, and the collection illustrates this well. There is also a sizable amount of material on farming, ranching, lumbering, and mining in the area.

Museum on Premises: Yes

Museum Hours: F–Su 1–5, June–Aug, or by appt.; Su only in May and Sept; off season call 208-325-5000 for appt.

Cost of Entry to Museum: Donation

Museum Is Handicapped Accessible: No

Description of Museum: The town of Roseberry is being reconstructed with sample historic buildings from throughout the area. Each building will tell its own story but focuses on the Long Valley area of Idaho.

Parking: Free on-street diagonal parking and parking lot

Lunch: 1 mile west in Donnelly or at Roseberry General Store

Lodging: http://www.mccall-idchamber.org; Lodging in McCall, Idaho

Nearest Commercial Airport: Boise Air Terminal/Gowen Field (BOI) [104 miles]

Subjects

Historical Periods: Pre-1800; 1865–1900; 1900–1940; 1940–present

Eras: Fur Trade; Civil War; Indian Wars; Spanish American War; World War I; CCC; World War II

Natural Resources: Logging; Dams; Irrigation

Mining: Mining

Transportation: Railroads; Stagecoach/Freight; Ferry

Agriculture: Ranching/Livestock; Grains; Vegetable/Truck Crops; Dry Land Farming

Manufacturing: Grist/Flour Mills; Sawmills; Creamery; Brickmaking

Government: City; County

Organizations: Schools; Hospitals/Medical Facilities; Civic and Fraternal; Women's; Labor and Union

Ethnic Groups: Basque; Finnish; German; French; Chinese

Religious Sites and Organizations: Protestant

Date of Reviewer's Visit: 7/30/2002

Profile Updated by Institution: 1/15/2005

EMMETT

Name: Gem County Historical Society and Museum   **County:** Gem

Mailing Address: PO Box 312

City: Emmett   **State:** ID   **Postal Code:** 83617-0000

Street Address: 501 E. 1st St.

Institution Email: gemcohs@bigskytel.com

Telephone Number: (208) 365-9530

Contact Name: Meg Davis

Institution Type: Local Museum

Web site URL: http://www.gemcohs.org

Hours: Summer W–F 10:30–5:30, Sa 12–5; winter W–F 10:30–4:00

Staff in Archives: 1p 8v

Archives Are Handicapped Accessible: Yes

Access Description: Through back door

List of Researchers Available: Yes

Review of Facilities: The Gem County Historical Society is located in a former storefront with several historic buildings on the property. There is not a research area set aside in this institution. Some materials are stored at the front desk on the main floor of the museum. Workspace could be provided for researchers in this area. Photographs, maps, and many other collections are on display in the museum.

Vertical Files: Yes   **Vertical Files in Cubic Feet:** 5

  Vertical File Description and Subjects: Clippings and ephemera of local interest

Manuscripts: Yes   **Manuscripts Volume in Cubic Feet:** 6

  Manuscript Types: Scrapbooks

  Manuscript Subjects: Personal and organizational scrapbooks and files

Photographs: Yes   **Number of Photographs:** 500

  Storage of Photographs: Photos are stored loose in file cabinets. Institution is starting a digitization project.

  Photograph Subjects: All aspects of Gem County history. Particularly good collection of businesses and storefronts, mining and lumbering. Also the fruit and dairy industry of the area. Aerial Maps of county from 1948–1970s.

  Photograph Reproductions Are Available: Yes

    Photographic Prints: No   **Digital Prints:** Yes

Books: Yes

  Description of Books: Local history, yearbooks

Newspapers: No

Oral Histories: No

Maps and Drawings: No

Genealogy Sources: No

Special Collections: No

Indexes: There is currently no indexing to the collection.

Review of Collections: The Gem County Historical Society has a very small research collection. It has some unique items, however, that would be an important addition to any research on the Gem County vicinity. The photographs of local businesses were particularly noteworthy. Most of their collection is not duplicated elsewhere. There are a great deal of photographs and some other information that deal with the irrigation systems and fruit industry of the region.

Museum on Premises: Yes

Museum Hours: Summer W–F 10:30–5:30, Sa noon–5; winter W–F 10:30–4

Cost of Entry to Museum: donation

Museum Is Handicapped Accessible: No

Description of Museum: Museum is spread out over a five-building complex that includes a historic house (1903), blacksmith shop, and one-room school house.

Parking: Free on-street parallel parking and lot across street

Lunch: Local restaurants and fast-food chains driving distance

Lodging: http://www.emmettidaho.com

Nearest Commercial Airport: Boise Air Terminal/Gowen Field (BOI) [34 miles]

Subjects

Historical Periods: 1865–1900; 1900–1940; 1940–present

Natural Resources: Logging

Mining: Mining

Agriculture: Dairy; Vegetable/Truck Crops; Orchards

Business: Retail

Manufacturing: Sawmills

Date of Reviewer's Visit: 7/30/2002

Profile Updated by Institution: None

HAGERMAN

Name: Hagerman Valley Historical Society   **County:** Gooding

Mailing Address: PO Box 86

   City: Hagerman   **State:** ID   **Postal Code:** 83332-0000

Street Address: 100 S. State St.

Institution Email: None

Telephone Number: (208) 837-6288

Contact Name: Bob Wonderle, President

Institution Type: Local Museum

Web site URL: None

Hours: W–Su 1–4

Staff in Archives: 5v

Archives Are Handicapped Accessible: No

Access Description: Four steps into building

Review of Facilities: The Hagerman Valley Historical Society is located in the old Hagerman State Bank. It was a small bank and this is the smallest museum visited. What space they have is well utilized. There is a small research area set aside near the back of the one-room museum. It has a counter for workspace and shelves above and below where the majority of the documents and photographs are housed.

Vertical Files: Yes   **Vertical Files in Cubic Feet:** 8

    Vertical File Description and Subjects: Family history files and general subject files in file cabinets

Manuscripts: Yes   **Manuscripts Volume in Cubic Feet:** 4

    Manuscript Types: Business records, government records, organizational records

    Manuscript Subjects: Bliss Mercantile Ledger 1917; Hagerman Bank cashier records 1915–1940s (mostly records of where the bank's money was invested); water collection records 1920s; city receipts 1941–1943

Photographs: Yes   **Number of Photographs:** 500

    Storage of Photographs: Plastic sleeves in loose-leaf binders

    Photograph Subjects: Schools, scenery, groups and events, towns of Bliss and Hagerman, and Hagerman Valley

    Photograph Reproductions Are Available: Yes

Books: Yes   **Number of Books in Collection:** 40

    Description of Books: Local interest and old books

Newspapers: No

Oral Histories: No

Maps and Drawings: No

Genealogy Sources: Yes

    Genealogy Sources Description: Family history files and cemetery records

Special Collections: No

Indexes: No

Review of Collections: The collections are small and relate to the Hagerman Valley, including the towns of Hagerman and Bliss. Photographs are filed in subject notebooks along with copies of documents or newspaper articles that relate to the same family, or subject matter. Other materials are arranged in subject files in file cabinets. The institution is small but well worth a visit if doing history on the Hagerman Valley settlement periods.

Museum on Premises: Yes

Museum Hours: W–Su 1–4

Cost of Entry to Museum: Donation

Museum Is Handicapped Accessible: No

Description of Museum: This museum is extremely small but well done. They have used every available space including reconstructing a cabin in the old bank vault. A display on the Hagerman Fossil beds was beautifully done.

Parking: Free on-street vertical parking

Lunch: Several local restaurants within short walking distance

Lodging: http://www.inidaho.com; Hagerman Valley Inn (208) 837-6196

Nearest Commercial Airport: Joslin Field–Magic Valley Regional (Twin Falls) (TWF) [38 miles]; Boise Air Terminal/Gowen Field (BOI) [95 miles]

Subjects

Historical Periods: Pre-1800; 1800–1865; 1865–1900; 1900–1940; 1940–present

Natural Resources: Fishing; Hunting

Business: Retail; Hotels/Restaurants

Organizations: Schools; Nonreligious Organizations

Date of Reviewer's Visit: 5/30/2003

Profile Updated by Institution: None

HAILEY

Name: Blaine County Historical Museum   **County:** Blaine

Mailing Address: PO Box 124

City: Hailey   **State:** ID   **Postal Code:** 83333-0000

Street Address: 218 N. Main St.

Institution Email: bcmuseum@mindspring.com

Telephone Number: (208) 788-1801   **Fax Number:** (208) 725-5811

Contact Name: Teddie Daley

Institution Type: Local Museum

Affiliation: City of Blaine

Web site URL: http://www.bchistoricalmuseum.org

Hours: Summer M–Sa 11–5, Su 1–5; rest of year by appt.

Staff in Archives: 2p, 5v

Archives Are Handicapped Accessible: Yes

Review of Facilities: The Blaine County Historical Museum is housed in an 1883 building, originally adobe. It is on the main street of town in a business area. This is a museum with little space to spare. The museum galleries are filled to capacity. There is no area set aside for research and workspace is very limited. Photographs and other materials are stored at various locations in the front of the museum. A staff workstation holding the computer database is located behind the front desk. The political button collection is 100 percent displayed on the walls and in glass flat cases.

Vertical Files: No

Manuscripts: Yes   **Manuscripts Volume in Cubic Feet:** 5

  Manuscript Types: Ledgers, government records

  Manuscript Subjects: Alturas County records from 1887

Photographs: Yes   **Number of Photographs:** 1,500

  Storage of Photographs: Photographs are stored in 14 loose-leaf binders with originals in plastic sleeves; plan to scan photos into PastPerfect.

  Photograph Reproductions Are Available: Yes

Books: Yes   **Number of Books in Collection:** 50

  Description of Books: Local history and professional collection

Newspapers: Yes

  Newspapers in Paper Format: Yes

  Papers and Dates: *Wood River Times;* assorted runs, not continuous

Oral Histories: No

Maps and Drawings: Yes

Description of Maps and Drawings: Assorted mining maps stored rolled and flat

Genealogy Sources: No

Special Collections: Yes

  Special Collections Description: Interesting political ephemera collection of primarily pin-back buttons, but also contains other campaign materials from 1840s to the present, though later years are sparse. Majority of collection is Republican Party candidates. Around 6,000 items. Joe Fuld's (born 1878) collection was started in the early twentieth century. Fuld was one of the founders of the American

Political Items Collectors Association and served as its first president in 1945; the organization now has 2,000 members.

Indexes: Computer index to photo collection

Review of Collections: This is a small historical society. The research collections are likewise very limited. The collections are limited to the development of Hailey and the surrounding areas. The most significant part of the collection is the political ephemera, which is possibly one of the largest single-person collections currently available for research. The 6,000 items in the collection are primarily pin-back buttons, but it contains other political memorabilia. The items date from the 1840s and were actively collected until the1960s. Newer pieces have been added, though not comprehensively.

Museum on Premises: Yes

   Museum Hours: Summer M, W, Th, and F, Sa 11–5, Su 1–5

   Cost of Entry to Museum: Donation

   Museum Is Handicapped Accessible: Yes

   Description of Museum: The museum is small and illustrates the history of the Wood River Valley area. The galleries are traditional museum displays for a small town.

Parking: Free on-street vertical parking

Lunch: Various local cafes and chain restaurants a few blocks' drive

Lodging: http://www.haileyidaho.com; Hailey or Sun Valley/Ketchum, 11 miles

Nearest Commercial Airport: Friedman Memorial (Hailey, ID) (SUN) [2 miles]

Subjects

   Historical Periods: 1865–1900; 1900–1940; 1940–present

   Natural Resources: Hunting

   Mining: Tunnel Mining

   Agriculture: Ranching/Livestock

   Business: Retail; Legal/Medical Services; Hotels/Restaurants

Date of Reviewer's Visit: 5/28/2003

Profile Updated by Institution: 12/16/2004

IDAHO FALLS

Name: Museum of Idaho   **County:** Bonneville

Mailing Address: 200 N. Eastern Ave.

   City: Idaho Falls   **State:** ID   **Postal Code:** 83403-1784

Street Address: 200 N. Eastern Ave.

Institution Email: david.pennock@museumofidaho.org

Telephone Number: (208) 522-1400   **Fax Number:** (208) 524-5060

Contact Name: David Pennock, Museum Director, or Judy House

Contact Email: davidpennock@museumofidaho.org

Institution Type: Regional Museum

Affiliation: Bonneville County Historical Society

Web site URL: http://www.museumofidaho.org

Hours: M–F 10–4

Staff in Archives: 2v

Archives Are Handicapped Accessible: Yes

Access Description: Archives are accessible through new addition

Cost for Researcher—Remote: $10

Review of Facilities: The Museum of Idaho is located in Idaho Falls, east on Broadway, just over the railroad tracks. Formerly known as the Bonneville Museum, the facility underwent extensive renovation/addition to the original 1916 Carnegie Library building in 2002. The reading and reference room is located toward the back of the original building. The room is pleasant, with bookcases filling the walls. A big worktable dominates the center of the room. Most of the research materials are housed on shelves and cabinets in the room.

Vertical Files: No

Manuscripts: Yes

    Manuscript Types: Business records, government records, personal papers, scrapbooks

    Manuscript Subjects: Agriculture, irrigation; 1900 to 1920 sheriff arrest records, 200 items

Photographs: Yes   **Number of Photographs:** 4,000

    Storage of Photographs: Originals are stored in document boxes in Mylar sleeves.

    Photograph Subjects: Bonneville County, Idaho Falls, and surrounding areas

    Photograph Reproductions Are Available: Yes

      Photographic Prints: Yes

Books: Yes   **Number of Books in Collection:** 200

    Description of Books: Local history, annuals, and professional collection

Newspapers: Yes

Newspapers in Paper Format: Yes

Papers and Dates: Scattered issues of papers from 1891 to 1990s

Oral Histories: Yes   **Oral Histories Number:** 58

Oral Histories Description: Audiocassette interviews of early people of the area, including schoolteachers and a former mayor. Interviews mostly done from 1975–1985.

Maps and Drawings: Yes

Description of Maps and Drawings: Local and regional maps on various subjects, irrigation maps. Stored flat or large rolled.

Genealogy Sources: Yes

Genealogy Sources Description: Refer researchers to local LDS Family History Center

Special Collections: No

Indexes: Collection is indexed in both a card file and on a local computer

Published Guides: Subject guide of collections

Review of Collections: The Museum of Idaho research collection is well cared for by volunteers and staff. The collections are easily accessible to a researcher. Agriculture, irrigation, and related topics are a strength of this collection. The manuscript items are arranged by format and then by subject. There are subject guides to history topics in agriculture, irrigation, people, history, churches, and communities.

Museum on Premises: Yes

Museum Hours: Mon–Fri 9–8, Sat 10–5

Cost of Entry to Museum: $5

Museum Is Handicapped Accessible: Yes

Description of Museum: The Museum of Idaho focuses on the history of the area and has some very well done displays on natural history, mining, and nuclear energy. Many of the exhibits are interactive.

Parking: Free parking lot across street

Lunch: Driving distance to a variety of restaurants

Lodging: http://www.inidaho.com/

Nearest Commercial Airport: Idaho Falls Regional (IDA) [3 miles]

Subjects

    Historical Periods: 1865–1900; 1900–1940; 1940–present

    Eras: Exploration; Fur Trade; World War II

    Natural Resources: Water; Dams; Irrigation

    Transportation: Railroads; Stagecoach/Freight

Agriculture: Ranching/Livestock

Business: Banking; Retail; Entertainment/Theaters

Government: City; County

Organizations: Schools; Hospitals/Medical Facilities

Ethnic Groups: Native American; Japanese

Religious Sites and Organizations: Protestant; Catholic; LDS (Mormon)

Date of Reviewer's Visit: 8/13/2002

Profile Updated by Institution: 11/22/2004

JEROME

Name: Jerome County Historical Society, Inc.   **County:** Jerome

Mailing Address: PO Box 50

   City: Jerome   **State:** ID   **Postal Code:** 83338-0000

Street Address: 220 N. Lincoln

Institution Email: info@historicaljeromecounty.com

Telephone Number: (208) 324-5641

Contact Name: Clair and Virginia Ricketts, Marguerite Roberson

Institution Type: Local Museum

Web site URL: http://www.historicaljeromecounty.com/museum.dsp

Hours: T–Sa 1–5

Staff in Archives: 8v

Archives Are Handicapped Accessible: No

Access Description: Ramp in back to access museum. Wooden stairs to research materials in basement

Cost for Researcher—Remote: fee schedule

Review of Facilities: The Jerome County Historical Society is housed in a historic (unrestored) building in downtown Jerome. Museum exhibits are on the first floor. The research area is in the basement, down a steep staircase. The main research room has large tables in the center of the room and cabinets, bookshelves, and various materials stacked everywhere. It is in the unfinished basement of an old building and has the feeling of an overstuffed storage shed. Off the main room is a smaller room, also filled with materials. The remainder of the collections is stored in shelving that fills every empty corner of the basement. The historical society is hoping for a new building eventually and hopefully they will invest in properly housing this impressive collection of primary source materials.

Vertical Files: No

Manuscripts: Yes   **Manuscripts Volume in Cubic Feet:** 100

   Manuscript Types: Business records, organizational records, scrapbooks, land records

   Manuscript Subjects: Hillsdale Irrigation Co. papers; Jerome Co-op Creamery papers; Northside Canal Company papers; Jerome (Flour) Milling Company; Minidoka War Relocation Camp at Hunt, papers and artifacts; Early Jerome County records and land/title records; other local businesses and club records

Photographs: Yes   **Number of Photographs:** 2,000

   Storage of Photographs: Photos stored in plastic sleeves in binders

   Photograph Subjects: Jerome County and towns within

   Photograph Reproductions Are Available: Yes

      Photographic Prints: Yes

Books: Yes   **Number of Books in Collection:** 350

   Description of Books: Annuals; telephone books; agricultural books; local interest, and professional collection

Newspapers: Yes

   Newspapers in Paper Format: Yes

   Papers and Dates: *Northside News,* 1907–present and other county papers from surrounding areas

Oral Histories: No

Maps and Drawings: Yes

   Description of Maps and Drawings: Early survey of irrigation project, towns, highways

Genealogy Sources: Yes

   Genealogy Sources Description: Obituary file, cemetery records

Special Collections: Yes

   Special Collections Description: Materials from and about the Minidoka War Relocation Camp at Hunt, Idaho. This includes such papers and documents as the camp newspapers, annuals, photographs, some memoirs, and Hunt High School annuals, as well as artifacts from the camps.

Indexes: No

Review of Collections: Although the institution is small, the research collection is surprisingly large. There is more collection than space, however, so the filing system seems random, with similar types of materials being stored at multiple places in the several-room basement. There is much more to the collection than one would guess at first glance, including quite a bit of unique historical documents. The areas of most significant note would be the materials dealing with the Minidoka Relocation Camp, including a number of artifacts that were rescued from the garbage dumps after the camp was closed. There are quite a few collections of business records of local industries. This is a bare-bones operation with wonderful possibilities for researchers.

Museum on Premises: Yes

> **Museum Hours:** Tu–Sa 1–5
>
> **Cost of Entry to Museum:** Donation
>
> **Museum Is Handicapped Accessible:** Yes
>
> **Description of Museum:** This is a small museum which has displays on the Northside Irrigation Project, the Minidoka Relocation Camp, and the general history of Jerome County.

Parking: Free on-street parallel or small parking lot behind museum

Lunch: Mexican and Chinese restaurants within two blocks; others are within driving distance

Lodging: http://www.visitjerome.com

Nearest Commercial Airport: Joslin Field–Magic Valley Regional (Twin Falls) (TWF) [14 miles]; Pocatello Regional (PIH) [122 miles]

Subjects

> **Historical Periods:** 1800–1865; 1865–1900; 1900–1940; 1940–present
>
> **Eras:** World War I; World War II
>
> **Natural Resources:** Irrigation; Fishing; Hunting
>
> **Mining:** Gold
>
> **Transportation:** Railroads; Stagecoach/Freight; Ferries
>
> **Agriculture:** Dairy; Ranching/Livestock; Vegetable/Truck Crops; Grains
>
> **Business:** Banking; Retail; Legal/Medical Services; Hotels/Restaurants; Entertainment/Theaters
>
> **Manufacturing:** Creamery
>
> **Government:** City; County
>
> **Organizations:** Schools; Hospitals/Medical Facilities; Charities; Nonreligious Organizations; Civic and Fraternal; Women's
>
> **Ethnic Groups:** Latin American; Japanese; Chinese; German
>
> **Religious Sites and Organizations:** Protestant; Catholic; LDS (Mormon)

Date of Reviewer's Visit: 5/30/2003

Profile Updated by Institution: 11/15/2004

KELLOGG

Name: Kellogg Public Library   **County:** Shoshone

Mailing Address: 16 Market Ave.

  City: Kellogg   **State:** ID   **Postal Code:** 83837-2499

Street Address: 16 Market Ave.

Institution Email: kellogglibrary@usamedia.tv

Telephone Number: (208) 786-7321   **Fax Number:** (208) 784-1100

Contact Name: Debora Gibler, Director

Institution Type: Public Library

Affiliation: City of Kellogg

Web site URL: None

Hours: M 12:30–8, Tu–F 12:30–5:30

Staff in Archives: 1f 1p

Archives Are Handicapped Accessible: No

Access Description: Main floor of library accessible by steep ramp

Review of Facilities: Kellogg Public Library is located in the main business district of Kellogg in a building shared with North Idaho College and the Fire Department. The library, though small, is two stories. The photograph and other research collections are stored in a staff-only area on the lower level of the library. In the library itself there are standard library tables and workspaces available for researchers. Staff assistance is necessary to view any part of the research collection. The photographs are stored in various ways, from acid-free photo albums to file cabinets to cardboard boxes.

Vertical Files: Yes   **Vertical Files in Cubic Feet:** 4

  Vertical File Description and Subjects: Area history and clipping files

Manuscripts: Yes   **Manuscripts Volume in Cubic Feet:** 12

  Manuscript Types: Business records, organizational records, scrapbooks

  Manuscript Subjects: Annual reports of the Bunker Hill and Sullivan Mines 1907–1967, YMCA minutes, and scrapbooks of various civic organizations

Photographs: Yes   **Number of Photographs:** 8,000

  Storage of Photographs: Photographs are stored in various ways, mostly in the original containers/binders in which they were donated. These include cardboard and metal boxes, acid-free or non-acid-free binders, file cabinets, and scrapbooks. The collection includes prints, panoramas, glass lantern slides, slides, and negatives.

Photograph Subjects: The majority of the photographs are of the various plants and people of the Bunker Hill Company from 1885 to 1982. These are from the official company records. There is also a collection of photographs from a Kellogg area portrait studio from the 1940s.

Photograph Reproductions Are Available: Yes

   Photographic Prints: Yes

Books: Yes   **Number of Books in Collection:** 100

   Description of Books: Local history, annuals

Newspapers: No

Oral Histories: No

Maps and Drawings: No

Genealogy Sources: No

Special Collections: No

Indexes: No

Review of Collections: The collections at Kellogg Public Library are very significant to the history of the region and the mining industry in general. When the Bunker Hill Mining Company went out of business, it divided the corporate records among several institutions. The payroll ledgers went to the Staff House Museum (see entry). Most of the corporation records went to the University of Idaho (see entry), and the photograph collection went to the Kellogg Public Library. The division of business records may be curious or even unfortunate but it is understandable and far from being uncommon. The photographs are largely unprocessed, many are unidentified and the collection is mostly unorganized. Finding a specific type of photo in this collection would be time-consuming. The institution is aware of the problem, however, and is looking for funding to properly process and store the collection.

Museum on Premises: No

Parking: Free on-street parallel parking

Lunch: Ethnic restaurants within walking distance, driving distance to several fast-food chains and other restaurants.

Lodging: http://www.historicsilvervalleychamberofcommerce.com

Nearest Commercial Airport: Spokane International (Spokane, WA) (GEG) [76 miles]

Subjects

   Historical Periods: 1865–1900; 1900–1940; 1940–present

   Mining: Silver; Tunnel Mining; Lead; Zinc

Date of Reviewer's Visit: 8/19/2004

Profile Updated by Institution: 11/12/2004

Name: Staff House Museum **County:** Shoshone

Mailing Address: PO Box 783

City: Kellogg **State:** ID **Postal Code:** 83837-0000

Street Address: 820 McKinley Ave.

Institution Email: mail@staffhousemuseum.com

Telephone Number: (208) 786-4141

Contact Name: Rebecca Powers **Contact Email:** bpower68@verizon.net

Institution Type: Local Museum

Affiliation: Shoshone County Mining and Smelting Museum

Web site URL: http://www.staffhousemuseum.com

Hours: Daily 10–5, May to Sept

Staff in Archives: 3p

Archives Are Handicapped Accessible: Yes

Review of Facilities: The Staff House Museum is located in a house built for the manager of the Bunker Hill Mining Corporation in 1906. It was later used for lodging mining staff, hence the name. The museum is three stories. The photograph collections are mostly displayed on the walls and throughout the exhibit rooms of the house. The main research collection is the Bunker Hill and Sullivan Mine payroll records. These records are currently stored on the third floor in a long narrow room. Wide shelves lining one wall hold the oversize volumes. A folding table is at one end, and benches line another wall where sample ledgers are displayed as part of the museum. The institution has plans to move the ledgers to the lower level of the museum, which will have much more desirable storage conditions for these important volumes. The daylight basement location should be handicapped-accessible as well.

Vertical Files: No

Manuscripts: Yes **Manuscripts Volume in Cubic Feet:** 88

Manuscript Types: Ledgers

Manuscript Subjects: Payroll ledgers from the Bunker Hill and Sullivan Mines from 1899 to 1962. From the Sullivan Mines before it merged with Bunker Hill and also some early ledgers from the Caledonia Mine. There are also some equipment-ordering records from select years. The Bunker Hill Mine Inventory of Ores and Concentrates from 1944 to 1969 is also housed here.

Photographs: Yes **Number of Photographs:** 400

Storage of Photographs: Photographs are part of the museum displays

Photograph Subjects: Local area and mining history

Photograph Reproductions Are Available: Yes

Photographic Prints: Yes

Books: No

Newspapers: Yes

Newspapers in Paper Format: Yes

Papers and Dates: *News Miner* (Kellogg) 1950–1970

Oral Histories: No

Maps and Drawings: Yes   **Estimated Number of Maps and Drawings:** 2

Description of Maps and Drawings: Three-dimensional engineer's drawings of the local mining district

Genealogy Sources: No

Special Collections: No

Indexes: No

Review of Collections: The research collections of the Staff House Museum are limited entirely to business ledgers of the Bunker Hill and Sullivan Mining Company. Although useful only for a narrow research focus, the collections are a significant piece in the history of the area. The remaining business records of the company are at the University of Idaho (see entry), while the photographs were given to the Kellogg Public Library (see entry). The ledgers are oversize and some are extremely heavy. There are nearly 200 individual volumes of various shapes and sizes; although most are payroll records, there are also a few ledgers of other types. The early ones are handwritten and often difficult to read and the later ones typed. An inventory of all volumes needs to be undertaken, which hopefully will be completed when they are moved to their basement home.

Museum on Premises: Yes

Museum Hours: 10–5 May to Sept

Cost of Entry to Museum: $4

Museum Is Handicapped Accessible: No

Description of Museum: Historic building with exhibits placed in various rooms of this two-story museum.

Parking: Free parking in lot down the block

Lunch: Driving distance to a variety of restaurants and some fast-food chains

Lodging: http://www.historicsilvervalleychamberofcommerce.com

Nearest Commercial Airport: Spokane International (Spokane, WA) (GEG) [76 miles]

Subjects

Historical Periods: 1900–1940; 1940–present

Mining: Gold; Silver; Tunnel Mining

Business: Banking; Legal/Medical Services

Date of Reviewer's Visit: 8/19/2004

Profile Updated by Institution: 1/10/2005

KETCHUM

✳✳✳✳

Name: The Community Library Association–Regional History Department

County: Blaine

Mailing Address: PO Box 2168

City: Ketchum   **State:** ID   **Postal Code:** 83340-0000

Street Address: 415 N. Spruce Ave.

Institution Email: reghist@thecommunitylibrary.org

Telephone Number: (208) 726-3493   **Fax Number:** (208) 726-0050

Contact Name: Chris Millspaugh

Institution Type: Public Library

Web site URL: http://www.thecommunitylibrary.org

Hours: M–Sa 9–12 and 1–6

Staff in Archives: 1f 1p

Archives Are Handicapped Accessible: Yes

Access Description: Ramp, flat

Review of Facilities: The Regional History Department of The Community Library is truly one of the best facilities in the Northwest. The reading room is spacious and well lit with the books, computers, microfilm, and photograph collections available to the researcher. Manuscript materials are stored in an adjacent climate-controlled room. Photographs are stored in a large bank of fireproof file cabinets. This facility is a good example of what most of the institutions being visited strive to achieve. Most archivists in the country in small and medium sized institutions would covet the staff workspace and bright cheery research room.

Vertical Files: Yes   **Vertical Files in Cubic Feet:** 16

   Vertical File Description and Subjects: Arranged by accession number listed in general library catalog

Manuscripts: Yes   **Manuscripts Volume in Cubic Feet:** 36

   Manuscript Types: Business records, personal papers

   Manuscript Subjects: Avalanches, local businesses, mining records

Photographs: Yes   **Number of Photographs:** 9,350

Storage of Photographs: On photoboards in file cabinets with complete photo information arranged by accession number; also on computer database (Filemaker Pro)

Photograph Subjects: Wood River Valley, Sun Valley, Ketchum, Hailey, Bellevue, and surrounding communities; Union Pacific Railroad promotional photographs

Photograph Reproductions Are Available: Yes

    Photographic Prints: Yes   **Digital Prints:** Yes

Books: Yes   **Number of Books in Collection:** 800

    Description of Books: Regional interest books, all in library catalog

Newspapers: Yes

    Newspapers in Paper Format: Yes

    Papers and Dates: Assorted historical copies

    Newspapers on Microfilm: Yes

    Microfilm and Dates: Ketchum, Hailey, and other area papers from 1880s to present

Oral Histories: Yes   **Oral Histories Number:** 730

    Oral Histories Description: Interviews of local residents on subjects such as pioneer life, mining, sheep industry, Forest Service in area, early Sun Valley, and Ernest Hemingway in Idaho

Maps and Drawings: Yes   **Estimated Number of Maps and Drawings:** 212

    Description of Maps and Drawings: Topographical, city plats, forest service

Genealogy Sources: No

Special Collections: Yes

    Special Collections Description: The library is actively collecting for preservation audio/visual materials produced in or about the area. There is a large VHS video tape collection of films on the region. Many were originally 8 and 16 mm. Also a large collection of audiotapes of conferences held in the Sun Valley Area since 1982.

Indexes: Part of the collection is available online in library catalog. A in-house computer allows computerized searching on Filemaker Pro of the collection materials.

Review of Collections: The Regional History Department collections focus on the history of Alturas and Blaine counties. The collections are professionally stored and maintained. Because the collection and retention of two-dimensional history is a major part of the mission of the library, it has stricter rules for using the collections than most like-sized libraries (justifiably). There are some restrictions on use of some materials in the collection, primarily those items dealing with the rich or famous residents or visitors of the area. Overall, the collection has a little bit of everything. Large oral history tape collections, impressive photograph collections, and some manuscript and other materials are complemented by the large audiovisual collection on local subjects.

Museum on Premises: No

Parking: Free on-street diagonal parking

Lunch: Many local restaurants and upscale eateries nearby

Lodging: http://www.visitsunvalley.com

Nearest Commercial Airport: Friedman Memorial (Hailey, ID) (SUN) [99 miles]

Subjects

> **Historical Periods:** 1800–1865; 1865–1900; 1900–1940; 1940–present
>
> **Eras:** Fur Trade; Indian Wars; World War I; WPA; CCC; World War II
>
> **Natural Resources:** Water; Irrigation; Fishing; Hunting; Logging
>
> **Mining:** Silver; Placer Mining; Tunnel Mining; Boxite; Galena
>
> **Transportation:** Railroads; Aviation
>
> **Agriculture:** Ranching/Livestock; Dry Land Farming
>
> **Business:** Banking; Retail; Legal/Medical Services; Hotels/Restaurants; Entertainment/Theaters
>
> **Manufacturing:** Technology/Computers; Sawmills
>
> **Government:** City; County
>
> **Organizations:** Schools; Colleges/Universities; Nonreligious Organizations; Civic and Fraternal; Women's; Business
>
> **Ethnic Groups:** Native American; Latin American; Peruvian; Chinese; Basque; English; Irish; Italian; Scottish; Spanish; Austrian
>
> **Religious Sites and Organizations:** Protestant; Catholic; LDS (Mormon); Jewish

Date of Reviewer's Visit: 5/27/2003

Profile Updated by Institution: 11/8/2004

LAVA HOT SPRINGS

Name: South Bannock County Historical Center Museum   **County:** Bannock

Mailing Address: PO Box 387

  City: Lava Hot Springs   **State:** ID   **Postal Code:** 83246-0000

Street Address: 110 E. Main St.

Institution Email: Lavamus@dcdi.net

Telephone Number: (208) 776-5254   **Fax Number:** (208) 776-5228

Contact Name: Ruth Ann Olson, Administrator

Institution Type: Local Museum

Web site URL: http://www.lavahotsprings.com/museum.htm

Hours: Daily 12–5

Staff in Archives: 3p, 4v

Archives Are Handicapped Accessible: Yes

Review of Facilities: The South Bannock County Historical Center Museum is housed in a former bank building (1970s) in the center of town. The collection is divided and stored in two locations in the moderately sized museum. Documents and photographs are stored in the office area in the front of the building, where some workspace is available. The book collection is stored in a small library to the back of the building. A long worktable is available in that room, which doubles as a lunch/ conference room. The museum is fairly small and facilities are adequate for the size of the institution.

Vertical Files: Yes   **Vertical Files in Cubic Feet:** 10

   Vertical File Description and Subjects: Family histories, general subject files

Manuscripts: Yes

   Manuscript Types: variety of unknown quantity

Photographs: Yes   **Number of Photographs:** 6,000

   Storage of Photographs: Original and copy photographs are housed in file folders, some with plastic sleeves, and filed in cabinets by accession number; a computer subject list exists.

   Photograph Subjects: South Bannock County, mostly Lava Hot Springs

   Photograph Reproductions Are Available: Yes

      Photographic Prints: Yes

Books: Yes   **Number of Books in Collection:** 200

   Description of Books: Local history; family histories, and old books

Newspapers: Yes

   Newspapers in Paper Format: Yes

   Papers and Dates: *Lava Lyer, McEammon News, Salt Lake Tribune,* and *Idaho State Journal*

Oral Histories: Yes   **Oral Histories Number:** 12

   Oral Histories Description: Oral histories of local residents on audiocassette with transcriptions.

Maps and Drawings: Yes

   Description of Maps and Drawings: Assorted local area maps

Genealogy Sources: Yes

Genealogy Sources Description: Family history files and cemetery records

Special Collections: No

Indexes: A computer index

Review of Collections: Collections at the South Bannock County Historical Center are small and scattered in several locations throughout the building. The finding aids are minimal, but the staff was helpful. The computer index was unavailable at the time of the visit. Collections deal with Lava Hot Springs and the South Bannock County areas The institution has applied for grant money to digitize part of the collection and put it online.

Museum on Premises: Yes

 Museum Hours: Daily 12–5

 Cost of Entry to Museum: Donation

 Museum Is Handicapped Accessible: Yes

 Description of Museum: Small local museum

Parking: Free on-street parallel parking

Lunch: Local eateries across the street and within short walking distance

Lodging: http://www.lavahotsprings.org; numerous B&B's and small hotels

Nearest Commercial Airport: Pocatello Regional (PIH) [46 miles]

Subjects

 Historical Periods: 1865–1900; 1900–1940; 1940–present

 Eras: Fur Trade; World War I; World War II

 Natural Resources: Irrigation; Logging

 Mining: Manganese

 Agriculture: Dairy; Ranching/Livestock; Dry Land Farming

 Business: Banking; Retail; Legal/Medical Services; Hotels/Restaurants; Entertainment/Theaters

 Manufacturing: Sawmills

 Government: City; County

 Organizations: Schools; Hospitals/Medical Facilities; Nonreligious Organizations; Civic and Fraternal; Women's

 Ethnic Groups: Native American; Basque; Danish; Dutch; English; Finnish; French; German; Irish; Italian; Norwegian; Russian; Scottish; Spanish; Swedish

 Religious Sites and Organizations: Protestant; Catholic; LDS (Mormon)

Date of Reviewer's Visit: 5/29/2003

Profile Updated by Institution: 11/8/2004

LEWISTON

Name: Nez Perce County Museum   **County:** Nez Perce

Mailing Address: 0306 Third St.

   City: Lewiston   **State:** ID   **Postal Code:** 83501-0000

Street Address: 0306 Third St. (3rd and C Streets)

Institution Email: registrar@npchistsoc.org

Telephone Number: (208) 743-2535   **Fax Number:** (208) 743-2535

Contact Name: Lora Feucht

Institution Type: Local Museum

Affiliation: Nez Perce County Historical Society

Web site URL: http://www.npchistsoc.org

Hours: Tu–Sa 10 to 4, Mar–Dec

Staff in Archives: 1f 1p

Archives Are Handicapped Accessible: Yes

Access Description: Handicapped ramp at separate but well-marked entrance

Cost for Researcher—Remote: Fee schedule

Review of Facilities: The Nez Perce County Museum is housed in a unique art deco building originally built by the WPA. The research area is in the staff office area. The library has a large worktable and bookshelves, with the book collections surrounding the walls. The room is small but functional. With the exception of the books, most of the research materials are stored in an adjoining staff office. The manuscript materials and larger collections are stored in the basement in a staff-only area.

Vertical Files: Yes   **Vertical Files in Cubic Feet:** 6

   Vertical File Description and Subjects: General history and clipping files

Manuscripts: Yes   **Manuscripts Volume in Cubic Feet:** 66

   Manuscript Types: Personal papers, organizational records, business records

   Manuscript Subjects: Nez Perce County

Photographs: Yes   **Number of Photographs:** 4,200

   Storage of Photographs: Photocopies of photographs are arranged in 30 subject-arranged notebooks. Original photographs are arranged by accession number in acid-free envelopes in file cabinets.

   Photograph Subjects: Nez Perce County, Lewiston, and surrounding areas

   Photograph Reproductions Are Available: Yes

      Photographic Prints: Yes

Books: Yes   **Number of Books in Collection:** 300

Description of Books: Local history, city directories, professional collection

Newspapers: No

Microfilm and Dates: Lewis and Clark State College has microfilm of local newspapers

Oral Histories: Yes   .   **Oral Histories Number:** 30

Oral Histories Description: Interviews of local residents. Some are indexed and a few are transcribed.

Maps and Drawings: Yes   **Estimated Number of Maps and Drawings:** 25

Description of Maps and Drawings: Miscellaneous maps of the area are stored rolled, but are not indexed.

Genealogy Sources: Yes

Genealogy Sources Description: Cemetery records

Special Collections: No

Indexes: Yes

Manuscript Finding Aids: Finding aid for all manuscript collections are filed in notebooks and available for researcher and staff use.

Review of Collections: The collections of Nez Perce County Historical Society are well cared for. The photograph collection is strong, the manuscript materials somewhat limited. The manuscript materials are listed to the folder level but there is no comprehensive index to locate a specific subject. They do not collect materials of a genealogical nature. The collection focuses on the city of Lewiston, Nez Perce County, and the surrounding areas including the neighboring communities.

Museum on Premises: Yes

Museum Hours: Tu–Sa 10–4, Mar–Dec

Cost of Entry to Museum: Donation

Museum Is Handicapped Accessible: Yes

Description of Museum: The museum presents the chronological highlights of Nez Perce County history in a number of professionally designed galleries.

Parking: Free parking lot adjacent

Lunch: Number of upscale restaurants within two blocks

Lodging: http://www.lewistonchamber.org; http://www.northcentralidaho.info

Nearest Commercial Airport: Lewiston–Nez Perce County (LWS) [4 miles]

Subjects

Historical Periods: 1865–1900; 1900–1940; 1940–present

Eras: Indian Wars; World War I; CCC

Natural Resources: Dams; Irrigation; Logging

Mining: Gold

Transportation: Railroads; Ferries

Agriculture: Dairy; Vegetable/ Truck Crops; Orchards

Business: Hotels/Restaurants; Entertainment/Theaters

Manufacturing: Brewery; Grist/Flour Mills; Sawmills; Wood Products

Organizations: Schools; Colleges/Universities; Hospitals/ Medical Facilities; Nonreligious Organizations; Women's

Ethnic Groups: Native American

Date of Reviewer's Visit: 9/12/2003

Profile Updated by Institution: 11/4/2004

MACKAY

Name: Lost Rivers Museum   **County:** Custer

Mailing Address: PO Box 572

  City: Mackay   **State:** ID   **Postal Code:** 83251-0000

Street Address: 310 Capitol St.

Institution Email: None

Telephone Number: (208) 588-3148

Contact Name: Earl A. Lockie   **Contact Email:** earllockie@atcnet.net

Institution Type: Local Museum

Affiliation: South Custer Historical Society

Web site URL: None

Hours: Sa–Su 1–5, May–Sept

Staff in Archives: 10v

Archives Are Handicapped Accessible: No

Access Description: Stairs at entrance

Review of Facilities: The Lost Rivers Museum is located in an old frame church a few blocks off the highway in downtown Mackay. There are steps up to enter the building. The facilities are sparse. The museum display area is spread out over several rooms and the research collections are interspersed with the exhibit materials. Many of the archival materials are actually part of the displays. There is no specific research table, but space is available to accommodate a researcher. This collection is small, but significant, because it covers a large geographic and sparsely settled area. The Lost River Valley of Idaho and the South Custer County area are the main areas of focus.

Vertical Files: Yes   **Vertical Files in Cubic Feet:** 1

Vertical File Description and Subjects: Family history files, mostly uncataloged

Manuscripts: Yes   **Manuscripts Volume in Cubic Feet:** 10

Manuscript Types: Scrapbooks

Manuscript Subjects: Local organizations; High Country Cowbells (Idaho Cattle Women) 1965–1981 scrapbook collection

Photographs: Yes

Number of Photographs: 700

Storage of Photographs: Displays of photocopies of photos, many scanned; no index to the photos.

Photograph Subjects: Mostly mining and businesses in early Mackay

Photograph Reproductions Are Available: Yes

Photographic Prints: No   **Digital Prints:** Yes

Books: No

Newspapers: Yes

Newspapers in Paper Format: Yes

Papers and Dates: *Mackay Telegraph,* 1901–1905, and *Mackay Miner,* 1906–1975

Newspapers on Microfilm: No

Microfilm and Dates: Mackay District Library has microfilm of local paper, *Mackay Miner,* 1906–1975

Oral Histories: No

Maps and Drawings: No

Genealogy Sources: Yes

Genealogy Sources Description: Family history files

Special Collections: No

Indexes: No

Review of Collections: The Lost River Museum collection is very small and severely underfunded. At present all inquiries and research material requests are handled by the Museum/Historical Society contact person. He is dedicated to helping to every degree possible anyone requiring research material. There are some magnificent early photographs of the area in the collection. The photographs are not easily searched by subject or otherwise. They are working to process some of the materials, but at present the collection is mostly unindexed. The volunteers are dedicated, however, and the collection shows great promise and covers an area of the state not well represented in any other collection. Indexing and cataloging of all archives, including historical photographs and documents, is scheduled for completion within the next year.

Museum on Premises: Yes

Description of Museum: Small, volunteer-run museum displaying historical artifacts from the history of the area.

Parking: Free vertical street parking

Lunch: Several local eateries and small market within a few blocks

Lodging: http://www.mackayidaho.com; or in Arco, 27 miles

Nearest Commercial Airport: Idaho Falls Regional (IDA) [94 miles]

Subjects

Historical Periods: 1800–1865; 1865–1900; 1900–1940; 1940–present

Eras: World War I; WPA

Natural Resources: Water; Dams

Mining: Copper; Tunnel Mining

Transportation: Railroads; Stagecoach/Freight

Agriculture: Ranching/Livestock

Business: Retail; Hotels/Restaurants; Entertainment/Theaters

Government: Federal

Organizations: Schools; Civic and Fraternal; Women's

Religious Sites and Organizations: Protestant; Catholic; LDS (Mormon)

Date of Reviewer's Visit: 5/28/2003

Profile Updated by Institution: 11/15/2004

MOSCOW

✯✯✯✯

Name: Latah County Historical Society **County:** Latah

Mailing Address: 327 E. Second

City: Moscow **State:** ID **Postal Code:** 83843-0000

Street Address: 327 E. Second

Institution Email: lchlibrary@moscow.com

Telephone Number: (208) 882-1004 **Fax Number:** (208) 883-0759

Contact Name: Ann Catt   **Contact Email:** lchsoffice@moscow.com

Institution Type: Historical Society Archives

Web site URL: http://users.moscow.com/lchs/resources/

Hours: Tu–F 9–5

Staff in Archives: 1f 2p 6v

Archives Are Handicapped Accessible: No

Access Description: Stairs to enter building. Staff will take materials to Moscow Public Library by arrangement if necessary.

Cost for Researcher—In-house: Fee for extra staff time

Cost for Researcher—Remote: Fee schedule

Review of Facilities: The Latah County Historical Society Research Library is located across the street from the McConnell Mansion Museum in a residential area close to downtown. The research library shares a building with the administrative offices of the historical society. The former apartment building has been opened up to serve as offices, storage, and the research room. A large tile fireplace dominates the research room. Hardwood floors, glass-fronted bookcases, and a large worktable fill out the very pleasant research room. A card file cabinet, books, and genealogical indexes are the only items stored in the research room. Photographs are housed nearby. A storage room in the back holds short rows of compact shelving and the majority of the collection.

Vertical Files: Yes   **Vertical Files in Cubic Feet:** 8

　Vertical File Description and Subjects: Vertical files include sections of biography, towns, and general files.

Manuscripts: Yes   **Manuscripts Volume in Cubic Feet:** 220

　Manuscript Types: Business records, family papers, scrapbooks, legal records, organizational records

　Manuscript Subjects: Probate records of Latah County from 1888 to 1908. Family histories and papers of local residents of all time periods, doctors' records

Photographs: Yes   **Number of Photographs:** 13,000

　Storage of Photographs: Photocopies of photos are in binders and filed by subject number. The original photographs are stored in file cabinets in Mylar sleeves. There are also 74 photograph albums and 1,000 slides

　Photograph Subjects: Latah County and surrounding area

　Photograph Reproductions Are Available: Yes

　　Photographic Prints: Yes

Books: Yes   **Number of Books in Collection:** 550

　Description of Books: Local history, professional collection, genealogy

Newspapers: No

Oral Histories: Yes   **Oral Histories Number:** 950

  Oral Histories Description: There are 746 reel-to-reel tapes of oral history interviews done from 1974 to 1976 with local area residents. There are 172 audiocassette interviews as well. The museum does not have a reel-to-reel player but 282 of the interviews have transcriptions.

Maps and Drawings: Yes   **Estimated Number of Maps and Drawings:** 165

  Description of Maps and Drawings: Local area maps and atlases

Genealogy Sources: Yes

  Genealogy Sources Description: Cemetery records; birth, death and marriage records, 1885–1950

Special Collections: Yes

  Special Collections Description: The research library has an extensive pamphlet and ephemera collection of local area subjects. Included are church histories, promotional brochures, business materials, trade catalogs, and posters. This totals nearly 11 cu. ft.

Indexes: Local historical card file lists both subjects and individuals by name. Index of archives. Obituary index. In-house local computer database listing photographs and manuscript items.

Review of Collections: The Latah County Historical Society has materials representing the history of the area, from the first white settlement in 1871 to the present. A diversity of cultures is represented, including the Native American tribes of the area. The collection is large for the size of the county. The collection is also well rounded and professionally handled. The pamphlet file is significant for its size and content. The photographs represent a diverse subject and cultural range.

Museum on Premises: No

Parking: Free on-street parallel parking. Some areas marked "one hour only." Narrow residential street.

Lunch: Variety of ethnic and upscale restaurants in downtown Moscow a short drive away

Lodging: http://www.moscowchamber.com

Nearest Commercial Airport: Pullman/Moscow Regional (Pullman, WA) (PUW) [7 miles]

Subjects

  Historical Periods: 1865–1900; 1900–1940; 1940–present

  Eras: Indian Wars

  Natural Resources: Logging

Mining: Gold; Tunnel Mining

Transportation: Railroads

Agriculture: Ranching/Livestock; Orchards; Dry Land Farming

Business: Banking; Retail; Legal/Medical Services

Manufacturing: Brewery; Brick Making; Sawmills

Government: County

Organizations: Schools; Colleges/Universities; Hospitals/ Medical Facilities; Charities; Nonreligious Organizations; Civic and Fraternal; Women's; Business; Children's

Date of Reviewer's Visit: 1/29/2004

Profile Updated by Institution: 12/2/2004

✳✳✳✳✳

Name: University of Idaho Library, Special Collections and Archives
County: Latah

Mailing Address: P.O. Box 442351

City: Moscow   **State:** ID   **Postal Code:** 83844-2351

Street Address: Rayburn St.

Institution Email: libspec@uidaho.edu

Telephone Number: (208) 885-7951   **Fax Number:** (208) 855-6817

Contact Name: Terry Abraham

Institution Type: Academic Library

Affiliation: University of Idaho

Web site URL: http://www.lib.uidaho.edu/special-collections

Hours: M–F 8–12, 1–5

Staff in Archives: 3f

Archives Are Handicapped Accessible: Yes

Access Description: On side of building, has buzzer outside door

Review of Facilities: The Special Collections and Archives is located on the ground floor of the University of Idaho Library, on Rayburn Street, on campus. The main floor entrance to the special collections door leads directly to a flight of stairs downward. The research room is moderate in size and ornamentation. There are two large tables, each with four chairs, and bookshelves with guides to materials. Staff offices and work areas flank the research room. Personal items can be stored on unsecured shelves in the staff area. Materials are housed in compact shelving in an adjacent storage area.

Collection housed onsite. Their Web site has a particularly helpful Visitor's Guide with detailed information about the institution.

Vertical Files: Yes   **Vertical Files in Cubic Feet:** 40

   Vertical File Description and Subjects: Idaho and the Pacific Northwest

Manuscripts: Yes   **Manuscripts Volume in Cubic Feet:** 6,000

   Manuscript Types: All manuscript types

   Manuscript Subjects: Lumber, railroad, mining and other companies; religions; fraternal and civic organizations; papers of government officials, educators, and authors. Conservation of Idaho's natural resources.

Photographs: Yes   **Number of Photographs:** 100,000

   Photograph Subjects: Idaho state history, University of Idaho, Moscow, Wallace, and Northern Idaho.

   Photograph Reproductions Are Available: Yes

      Photographic Prints: Yes   **Digital Prints:** Yes

Books: Yes   **Number of Books in Collection:** 16,500

   Description of Books: Idaho State, Pacific Northwest published materials in the Day-Northwest collection. They are searchable from the library electronic catalog.

Newspapers: No

   Microfilm and Dates: Idaho papers in periodicals department, second floor.

Oral Histories: Yes   **Oral Histories Number:** Unknown

   Oral Histories Description: Collect copies of some oral histories from other areas in the state.

Maps and Drawings: Yes

   Description of Maps and Drawings: Early maps of the area prior to 1900

Genealogy Sources: No

Special Collections: Yes

   Special Collections Description: Barnard-Stockbridge photo collection

Indexes: Microsoft Access database for photographs

   Manuscript Finding Aids: Inventories of manuscripts stored in document boxes in reference room. Finding aids available online from Web site.

   Published Guides: List of published guides available at http://www.lib.uidaho.edu/special-collections/libbib.htm

   Online Sources: Information regarding manuscript collections can be found in the library electronic catalog. Inventories, lists, and bibliographies of some collections are available from Web site.

Review of Collections: The collections of the University of Idaho are well documented on the Web site, several hundred having complete finding aids. Photograph collections focus on the university and the state of Idaho. The Day-Northwest collection of published materials is one of the most comprehensive in the region. The collections are well processed, professionally maintained, and extremely important to the history of the state of Idaho.

Museum on Premises: No

Parking: Check at visitor center on Highway 8; parking passes available for lots near library

Lunch: Various dining options in the Student Union or drive to a variety of restaurants

Lodging: http://www.moscowchamber.com

Nearest Commercial Airport: Pullman/Moscow Regional (Pullman, WA) (PUW) [6 miles]

Subjects

> **Historical Periods:** 1800–1865; 1865–1900; 1900–1940; 1940–present
>
> **Eras:** Exploration; Fur Trade; Indian Wars; Spanish American War; World War I; CCC; World War II
>
> **Natural Resources:** Water; Dams; Irrigation; Fishing; Hunting; Logging
>
> **Mining:** Gold; Silver; Copper; Placer Mining; Surface Mining; Tunnel Mining
>
> **Transportation:** Railroads; Aviation
>
> **Agriculture:** Ranching/Livestock; Grains; Dry Land Farming;
>
> **Business:** Banking; Retail; Legal/Medical Services; Hotels/Restaurants
>
> **Manufacturing:** Grist/Flour Mills; Sawmills; Wood Products
>
> **Government:** City; County; State; Federal
>
> **Organizations:** Schools; Colleges/Universities; Hospitals/Medical Facilities; Charities; Nonreligious Organizations; Civic and Fraternal; Women's; Business; Labor and Union

Date of Reviewer's Visit: 1/28/2004

Profile Updated by Institution: 11/5/2004

OROFINO

Name: Clearwater Historical Museum   **County:** Clearwater
Mailing Address: PO Box 1454

City: Orofino   **State:** ID   **Postal Code:** 83544-1454

Street Address: 315 College Ave.

Institution Email: chmuseum@clearwater.net

Telephone Number: (208) 476-5033

Institution Type: Local Museum

Affiliation: Clearwater Historical Society

Web site URL: http://www.clearwatermuseum.org

Hours: Tu–Sa 1:30–4:30, Oct–May; 1:30–5:30, Jun–Sept

Staff in Archives: 1p 1v

Archives Are Handicapped Accessible: No

Access Description: 5 stairs up into museum

Cost for Researcher—Remote: Donation

Review of Facilities: The Clearwater Historical Museum is on the ground floor of an old house a few blocks from the center of town. Entry to the house is up five cement stairs. The remainder of the public area is on one level. There is no particular area set aside for research, although the majority of the materials is housed in one section. There is no table space for researchers and all the collections and indexes are staff reference help only. There is one possible worktable in the main display area but it is not always available.

Vertical Files: Yes   **Vertical Files in Cubic Feet:** 12

Vertical File Description and Subjects: General clipping and ephemera files

Manuscripts: Yes   **Manuscripts Volume in Cubic Feet:** Unknown

Manuscript Types: Business ledgers, scrapbooks

Manuscript Subjects: Business, U.S. Forest Service (1960s) 4H; Commercial Club; Chamber of Commerce; Shoshone County court records, 1875–1900; school district records, 1911–1950; water rights court claims; mining record books, 1861–1930s; collection of handwritten gold mining record books from the area

Photographs: Yes   **Number of Photographs:** 4,500

Storage of Photographs: Photos stored by accession number in plastic sleeves in file folders

Photograph Subjects: Local interest

Books: Yes   **Number of Books in Collection:** 500

Description of Books: Idaho history, local interest, logging

Newspapers: Yes

Newspapers in Paper Format: Yes

Papers and Dates: Orofino papers from 1899–1950 (scattered issues) and from 1950–present (complete run)

Oral Histories: Yes   **Oral Histories Number:** 100

Oral Histories Description: Local area residents' interviews; some have transcriptions

Maps and Drawings: Yes

Description of Maps and Drawings: Local area maps, 1917 and newer

Genealogy Sources: Yes

Genealogy Sources Description: Family and genealogy files; obituary and marriage indexes

Special Collections: Yes

Special Collections Description: Starr Maxwell Papers: papers from the early 1900s, including Maxwell's work on the subject of tribal allotments, several trips to Washington, D.C., on behalf of the Nez Perce tribe, and correspondence regarding the tribal interests of the Nez Perce.

Indexes: Separate subject card indexes for the photograph collection (4 x 6 cards with subjects and cross references), manuscript materials, obituary files, and book collection

Review of Collections: The collections in this small historical society museum are interesting and include a few notable and very important manuscript collections. The Starr Maxwell Papers regard the Indian allotments of the early part of the twentieth century. These papers include legal and personal correspondence regarding this and other subjects from a man with Nez Perce heritage. The set of original gold mining records books from the area is also a notable collection. The earliest dates from 1861 and the latest from the 1930s. There are also a small number of Chinese artifacts and some documents from the mining area in the nineteenth century. Even though the research area is not developed, these gems are a significant part of the historical record and should not be overlooked.

Museum on Premises: Yes

Museum Hours: Tu–Sat 12:30–5:30, Jun– Sept; 1:30–4:30, Oct–May

Cost of Entry to Museum: Donation

Museum Is Handicapped Accessible: No

Description of Museum: Small local history museum with multiple display rooms depicting the history of the area.

Parking: On-street free parallel parking

Lunch: Several cafes and local restaurants in downtown area, 3–6 blocks away.

Lodging: http://www.orofino.com; Helgeson Place Suites Hotel few blocks away

Nearest Commercial Airport: Lewiston–Nez Perce County (LWS) [46 miles]

Subjects

    Historical Periods: 1800–1865; 1865–1900; 1900–1940; 1940–present

    Natural Resources: Water; Dams; Logging

    Mining: Gold

    Business: Hotels/Restaurants

    Government: County; Tribal

    Organizations: Schools

    Ethnic Groups: Native American; Chinese

Date of Reviewer's Visit: 9/11/2003

Profile Updated by Institution: None

POCATELLO

Name: Bannock County Historical Museum   **County:** Bannock

Mailing Address: PO Box 253

    City: Pocatello   **State:** ID   **Postal Code:** 83204-0253

Street Address: 3000 Alvord Loop

Institution Email: None

Telephone Number: (208) 233-0434

Contact Name: Margaret A. Barrett

Institution Type: Local Museum

Affiliation: Bannock County and Bannock County Historical Society

Web site URL: None

Hours: T–Sa 10–2, Sept–May; 10–6, June–Aug

Staff in Archives: 1f, 1p, 3v

Archives Are Handicapped Accessible: Yes

Review of Facilities: The Bannock County Historical Museum is located on the upper level of Ross Park across from the Fort Hall replica. The museum is housed in a newer, but too-small building. The library space has been taken over for storage, so space in the office is made available to researchers.

Vertical Files: Yes

    Vertical File Description and Subjects: Clippings, ephemera, copies and some originals of documents on Bannock County

Manuscripts: Yes

Manuscript Types: Organizational records, ledgers, scrapbooks, personal papers

Manuscript Subjects: Bannock County history

Photographs: Yes   **Number of Photographs:** 3,000

Storage of Photographs: Photographs stored in file cabinets in folders filed by accession number. Subject list is available.

Photograph Subjects: Pocatello, downtown business district, railroad, other Pocatello sites

Photograph Reproductions Are Available: Yes

  Photographic Prints: Yes   **Digital Prints:** No

Digital Images on CD or Electronically: Yes

Books: Yes   **Number of Books in Collection:** 600

Description of Books: Local history, Polk directories 1901–current, Pocatello High School yearbooks 1907–1990s, professional collections.

Newspapers: No

Microfilm and Dates: Local Libraries have microfilm of newspapers

Oral Histories: Yes   **Oral Histories Number:** 20

Oral Histories Description: Local area resident interviews. Transcriptions are available for most interviews.

Maps and Drawings: Yes   **Estimated Number of Maps and Drawings:** 20

Description of Maps and Drawings: Some early local area maps, Sanborn maps

Genealogy Sources: Yes   **Genealogy Sources Description:** Cemetery records

Special Collections: No

Indexes: Subject listing of the photograph collection

Review of Collections: The collections at the Bannock County Historical Museum are limited in scope. The focus of the collections are the 3,000 photographs of Bannock County and the surrounding area. Books and some manuscript materials make up the remainder of the collection. They have a vertical file, which includes clippings, paper ephemera, originals and copies of documents, and other assorted items. They also have scrapbooks, ledgers, letters, minutes of organizations, master's theses, and so on.

Museum on Premises: Yes

  Museum Is Handicapped Accessible: Yes

  Description of Museum: Moderate-sized local museum with exhibits on Pocatello's early railroad history and Native American tribes.

Parking: Free parking lot

Lunch: Driving distance 1 mile to various chains on 5th Ave. by Idaho State University

Lodging: http://www.pocatellocvb.com

Nearest Commercial Airport: Pocatello Regional (PIH) [14 miles]

Subjects

    Historical Periods: 1865–1900; 1900–1940; 1940–present

    Eras: WPA; CCC; World War II

    Transportation: Railroads; Stagecoach/Freight

    Business: Retail; Legal/Medical Services; Hotels/Restaurants; Entertainment/ Theaters

    Manufacturing: Brewery; Brick Making

    Organizations: Schools; Colleges/Universities; Hospitals/Medical Facilities; Civic and Fraternal; Women's

    Ethnic Groups: Native American; African; Bannock; Shoshone; Japanese; Chinese

    Religious Sites and Organizations: Protestant; Catholic; LDS (Mormon)

Date of Reviewer's Visit: 5/28/2003

Profile Updated by Institution: 11/12/2004

✵✵✵✵✵

Name: Idaho State University, Special Collections, Eli M. Oboler Library
County: Bannock

Mailing Address: PO Box 8089

  City: Pocatello   **State:** ID   **Postal Code:** 83209-8089

Street Address: 850 S. 9th Ave.

Institution Email: None

Telephone Number: (208) 236-2997

Contact Name: Karen Kearns   **Contact Email:** kearkare@isu.edu

Institution Type: Academic Library

Affiliation: Idaho State University

Web site URL: http://www.isu.edu/library/special/home.htm

Hours: 8–4:30

Staff in Archives: 2

Archives Are Handicapped Accessible: Yes

Access Description: Electric doors and elevators

Cost for Researcher—Remote: Fee schedule $5 min.

Review of Facilities: Special Collections is located in the basement of the Oboler Library on the Idaho State University Campus. The research room has four large worktables. The area is open and well lit. The book collections are housed in the research room. Maps in a large map case with eight drawers provide the only other materials available in the research room. Only pencils are allowed in the research room. The bulk of the collection is maintained in an adjacent storage area.

Vertical Files: Yes   **Vertical Files in Cubic Feet:** 8

Vertical File Description and Subjects: Local newspaper clippings and ephemera

Manuscripts: Yes   **Manuscripts Volume in Cubic Feet:** Unknown

Manuscript Types: All manuscript types

Manuscript Subjects: Related to people and institutions of southern Idaho and Native American populations. University Archives from 1902–present. More than 100 collections.

Photographs: Yes   **Number of Photographs:** 5,000

Storage of Photographs: In manuscript boxes

Photograph Subjects: Collection of local newspaper negatives after 1950. Most of the photographs have been pulled from the manuscript collections. Early Pocatello history and the railroads are two of the main topics.

Photograph Reproductions Are Available: Yes

Photographic Prints: Yes   **Digital Prints:** Yes

Books: Yes   **Number of Books in Collection:** 5,150

Description of Books: Intermountain West Collection, local interest, and rare books. All listed in library catalog.

Newspapers: Yes

Newspapers in Paper Format: Yes

Papers and Dates: Student newspapers for campus from 1910. Other newspapers for local area upstairs in the periodicals department. Newspaper holdings are listed on the library catalog.

Oral Histories: Yes   **Oral Histories Number:** 150

Oral Histories Description: Interviews were collected by students on various projects and deal with local historical interest. Most have transcripts.

Maps and Drawings: Yes

Description of Maps and Drawings: Local interest maps and historical maps and Metsker atlases. Large cabinet with 8 drawers in reading room.

Genealogy Sources: Yes

Genealogy Sources Description: Cemetery records, city directories

Special Collections: No

Indexes: Books are listed in the general library catalog. Finding aids available to researchers in the research room.

Manuscript Finding Aids: Majority of manuscript collections have finding aids. Some are available through the Web site.

Online Sources: A small number of the finding aids are available through the Web site. Some collections are listed in the general library computer catalog.

Review of Collections: The Special Collections and University Archives at Idaho State University have collections related to the area or to Idaho history in general. The Albion State Normal School Records collection documents the history of the normal school from 1893 to 1951. There are over 100 separate manuscript collections from 1/2 cu. ft. to 40 cu. ft. in size per collection. Two notable collections are a 27-cu.-ft. collection from Dr. Minnie Howard, an early Pocatello physician, and another collection of papers from Dr. Vincent Schultz on the subject of radioecology.

Museum on Premises: No

Parking: On-street or day parking permit available from parking kiosk at Administration Building

Lunch: Variety of fast-food and family restaurants on 5th St.

Lodging: http://www.pocatellocvb.com; Econolodge adjacent to campus

Nearest Commercial Airport: Pocatello Regional (PIH) [10 miles]

Subjects

> **Historical Periods:** 1865–1900; 1900–1940; 1940–present
>
> **Eras:** Indian Wars; WPA
>
> **Transportation:** Railroads
>
> **Agriculture:** Dry Land Farming
>
> **Business:** Legal/Medical Services
>
> **Government:** City; Federal
>
> **Organizations:** Colleges/Universities; Women's
>
> **Ethnic Groups:** Native American
>
> **Religious Sites and Organizations:** LDS (Mormon)

Date of Reviewer's Visit: 5/29/2003

Profile Updated by Institution: 12/9/2004

REXBURG

✹✹✹✹

Name: BYU–Idaho Library—Special Collections   **County:** Madison

Mailing Address: McKay Library

City: Rexburg   **State:** ID   **Postal Code:** 83460-0405

Street Address: McKay Library, 525 South Center

Institution Email: familyhistory@byui.edu

Telephone Number: (208) 496-2986   **Fax Number:** (208) 356-2390

Contact Name: Blaine R Bake, Archivist

Institution Type: Academic Library

Affiliation: Brigham Young University—Idaho

Web site URL: http://abish.byui.edu/specialCollections/spchome.htm

Hours: M–F 9–4, Sa by appt. only

Staff in Archives: 1f 1p

Archives Are Handicapped Accessible: Yes

Review of Facilities: The Special Collections, University Archives, and a branch of the Family History Center are located on the second floor in the west wing of the McKay Library near the center of campus. The Special Collections reading room was in transition at the time of the visit, but the room was large and well lit with large worktables. The collections are stored elsewhere in the building in a secure area.

Vertical Files: Yes   **Vertical Files in Cubic Feet:** 8

  Vertical File Description and Subjects: Various topics of local interest

Manuscripts: Yes   **Manuscripts Volume in Cubic Feet:** 135

  Manuscript Types: Business records, organizational records, family papers, archives

  Manuscript Subjects: Upper Snake River Valley; Daughters of Utah Pioneers; Great Feeder Canal Co. and Rexburg Canal Co.; C.C. Moore (former Idaho governor) papers

Photographs: Yes   **Number of Photographs:** 20 linear feet

  Storage of Photographs: Photographs are stored archivally in boxes.

  Photograph Subjects: Ricks College, BYU–Idaho, Upper Teton Valley, Rexburg, Teton Flood

  Photograph Reproductions Are Available: Yes

    Photographic Prints: Yes   **Digital Prints:** Yes

Books: Yes

  Description of Books: Local history, regional history

Newspapers: No

Oral Histories: Yes   **Oral Histories Number:** 41

  Oral Histories Description: Oral histories done for history class interviewing individuals who experienced World War II, Korea, or Vietnam wars. Transcripts for most interviews.

Maps and Drawings: No

Genealogy Sources: Yes

> **Genealogy Sources Description:** Family History Center is located in another room on the same floor with a full genealogy collection.

Special Collections: No

Indexes: Yes

> **Manuscript Finding Aids:** The manuscript collections each have a register, many of these are available on the Web site.

> **Online Sources:** Online listing of some of the manuscript collections available from Web site. Also the CES Digital Collections (with BYU–Provo) has digitized versions of the collection titled Historical Sketches of the Upper Snake River Valley Pioneers; historical photographs of Ricks College and BYU–Idaho. Available at http://www.lib.byui.edu/cesdigCollectionsEntry.htm.

Review of Collections: The collection covers the area of the Upper Snake River Valley and eastern Idaho. The collections include personal and business papers of the early settlement of Rexburg and the area. History of the Mormon settlement, life, and activities in the area is particularly strong. A collection of LDS church historical materials is also available. One of the most significant collections, Historical Sketches of the Upper Snake River Valley Pioneers, is available online (see online sources). The history of Ricks College from the beginning and its transformation into BYU–Idaho is recorded in the University Archives; some of the collections in these archives are closed to researchers.

Museum on Premises: No

Parking: Free on-street parallel parking or visitors parking

Lunch: Cafeteria and deli in the adjacent Student Union Building

Lodging: http://www.rexcc.com

Nearest Commercial Airport: Idaho Falls Regional (IDA) [29 miles]

Subjects

> **Historical Periods:** 1865–1900; 1900–1940; 1940–present

> **Organizations:** Colleges/Universities

> **Religious Sites and Organizations:** LDS (Mormon)

Date of Reviewer's Visit: 8/13/2002

Profile Updated by Institution: None

Name: Upper Snake River Valley Historical Society   **County:** Madison

Mailing Address: PO Box 244

City: Rexburg   **State:** ID   **Postal Code:** 83440-0000

Street Address: 51 N. Center

Institution Email: None

Telephone Number: (208) 356-9101   **Fax Number:** (208) 356-3379

Contact Name: Lewis Clemens

Institution Type: Local Museum

Affiliation: Teton Flood Museum

Web site URL: None

Hours: By appt. only (hours for appts. M–Sa 9–4, June–Aug; 10–3, Sept–May)

Staff in Archives: 5v

Archives Are Handicapped Accessible: No

Access Description: Stairs to archives room

Review of Facilities: The Teton Flood Museum is housed in the basement of the historic Rexburg Tabernacle. The Upper Snake River Valley Historical Society has a room adjacent to the museum but not part of the museum. The door to the research room is off a stairway with several steps leading to the room itself. The research room is small with tables in the center and materials ringing the room.

Vertical Files: Yes   **Vertical Files in Cubic Feet:** 12

  Vertical File Description and Subjects: Clipping files and miscellaneous ephemera

Manuscripts: Yes   **Manuscript Types:** Legal records, scrapbooks, personal papers, organizational records

  Manuscript Subjects: Upper Snake River Valley, Teton Flood, Rexburg

Photographs: Yes   **Number of Photographs:** 2,700

  Storage of Photographs: Photos are in photosleeves in binders. Arrangement by accession number.

  Photograph Subjects: Fremont County and Madison County subjects; Teton Flood photographs

Books: Yes

Newspapers: Yes

Oral Histories: Yes   **Oral Histories Number:** 620

  Oral Histories Description: Interviews with local area residents starting in 1968. Originally on audiocassette and transferred to CD format. Transcriptions of tapes in process.

Maps and Drawings: No

Genealogy Sources: Yes

Genealogy Sources Description: Collection of family histories

Special Collections: No

Indexes: Collection is cataloged on card files and a computer index

Review of Collections: This collection is small but significant. The collection covers the early history of the Upper Snake River Valley, Rexburg, and surrounding communities and the Teton Flood of 1976. There are materials dealing with the mountain men and the early fur trade. Some of the early Fremont County documents are also in the collection. Although the neighboring museum focuses mainly on Teton Flood, the archival collections are much broader-based. The oral history collection is large and spread over many years.

Museum on Premises: Yes

> **Museum Hours:** M–Sa 9–4, Jun–Sept; M–F 10–3, Oct–May
>
> **Cost of Entry to Museum:** $1
>
> **Museum Is Handicapped Accessible:** Yes
>
> **Description of Museum:** Teton Flood Museum is adjacent to the Upper Snake River Historical Society, but they are separately run.

Parking: Free parking lot adjacent

Lunch: Driving distance to variety of restaurants

Lodging: http://www.rexcc.com

Nearest Commercial Airport: Idaho Falls Regional (IDA) [9 miles]

Subjects

> **Historical Periods:** 1900–1940; 1940–present
>
> **Eras:** Fur Trade; World War I; World War II
>
> **Natural Resources:** Water; Dams
>
> **Government:** City
>
> **Organizations:** Nonreligious Organizations

Date of Reviewer's Visit: 8/13/2002

Profile Updated by Institution: None

RUPERT

Name: Minidoka County Historical Society   **County:** Minidoka

Mailing Address: PO Box 21

City: Rupert   **State:** ID   **Postal Code:** 83350-0000

Street Address: 100 E. Baseline

Institution Email: rupertmuseum@yahoo.com

Telephone Number: (208) 436-0336

Contact Name: Anne Schenk

Institution Type: Local Museum

Web site URL: None

Hours: M–Sa 1–5

Staff in Archives: 2p

Archives Are Handicapped Accessible: Yes

Access Description: Worktable height may be a problem for some researchers

Cost for Researcher—In-house: Donation

Cost for Researcher—Remote: Donation

Review of Facilities: The Minidoka County Historical Society Museum is a one-story building one mile east of Rupert, in a rural area. Research area is in the middle of the museum display floor. The research table itself is a high court clerk's desk with bookcases above the work area that house all of the research materials. This desk, though interesting, necessitates the use of high stools. Notebooks of various subjects, yearbooks, photographs, and other research materials are easily reached from the desk.

Vertical Files: Yes   **Vertical Files in Cubic Feet:** 2

     Vertical File Description and Subjects: Family histories and specific subjects filed in color-coded paper three-hole folders

Manuscripts: No

Photographs: Yes   **Number of Photographs:** 300

     Storage of Photographs: Arranged in subject books and photo albums in plastic sleeves

     Photograph Subjects: Towns of Paul, Heyburn, Rupert, Minidoka Dam, Civilian Conservation Corps camps, Hunt Camp (Japanese Internment), Camp Rupert (German POW), World War II

     Photograph Reproductions Are Available: Yes

         Photographic Prints: Yes   **Digital Prints:** Yes

Books: Yes   **Number of Books in Collection:** 24

     Description of Books: Local history

Newspapers: Yes

     Newspapers in Paper Format: Yes

Papers and Dates: Some early bound newspapers (1905–1906)

Oral Histories: Yes   **Oral Histories Number:** 25

Oral Histories Description: Interviews of local area residents done in the late1970s

Maps and Drawings: No

Genealogy Sources: Yes

Genealogy Sources Description: Limited to manuscripts submitted by families

Special Collections: Yes

Special Collections Description: Camp Rupert (World War II POW camp)

Indexes: Items are arranged by general subjects, no indexes to the collections

Review of Collections: This collection is fairly small but does have some special-interest items. One of these is a collection of the irrigation history of the valley. Also they have information on the Rupert POW camp from World War II. They have few photos of the camp because photography of the camp was prohibited. A third collection of interest is the Veterans' Homestead Program following World War II. There is also information on the Minidoka Dam. The photo collection is not large and is not readily searchable. Manuscript collections are also limited, but subject matters make them of particular interest.

Museum on Premises: Yes

Museum Hours: Daily 1–5

Cost of Entry to Museum: Donation

Museum Is Handicapped Accessible: Yes

Description of Museum: The museum is small and illustrates the history of Minidoka County.

Parking: Free gravel parking lot adjacent

Lunch: Driving distance into town of Rupert with several small local cafes

Lodging: http://www.minicassiachamber.org

Nearest Commercial Airport: Joslin Field–Magic Valley Regional (Twin Falls, ID) (TWF) [53 miles]

Subjects

Historical Periods: 1865–1900; 1900–1940; 1940–present

Eras: World War I; CCC; World War II

Natural Resources: Dams; Irrigation; Logging

Mining: Gold; Placer Mining

Transportation: Railroads

Agriculture: Ranching/Livestock; Vegetable/ Truck Crops; Grains; Dry Land Farming

Business: Retail

Ethnic Groups: Japanese; English; German; Russian; Spanish; Swedish

Religious Sites and Organizations: Protestant; Catholic; LDS (Mormon)

Date of Reviewer's Visit: 5/29/2003

Profile Updated by Institution: 11/8/2004

SALMON

Name: Lemhi County Historical Society   **County:** Lemhi

Mailing Address: 210 Main

   City: Salmon   **State:** ID   **Postal Code:** 83467-0000

Street Address: 210 Main

Institution Email: lemhimuseum@salmoninternet.com

Telephone Number: (208) 756-3342

Institution Type: Local Museum

Affiliation: Lemhi County Historical Society, Inc.

Web site URL: http://www.sacajaweahome.com

Hours: M–Sa 10–5, Apr–Oct

Staff in Archives: 5p

Archives Are Handicapped Accessible: Yes

List of Researchers Available: Yes

Review of Facilities: The Lemhi County Historical Society Museum is located on the main street of Salmon, next door to the public library. The single-story brick building has a ramp entrance. The research area is divided into two parts. Part of the collection is available in the main section of the museum and other parts are housed in a back room. Both areas have workspace.

Vertical Files: Yes   **Vertical Files in Cubic Feet:** 3

   Vertical File Description and Subjects: General clippings and ephemera filed by subject

Manuscripts: Yes   **Manuscripts Volume in Cubic Feet:** 3

   Manuscript Types: Family papers, business records

   Manuscript Subjects: Miscellaneous Lemhi County history

Photographs: Yes   **Number of Photographs:** 500

    Storage of Photographs: Stored in file folders in file cabinets arranged by subject, moving to acid-free storage

    Photograph Reproductions Are Available: Yes

        Photographic Prints: Yes   **Digital Prints:** Yes

Books: Yes

    Description of Books: Local history, Lewis and Clark journals, and old books

Newspapers: No

    Microfilm and Dates: Microfilm of local Newspapers available at Salmon Public Library next door

Oral Histories: No

Maps and Drawings: No

Genealogy Sources: Yes

    Genealogy Sources Description: Biography files

Special Collections: No

Indexes: No

Review of Collections: The Lemhi County Historical Society and Museum archive and library collections are small and growing. They are moving to a system of storage that is more archivally based. At the time of the visit, most of the unprocessed manuscript collections were stored offsite. They do have an inventory of those items, but access to them is limited. There is a 12-volume unpublished set of assorted local history articles and photographs of the area. The high school also does an annual local history magazine with articles researched and written by the students.

Museum on Premises: Yes

    Museum Hours: M–Sa 9–5

    Cost of Entry to Museum: $1

    Museum Is Handicapped Accessible: Yes

    Description of Museum: The museum illustrates frontier life during the 1800s and early 1900s in the Lemhi Valley. The museum also has the largest collection of Lemhi Shoshone artifacts known and the Ray Edwards Asian Collection of antiquities from China and Japan.

Parking: Free parallel on-street parking also a free adjacent parking lot

Lunch: Several local bars within walking distance. Chain fast food within short drive.

Lodging: http://www.salmonidaho.com; several chain hotels and local motels

Nearest Commercial Airport: Missoula International Airport (Missoula, MT) (MSO) [144 miles]

Subjects

Historical Periods: 1800–1865; 1865–1900; 1900–1940

Mining: Mining

Transportation: Railroads; Stagecoach/Freight

Agriculture: Ranching/Livestock

Organizations: Schools; Nonreligious Organizations

Ethnic Groups: Native American

Date of Reviewer's Visit: 8/12/2002

Profile Updated by Institution: 11/12/2004

SANDPOINT

✯✯✯✯

Name: Bonner County Historical Society **County:** Bonner

Mailing Address: 611 S. Ella St.

City: Sandpoint **State:** ID **Postal Code:** 83864-0000

Street Address: 611 S. Ella St.

Institution Email: bchsmuseum@imbris.net

Telephone Number: (208) 263-2344

Contact Name: Ann Ferguson

Institution Type: Local Museum

Web site URL: http://www.bonnercountyhistory.org

Hours: Tu, Th, and F 10–3

Staff in Archives: 1f 3v

Archives Are Handicapped Accessible: Yes

Access Description: Newer single-level building with no obvious barriers

Cost for Researcher—In-house: Museum admission

Cost for Researcher—Remote: Fee schedule

Review of Facilities: The museum is in a newer building in Lakeview City Park in Sandpoint. The archives area is spread over three large adjoining rooms. Large worktables are available with adequate lighting. File cabinets, bookshelves, and collections are spread over the walls of the room. Manuscript and newspaper collections are stored in adjacent room with other museum collections. Although the staff feels crunched for space, they actually have more than most like-sized museums visited. Research area better than average.

Vertical Files: Yes **Vertical Files in Cubic Feet:** 20

Vertical File Description and Subjects: Biography, communities, general subject files

Manuscripts: Yes   **Manuscripts Volume in Cubic Feet:** 40

Manuscript Types: Business records, family papers, government records

Manuscript Subjects: Civic Club records, David Thompson history in Wendell Collection from Kalispel House; Collection of Humbird Lumber Company, 1901–1933; City of Sandpoint records

Photographs: Yes   **Number of Photographs:** 40,000

Storage of Photographs: Photocopies of photographs in binders and arranged by subject. Originals are filed in plastic sleeves on hanging folders. Collection includes 17,000 negatives or slides; most not cataloged.

Photograph Subjects: Warren "Chuck" Peterson Collection of old photographs, which are copies of those owned by early residents; *Bonner County Bee* (newspaper) photos from 1970s–1980s; Sandpoint photos from 1940–1950s.

Books: Yes   **Number of Books in Collection:** 400

Description of Books: Local history, professional collection, yearbooks, phone books

Newspapers: Yes

Newspapers in Paper Format: Yes

Papers and Dates: 1899–present; most of the papers in Bonner County

Newspapers on Microfilm: Yes

Microfilm and Dates: Most papers on microfilm as well as paper

Oral Histories: Yes   **Oral Histories Number:** 120

Oral Histories Description: Interviews with local residents starting in the 1970s. Most have transcriptions.

Maps and Drawings: Yes

Description of Maps and Drawings: Sanborn Fire property records, miscellaneous local area maps

Genealogy Sources: Yes

Genealogy Sources Description: Obituary file

Special Collections: No

Indexes: Card file for photos (staff use) select newspaper card file and obituary file

Review of Collections: The collections are varied and contain most of the history throughout the county. Collections are well maintained and a skilled group of volunteers is processing and indexing the materials. Collections of note are the history of David Thompson in Wendell Collection from his time at Kalispel House and the collection of Humbird Lumber Company records from the years 1901 to

1933. Also important is a collection of photographs by a local man, Warren "Chuck" Peterson, who made copies of local family photographs for the purpose of archiving the images.

Museum on Premises: Yes

> **Museum Hours:** Tu–Sa 10–4

> **Cost of Entry to Museum:** $2

> **Museum Is Handicapped Accessible:** Yes

> **Description of Museum:** 7,000-sq.-ft. museum depicting the history of Bonner County and the Sandpoint area

Parking: Free parking lot adjacent

Lunch: Driving distance to variety of local and chain eateries

Lodging: http://sandpointchamber.org/

Nearest Commercial Airport: Spokane International WA (Spokane, WA) (GEG) [83 miles]

Subjects

> **Historical Periods:** 1800–1865; 1865–1900; 1900–1940; 1940–present

> **Natural Resources:** Fishing; Logging

> **Mining:** Placer Mining; Tunnel Mining

> **Transportation:** Railroads; Ferries

> **Agriculture:** Dairy; Ranching/Livestock

> **Manufacturing:** Sawmills; Wood Products

> **Organizations:** Schools

> **Ethnic Groups:** Native American; Chinese; Irish; Norwegian; Scottish; Swedish

Date of Reviewer's Visit: 7/11/2003

Profile Updated by Institution: None

SPALDING

�✩✩✩✩✩

Name: Nez Perce National Historic Park   **County:** Nez Perce

Mailing Address: 39063 U.S. Highway 95

> **City:** Spalding   **State:** ID   **Postal Code:** 83540-9715

Street Address: 39063 U.S. Highway 95 (3 miles north of Lapwai)

Institution Email: None

Telephone Number: (208) 843-2261   **Fax Number:** (208) 843-2001

Contact Name: Robert Applegate   **Contact Email:** robert_applegate@nps.gov

Institution Type: Historic Site

Affiliation: National Park Service

Web site URL: http://www.nps.gov/nepe

Hours: Daily 9–3 by appt.

Staff in Archives: 1f

Archives Are Handicapped Accessible: Yes

Access Description: Access is available through back door on lower level upon arrangement

Cost for Researcher—In-house: No charge

Cost for Researcher—Remote: Case-determined

List of Researchers Available: Yes

Review of Facilities: The Nez Perce National Historic Park is located in a remote area off Highway 95. The visitor center is modern, with museum displays on the main floor and staff offices in the basement. The research room is located in the basement as well. Visitors need to check in at the visitor center desk and be escorted to the research room. The room is large with ample, well lit table space. One section of the room holds the book collections, other areas have map cases, file cabinets, audiovisual equipment, and staff desks and work areas. Off the main research room is a climate-controlled storage area where the majority of manuscripts is kept. The facility is professionally managed with a certified archivist.

Vertical Files: Yes   **Vertical Files in Cubic Feet:** 20

   Vertical File Description and Subjects: Biography, Nez Perce history and culture,

Manuscripts: Yes   **Manuscripts Volume in Cubic Feet:** 360

   Manuscript Types: Government records, land records, family papers, organizational records, archives

   Manuscript Subjects: Nez Perce tribes, neighboring tribes, Nez Perce Trail, some original Spalding collections, War of 1877, White Bird Battle, Big Hole Battle, administrative records of Nez Perce National Historic Park, resource management of park sites, archeology records (some restricted access)

Photographs: Yes   **Number of Photographs:** 7,000

   Storage of Photographs: Electronic and index file cards

   Photograph Subjects: Nez Perce tribes, Spalding Mission; local area history; Nez Perce National Historic Park

   Photograph Reproductions Are Available: Yes

Photographic Prints: Yes   **Digital Prints:** Yes

Digital Images on CD or Electronically: Yes

Books: Yes

Number of Books in Collection: 3,000

Description of Books: Local area history, Nez Perce and Native American tribal history, archeology, and environmental issues

Newspapers: No

Oral Histories: Yes   **Oral Histories Number:** 200

Oral Histories Description: Nez Perce tribal members' oral histories on audiocassette or VHS videocassette. Some of the interviews are restricted.

Maps and Drawings: Yes   **Estimated Number of Maps and Drawings:** 400

Description of Maps and Drawings: Local area historical and modern maps, Some maps of Fort Lapwai.

Genealogy Sources: Yes

Genealogy Sources Description: Biography vertical files

Special Collections: No

Indexes: Computerized index to book collections and some photos

Manuscript Finding Aids: Finding aids available for manuscript collections

Review of Collections: The Nez Perce National Historic Park Research Center is managed by the National Park Service. This specialized collection is managed by a Certified Archivist. The collection encompasses the historic and current lives of the Nez Perce. It also collects on the subjects of missionary influences, the Nez Perce War of 1877, and the environmental effects of commercial ventures on the Nez Perce. Manuscript collections of various sizes illustrate this history. The collection on the Big Hole Battle alone is 100 linear feet. The book collections are noncirculating, Some collections are restricted, or use may be dependent on the permission of the Nez Perce tribal elders.

Museum on Premises: Yes

Museum Is Handicapped Accessible: Yes

Description of Museum: Professionally curated displays on Nez Perce history, rotating displays, and artwork

Parking: Free parking lot adjacent with long walkway

Lunch: Donald's Café in Lapwai, 3 miles south, or Lewiston, 10 miles north

Lodging: http://www.northcentralidaho.info; Lewiston, Idaho, 10 miles north

Nearest Commercial Airport: Lewiston–Nez Perce County (LWS) [18 miles]

Subjects

Historical Periods: Pre-1800; 1800–1865; 1865–1900; 1900–1940; 1940–present

Eras: Exploration; Fur Trade; Indian Wars

Natural Resources: Logging

Mining: Gold

Transportation: Railroads; Ferries

Business: Retail

Government: Federal; Tribal

Organizations: Schools

Ethnic Groups: Native American

Religious Sites and Organizations: Protestant; American Indian

Date of Reviewer's Visit: 7/29/2002

Profile Updated by Institution: 11/5/2004

TWIN FALLS

Name: Twin Falls Public Library—Idaho and Pacific Northwest History Room

County: Twin Falls

Mailing Address: 201 4th Ave. E.

  City: Twin Falls   **State:** ID   **Postal Code:** 83301-6397

Street Address: 201 4th Ave. E.

Institution Email: twinfalls@idaho-lynx.org

Telephone Number: (208) 733-2964   **Fax Number:** (208) 733-2965

Contact Name: Susan Ash, Assistant Director

Institution Type: Public Library

Affiliation: City of Twin Falls

Web site URL: http://www.twinfallspubliclibrary.org

Hours: M, F, and Sa 9–6; Tu, W, and Th 9–9

Staff in Archives: 1f

Archives Are Handicapped Accessible: Yes

Access Description: Covered ramp and electric doors on exterior of building

Review of Facilities: Twin Falls Public Library is located in the center of town across from the city park. The entrance to the library is up numerous stairs, but a ramp is provided. The building is modern and very pleasant. Access to the Idaho and Pacific Northwest History room is available only by permission. Check-in is at the circulation desk, where they will request that you sign a use form and leave a piece of identification. The IR (for "Idaho References") room, as the staff calls it, has two large worktables and is surrounded by the special collections materials. These materials include books on Pacific Northwest history, manuscripts, pamphlets, scrapbooks, oral histories, and other items relating to the history of the area.

Vertical Files: Yes

Vertical File Description and Subjects: Vertical file materials are all cataloged and interfiled with the book collection.

Manuscripts: Yes

Manuscript Types: Scrapbooks, personal papers

Manuscript Subjects: Scrapbooks, reminiscences, letters, and personal papers (manuscripts cataloged and interfiled with the books)

Photographs: Yes   **Number of Photographs:** 4,000

Storage of Photographs: 1,500 of the images are in three large file cabinets. Most are mounted on cardboard. Many originals are on glass plate negatives stored elsewhere.

Photograph Subjects: The Bisbee Collection contains 2,400 images taken 1904 through the 1920s. Nearly every building of importance in Twin Falls, Jerome, Buhl, and Kimberly were recorded during those years. There are also hundreds of photographs taken to promote the newly irrigated region.

Photograph Reproductions Are Available: Yes

Photographic Prints: Yes

Books: Yes   **Number of Books in Collection:** 20,000

Description of Books: Local history, Idaho history, Pacific Northwest history, city directories. All are cataloged and searchable on the Web site.

Newspapers: Yes

Newspapers on Microfilm: Yes

Microfilm and Dates: The *Times-News* (Twin Falls), 1904–present. Located in reference department.

Oral Histories: Yes   **Oral Histories Number:** 350

Oral Histories Description: Interviews with local residents on audiocassette. Most have transcriptions.

Maps and Drawings: Yes   **Estimated Number of Maps and Drawings:** 500

Description of Maps and Drawings: Large 10-drawer map file. Pacific Northwest maps, plat maps, highway maps, and local and regional interest maps

Genealogy Sources: No

Special Collections: Yes

Special Collections Description: The Bisbee collection of photographs is significant because they illustrate the Magic Valley area at the time of its greatest growth. Commercial photographer Clarence E. Bisbee was hired by the Twin Falls Land and Water Company to promote the newly irrigated farmland. In addition to recording the agricultural development of the area, he recorded the architectural and cultural history of the community.

Indexes: Most all materials including vertical file, manuscripts, books, and scrapbooks are cataloged and listed on the library electronic catalog.

Review of Collections: The collections at the Twin Falls Public Library are difficult to quantify because of the way the materials are arranged. The materials that in most institutions would be in a vertical file are housed alongside the book collection. These items are completely cataloged in the library system, even though an item may be as simple as a newspaper clipping, an oral history transcription, or numerous other types of materials. Everything is shelved in Dewey order on the bookshelves or oversize bookshelves. The one exception is the photograph files, which are in file cabinets. The Bisbee collection is the most significant and nationally important part of the collection. There are a detailed description and sample photographs on the Web site.

Museum on Premises: No

Parking: Free parking lot adjacent

Lunch: Driving distance

Lodging: http://www.inidaho.com

Nearest Commercial Airport: Joslin Field–Magic Valley Regional (Twin Falls, ID) (TWF) [6 miles]

Subjects

　　Historical Periods: 1865–1900; 1900–1940; 1940–present

　　Eras: World War II

　　Natural Resources: Water; Dams; Irrigation; Fishing; Hunting

　　Mining: Gold; Placer Mining

　　Transportation: Railroads; Stagecoach/Freight

　　Agriculture: Dairy; Ranching/Livestock; Vegetable/Truck Crops; Grains; Orchards

　　Business: Retail; Legal/Medical Services; Hotels/Restaurants; Entertainment/Theaters

　　Government: City

　　Organizations: Schools; Colleges/Universities; Hospitals/Medical Facilities; Charities; Nonreligious Organizations; Women's

　　Ethnic Groups: Native American; Chinese; Basque

Date of Reviewer's Visit: 5/30/2003

Profile Updated by Institution: 11/8/2004

VICTOR

Name: Valley of the Tetons District Library   **County:** Teton

Mailing Address: PO Box 37

   City: Victor   **State:** ID   **Postal Code:** 83455-0037

Street Address: 56 N. Main

Institution Email: library@tetontel.com

Telephone Number: (208) 787-2201   **Fax Number:** (208) 787-2201

Contact Name: Carla Sherman   **Contact Email:** library@tetontel.com

Institution Type: Public Library

Web site URL: http://www.teton.lib.id.us

Hours: M, F, and Sa 1–5; Tu, Th 10–5; W 1–7

Staff in Archives: 1f, 1p

Archives Are Handicapped Accessible: Yes

Review of Facilities: Valley of the Tetons District Library is located in a one-story building in the heart of downtown Victor, Idaho. The research collections are located in the library. The building is small but pleasant with some nice oversize historical photographs on the walls. There are computers and a worktable available, and researchers will share space with other library patrons.

Vertical Files: Yes   **Vertical Files in Cubic Feet:** 8

   Vertical File Description and Subjects: Vertical file materials are filed by subject or last name. There is an index to the vertical file materials.

Manuscripts: No

Photographs: Yes   **Number of Photographs:** 2,000

   Storage of Photographs: Photographs are stored in plastic sleeves in binders.

   Photograph Subjects: Photographs on agriculture, people, churches, and schools from the Driggs, Victor, and Teton Valley areas

   Photograph Reproductions Are Available: Yes

   Photographic Prints: Yes   **Digital Prints:** No

   Digital Images on CD or Electronically: Yes

Books: Yes   **Number of Books in Collection:** 75

   Description of Books: Local history, family histories

Newspapers: Yes   **Newspapers in Paper Format:** Yes

   Papers and Dates: *Teton Valley News,* 1909–present

   Newspapers on Microfilm: Yes

   Microfilm and Dates: *Teton Valley News,* 1909–present

Oral Histories: Yes   **Oral Histories Number:** 64

   Oral Histories Description: Oral history interviews with area residents. Transcripts only. Audiotapes in the museum in Driggs.

Maps and Drawings: Yes   **Estimated Number of Maps and Drawings:** 4

   Description of Maps and Drawings: Teton County, city maps

Genealogy Sources: Yes

   Genealogy Sources Description: Area cemetery records for Cedron and Victor

Special Collections: No

Indexes: Indexes available for the photographs and vertical file

Review of Collections: The collections of the Valley of the Tetons District Library are small but significant because of the remoteness of the area. The population of the county is 6,000. The city of Victor has only 840. The photographs are well cared for and most are not duplicated in collections elsewhere. They have recently purchased their local newspaper on microfilm. The collections are limited in scope, but the staff is helpful.

Museum on Premises: No

Parking: Free on-street parking

Lunch: Several local cafes within walking distance

Lodging: http://www.tetonvalleychamber.com

Nearest Commercial Airport: Jackson Hole Airport (Jackson Hole, WY) (JAC) [34 miles]

Subjects

   Historical Periods: 1800–1865; 1865–1900; 1900–1940; 1940–present

   Natural Resources: Water; Irrigation; Fishing; Hunting

   Agriculture: Dairy; Ranching/Livestock

   Business: Banking; Retail; Legal/Medical Services; Hotels/restaurants

   Manufacturing: Brewery; Sawmills

   Government: City; County

   Organizations: Schools; Hospitals/Medical Facilities; Charities; Nonreligious Organizations; Business; Children's

Ethnic Groups: Latin American; English; Spanish

Religious Sites and Organizations: Protestant; Catholic; LDS (Mormon)

Date of Reviewer's Visit: 8/14/2002

Profile Updated by Institution: 11/9/2004

WALLACE

Name: Wallace District Mining Museum   **County:** Shoshone

Mailing Address: PO Box 469

   City: Wallace   **State:** ID   **Postal Code:** 83873-0000

Street Address: 509 Bank St.

Institution Email: None

Telephone Number: (208) 556-1592   **Fax Number:** (208) 556-1592

Contact Name: John Amonson

Institution Type: Local Museum

Web site URL: None

Hours: Summer daily 9–6, winter M–F 9–4

Staff in Archives: 1f, 3p

Archives Are Handicapped Accessible: Yes

Cost for Researcher—Remote: Fee schedule

Review of Facilities: The Wallace District Mining Museum is located in downtown Wallace on Bank Street. The museum itself is on two levels, with the entrance and research room on the street level and the museum exhibit area one-half flight down to the rear of the building (there is a ramp). The research room is to the left of the entrance. One wall holds file cabinets and a map case; an antique wooden conference table piled with various papers and materials is in the center of the room. Notebooks holding photocopies of photos and documentary materials are housed behind the staff desk in the gift shop area. The area is sufficient for the collections, but a reorganization of the materials would make everything much more user-friendly.

Vertical Files: Yes   **Vertical Files in Cubic Feet:** 4

   Vertical File Description and Subjects: Binders of newspaper clippings arranged by subject

Manuscripts: Yes   **Manuscripts Volume in Cubic Feet:** 15

   Manuscript Types: Business records, land records

Manuscript Subjects: Ledgers from the First National Bank of Wallace from 1890s—1910, mining and land survey records, payroll records, mining company stock records, and supply records

Photographs: Yes   **Number of Photographs:** 3,000

Storage of Photographs: Photocopies of photographs have been arranged by subject order in binders. Original photographs stored in file cabinets.

Photograph Subjects: Photographs for Wallace, Kellogg, Burke, Murray, and Mullan. Mining is the major subject area, but collection includes all aspects of life in Shoshone County. Also have the Harry Graff photo collection from the years 1889 to the 1940s.

Photograph Reproductions Are Available: Yes

   Photographic Prints: Yes

Books: Yes   **Number of Books in Collection:** 100

Description of Books: Local history, mining industry, geology, annuals, city directories, and old books

Newspapers: Yes

   Newspapers in Paper Format: Yes

   Papers and Dates: North Idaho papers from 1963 to 1985. Scattered issues and papers from 1880s—1890s.

Oral Histories: Yes   **Oral Histories Number:** 50

Oral Histories Description: Mostly videotaped interviews with local area residents. About 15 of total number are audio only. Most interviews are from the 1980s and some from the 1990s. A few of the audiotapes have transcriptions, but none available for the video interviews.

Maps and Drawings: Yes   **Estimated Number of Maps and Drawings:** 500

Description of Maps and Drawings: Mining maps and railroad maps of the mining area. Many have copies for sale. Also have Sanborn fire maps. Maps stored rolled or flat in various locations.

Genealogy Sources: Yes

   Genealogy Sources Description: Some cemetery records are available

Special Collections: No

Indexes: No

Review of Collections: The collections focus mainly on the mining history of the area. There is little indexing to the collections and use of them relies on the knowledge of the director. The photograph collection illustrates the changing face of mining in northern Idaho from the earliest years to the present. Manuscript materials include various single sheets or collections of letters, deeds, surveys, supply lists, and so on. Photocopied documents are available for searchers; some are copies from other institutions but most are held locally in fragile condition. Good collection for northern Idaho mining history.

Museum on Premises: Yes

Museum Hours: Summer daily, 9–6; winter M–F, 9–4

Cost of Entry to Museum: $2

Museum Is Handicapped Accessible: Yes

Description of Museum: Small museum with displays on the mining history of the region

Parking: Free parallel on-street parking

Lunch: Several restaurants in historic buildings and hotels in same and neighboring blocks

Lodging: http://www.historic-wallace.org

Nearest Commercial Airport: Spokane International (Spokane, WA) (GEG) [88 miles]

Subjects

Historical Periods: 1865–1900; 1900–1940; 1940–present

Natural Resources: Water; Dams

Mining: Gold; Silver; Copper; Coal; Placer Mining; Surface Mining; Tunnel Mining

Transportation: Railroads

Business: Retail; Legal/Medical Services

Government: County

Date of Reviewer's Visit: 8/19/2004

Profile Updated by Institution: 11/3/2004

5

~

Oregon Profiles

Population (2003 estimate): 3,559,596

Land area: 95,997 square miles

Persons per square mile (2000 estimate): 35.6

ASHLAND

Name: Southern Oregon University Library   **County:** Jackson

Mailing Address: 1250 Siskiyou Blvd.

City: Ashland   **State:** OR   **Postal Code:** 97520-5076

Street Address: 1250 Siskiyou Blvd.

Institution Email: None

Telephone Number: (541) 552-6836   **Fax Number:** (541) 552-6429

Contact Name: Mary Jane Cedar Face   **Contact Email:** cedarface@sou.edu

Institution Type: Academic Library

Web site URL: http://www.sou.edu/library

Hours: 9–4 or by appt.

Staff in Archives: 1f, 1p

Archives Are Handicapped Accessible: Yes

Review of Facilities: The Southern Oregon University Special Collections/ University Archives is located in the Lenn and Dixie Hannon Library in the central part of campus. The Special Collections/University Archives opened in 2004 and is located on the second floor. Brightly lit, the research and special collections area, with compact shelving and storage, is pleasant and functional. Adjacent to the secure, climate-controlled storage is a reading room that houses several large worktables, easy chairs, and shelving. (The shelving in the reading area houses the circulating Margery Bailey Renaissance and Shakespeare Collection.) The University Archives has been moved to share space with the Special Collections in the new facility.

Vertical Files: Yes   **Vertical Files in Cubic Feet:** 48

Vertical File Description and Subjects: University records, Shakespeare

Manuscripts: Yes   **Manuscripts Volume in Cubic Feet:** 647

Manuscript Types: University records, personal papers

Manuscript Subjects: Redbird Collection (Native American), Shakespeare, local history. 600 cu. ft. are University Archives; the remainder is the manuscript collection.

Photographs: Yes   **Number of Photographs:** 10,000

Storage of Photographs: Boxes

Photograph Subjects: Peter Britt collection (2,067 southern Oregon history), university glass plate negatives and photographs.

Photograph Reproductions Are Available: Yes

  Photographic Prints: Yes

Books: Yes   **Number of Books in Collection:** 5,650

Description of Books: Books listed in library catalog and Summit

Newspapers: Yes

Newspapers on Microfilm: Yes

Microfilm and Dates: Microfilm of southern Oregon newspapers beginning in 1850 to present

Oral Histories: Yes   **Oral Histories Number:** 15

Oral Histories Description: University Presidential Interviews by Kay Atwood

Maps and Drawings: Yes **Estimated Number of Maps and Drawings:** 300

Description of Maps and Drawings: Historical maps on Oregon in special collections, others in general map collections

Genealogy Sources: No

Special Collections: Yes

Special Collections Description: The Margery Bailey Renaissance Collection contains over 8,000 volumes on William Shakespeare, his times, and his works, including the 2nd and 4th folios. Also contains production histories, promptbooks, and literature generated by and about the Oregon Shakespeare Festival in Ashland. Some of the Bailey collection circulates. The regional collection contains over 2,000 books and documents relating to southwestern Oregon and northern California.

The Adrienne Lee Ferte Collection contains 968 literary publications, mostly first edition, including northwest poetry. Recently the Will Brown Wine Collection was added, with nearly 1,000 books on enology and viticulture.

Indexes: Listing of books and most maps are available on the library computer through the Web site

> **Manuscript Finding Aids:** There are eight different finding aids to the collection

> **Published Guides:** *Early Printed Books in the Margery Bailey Renaissance Collection*, by Cecil L. Chase, 1983, 46 p.

> **Online Sources:** Southern Oregon Digital Archives Bioregion Collection and First Nations Collection, http://soda.sou.edu

Review of Collections: The collections at Southern Oregon University are limited in size and focus. There are five areas of collection emphasis: regional materials including environmental/bioregional and local history; Shakespeare; enology and viticulture; northwest poetry, and Native Americans. Full-text access is provided to over 1,600 regional documents in the Southern Oregon Digital Archives with the Bioregion Collection and the First Nations Collection (soda.sou.edu). The Southern Oregon University Archives amount to 600 cu. ft. of the collection.

Museum on Premises: No

Parking: Limited visitor parking, parking in a metered visitors' lot, or obtain parking permit from parking services

Lunch: First-floor coffee shop

Lodging: http://www.ashlandchamber.com

Nearest Commercial Airport: Rogue Valley International–Medford (MFR) [20 miles]

Subjects

> **Historical Periods:** 1800–1865; 1865–1900; 1900–1940; 1940–present

> **Eras:** Indian Wars

> **Natural Resources:** Water; Dams; Irrigation; Fishing; Logging

> **Mining:** Mining

> **Agriculture:** Orchards; Vineyard

> **Business:** Entertainment/Theaters

> **Manufacturing:** Sawmills

> **Government:** City; State; Federal; Tribal

> **Organizations:** Colleges/Universities

> **Ethnic Groups:** Native American

Date of Reviewer's Visit: 8/14/2003

Profile Updated by Institution: 11/16/2004

ASTORIA

Name: Columbia River Maritime Museum   **County:** Clatsop

Mailing Address: 1792 Marine Dr.

  City: Astoria   **State:** OR   **Postal Code:** 97103-0000

Street Address: 1792 Marine Dr.

Institution Email: None

Telephone Number: (503) 325-2323   **Fax Number:** (503) 325-2331

Contact Name: Dave Pearson   **Contact Email:** pearson@crmm.org

Institution Type: Regional Museum

Web site URL: http://www.crmm.org

Hours: By appt. M–F 9:30—4:30

Staff in Archives: 2f 1p 4v

Archives Are Handicapped Accessible: Yes

Review of Facilities: The Columbia River Maritime Museum is located on the waterfront just blocks from downtown Astoria. The research room is currently housed in the staff area to the very back of the building. Visitors need to have an appointment and check in at the museum desk. The research room itself is large and well lit. One-half of the room is devoted to file cabinets, map cases, and six compact shelving ranges, with room for expansion. There are two medium-sized tables available for researchers, and workspace for staff and volunteers in the other half of the room. An alcove holds their new periodical display and a long table with a research computer station. A climate-controlled vault is adjacent to the research room. The room is large, airy, functional, and pleasant—it is the type of research/storage space to which a large number of the institutions surveyed aspire.

Vertical Files: Yes   **Vertical Files in Cubic Feet:** 16

  Vertical File Description and Subjects: General and clipping files also filed separately by biography, vessel name, or shipwrecks. Pamphlet files are cataloged and housed with the books but number an additional 100 cu. ft.

Manuscripts: Yes   **Manuscripts Volume in Cubic Feet:** 300

  Manuscript Types: Business records, ships logs, union records, personal papers, organizational papers

  Manuscript Subjects: Columbia River Bar Pilots, Union Fish Company, Berenson Collection on Sailing Ships, ships logs, steamer logs

Photographs: Yes   **Number of Photographs:** 15,000

  Storage of Photographs: Photographs stored in document cases by subject arrangement. Photographs from the Columbia River Packers Association are also searchable on the computer.

Photograph Subjects: Fisheries, Columbia River or Maritime subjects dealing with Oregon

Photograph Reproductions Are Available: Yes

    Photographic Prints: Yes   **Digital Prints:** Yes

    Digital Images on CD or Electronically: Yes

Books: Yes   **Number of Books in Collection:** 8,000

Description of Books: General maritime, regional history, Lloyds Register 1764–present (incomplete). Books are cataloged using Library of Congress classification and listed on electronic catalog.

Newspapers: No

Oral Histories: Yes   **Oral Histories Number:** 76

Oral Histories Description: Group of interviews with local fishermen of the Columbia River Gillnetters. Interviews from 0s1980s on reel-to-reel and cassette tapes. Interviews used to make film *Work Is Our Joy.* Random collection of other interviews.

Maps and Drawings: Yes   **Estimated Number of Maps and Drawings:** 250

Description of Maps and Drawings: Local area maps of maritime interest, ships' plans from local shipyard, navigational charts, regional maps (most local but some larger), West coast area from 1940s and 1950s.

Genealogy Sources: No

Special Collections: Yes

    Special Collections Description: Includes the Columbia River Packers Association (CRPA) business papers from the early twentieth century to the mid-1970s. The CRPA was a consolidation of a number of fish packing companies and eventually was known by the name Bumblebee. The collection of 120 cu. ft. of materials includes business records and original documents of the company. The 3,000 images in the CRPA photo collection include the plants, people, and boats that were involved in the various aspects of the business. Most photos are from the 1930s to the 1960s. There is a detailed finding aid to this collection.

Indexes: Books and pamphlets are searchable through a staff computer. The CRPA photographs are searchable on the research room computer.

    Manuscript Finding Aids: The CRPA and Bumblebee collection have an inventory.

Review of Collections: The collections of the Columbia River Maritime Museum Ted M. Natt Library are regionally and nationally significant. The collecting area is limited to the history of the Columbia River maritime and Pacific Northwest maritime history. The Columbia River Packers Association (see Special Collections Description, above) collection is of special significance to the area. The Union Fish

Company papers (fisherman cooperative and canneries), which are as yet unprocessed, may provide a perfect research compliment to the CRPA and illuminate further the complex relationships of fishing, canning, and marketing. Another collection of special note consists of the architectural plans from the Astoria Marine Construction Company for many types of wooden vessels, including tugboats, fishing boats, yachts, and World War II mine sweepers. They also have a large collection of artwork, prints, photos and posters of maritime subjects. A collection of films (VHS, Beta, 8 mm and 16 mm) are on topics including Coast Guard training, fishing, and boatbuilding. The collection is professionally processed and housed.

Museum on Premises: Yes

Museum Hours: Daily 9:30–5:00

Cost of Entry to Museum: $8

Museum Is Handicapped Accessible: Yes

Description of Museum: Large beautiful building with numerous ships displayed with interpretive materials professionally curated. Covers the history of the Columbia River and the coastal maritime experience. One of the top museums in the Northwest.

Parking: Free paved and gravel parking lots adjacent

Lunch: Variety of restaurants several blocks' walk or a short·drive away

Lodging: http://www.oldoregon.com

Nearest Commercial Airport: Portland International (PDX) [96 miles]

Subjects

Historical Periods: 1865–1900; 1900–1940; 1940–present

Eras: World War II

Natural Resources: Fishing; Whaling; Logging

Transportation: Ships and Shipping; Ferries

Manufacturing: Cannery; Boatbuilding/Shipyard

Date of Reviewer's Visit: 7/29/2004

Profile Updated by Institution: 11/12/2004

Name: Heritage Museum of the Clatsop County Historical Society

County: Clatsop

Mailing Address: PO Box 88

City: Astoria   **State:** OR   **Postal Code:** 97103-0000

Street Address: 1618 Exchange

Institution Email: cchs@seasurf.net

Telephone Number: (503) 325-2203   **Fax Number:** (503) 338-6265

Contact Name: Liisa Penner   **Contact Email:** liisa-cchs@seasurf.net

Institution Type: Local Museum

Affiliation: Clatsop County Historical Society

Web site URL: http://www.clatsophistoricalsociety.org/

Hours: Winter Tu–F 11–4; summer Tu– F 10–5; year-round by appt.

Staff in Archives: 2f, 4v

Archives Are Handicapped Accessible: Yes

Access Description: Ramp on Exchange St. entrance

Cost for Researcher—In-house: $3, 2-week pass, $5

Cost for Researcher—Remote: Fee schedule

Review of Facilities: The Archives and Research Library of the Clatsop County Historical Society is located in the neoclassical Heritage Museum adjacent to downtown Astoria. The museum is housed in a former city hall (built 1904). The research room is located on the main floor of the two-story building. The room is large, with bookcases used as partitions. There are long windows providing light in the corner room overlooking the harbor. The room has a staff desk work area along one wall. A nearby vault provides some storage area, as do the file cabinets and bookcases along the walls. Adequate research space is provided in this room with high ceilings. The bulk of the collections is stored upstairs in staff work areas. The facility was undergoing renovation at the time of the visit. It is hoped that some reorganization of the research room and collections will occur to make it a more functional collection.

Vertical Files: Yes   **Vertical Files in Cubic Feet:** 22

   Vertical File Description and Subjects: Biography file, subject file

Manuscripts: Yes   **Manuscripts Volume in Cubic Feet:** 218

   Manuscript Types: Business records, government records, organizational records, school records, scrapbooks, diaries

   Manuscript Subjects: Union Fisherman's Cooperative, fisherman's union records, superintendent of school records, hotel registers (Occident Hotel, hotel in Seaside), prescription records, Astoria police records (ledgers), Finnish Congregational Lutheran, Town of Hammond, Timber Cruisers records, Port of Astoria records, diaries including some that go back to the 1860s.

Photographs: Yes   **Number of Photographs:** 50,000

   Storage of Photographs: Photos filed in file cabinets by general subject, number

Photograph Subjects: Clatsop County life, also special photograph collections from *Daily Astorian* archives (1973–1989), Wilson Studio collection (ca. 1911–1939), Ralph Horton collection (ca. 1909–1964), Reuben Jensen collection (ca. 1920–1940)

Photograph Reproductions Are Available: Yes

 Photographic Prints: Yes   **Digital Prints:** Yes

 Digital Images on CD or Electronically: Yes

Books: Yes   **Number of Books in Collection:** 330

Description of Books: Local and regional history, city directories, annuals, phone books, old books. Arranged by general subject.

Newspapers: Yes

 Newspapers in Paper Format: Yes

 Papers and Dates: *Daily Astorian,* Astoria papers 1880–present, incomplete

 Newspapers on Microfilm: No

 Microfilm and Dates: Microfilm at Astoria Public Library, which has a card catalog index to the papers

Oral Histories: Yes   **Oral Histories Number:** 200

 Oral Histories Description: Some videotapes, reel-to-reels, 1960s–1970s, no transcriptions. Working on project of Native American Tribes of region.

Maps and Drawings: Yes   **Estimated Number of Maps and Drawings:** 200

 Description of Maps and Drawings: Sanborn maps, early area maps, Timber Cruisers maps

Genealogy Sources: Yes

 Genealogy Sources Description: Cemetery, death, biographies, marriage, family histories, Episcopal Church records, census, Finnish Congregational Church records

Special Collections: No

Indexes: Subject index to photos on card file, migrating to PastPerfect

Review of Collections: The collections of the Clatsop County Historical Society are varied and historically significant. Organization, description, and arrangement of the collection needs to be improved before it begins to meet its potential; the fishing industry is one of the strongest topics, but forestry is also represented. As Astoria was settled early, the history represents the full range of nineteenth-century topics. Finnish Americans are the major identifiable ethnic group in the collection, although they have a wonderful compilation of information of the five Native American tribes in the region. Their collection of 61 scrapbooks has all been indexed with the newspapers and is searchable in card files.

Museum on Premises: Yes

Museum Hours: Winter Tu–Sa 11–4; summer Su–Sa 10–5

Cost of Entry to Museum: $3

Museum Is Handicapped Accessible: Yes

Description of Museum: Museum galleries feature changing and permanent exhibits and displays of Astoria and Clatsop County history

Parking: On-street free parallel parking

Lunch: Variety of restaurants within blocks

Lodging: http://www.oldoregon.com

Nearest Commercial Airport: Portland International (PDX) [97 miles]

Subjects

Historical Periods: 1800–1865; 1865–1900; 1900–1940; 1940–present

Eras: Civil War; World War I; CCC; World War II

Natural Resources: Fishing; Logging

Mining: Silver; Coal

Transportation: Railroads; Ships and Shipping; Ferries

Agriculture: Dairy; Ranching/Livestock; Vegetable/Truck Crops

Business: Retail; Legal/Medical Services; Hotels/Restaurants; Entertainment/Theaters

Manufacturing: Cannery; Brewery; Grist/Flour Mills; Creamery; Boatbuilding/Shipyard; Sawmills; Wood Products

Government: City; County

Organizations: Schools; Hospitals/Medical Facilities; Nonreligious Organizations; Civic and Fraternal; Women's; Business; Labor and Union

Ethnic Groups: Native American; African; Pacific Islander; Japanese; Chinese; Sikhs; Danish; Dutch; English; Finnish; French; German; Irish; Italian; Norwegian; Russian; Scottish; Swedish; Yugoslavs

Religious Sites and Organizations: Protestant; Catholic; Jewish; Buddhist

Date of Reviewer's Visit: 7/29/2004

Profile Updated by Institution: 11/18/2004

✯✯✯✯

Name: Lewis and Clark National Historical Park

County: Clatsop

Mailing Address: 92343 Fort Clatsop Rd.

City: Astoria **State:** OR **Postal Code:** 97103-0000

Street Address: 92343 Fort Clatsop Rd.

Institution Email: focl_administration@nps.gov

Telephone Number: (503) 861-2471   **Fax Number:** (503) 861-2585

Contact Name: Deborah S. Wood, Cultural Resource Manager

Contact Email: Deborah_S_Wood@nps.gov

Institution Type: Historic Site

Affiliation: National Park Service

Web site URL: http://www.nps.gov/focl/home.htm

Hours: M–F 9–5 by appt. only

Staff in Archives: 2f 2v

Archives Are Handicapped Accessible: Yes

Review of Facilities: The Lewis and Clark National Historical Park is located southwest of Astoria. The research collections of Lewis and Clark National Historical Park are located in the research library of the visitor center. The research room is moderate-sized, pleasant, and efficient. A staff desk is directly next to the door, and a large table with six chairs is in the center of the room. Bookcases fill several walls; one corner holds a computer workstation and a low shelf holds the periodical collections. The archival materials are either stored in large metal locked "archive" cabinets in the main research room or in the adjoining museum collection storage area. The area is climate controlled and contains several rows of large metal cabinets. The Herbarium and the park's museum collections are stored in this area, as well as the documents. Researchers have access to the museum collections, archives, and library materials by appointment.

Vertical Files: No

Manuscripts: Yes   **Manuscripts Volume in Cubic Feet:** 32

  Manuscript Types: Administrative records, historic documents

  Manuscript Subjects: Reports, field documents, archeological records, herbarium records

Photographs: Yes   **Number of Photographs:** 5,200

  Storage of Photographs: Photographs stored in plastic sleeves in document boxes

  Photograph Subjects: Fort Stevens, Cape Disappointment, Station Camp, Dismal Nitch, Pacific Northwest, Fort Clatsop, Astoria(OR), Clatsop Nation, Chinook Tribe and Fort to Sea Trail, National Park Service.

  Photograph Reproductions Are Available: Yes

    Photographic Prints: Yes   **Digital Prints:** Yes

    Digital Images on CD or Electronically: Yes

Books: Yes   **Number of Books in Collection:** 2,250

Description of Books: Early exploration, Lewis and Clark, Thomas Jefferson, ethnology, natural history of area. Books cataloged using Library of Congress classification and listed in card catalog and in an electronic database on the computer.

Newspapers: No

Oral Histories: No

Maps and Drawings: Yes   **Estimated Number of Maps and Drawings:** 75

Description of Maps and Drawings: Pacific Northwest, Fort Clatsop, regional maps, Columbia River, watersheds, Pacific coastline, Point Adams, Oregon, Cape Disappointment, Station Camp, Dismal Nitch, Ecola State Park, Fort Stevens, Fort to Sea Trail.

Genealogy Sources: No

Special Collections: Yes

Special Collections Description: Robert E. Lange collection of Lewis and Clark information, along with a master index of Lange's books and research papers, notes, and miscellaneous items. 20-cu.-foot collection.

Indexes: Card index to photographs, with copies of thumbnail images. Card catalog of books.

Online Sources: National Park Service Library site listing the items in the collection and photographs with catalog records

Review of Collections: The collections of Fort Clatsop focus on Lewis and Clark Corps of Discovery (1803–1806); area Native American tribes; early settlers and explorers; and military history in the area. Microfiche of Lewis and Clark journals and copies of documents (on these subjects) held in the National Archives system are also available. There are originals of primary sources available to researchers as well. Fort Clatsop was specifically established to preserve the site of the Lewis and Clark 1805–1806 Winter Camp, and the natural and cultural resources of the park and the archives reflect this aim. Secondary research notes and papers are also available.

Museum on Premises: Yes

Museum Hours: Summer 9–7, other seasons 9–5

Museum Is Handicapped Accessible: Yes

Description of Museum: An interpretive center with exhibits located in the visitor center. On site is a replica of the fort built by Lewis and Clark in 1805–1806.

Parking: Paved parking adjacent to the building. Bus transit is also available from towns of Astoria, Warrenton, and Seaside.

Lunch: Picnic areas available, or drive to Astoria or other nearby towns.

Lodging: http://www.oldoregon.com

Nearest Commercial Airport: Portland International (PDX) [102 miles]

Subjects

    Historical Periods: Pre-1800; 1800–1865; 1865–1900; 1900–1940; 1940–present

    Eras: Exploration; Fur Trade

    Natural Resources: Water; Fishing; Hunting; Whaling; Shellfish; Logging

    Mining: Clay Mining

    Transportation: Railroads; Stagecoach/Freight; Ferries

    Manufacturing: Cannery; Brick Making; Boatbuilding/Shipyard; Sawmills

    Government: Federal

    Organizations: Civic and Fraternal

    Ethnic Groups: Native American; Danish; English; Finnish; Norwegian; Swedish

Date of Reviewer's Visit: 7/29/2004

Profile Updated by Institution: 11/12/2004

BAKER CITY

Name: Baker County Public Library   **County:** Baker

Mailing Address: 2400 Resort St.

  City: Baker City   **State:** OR   **Postal Code:** 97814-2798

Street Address: 2400 Resort St.

Institution Email: alethab@oregontrail.net

Telephone Number: (541) 523-6419   **Fax Number:** (541) 523-9088

Contact Name: Aletha Bonebrake

Contact Email: alethab@oregontrail.net

Institution Type: Public Library

Affiliation: Library District

Web site URL: None

Hours: M–Th 10–8, F 10–5, Sa 10–4, Su 12–4

Staff in Archives: 1f

Archives Are Handicapped Accessible: Yes

Review of Facilities: Baker County Library is located in a beautiful one-story building on the edge of the city park. The research area really consists of several rooms depending on the type of research being done. The Oregon Room is open to the public generally and has a large table and comfortable chairs. The room is ringed by bookcases that hold the general collection of Oregon books. Most are on open shelves. The harder-to-replace items are in locked cabinets in the room. Most of the manuscript materials are housed in a conference room nearby in locked cabinets, but with a long worktable. Vertical files are stored in the staff area, and use is controlled. The building is modern and pleasant with a beautiful view of the park.

Vertical Files: Yes   **Vertical Files in Cubic Feet:** 13

Vertical File Description and Subjects: Vertical files divided into people files and general subject files of Baker County history and Oregon subjects.

Manuscripts: Yes   **Manuscripts Volume in Cubic Feet:** 10

Manuscript Types: Business records, scrapbooks, family papers

Manuscript Subjects: Ledgers from local stores, memorabilia from local businesses

Photographs: Yes   **Number of Photographs:** 6,000

Storage of Photographs: Copies of photographs are stored in three-ring binders in plastic sleeves. Originals stored elsewhere. Several hundred images available from Web site.

Photograph Subjects: Baker County history, mining, schools, agriculture, logging, organizations, transportation, military, and people. From 1866 to present.

Photograph Reproductions Are Available: No

   Photographic Prints: Yes

   Digital Prints: Yes

   Digital Images on CD or Electronically: No

Books: Yes   **Number of Books in Collection:** 2,000

Description of Books: Local and regional history, city directories, annuals

Newspapers: Yes

   Newspapers in Paper Format: Yes

   Papers and Dates: *East Oregonian* (Pendleton) 1889–present; *Record-Courier* (Baker City) 1930–present

   Newspapers on Microfilm: Yes

   Microfilm and Dates: *Baker City Herald,* 1901–1917; 1992–1995; *Baker Democrat Herald*, 1929–1992;

Oral Histories: No

Maps and Drawings: Yes   **Estimated Number of Maps and Drawings:** 200

   Description of Maps and Drawings: Local area maps in flat files. Most are USGS or U.S. Forest Service.

Genealogy Sources: Yes

Genealogy Sources Description: Obituary index to 1970, people files

Special Collections: No

Indexes: Library card file of local history topics, obituaries, and indexing to contents of book collection. Paper printout of index to photographs.

Online Sources: Book collection information on general library computer system. Online access to selected photographs available from the Web site, mostly of the historic downtown area.

Review of Collections: The collections at Baker County Public Library are limited in size but regionally important. The library has been digitizing some of the photograph collection and hundreds of images are now available through the Web site, searchable by subject. As is true for many public libraries, the manuscript and original materials are not of the highest priority, and so there is possibly more buried in this collection than the reviewer has seen.

Museum on Premises: No

Parking: Free on-street parallel parking and small off-street lot behind building

Lunch: There are a few restaurants within walking distance and a full variety of chain and local restaurants within driving distance.

Lodging: http://www.visitbaker.com

Nearest Commercial Airport: Eastern Oregon Regional at Pendleton (PDT) [95 miles]; Boise Air Terminal/Gowen Field (BOI) [128 miles]

Subjects

    Historical Periods: 1865–1900; 1900–1940

    Eras: CCC

    Natural Resources: Logging

    Mining: Gold; Silver; Placer Mining; Surface Mining; Tunnel Mining

    Transportation: Railroads; Stagecoach/Freight

    Agriculture: Ranching/Livestock

    Business: Hotels/Restaurants

    Manufacturing: Wood Products

    Government: City; County

    Organizations: Schools

    Ethnic Groups: Chinese; Belgian

    Religious Sites and Organizations: Protestant; Catholic; LDS (Mormon); Jewish

Date of Reviewer's Visit: 9/24/2003

Profile Updated by Institution: 11/10/2004

✳✳

Name: Oregon Trail Regional Museum   **County:** Baker

Mailing Address: 2480 Grove St.

   City: Baker City   **State:** OR   **Postal Code:** 97814-0000

Street Address: 2480 Grove St.

Institution Email: None

Telephone Number: (541) 523-9308   **Fax Number:** (541) 523-9308

Contact Name: Chary Mires, Director   **Contact Email:** cmotrm@oregontrail.net

Institution Type: Local Museum

Affiliation: Baker County

Web site URL: http://www.bakercounty.org/museum/museum.html

Hours: Daily 9–5 Mar 20–Oct 31; winter 9–12 by appt.

Staff in Archives: 1f 1p 7v

Archives Are Handicapped Accessible: Yes

Cost for Researcher—In-house: No charge

Cost for Researcher—Remote: Donation

List of Researchers Available: Yes

Review of Facilities: The Oregon Trail Regional Museum is located in a 1920 natatorium building just outside the main business district. The research room is located in a fairly large room to the back of the gift shop. The room is long and narrow with bookshelves throughout the room. There is a worktable in the middle of the room, but the lighting is inadequate at that location. Research materials are housed on the bookshelves and in file cabinets and map cases in the room.

Vertical Files: Yes   **Vertical Files in Cubic Feet:** 2

   Vertical File Description and Subjects: Vertical files consist of family files and general clippings.

Manuscripts: Yes   **Manuscripts Volume in Cubic Feet:** 30

   Manuscript Types: Business records, organizational records

   Manuscript Subjects: Shriners records, hotel registers from the Imperial Hotel 1940–1944, drugstore records from 1939–1944 with books of prescriptions, Lewis and Clark Expedition centennial 1905, Oregon Educational Exhibit A.Y.P.E. 1909, Oregon Educational Exhibit in St. Louis in 1904.

Photographs: Yes   **Number of Photographs:** 4,000

   Storage of Photographs: Photographs are stored in Mylar sleeves in file cabinets. The museum is scanning the photographs into PastPerfect software.

   Photograph Subjects: Baker County people, events, and scenes

Photograph Reproductions Are Available: Yes

    Photographic Prints: Yes   **Digital Prints:** Yes

Books: Yes   **Number of Books in Collection:** 2,100

    Description of Books: Local history, city directories, phone books, annuals, and old books. This collection is unfortunately heavy in the "old book category," which accounts for maybe three-quarters of the collection.

Newspapers: No

Oral Histories: Yes

    Oral Histories Description: Oral history project was being planned at the time of visit.

Maps and Drawings: Yes   **Estimated Number of Maps and Drawings:** 200

    Description of Maps and Drawings: There are 200 processed maps of local and regional interest. They also hold another several hundred maps that are unprocessed.

Genealogy Sources: Yes

    Genealogy Sources Description: Cemetery records

Special Collections: No

Indexes: Books, manuscript materials, and photographs are indexed only on Past-Perfect program.

Review of Collections: The collections at the Oregon Trail Regional Museum focus on the history of Baker County, Baker City, and the influences of the Oregon Trail on the region. The book collection is very heavily laden with old books and hopefully this has been weeded since the reviewer's visit to make a useable history book collection. The prescription drug records from the World War II era may be of particular note to the proper researcher. The 1940s is the decade that really has the strongest manuscripts in this collection, most of which are related to the local life (nonmilitary). Regardless of the name of the institution, the historical information of the Oregon Trail experience is extremely limited. Although some information dates back to 1861, it is not a must-see collection for that time period. Collection and processing is in progress.

Museum on Premises: Yes

    Museum Hours: M–F 9–5

    Cost of Entry to Museum: $5

    Museum Is Handicapped Accessible: No

    Description of Museum: Museum housed in old natatorium with displays on Baker County history

Parking: Free gravel parking lot and on-street parallel parking

Lunch: There are a few restaurants within walking distance and a full variety of chain and local restaurants within driving distance.

Lodging: http://www.visitbaker.com

Nearest Commercial Airport: Eastern Oregon Regional at Pendleton (PDT) [95 miles]; Boise Air Terminal/Gowen Field (BOI) [128 miles]

Subjects

    Historical Periods: 1800–1865; 1865–1900; 1900–1940; 1940–present

    Eras: World War I; World War II; Vietnam War

    Natural Resources: Dams; Irrigation; Logging

    Mining: Gold; Silver; Copper; Placer Mining; Surface Mining; Tunnel Mining

    Transportation: Railroads; Stagecoach/Freight; Aviation

    Agriculture: Dairy; Ranching/Livestock; Grains; Dry Land Farming

    Business: Retail; Legal/Medical Services

    Manufacturing: Brick Making; Sawmills; Wood Products

    Government: City; County

    Organizations: Schools; Hospitals/Medical Facilities; Charities; Civic and Fraternal; Women's

    Ethnic Groups: Native American; Chinese; Dutch; English; German; Irish; Russian; Scottish

    Religious Sites and Organizations: Protestant; Catholic; LDS (Mormon); Jewish

Date of Reviewer's Visit: 9/24/2003

Profile Updated by Institution: 11/10/2004

BANDON

Name: Bandon's Coquille River Museum   **County:** Coos

Mailing Address: PO Box 737

  City: Bandon   **State:** OR   **Postal Code:** 97411-0000

Street Address: 270 Fillmore and Hwy. 101

Institution Email: None

Telephone Number: (541) 347-2164   **Fax Number:** (541) 347-2164

Contact Name: Judy Knox, Executive Director

Contact Email: jnrknox@harborside.com

Institution Type: Local Museum

Affiliation: Bandon Historical Society

Web site URL: http://www.bandonhistoricalmuseum.org

Hours: M–Sa 10–4 and by appt.

Staff in Archives: 1f, 10v

Archives Are Handicapped Accessible: Yes

Review of Facilities: The Coquille River Museum is located on Highway 101 just blocks from the center of Bandon. The single-story frame building was formerly the Bandon City Hall. The research room is narrow, well-lit, and dominated by a long wooden table. Books and some research collections are available in the room. Other materials are stored elsewhere in the building.

Vertical Files: Yes   **Vertical Files in Cubic Feet:** 100

   Vertical File Description and Subjects: Vertical file has materials on people and locations filed by accession number. Clipping files from local residents in scrapbooks.

Manuscripts: Yes   **Manuscripts Volume in Cubic Feet:** 50

   Manuscript Types: Scrapbooks, personal papers, business records, school records

Photographs: Yes   **Number of Photographs:** 3,000

   Storage of Photographs: The photographs have no subject arrangement; some have negatives. They are not available for browsing. Originals stored in document boxes in staff area. Negatives are stored off site.

   Photograph Subjects: Bandon and Coquille River history.

   Photograph Reproductions Are Available: Yes

     Photographic Prints: Yes

Books: Yes   **Number of Books in Collection:** 200

   Description of Books: Local history and old books

Newspapers: Yes

   Newspapers in Paper Format: Yes

   Papers and Dates: Local area papers from 1900 to 1920, also selected older issues

   Microfilm and Dates: Some microfilm available at University of Oregon.

Oral Histories: Yes   **Oral Histories Number:** 50

   Oral Histories Description: Interviews with local area residents taken in the 1980s on audiocassette and/or videocassette. Some interviews have transcriptions. Public access not available without staff.

Maps and Drawings: Yes   **Estimated Number of Maps and Drawings:** 10

   Description of Maps and Drawings: Local township maps

Genealogy Sources: Yes

Genealogy Sources Description: Marriage records 1840–1905, obituary index, burial index, and detailed list of cemeteries in area with obituaries of all buried there

Special Collections: No

Indexes: Computer index for staff use of part of the collection. Use PastPerfect Software. Indexes for books, photographs, some finding aids.

Manuscript Finding Aids: Some finding aids to manuscript collections stored in staff areas.

Online Sources: Several online displays available from Web site, including a timeline and cemetery tours

Review of Collections: The collections at the Coquille River Museum are limited in scope and size. The collecting focus is the history of Bandon and the Coquille River area, both documentary and photographic. The strongest part of the collection is the volunteer-researched history. Binder after binder of collected information on previous residents of the area with cemetery records that include not only listings of headstones, but obituaries and histories of those buried there. Countless hours of work went into this compilation. The marriage records are also available. A small collection and small institution but great potential.

Museum on Premises: Yes

Museum Hours: Daily 10–4 (closed Sunday in winter)

Cost of Entry to Museum: $2

Museum Is Handicapped Accessible: Yes

Description of Museum: Moderate-sized museum on the Coquille River region with focus on the logging, fishing, and cranberry farming of the area

Parking: Free parking lot adjacent or on-street parallel parking

Lunch: Variety of local restaurants within a few blocks.

Lodging: http://www.bandon.com

Nearest Commercial Airport: Mahlon Sweet Field (Eugene) (EUG) [132 miles]; Rogue Valley International–Medford (MFR) [165 miles]

Subjects

Historical Periods: 1800–1865; 1865–1900; 1900–1940; 1940–present

Eras: Civil War; World War I

Natural Resources: Fishing; Logging

Mining: Gold; Coal; Placer Mining

Transportation: Ships and Shipping; Ferries

Agriculture: Dairy; Ranching/Livestock

Manufacturing: Creamery; Sawmills; Wood Products

Organizations: Schools

Ethnic Groups: Native American

Date of Reviewer's Visit: 8/16/2003

Profile Updated by Institution: 11/12/2004

BEND

Name: Deschutes County Historical Society   County: Deschutes

Mailing Address: 129 NW Idaho Ave.

City: Bend   State: OR   Postal Code: 97701-2602

Street Address: 129 NW Idaho Ave.

Institution Email: None

Telephone Number: (541) 389-1813   Fax Number: (541) 317-9354

Contact Name: Curt Lantz   Contact Email: CURTL@deschutes.historical.
museum

Institution Type: Local Museum

Web site URL: http://deschutes.historical.museum

Hours: Tu–Sa 10–4:30

Staff in Archives: 4p 15v

Archives Are Handicapped Accessible: Yes

Access Description: Small ramp to get in building

Review of Facilities: The Deschutes County Historical Museum is housed in a
three-story schoolhouse. The research library is on the main floor of the museum.
The room is large with a large workspace in the middle. Around the perimeter of
the room are bookcases, indexes, file cabinets, and assorted research material. The
lighting is adequate. Manuscript collections are stored on another floor, in a staff-
only area.

Vertical Files: Yes   Vertical Files in Cubic Feet: 20

   Vertical File Description and Subjects: Places and communities, people and
   subjects consisting of mostly clipping files

Manuscripts: Yes

   Manuscript Types: Scrapbooks

Photographs: Yes   Number of Photographs: 20,000

   Storage of Photographs: Index to photographs consists of 3 x 5 copies of images
   sorted by subject and filed in card file cabinets. Only a portion of the images in this
   collection are available. Originals of the photographs are stored in acid-free boxes

away from the research room in a new climate-controlled vault. The Deschutes County Historical Society has started a digitization project and at the time of writing, had about 3,000 images scanned to a PastPerfect database.

Photograph Subjects: Deschutes County and the central Oregon region is the focus of the collection.

Photograph Reproductions Are Available: Yes

   Photographic Prints: Yes

   Digital Prints: Yes

   Digital Images on CD or Electronically: Yes

Books: Yes   **Number of Books in Collection:** 1,000

   Description of Books: Central Oregon history

Newspapers: Yes

   Newspapers in Paper Format: Yes

   Papers and Dates: *Bend Bulletin* for 1909–1919 (incomplete) and after 1919 to present

   Microfilm and Dates: Microfilm of papers available at the local public library

Oral Histories: Yes   **Oral Histories Number:** 200

   Oral Histories Description: Most oral history interviews do not have transcriptions available.

Maps and Drawings: Yes   **Estimated Number of Maps and Drawings:** 50

   Description of Maps and Drawings: Water resources of area

Genealogy Sources: Yes

Special Collections: Yes

   Special Collections Description: Map collection with significant information on water resources of the area

Indexes: Card files on scrapbooks; card catalog of books; marriage file of county marriage records; card index of high school students

Review of Collections: The Deschutes County Historical Museum has a wonderful, if underprocessed, collection. The photographic images that are available to researchers are only a small percentage of those stored in the building, maybe numbering close to half a million images. Hopefully more will be made available. The staff is small but hard working and good progress is being made in the collection. The collection is particularly strong in the area of water resources.

Museum on Premises: Yes

   Museum Hours: Tu–Sa 10–4:30

   Cost of Entry to Museum: $5

   Museum Is Handicapped Accessible: Yes

Description of Museum: Located in a three-story old stone schoolhouse, the museum displays artifacts and vignettes of local history subjects.

Parking: Free parking lot adjacent

Lunch: Ethnic downtown restaurants close by; short drive to most major chain and fast-food chains

Lodging: http://www.visitbend.com

Nearest Commercial Airport: Roberts Field (Redmond, OR) (RDM) [17 miles]

Subjects

Historical Periods: 1800–1865; 1865–1900; 1900–1940; 1940–present

Eras: Indian Wars; Spanish American War; World War I; WPA; CCC; World War II

Natural Resources: Water; Irrigation; Fishing; Hunting; Logging

Mining: Gold; Silver; Placer Mining; Tunnel Mining

Transportation: Railroads; Stagecoach/Freight; Aviation

Agriculture: Dairy; Ranching/Livestock; Grains; Dry Land Farming

Business: Banking; Retail; Legal/Medical Services; Hotels/Restaurants; Entertainment/Theaters

Manufacturing: Brewery; Creamery; Brick Making; Technology/Computers; Sawmills; Wood Products

Government: City; County; State

Organizations: Schools; Colleges/Universities; Hospitals/Medical Facilities; Business

Ethnic Groups: Native American; Japanese; Chinese; Basque; English; German; Irish; Norwegian; Scottish; Spanish; Swedish

Religious Sites and Organizations: Protestant; Catholic

Date of Reviewer's Visit: 8/13/2003

Profile Updated by Institution: 12/7/2004

BROWNSVILLE

Name: Brownsville Community Library   **County:** Linn

Mailing Address: PO Box 68

City: Brownsville   **State:** OR   **Postal Code:** 97327-0068

Street Address: 146 Spalding

Institution Email: library@ci.brownsville.or.us

Telephone Number: (541) 466-5454   **Fax Number:** (541) 466-5454

Contact Name: Paul K. Smith, Librarian

Institution Type: Public Library

Affiliation: City of Brownsville

Web site URL: None

Hours: Tu, W, F 10–5; Th 1–7; Sa 10–2

Staff in Archives: 1p, 12v

Archives Are Handicapped Accessible: Yes

Review of Facilities: The Brownsville Community Library is located a block from the downtown area. When visited, the local history room was located off the periodical room. Plans are underway to move the history room to a slightly different space in the library. The new history room will have a computer station, the Northwest history collection books, and research tables.

Vertical Files: Yes   **Vertical Files in Cubic Feet:** 11

   Vertical File Description and Subjects: General subject vertical files 3 cu. ft.; family files 8 cu. ft.

Manuscripts: Yes

   Manuscript Types: Business records, organizational records, family papers

   Manuscript Subjects: Oregon Trail, wagon train roster from 1843, church records, Leslie Haskin collection of memories of pioneers and children of pioneers taken in the 1930s

Photographs: Yes   **Number of Photographs:** 500

   Storage of Photographs: Stored in files in file cabinets

   Photograph Subjects: Brownsville and Linn County history

   Photograph Reproductions Are Available: Yes

      Photographic Prints: Yes

Books: Yes   **Number of Books in Collection:** 100

   Description of Books: Local and regional history, genealogy

Newspapers: Yes

   Newspapers in Paper Format: Yes

   Papers and Dates: *Brownsville Times papers*

Oral Histories: No

Maps and Drawings: No

Genealogy Sources: Yes

   Genealogy Sources Description: Family files, cemetery records

Special Collections: No

Indexes: Indexes of immigrants from all years in a card file. Book index in card file.

Review of Collections: The collections of the Brownsville Community Library are small. Of particular interest to historians would be the collection of pioneer memories gathered in the 1930s, and thus covering an older period of history than most of the newer projects. There are some other early history pieces in the collection, as well, including a roster from a wagon train in 1843. Other Oregon Trail materials are available, but scattered. An oral history project is scheduled for 2005. The remainder of the Linn County history is available at the Linn County Historical Museum, which is in the same block as the library.

Museum on Premises: No

Parking: Free on-street parallel parking

Lunch: Local restaurant and coffee shop within two short blocks

Lodging: http://www.albanyvisitors.com. Motel 4 miles, 2 local bed and breakfasts, with one located across from the library

Nearest Commercial Airport: Mahlon Sweet Field (Eugene, OR) (EUG) [30 miles]

Subjects

    Historical Periods: 1800–1865; 1865–1900; 1900–1940; 1940–present

    Natural Resources: Logging

    Manufacturing: Woolen/Fabric Mills; Brick Making; Sawmills

    Ethnic Groups: Native American

    Religious Sites and Organizations: Protestant; Mennonite/Amish

Date of Reviewer's Visit: 8/19/2003

Profile Updated by Institution: 11/8/2004

Name: Linn County Historical Museum   **County:** Linn

Mailing Address: PO Box 607

    City: Brownsville   **State:** OR   **Postal Code:** 98327-0000

Street Address: 101 Park Ave.

Institution Email: jmoyer@peak.org

Telephone Number: (541) 466-3390   **Fax Number:** (541) 466-5312

Contact Name: Della Klinkebiel

Institution Type: Local Museum

Affiliation: Linn County and Linn County Historical Society

Web site URL: http://www.linnhistorical.com

Hours: M–Sa 11–4; Su 1–5

Staff in Archives: 2p, 10v

Archives Are Handicapped Accessible: Yes

Access Description: Separate handicapped entrance

Review of Facilities: The Linn County Historical Museum is housed in an old railway depot (transplanted) just a block off the main street. A small research corner is located in the main part of the museum up several steps from the entrance. The research area blends into the design of the museum. An antique round dining table dominates the small area and functions as the worktable. Nearby shelves house the basics of the research collections. The remaining collections are stored throughout the small building, in, under, and camouflaged by exhibits.

Vertical Files: Yes   **Vertical Files in Cubic Feet:** 10

Vertical File Description and Subjects: General subject vertical files and family files

Manuscripts: Yes   **Manuscripts Volume in Cubic Feet:** 25

Manuscript Types: Business records, school records, land records

Manuscript Subjects: Ledgers from local stores, Donation Land Claim records for Linn County

Photographs: Yes   **Number of Photographs:** 2,000

Storage of Photographs: Nine large binders of photocopies of photographs with description are available for researchers to use. Original photographs are stored in plastics sleeves in binders or boxes.

Photograph Subjects: Linn County history

Photograph Reproductions Are Available: Yes

Photographic Prints: Yes   **Digital Prints:** Yes

Digital Images on CD or Electronically: Yes

Books: Yes   **Number of Books in Collection:** 50

Description of Books: Local history, genealogy, city directories

Newspapers: No

Newspapers in Paper Format: No

Papers and Dates: At Brownsville Community Library—see separate entry

Newspapers on Microfilm: No

Microfilm and Dates: Microfilm available at University of Oregon

Oral Histories: Yes   **Oral Histories Number:** 20

Oral Histories Description: Interviews with long-time area residents on videocassettes

Maps and Drawings: Yes   **Estimated Number of Maps and Drawings:** 17

Description of Maps and Drawings: Sanborn maps, dated 1884 to 1912

Genealogy Sources: Yes

   Genealogy Sources Description: Cemetery records, family files

Special Collections: No

Indexes: Pioneer descendents file

Review of Collections: The collections of the Linn County Historical Society are small but significant to the local area history. The volunteer staff is developing a database of artifacts and research items using PastPerfect software. The genealogy portion of the collection is the strongest part, although there are other areas of strength, including the photograph collections. Manuscripts, in a traditional sense, are the weakest area of the collection. Some county records and land records are available.

Museum on Premises: Yes

   Museum Hours: M–Sa 11–5, Su 1–4

   Cost of Entry to Museum: Donation

   Museum Is Handicapped Accessible: Yes

   Description of Museum: Small, well-designed museum in historic depot that illustrates Linn County history and people

Parking: Free on-street parallel parking

Lunch: Several small local cafes within a block

Lodging: http://www.albanyvisitors.com

Nearest Commercial Airport: Mahlon Sweet Field (Eugene, OR) (EUG) [37 miles]

Subjects

   Historical Periods: Pre-1800; 1800–1865; 1865–1900; 1900–1940; 1940–present

   Eras: Indian Wars

   Natural Resources: Irrigation; Hunting; Logging

   Mining: Gold; Placer Mining; Tunnel Mining

   Transportation: Railroads; Ferries

   Agriculture: Dairy; Ranching/Livestock; Vegetable/Truck Crops; Grains; Orchards

   Business: Banking; Retail; Legal/Medical Services; Hotels/Restaurants; Entertainment/Theaters

   Manufacturing: Cannery; Grist/Flour Mills; Creamery; Woolen/Fabric Mills; Sawmills; Wood Products

   Government: City; County; State

   Organizations: Schools; Colleges/Universities; Civic and Fraternal

   Ethnic Groups: Native American

Religious Sites and Organizations: Protestant; Catholic; LDS (Mormon); Mennonite/Amish

Date of Reviewer's Visit: 8/19/2003

Profile Updated by Institution: 11/10/2004

BURNS

Name: Harney County Historical Museum   **County:** Harney

  Mailing Address: 18 W. D St.

  City: Burns   **State:** OR   **Postal Code:** 97720-1226

Street Address: 18 West D St.

Institution Email: HCHS@burnsmuseum.com

Telephone Number: (503) 573-5618   **Fax Number:** (541) 573-5618

Contact Name: Dorothea Purdy, Board President

Institution Type: Local Museum

Affiliation: Harney County Historical Society

Web site URL: http://www.burnsmuseum.com/

Hours: Tu–Sa 10–4, Apr–Sept; and by appt.

Staff in Archives: 2p, 25v

Archives Are Handicapped Accessible: No

Access Description: Step down into research room

Review of Facilities: The Harney County Historical Museum is located in a residential area just off the main highway, close to the public library. The museum is a two-story building originally built as a brewery. The research area is located on the main floor behind the entrance desk and gift shop. The research room is a step down from the main floor level. The research area is small, narrow, and has a single window at the end of the room. A narrow table is against the wall with bookshelves on the top. This creates a workspace only about a foot wide and six feet long. The materials are mostly stored on the shelves above the counter. Other items are stored under the counter. A locked bookcase stores the more valuable items.

Vertical Files: Yes   **Vertical Files in Cubic Feet:** 2

  Vertical File Description and Subjects: Some miscellaneous files in binders

Manuscripts: Yes   **Manuscripts Volume in Cubic Feet:** 6

  Manuscript Types: Business records, scrapbooks, family papers

  Manuscript Subjects: Cowbells, VFW, family histories, Camp Harney, land grants

Photographs: Yes   **Number of Photographs:** 500

Storage of Photographs: Photographs are stored in three-ring binders. Most photographs are on display in the museum on display boards. List of photographs, but no subject guide, and photos are not searchable by subject.

Photograph Subjects: Local history, schools

Photograph Reproductions Are Available: No

Books: Yes   **Number of Books in Collection:** 250

Description of Books: Local history, old books, annuals

Newspapers: No

Microfilm and Dates: Public Library has Microfilm of local papers.

Oral Histories: No

Oral Histories Description: The Harney County Library has 400 oral history interviews

Maps and Drawings: No

Genealogy Sources: Yes

Genealogy Sources Description: Cemetery records, family histories, marriage records, most in scrapbook form

Special Collections: No

Indexes: No

Review of Collections: The collections at the Harney County Historical Museum are available for research but are not very user-friendly. Indexing or cross-referencing is not available for any part of the collection. The order of storage seems to be quite random. That being said, this collection is important because it covers the history of a remote part of Oregon and most of this history exists nowhere else. The photograph collection is significant, if not large, but a subject arrangement would be welcomed. As a volunteer-run organization, the museum would do well to consider having their research collections organized by an archivist or local history librarian.

Museum on Premises: Yes

Museum Hours: Tu–Sa 10–4, Apr–Sept, and by appt.

Cost of Entry to Museum: $4

Museum Is Handicapped Accessible: No

Description of Museum: Local historical museum displaying the history of Harney County with the use of individual family display cases. This museum displays the artifacts of the history without attempting to interpret them.

Parking: Free parking lot adjacent

Lunch: Variety of restaurants driving distance

Lodging: http://www.harneycounty.com

Nearest Commercial Airport: Boise Air Terminal/Gowen Field (BOI) [186 miles]

Subjects

    Historical Periods: Pre-1800; 1865–1900; 1900–1940; 1940–present

    Natural Resources: Logging

    Mining: Mining

    Transportation: Railroads

    Agriculture: Ranching/Livestock

    Business: Retail; Legal/Medical Services; Hotels/Restaurants; Entertainment/Theaters

    Manufacturing: Sawmills

    Government: City

    Organizations: Schools; Hospitals/Medical Facilities

    Ethnic Groups: Native American; Japanese; Chinese; Basque; Spanish

    Religious Sites and Organizations: Protestant; Catholic; LDS (Mormon)

Date of Reviewer's Visit: 9/25/2003

Profile Updated by Institution: None

CANYON CITY

Name: Grant County Historical Museum   **County:** Grant

Mailing Address: PO Box 464

    City: Canyon City   **State:** OR   **Postal Code:** 97820-0000

Street Address: 101 S. Canyon Blvd., Hwy. 395

Institution Email: museum@ortelco.net

Telephone Number: (541) 575-0362

Contact Name: Jayne Primrose, Curator   **Contact Email:** museum@ortelco.net

Institution Type: Local Museum

Affiliation: Town of Canyon City

Web site URL: http://www.ortelco.net/~museum

Hours: M–Sa 9–4:30, May 15–Sept 30 only; off season call City Hall, 541-575-0509, for appt.

Staff in Archives: 1 p May 15–Sept 30 only

Archives Are Handicapped Accessible: No

Access Description: Ramp up to porch area, removable ramp at door

Cost for Researcher—In-house: Donation

Cost for Researcher—Remote: Fee Schedule

List of Researchers Available: Yes

Review of Facilities: The Grant County Historical Museum is located in the small town of Canyon City, aptly named for its location. Canyon City is located directly south of John Day. The museum receives funding from Canyon City. The main entrance to the museum serves as the research room as well. In addition to staff workspace, there are file cabinets, book cases, a computer, a copier, and wooden storage drawers designed to hold the research materials. There is a small portable table in the main area where researchers can sit. Although the quarters are cramped, from a researcher's point of view, the room is full of character. Wood paneled walls are adorned with oversize nineteenth-century portraits, and historical objects fill the remaining space.

Vertical Files: Yes   **Vertical Files in Cubic Feet:** 10

  Vertical File Description and Subjects: Vertical files of family files and general subjects

Manuscripts: Yes   **Manuscripts Volume in Cubic Feet:** 10

  Manuscript Types: Scrapbooks, business records

  Manuscript Subjects: Family scrapbooks, ledgers from Grant County Bank, business ledgers

Photographs: Yes   **Number of Photographs:** 3,200

  Storage of Photographs: Photographs are stored in file cabinets. Arranged by subject. Card file index to photographs.

  Photograph Subjects: Grant County region

  Photograph Reproductions Are Available: Yes

  Photographic Prints: Yes **Digital Prints:** Yes

Books: Yes   **Number of Books in Collection:** 75

  Description of Books: Local history

Newspapers: Yes   **Newspapers in Paper Format:** Yes

  Papers and Dates: Local papers 1884 to 1903 and later titles from the 1950s

  Newspapers on Microfilm: Yes

  Microfilm and Dates: *Grant County News,* Feb 1884–Dec 1887

Oral Histories: Yes   **Oral Histories Number:** 30

  Oral Histories Description: Interviews with local area residents. Transcripts only.

Maps and Drawings: Yes **Estimated Number of Maps and Drawings:** 4

  Description of Maps and Drawings: Gold mining regions

Genealogy Sources: Yes

  Genealogy Sources Description: Cemetery records, marriage records

Special Collections: No

Indexes: Card indexes for documents and books, with people index and topic index. Separate indexes for photographs, broken into people and topic.

Review of Collections: The research collections of the Grant County Museum focus on the various historical subjects of the region. The photograph collections cover a broad range of subjects. The collection of ledgers from the Grant County Bank are probably the most significant items from the manuscript area. Most of the rest of the collection is predictable small town history. This collection is stored safely if not archivally. The demand on the collection is mostly local historical interest.

Museum on Premises: Yes

Museum Hours: Mon–Sat 9:30–4:30, Su 1–5 (June 1–Sept 30 only)

Cost of Entry to Museum: $4.00

Museum Is Handicapped Accessible: No

Description of Museum: Old-style, traditional museum illustrating the history of Grant County. Main areas of display include the mining and ranching history of the region.

Parking: Vertical gravel parking in front of building

Lunch: There is a Chinese restaurant one mile up the road or other restaurants two miles away in John Day

Lodging: http://www.grantcounty.cc; in John Day

Nearest Commercial Airport: Eastern Oregon Regional at Pendleton (PDT) [129 miles]

Subjects

Historical Periods: 1865–1900; 1900–1940; 1940–present

Eras: Indian Wars

Natural Resources: Hunting; Logging

Mining: Gold; Placer Mining; Tunnel Mining; Chromium

Transportation: Stagecoach/Freight

Agriculture: Ranching/Livestock; Vegetable/Truck Crops

Business: Retail

Manufacturing: Brewery; Sawmills

Government: City; County

Organizations: Schools

Ethnic Groups: Native American; Chinese

Date of Reviewer's Visit: 9/24/2003

Profile Updated by Institution: 11/9/2004

CORVALLIS

Name: Oregon State University Archives   **County:** Benton

Mailing Address: 121 Valley Library

  City: Corvallis   **State:** OR   **Postal Code:** 97331-4501

Street Address: Jefferson and Waldo Place

Institution Email: archives@oregonstate.edu

Telephone Number: (541) 737-2165   **Fax Number:** (541) 737-0541

Contact Name: Lawrence A. Landis

Contact Email: larry.landis@oregonstate.edu

Institution Type: Academic Library

Affiliation: Oregon State University

Web site URL: http://osulibrary.oregonstate.edu/archives

Hours: M–F 9–5. Appt. recommended for out-of-town researchers.

Staff in Archives: 4f, 6p

Archives Are Handicapped Accessible: Yes

Review of Facilities: The Oregon State University Archives is located on the third floor of the Valley Library, located fairly centrally on the OSU campus. The Archives now share space with the maps and microforms area. Unlike most of the institutions profiled, the Special Collections are located on a separate floor in the building. (see separate profile) The Archives reading room is a large area partitioned off from the remainder of the library with a reference desk. Lockers are available at the entrance to the department for storing personal items other than pencils, papers, or laptops. The area has numerous oversize study tables and carrels some with electrical outlets. Most of the high-use items are stored in an adjoining staff area. The remaining collections are locked in compact shelving elsewhere on the floor.

Vertical Files: Yes   **Vertical Files in Cubic Feet:** 67

  Vertical File Description and Subjects: Memorabilia collection arranged by subject and containing information on Oregon State University and Benton County. Detailed description in library catalog.

Manuscripts: Yes   **Manuscripts Volume in Cubic Feet:** 3,105

  Manuscript Types: Business records, organizational records, personal papers, scrapbooks

  Manuscript Subjects: Corvallis businesses, school records, local organizations, agriculture and extension services

Photographs: Yes   **Number of Photographs:** 275,000

Storage of Photographs: Photographs are stored in document cases, flat oversize boxes, and flat files

Photograph Subjects: Crown Zellerbach photos, agriculture, and forestry products

Photograph Reproductions Are Available: Yes

Photographic Prints: Yes   **Digital Prints:** Yes

Digital Images on CD or Electronically: Yes

Books: Yes   **Number of Books in Collection:** 100

Description of Books: Annuals, professional collection

Newspapers: No

Newspapers on Microfilm: No

Microfilm and Dates: Historical newspapers in adjacent rooms

Oral Histories: Yes   **Oral Histories Number:** 250

Oral Histories Description: Oral history interviews mostly on audiotape; two-thirds have transcriptions. Also repository of oral history projects done on campus. Variety of subjects covered by interviews, some including Basques of Harney County, Oregon.

Maps and Drawings: Yes

Estimated Number of Maps and Drawings: 170,000

Description of Maps and Drawings: 170,000 maps in map collection, some historical Pacific Northwest, others worldwide, all subjects

Genealogy Sources: No

Special Collections: No

Indexes: Oregon State University Archives, 6 1/2 binders; MS collection, 3 binders; photo collection; 7 binders

Online Sources: Digital collections include: finding aids available at Northwest Digital Archives; Braceros in Oregon Photograph Collection; Willamette Basin Stream Survey (historic photos, 1939–1945); best of archives collection of selected online images; Linus Pauling research

Review of Collections: The archives at Oregon State University exist primarily to maintain the records and history of the university. In collecting their history, a significant amount of materials on Corvallis, Benton County, and the mid-Willamette Valley has been acquired as well. The area of strength is mostly in the photographs. Many of the community manuscript collections, though interesting, are relatively small. The papers of the numerous faculty members incorporate much of the history of the area and development of industries in the state. There is also a sizable videotape and motion picture collection from the college and extension offices.

Museum on Premises: No

Parking: Visitor parking permits are available at the information center on campus at 15th and Jefferson. Parking is $1 per hour or $5 per day. Metered parking lots near the library do not require a permit but allow only short-term parking.

Lunch: Coffee shop on lower level of library building

Lodging: http://www.visitcorvallis.com

Nearest Commercial Airport: Portland International (PDX) [83 miles]; Mahlon Sweet Field (Eugene) (EUG) [47 miles]

Subjects

Historical Periods: 1865–1900; 1900–1940; 1940–present

Eras: World War II

Natural Resources: Irrigation; Fishing; Logging

Transportation: Railroads; Ferries

Agriculture: Dairy; Ranching/Livestock; Vegetable/Truck Crops; Orchards

Business: Retail; Legal/Medical Services; Entertainment/Theaters

Manufacturing: Cannery; Sawmills; Wood Products

Government: City; State

Organizations: Schools; Colleges/Universities; Nonreligious Organizations

Ethnic Groups: Native American; Latin American; Basque

Religious Sites and Organizations: Protestant; Catholic

Date of Reviewer's Visit: 11/5/2003

Profile Updated by Institution: 11/15/2004

✱✱✱✱✱

Name: Oregon State University Special Collections **County:** Benton

Mailing Address: 121 Valley Library

City: Corvallis **State:** OR **Postal Code:** 97331-4501

Street Address: 15th and Jefferson

Institution Email: special.collections@orst.edu

Telephone Number: (541) 737-2075 **Fax Number:** (541) 737-8674

Contact Name: Cliff Mead **Contact Email:** cliff.mead@orst.edu

Institution Type: Academic Library

Affiliation: Oregon State University

Web site URL: http://osu.library.oregonstate.edu/specialcollections

Hours: M–F 8:30–4:30

Staff in Archives: 3f, 1p

Archives Are Handicapped Accessible: Yes

Access Description: ADA compliant

Review of Facilities: The Oregon State University Special Collections are located on the 5th floor of the Valley Library, near the center of the OSU campus. The Special Collections have a spacious, classy reading room with large conference tables, carrels, glass-fronted bookcases, and computer stations, in addition to the reference desk. Unlike most institutions surveyed, OSU retains a separation between the University Archives (see separate profile) and its Special Collections. Quite obviously, the Special Collections rate higher priority with administration and donors alike. The reading room leads to a staff study/work area amidst rows of compact shelving, all climate controlled. The collection is professionally managed. A large percentage of the sizable Special Collections area is devoted to the Linus Pauling Collection.

Vertical Files: No

Manuscripts: Yes   **Manuscripts Volume in Cubic Feet:** 5,450

    Manuscript Types: Personal papers

    Manuscript Subjects: Technology and science in the twentieth century, Atomic Energy Collection, Bernard Malamud papers, William Appleman William's papers, history of science collection

Photographs: Yes

    Storage of Photographs: Photos are maintained with document collections.

    Photograph Reproductions Are Available: Yes

        Photographic Prints: Yes   **Digital Prints:** Yes

Books: Yes

    Description of Books: The books are integrated into other collections, such as the History of Science Collection. In addition, Linus Pauling's personal library has over 4,000 books.

Newspapers: No

Oral Histories: No

Maps and Drawings: No

Genealogy Sources: No

Special Collections: Yes

    Special Collections Description: Ava Helen and Linus Pauling Papers consist of 500,000 items. The collection contains all of the Paulings' personal and scientific papers, research materials, correspondence, photographs, awards, and memorabilia. It also contains three-dimensional molecular models. The collection is 4,437 linear feet and 1,800 boxes.

Indexes: Yes

Manuscript Finding Aids: Finding aids to most collections available online from Web site

Online Sources: Exhibits, history, and digitalized copies of 46 research notebooks on Linus Pauling's work are available from the Web site.

Review of Collections: OSU Special Collections lists its main function as the preservation of the Linus Pauling papers. Nearly 80 percent of the holdings is this collection. It is doubtful that there is another collection of one person's accomplishments and life, both personal and professional, to match this one in breadth and depth. The remaining collections, although they may seem small by comparison, are also the papers of significant scientists, writers, and personalities. Most are connected to Oregon State University in some form. The Atomic Energy Collection and History of Science collection are growing and will eventually have finding aids online.

Museum on Premises: No

Parking: Visitor parking permits are available at the information center on campus at 15th and Jefferson. Metered parking lots near the library do not require a permit but allow only short-term parking.

Lunch: Coffee shop on lower level of library building

Lodging: http://www.visitcorvallis.com

Nearest Commercial Airport: Portland International (PDX) [83 miles]; Mahlon Sweet Field (Eugene) (EUG) [47 miles]

Subjects

   Historical Periods: 1900–1940; 1940–present

   Manufacturing: Technology/Computers

   Organizations: Colleges/Universities; Hospitals/Medical Facilities

Date of Reviewer's Visit: 11/5/2003

Profile Updated by Institution: 11/12/2004

CRATER LAKE

Name: Crater Lake National Park   **County:** Klamath

Mailing Address: PO Box 7

   City: Crater Lake   **State:** OR   **Postal Code:** 97604-0007

Street Address: Hwy. 62, Visitor Center, South Entrance

Institution Email: mary_benterou@nps.gov

Telephone Number: (541) 594-3095   **Fax Number:** (541) 594-3010

Contact Name: Mary Benterou   **Contact Email:** mary_benterou@nps.gov

Institution Type: Historic Site

Affiliation: National Park Service

Web site URL: None

Hours: Weekdays upon request

Staff in Archives: 1f

Archives Are Handicapped Accessible: No

Access Description: Archives are located on second floor

Review of Facilities: The historical collections are housed on the second floor of the visitor center near the south entrance to the park. The upstairs is closed, so notification of the staff in the visitor center will bring down a staff member to escort you to the upper level. The upstairs library would give the impression of being cramped, except for the charm of the place. Bookshelves fill the room, leaving only a moderate-sized table area. The library is obviously well used by the staff of the park. Vertical file type material is filed in clamshell boxes on the shelf of the library.

Vertical Files: Yes   **Vertical Files in Cubic Feet:** 40

   Vertical File Description and Subjects: General subject files stored in document boxes

Manuscripts: Yes   **Manuscripts Volume in Cubic Feet:** 120

   Manuscript Types: Archives, personal papers

   Manuscript Subjects: Crater Lake history, founders' papers, park rangers' papers, Interpreters paper, Building files of all structures in the park, botanical catalog

Photographs: Yes   **Number of Photographs:** 17,200

   Storage of Photographs: Reference copies of Interpreters photographs stored on 6 x 8 card files. Other photographs stored in archival enclosures.

   Photograph Subjects: Crater Lake history

   Photograph Reproductions Are Available: Yes

     Photographic Prints: Yes   **Digital Prints:** Yes

     Digital Images on CD or Electronically: Yes

Books: Yes   **Number of Books in Collection:** 1,500

   Description of Books: Park history, local history, interpretation, professional collection

Newspapers: Yes   **Newspapers in Paper Format:** Yes

   Papers and Dates: Park newspapers from 1970s to present

Oral Histories: Yes   **Oral Histories Number:** 30

   Oral Histories Description: Interviews with former park employees, particularly with rangers and superintendents. Interviews have transcriptions.

Maps and Drawings: Yes

> **Description of Maps and Drawings:** Maps, architectural drawings, large planning documents, blueprints; mostly stored flat, some rolled; 50 cu. ft.

Genealogy Sources: No

Special Collections: No

Indexes: Yes

> **Manuscript Finding Aids:** Manuscript collections have basic finding aids, which are also available electronically by collection

Review of Collections: The Crater Lake National Park collection focuses on the history of the park from the earliest period to the present. A significant part of the collection is on the establishment of the national park, and the history of the national park administration. The collection includes a large natural history collection of everything from soil samples to birds. This part of the collection is not included in the volume listed above. Oral histories and personal papers of the park personnel give a commentary on the life and work at the park through the years.

Parking: Free parking lot in front of building

Lunch: Lunch is available in the park at Rim Village three miles away. There is a cafeteria for burgers and short-order items for breakfast and lunch. A more formal lunch is available at Crater Lake Lodge, but reservations are suggested.

Lodging: http://www.craterlakelodges.com; Crater Lake Lodge (71 rooms), motel units at Mazama Village, camping available

Nearest Commercial Airport: Klamath Falls (LMT) [60 miles]

Subjects

> **Historical Periods:** 1900–1940; 1940–present
>
> **Eras:** CCC
>
> **Transportation:** Railroads
>
> **Government:** Federal

Date of Reviewer's Visit: 8/13/2003

Profile Updated by Institution: 11/9/2004

EUGENE

Name: Lane County Historical Museum/Archives   **County:** Lane

Mailing Address: 740 W 13th Ave.

> **City:** Eugene   **State:** OR   **Postal Code:** 97402-0000

Street Address: 740 W. 13th Ave.

Institution Email: lchm@efn.org

Telephone Number: (541) 682-4242 **Fax Number:** (541) 682-7361

Contact Name: Cheryl Roffe

Institution Type: Local Museum

Web site URL: http://www.lchmuseum.org

Hours: By appt. only, after filling out a museum Research Request Form

Staff in Archives: 1f 5p 8 v

Archives Are Handicapped Accessible: Yes

Cost for Researcher—In-house: Fee Schedule

Cost for Researcher—Remote: Fee Schedule

List of Researchers Available: No

Review of Facilities: The Lane County Historical Museum is housed in a single-story building on the county fairgrounds. The research room is to the right of the main entrance, past the museum store where they sell archival processing supplies. The research room itself is moderate to large but feels very dark and stuffed. There are research tables available in addition to volunteer and staff workspaces. The collection surrounds the room on bookcases and storage shelves. The collection is available only with staff assistance. The facility is one of the most restrictive of all the institutions in the survey.

Vertical Files: Yes **Vertical Files in Cubic Feet:** 6

Vertical File Description and Subjects: Vertical file of general subject (mostly newspaper clippings) and people files. Also have clipping collections in notebooks and filed by subject.

Manuscripts: Yes **Manuscripts Volume in Cubic Feet:** 250

Manuscript Types: Business records, family papers, organizational records, government records, land records

Manuscript Subjects: Businesses, families, schools, civic groups and other organizations. There are 335 separate manuscript collections; the largest has 27 boxes.

Photographs: Yes **Number of Photographs:** 20,000

Storage of Photographs: Photographs stored in plastic sleeves in boxes with a subject arrangement

Photograph Subjects: Eugene and Lane County history of industry, street scenes, portraits from 1860s to 1970s

Photograph Reproductions Are Available: Yes

Photographic Prints: Yes **Digital Prints:** Yes

Digital Images on CD or Electronically: Yes

Books: Yes **Number of Books in Collection:** 2,500

Description of Books: Local and regional history, professional collection, annuals, city directories. Indexed by card catalog.

Newspapers: No

Oral Histories: Yes   **Oral Histories Number:** 150

Oral Histories Description: Oral history interviews with local area residents on audiocassette tape. Most have transcripts.

Maps and Drawings: Yes   **Estimated Number of Maps and Drawings:** 350

Description of Maps and Drawings: Local area history, street maps filed in map case with an drawer inventory

Genealogy Sources: Yes

Genealogy Sources Description: People files. genealogy materials available at the Oregon Genealogical Society in Eugene, phone (541) 345-0399.

Special Collections: No

Indexes: Card catalog of the book collection. Surname index on card file indexing the manuscripts, people files, and contents of local historical books.

Manuscript Finding Aids: Manuscript collections have general description at a folder level listing.

Published Guides: "Catalog of Manuscripts in the Lane County Museum Library" by Edward W. Nolan, 1979.

Review of Collections: The collections of the Lane County Historical Archives are available by appointment only. The photograph collection is a significant one and covers the Eugene and Lane County area over a 100-year period. The local newspapers are not available at this facility in either paper or microfilm. The manuscript collections are only moderately sized but have some very significant contributions to the history of the state of Oregon.

Museum on Premises: Yes

Museum Hours: W–F 10–4, Sa–Su 12–4

Cost of Entry to Museum: $2

Museum Is Handicapped Accessible: Yes

Description of Museum: Lane County Historical Museum collects and displays the artifacts and history of Lane County.

Parking: Free parking lot adjacent

Lunch: Driving distance to variety of chain and local restaurants

Lodging: http://www.visitlanecounty.org

Nearest Commercial Airport: Mahlon Sweet Field (Eugene, OR) (EUG) [9 miles]

Subjects

Historical Periods: 1800–1865; 1865–1900; 1900–1940; 1940–present

Eras: Civil War

Natural Resources: Logging

Mining: Gold

Transportation: Railroads; Stagecoach/Freight; Ships and Shipping; Aviation

Agriculture: Dairy; Ranching/Livestock; Vegetable/Truck Crops; Grains; Orchards; Vineyard

Business: Retail; Legal/Medical Services; Entertainment/Theaters

Manufacturing: Sawmills

Government: City; County; State

Organizations: Schools; Colleges/Universities; Hospitals/Medical Facilities

Date of Reviewer's Visit: 8/19/2003

Profile Updated by Institution: 11/12/2004

�֎�֎�֎✖✖

Name: University of Oregon Library Special Collections and University Archives
County: Lane

Mailing Address: 1299 University of Oregon

City: Eugene   **State:** OR   **Postal Code:** 97403-1299

Street Address: Knight Library, 15th and Kincaid St.

Institution Email: spcarref@uoregon.edu

Telephone Number: (541) 346-3068   **Fax Number:** (541) 346-1882

Contact Name: James D. Fox   **Contact Email:** jdfox@uoregon.edu

Institution Type: Academic Library

Affiliation: University of Oregon

Web site URL: http://www.libweb.uoregon.edu/speccoll

Hours: M–F 10–4:30; Sa 11–4:30

Staff in Archives: 4f, 2p

Archives Are Handicapped Accessible: Yes

Access Description: Go to the circulation desk and ask for the elevator to special collections

Cost for Researcher—Remote: Fee schedule

List of Researchers Available: Yes

Review of Facilities: The University of Oregon Special Collections are located on the second floor of Knight Library. The research room is long and narrow with high ceilings. There are five large worktables with adequate lighting. A reference desk provides assistance and registration materials to access anything in the collection. Full archival restrictions are placed on use of materials, including limiting of personal items on tables. No secure storage area for personal belongings is provided. Pencils only and/or gloves are required when handling materials. The Special Collections area also provides access to the University of Oregon Archives.

Vertical Files: No

Manuscripts: Yes   **Manuscripts Volume in Cubic Feet:** 36,000

Manuscript Types: Personal papers, business records, organizational records, 2,000 processed collections

Manuscript Subjects: Oregon and regional history, politics and culture, missionaries to far east, children's literature, conservative and libertarian politics. University of Oregon Archives have 19,000 cubic feet of this 36,000 total.

Photographs: Yes   **Number of Photographs:** 400,000

Photograph Reproductions Are Available: Yes

Photographic Prints: Yes   **Digital Prints:** Yes

Books: Yes   **Number of Books in Collection:** 150,000

Description of Books: Oregon Collection, regional and local history, city directories, telephone books, annuals; most in closed stacks, books in regular catalog online; also has author, title and subject card catalog

Newspapers: No

Newspapers on Microfilm: No

Microfilm and Dates: Newspapers from throughout the state available downstairs in microfilm collection

Oral Histories: No

Oral Histories Description: Some oral histories are contained in general collections.

Maps and Drawings: No

Genealogy Sources: No

Special Collections: Yes

Special Collections Description: Manuscript collections documenting women in society—several hundred collections dealing with the roles women played in society listed by professions or their role in Western history

Indexes: Books and some manuscripts on library online catalog. Old card file of books and some manuscripts. Can search for subjects within the MS collection.

Manuscript Finding Aids: Folder-level inventories available in research room

Published Guides: *Catalogue of Manuscripts in the University of Oregon Library*, compiled by Martin Schmitt (published 1971)

Online Sources: Guides to manuscript collections available through Web site or searchable through the Northwest Digital Archive (see detail under Digital Sources, chapter 7). Some digital collections available from Web site.

Review of Collections: The collections at the University of Oregon are large and multifaceted. Prior planning is essential, as they often demand 48 hours' notice on materials usage, particularly for photographs and architectural drawings. Sub-collections include the large Oregon collection of history, life, and literature of Oregon from the territorial period onward. Manuscript collections focus on women's history, labor history, and politics. The University of Oregon Archives documenting the history of the institution are also available. The photograph collection is described as "Historic and Contemporary," many of the individual collections being listed on the Web site. A large, professionally managed collection with an increasing number of digital materials available.

Museum on Premises: No

Parking: Metered parking outside the library. Information kiosk at Beech St. and 13th Ave. for visitor permits. Parking map available from Web site.

Lunch: Various eating places on campus and walking distance to numerous local restaurants. Coffee shop located on lower level of library.

Lodging: http://www.visitlanecounty.org

Nearest Commercial Airport: Mahlon Sweet Field (Eugene, OR) (EUG) [13 miles]

Subjects

> **Historical Periods:** 1800–1865; 1865–1900; 1900–1940; 1940–present
>
> **Mining:** Gold; Silver; Copper; Placer Mining
>
> **Ethnic Groups:** Native American; Chinese
>
> **Religious Sites and Organizations:** Protestant

Date of Reviewer's Visit: 8/19/2003

Profile Updated by Institution: 12/8/2004

GRANTS PASS

Name: Josephine County Historical Society   **County:** Josephine

Mailing Address: 512 SW 5th St.

   City: Grants Pass   **State:** OR   **Postal Code:** 97526-0000

Street Address: 512 SW 5th St.

Institution Email: josephinehistorical@charter.net

Telephone Number: (541) 479-7827   **Fax Number:** (541) 472-8928

Contact Name: Rose Scott

Institution Type: Historical Society Archives

Web site URL: http://www.webtrail.com/jchs

Hours: Tu–F 10–4

Staff in Archives: 1 p 20v

Archives Are Handicapped Accessible: Yes

Cost for Researcher—In-house: $5

Cost for Researcher—Remote: Fee schedule

Review of Facilities: The research library of the Josephine County Historical Society is located in a house a few blocks from the historical district. The museum is on the same block but unconnected to the research library building. The research library takes up the front rooms of the old house. A staff desk is in the center directly opposite the door, with the museum bookstore to one side and a research area on the other. There is table space for researchers, and historical materials line the walls of the room. Materials are also housed in several other staff-only rooms in the building. The research room is pleasant, well used, and practical for a researcher. This institution has one of the best county-level historical research libraries in the survey.

Vertical Files: Yes   **Vertical Files in Cubic Feet:** 36

  Vertical File Description and Subjects: Newspaper clipping files by subject and people. Also 12 cu. ft. of pamphlet and ephemera files.

Manuscripts: Yes   **Manuscripts Volume in Cubic Feet:** 160

  Manuscript Types: Business records, personal papers, county records, school records

  Manuscript Subjects: Abstracts of title, personal papers of county residents, mining, schools

Photographs: Yes   **Number of Photographs:** 6,000

  Storage of Photographs: Photographs are stored in plastic sleeves in file folders; slides are on hanging file sleeves.

  Photograph Subjects: Josephine County and southern Oregon

  Photograph Reproductions Are Available: Yes

    Photographic Prints: Yes   **Digital Prints:** Yes

    Digital Images on CD or Electronically: Yes

Books: Yes   **Number of Books in Collection:** 400

  Description of Books: Local history, city directories, annuals. Books are in card catalog.

Newspapers: Yes   **Newspapers on Microfilm:** Yes

  Microfilm and Dates: *Grants Pass Bulletin* and *Rogue River Courier*, from 1895

Oral Histories: Yes   **Oral Histories Number:** 100

Oral Histories Description: Oral history project to record videotape histories of local area residents is ongoing. There are currently no transcriptions.

Maps and Drawings: Yes   **Estimated Number of Maps and Drawings:** 1,000

Description of Maps and Drawings: Local area maps, regional maps, land ownership and subdivision, road and assay, town plats

Genealogy Sources: Yes

Genealogy Sources Description: Family files with photographs, obituary files, cemetery records

Special Collections: No

Indexes: Card catalog of book collection

Review of Collections: The collections at the Josephine County Historical Society research library are varied and well maintained. The volume of manuscript-type materials is larger than many similarly sized communities. The map collection is sizable, with a wide variety of types of maps. Subjects of interest include Josephine County, Illinois Valley, Rogue River Valley, and southern Oregon. Collections are stored well and easily accessible to staff and researcher alike. The historical society obviously considers the preservation of the documents and photographs a priority, rather than an afterthought. Good collection.

Museum on Premises: No

Parking: Free small paved parking lot adjacent

Lunch: Driving distance to wide variety of local and chain restaurants

Lodging: http://www.visitgrantspass.org

Nearest Commercial Airport: Rogue Valley International–Medford (MFR) [27 miles]

Subjects

    Historical Periods: 1865–1900; 1900–1940; 1940–present

    Natural Resources: Fishing; Logging

    Mining: Gold; Silver; Placer Mining; Surface Mining

    Transportation: Railroads; Stagecoach/Freight

    Agriculture: Dairy; Ranching/Livestock; Orchards; Vineyard

    Business: Retail; Legal/Medical Services; Hotels/Restaurants

    Manufacturing: Sawmills

    Government: City; County

    Organizations: Schools; Hospitals/Medical Facilities; Charities; Nonreligious Organizations

    Religious Sites and Organizations: Protestant; Catholic; LDS (Mormon)

Date of Reviewer's Visit: 8/15/2003

Profile Updated by Institution: 11/22/2004

HOOD RIVER

Name: Hood River County Historical Museum   **County:** Hood River

Mailing Address: PO Box 781

   City: Hood River   **State:** OR   **Postal Code:** 97031-0000

Street Address: 300 E. Port Marina Dr.

Institution Email: hrchm@gorge.net

Telephone Number: (541) 386-6772

Contact Name: Connie Nice, Museum Coordinator

Institution Type: Local Museum

Affiliation: Hood River County Parks Department

Web site URL: http://www.co.hood-river.or.us/museum

Hours: M–F 10–4 by appt.

Staff in Archives: 1f, 15v

Archives Are Handicapped Accessible: Yes

Cost for Researcher—Remote: Fee schedule

Review of Facilities: The Hood River County Historical Museum is located in Marina Park. The building was built in 1978 and new sections added 20 years later. The main research room is off the lobby. This room houses the file cabinets with vertical files and photographs, periodicals in closed cabinets, photocopy machine, computer station, and small worktable and counter. In the back corner of the museum is the library area with the book collection in corner bookcases (some locked). There is also a small worktable for use with the books. The manuscript, papers, and other collections are stored in compact shelving in a back storage area.

Vertical Files: Yes   **Vertical Files in Cubic Feet:** 46

   Vertical File Description and Subjects: Biographical files and general subject files on local history with clippings, ephemera and miscellaneous materials

Manuscripts: Yes   **Manuscripts Volume in Cubic Feet:** 7

   Manuscript Types: Scrapbooks, family papers

   Manuscript Subjects: Hood River County

Photographs: Yes   **Number of Photographs:** 2,800

Storage of Photographs: Photographs are stored in file cabinets in plastic sleeves arranged by subject. A staff computer has Microsoft Access database file of indexing of photographs linked to digitized images.

Photograph Subjects: Hood River County subjects

Photograph Reproductions Are Available: Yes

   Photographic Prints: Yes   **Digital Prints:** Yes

Books: Yes   **Number of Books in Collection:** 250

Description of Books: Local history, professional collection, annuals, city directories

Newspapers: Yes

Newspapers in Paper Format: Yes

Papers and Dates: *Hood River Glacier,* 1894–1933 (incomplete)

Newspapers on Microfilm: No

Microfilm and Dates: Hood River papers on microfilm at local public library

Oral Histories: Yes   **Oral Histories Number:** 20

Oral Histories Description: New interviews in process. Some earlier interviews are available as transcriptions only (filed in vertical files)

Maps and Drawings: Yes   **Estimated Number of Maps and Drawings:** 20

Description of Maps and Drawings: Local area maps dating from early 1900s, including Sanborn maps of downtown area

Genealogy Sources: Yes

Genealogy Sources Description: Biography files included with vertical files have obituaries, family histories and biographical information, cemetery records

Special Collections: No

Indexes: Microsoft Access database index, some paper indexing, subject arrangement of vertical files

Review of Collections: The collections at Hood River County Museum are limited. The photograph collections and vertical files are the strongest features. The manuscript collections are extremely weak. This is reportedly due to staffing issues and space constraints. But like all institutions, it is a work in progress. Collections are professionally stored in compact shelving in the new addition to the museum. The strengths of the collection include the earlier-than-average collection of some materials from the Pioneer Association starting in 1903 and the historical society starting in 1948.

Museum on Premises: Yes

Museum Hours: M–Sa 10–4, Su 12–4 Apr–Aug; daily 12–4 Sept–Oct

Cost of Entry to Museum: Donation

Museum Is Handicapped Accessible: Yes

Description of Museum: Several galleries focusing on Hood River and mid-Columbia Gorge area history

Parking: Free parking lot adjacent

Lunch: Variety of restaurants in driving distance

Lodging: http://www.hoodriver.org

Nearest Commercial Airport: Portland International (PDX) [61 miles]

Subjects

    Historical Periods: 1800–1865; 1865–1900; 1900–1940; 1940–present

    Eras: Civil War; Spanish American War; World War I; WPA; World War II

    Natural Resources: Dams; Logging

    Transportation: Railroads; Ships and Shipping; Ferries

    Agriculture: Vegetable/Truck Crops; Orchards

    Business: Retail; Legal/Medical Services; Hotels/Restaurants; Entertainment/Theaters

    Manufacturing: Cannery; Sawmills

    Government: City; County; State

    Organizations: Schools; Hospitals/Medical Facilities

    Ethnic Groups: Native American; Latin American; Japanese; Finnish

Date of Reviewer's Visit: 3/24/2004

Profile Updated by Institution: 11/12/2004

JOHN DAY

Name: Kam Wah Chung & Co. Museum   **County:** Grant

Mailing Address: PO Box 10

  City: Mt. Vernon   **State:** OR   **Postal Code:** 97865-0000

Street Address: Canton Street, John Day, Oregon

Institution Email: None

Telephone Number: (541) 932-4453   **Fax Number:** (541) 932-4459

Contact Name: Dennis Bradley   **Contact Email:** Dennis.Bradley@state.or.us

Institution Type: Historic Site

Affiliation: Oregon State Parks and Recreation Department and City of John Day

Web site URL: None

Hours: By appt.

Archives Are Handicapped Accessible: No

Access Description: Uneven wooden floors, raised doorjambs

Cost for Researcher—In-house: Museum Donation

Review of Facilities: The Kam Wah Chung Museum is located in the city park in the center of John Day, Oregon. Not technically an archive, it is a unique museum with a special appeal for the researcher of late-nineteenth- and early-twentieth-century Chinese-American history. The museum building was built in 1867 as a trading post on The Dalles Military Road. The building was first purchased in 1887 by two Chinese immigrants, who in addition to living on the premises, opened a store, which functioned as a cultural and religious center for the Chinese community for decades. One of the owners, Ing "Doc" Hay, was a master of traditional Chinese medicine and he continued his practice until 1948, in the same building. Shuttered after his death in 1952, and not reopened until 1978, the contents remain as when it was occupied. The dark five-room building has paper collections on display throughout the museum and hidden in various nooks and crannies. As they restore the museum, hopefully, they will further catalog and preserve the documents found within this fascinating slice of little-recorded history.

Vertical Files: No

Manuscripts: Yes   **Manuscripts Volume in Cubic Feet:** 15

   Manuscript Types: Business records

   Manuscript Subjects: Records dealing with the business of the store, the medical practice, and local information. Collection of checks from 1909 to 1929, which were never cashed, written in amounts from 50 cents to several hundred dollars, totaling $23,000.

Photographs: Yes   **Number of Photographs:** 100

   Storage of Photographs: Photographs are stored in file folders in a file cabinet. Some are on display in museum.

   Photograph Subjects: Chinese community in John Day and the two proprietors, local history

   Photograph Reproductions Are Available: No

Books: No

Newspapers: No

Oral Histories: No

Maps and Drawings: No

Genealogy Sources: No

Special Collections: No

Indexes: 4 x 6 card file index for contents of the museum

Review of Collections: The collections of the Kam Wah Chung Museum are hard to compare with the rest of the institutions in this survey. Because of the unique nature of this collection, it stands in a category all its own. The documents are not processed or stored archivally, but at least they are being saved. There are 11 boxes of documents that had been given to the Oregon Historical Society and later returned to Kam Wah Chung (likely still unprocessed). There are photographs of the building, its inhabitants, and their clientele and friends. There are also a collection of theses and dissertations done on the subject. Some of the letters in the collection have been translated to English. There is also a small newspaper clipping collection. The focus of all subjects is appropriately narrow to cover the business and the Chinese community in eastern Oregon from the 1880s to 1940s. To research other historical topics dealing with the area around the town of John Day, the Grant County Historical Museum in nearby Canyon City houses those collections. (see profile).

Museum on Premises: Yes

   Museum Hours: 9–12 and 1–5 M–Su, May 1– Oct 31

   Cost of Entry to Museum: Donation

   Museum Is Handicapped Accessible: No

   Access Description: Uneven floors, doorjambs, and steps

   Description of Museum: This museum has been described as a time capsule but it is even more than that. Everything has been left the same as when the previous occupants left. An important remnant of Chinese-American history and a must-see museum.

Parking: Free parking lot adjacent

Lunch: Several local restaurants within a short drive or use adjacent picnic area

Lodging: http://www.grantcounty.cc

Nearest Commercial Airport: Eastern Oregon Regional at Pendleton (PDT) [128 miles]

Subjects

   Historical Periods: 1865–1900; 1900–1940

   Business: Retail; Legal/Medical Services

   Ethnic Groups: Chinese

   Religious Sites and Organizations: Buddhist

Date of Reviewer's Visit: 9/24/2003

Profile Updated by Institution: 11/16/2004

JOSEPH

Name: Wallowa County Museum   **County:** Wallowa

Mailing Address: 110 S. Main St.

  City: Joseph   **State:** OR   **Postal Code:** 97846-0000

Street Address: 110 S. Main St.

Institution Email: None

Telephone Number: (541) 432-6095   **Fax Number:** (541) 432-4834

Contact Name: Caryl Coppin or Anne Hayes   **Institution Type:** Local Museum

Affiliation: Wallowa County

Web site URL: None

Hours: M–Su 10–5, May 30–3d weekend in Sept; call ahead for appt.

Staff in Archives: 5v

Archives Are Handicapped Accessible: No

Access Description: Several steps at entrance, elevator to second floor

Cost for Researcher—Remote: Donations

Review of Facilities: The Wallowa County Museum is located at the edge of the business district in a former bank building. There are several worktables in the main part of the museum, where a researcher could work. These are in the main traffic area, and during open business hours, research is not allowed because of space problems. The building is unheated, so winter research is not possible. The collections are stored in the bank vault or storage closet off the main downstairs room of the museum. They are planning to build a new facility in a few years that will have a dedicated research room.

Vertical Files: Yes   **Vertical Files in Cubic Feet:** 4

  Vertical File Description and Subjects: Clipping files, single documents, and miscellaneous records

Manuscripts: Yes   **Manuscripts Volume in Cubic Feet:** 30

  Manuscript Types: City records, business records, personal papers, school records, scrapbooks

  Manuscript Subjects: Hornor papers, diaries from area, homestead certificates, military papers, mining and stock certificates from local mines, City of Joseph records, court proceedings of Chinese Massacre.

Photographs: Yes   **Number of Photographs:** 2,000

  Storage of Photographs: Most photographs are stored in archival envelopes. Some are in photo albums.

Photograph Subjects: Wallowa County, local area history scenes and events

Photograph Reproductions Are Available: Yes

Photographic Prints: Yes

Books: No

Newspapers: Yes

Newspapers in Paper Format: Yes

Papers and Dates: Scattered issues of local Wallowa County papers and unorganized stacks.

Microfilm and Dates: Microfilm of newspapers available at Wallowa County Library. Wallowa County Chieftain newspaper office has full run.

Oral Histories: Yes   **Oral Histories Number:** 50

Oral Histories Description: Oral histories are on VHS tape, audiocassette, and some reel-to-reel. Some have been transcribed. Interviews of local area residents.

Maps and Drawings: Yes   **Estimated Number of Maps and Drawings:** 6

Description of Maps and Drawings: Local area maps

Genealogy Sources: Yes

Genealogy Sources Description: A collection of family histories of Wallowa County

Special Collections: No

Indexes: An index to the collection is on 5 x 7 cards. It is for staff use only, however.

Review of Collections: The research collections are fairly small but there are greater possibilities for historical "gems." The collection is still in the early stages of organization. Significant pieces in this collection include court proceedings of the Chinese Massacre, early history and ledgers from the City of Joseph (10 cu. ft.), and many other local historical records.

Museum on Premises: Yes

Cost of Entry to Museum: Donations

Museum Is Handicapped Accessible: No

Parking: Free diagonal on-street parking

Lunch: Restaurant adjacent and numerous tourist restaurants nearby

Lodging: http://www.chiefjosephdays.com/home.html

Nearest Commercial Airport: Lewiston–Nez Perce County (LWS) [94 miles]; Eastern Oregon Regional at Pendleton (PDT) [121 miles]

Subjects

Historical Periods: 1865–1900; 1900–1940; 1940–present

Natural Resources: Water; Dams; Fishing; Hunting; Logging

Transportation: Railroads; Stagecoach/Freight

Agriculture: Dairy; Ranching/Livestock; Vegetable/Truck Crops; Grains

Business: Retail

Manufacturing: Grist/Flour Mills; Sawmills; Wood Products

Government: City; County

Organizations: Schools; Nonreligious Organizations

Ethnic Groups: Native American

Religious Sites and Organizations: Protestant; Catholic; LDS (Mormon)

Date of Reviewer's Visit: 9/23/2003

Profile Updated by Institution: 11/15/2004

KLAMATH FALLS

Name: Klamath County Museum   **County:** Klamath

Mailing Address: 1451 Main St.

  City: Klamath Falls   **State:** OR   **Postal Code:** 97601-0000

Street Address: 1451 Main St.

Institution Email: None

Telephone Number: (541) 883-4208   **Fax Number:** (541) 884-0219

Contact Name: Judith Hassen, Curator

Institution Type: Local Museum

Affiliation: Klamath County

Web site URL: None

Hours: Tu–Sa 9–6, June–Labor Day; winter 9–5

Staff in Archives: 2f 2p 4v

Archives Are Handicapped Accessible: No

Access Description: Research room is up several flights of stairs.

Cost for Researcher—In-house: $5

Cost for Researcher—Remote: Fee Schedule

List of Researchers Available: Yes

Review of Facilities: Museum is housed in an old armory building. The research room is up several flights of stairs. There is a big worktable, but the lighting is barely sufficient. The collections are stored on various levels and landings with insufficient organization.

Vertical Files: Yes   **Vertical Files in Cubic Feet:** 6

Vertical File Description and Subjects: Biography files

Manuscripts: Yes   **Manuscripts Volume in Cubic Feet:** 18

Manuscript Types: Scrapbooks

Manuscript Subjects: Local clubs, clipping files of various local groups and events

Photographs: Yes   **Number of Photographs:** 10,000

Storage of Photographs: Photo files are on main floor in staff office area. Files are a mixture of documents and photocopies of photographs. Originals and some negatives stored in vault.

Photograph Subjects: Klamath County and surrounding areas

Books: Yes   **Number of Books in Collection:** 7,000

Description of Books: Oregon history, city directories, catalogs, professional collection, and lots of old books

Newspapers: Yes   **Newspapers in Paper Format:** Yes

Papers and Dates: Bound volumes of most of the newspapers from the area

Newspapers on Microfilm: No

Microfilm and Dates: Klamath County Library has most of the microfilm of the papers.

Oral Histories: No

Maps and Drawings: No

Genealogy Sources: Yes

Genealogy Sources Description: Scrapbook obituary files from 1970s–1990s measuring 12 linear ft.

Special Collections: Yes

Special Collections Description: County records, wills and deeds, assessment records, and tax rolls. Collection is hundreds of cubic feet in size. Also map files and blueprints of area subjects; an inventory of these is currently in process.

Indexes: No

Review of Collections: This collection is full of wonderful material but is seriously underindexed and falls far short of its potential, for both the staff and the researcher. The collections are spread throughout the building, not for space concerns, but lack of organized plan.

Museum on Premises: Yes

Museum Is Handicapped Accessible: Yes

Description of Museum: Local museum of natural and local history of the Klamath Basin

Parking: Free on-street parallel parking or small parking lot behind museum

Lunch: Driving distance to local and chain eateries

Lodging: http://klamathcounty.net

Nearest Commercial Airport: Klamath Falls (LMT) [6 miles]

Subjects

> **Historical Periods:** 1865–1900; 1865–1900; 1865–1900
>
> **Natural Resources:** Logging
>
> **Mining:** Mining
>
> **Organizations:** Schools

Date of Reviewer's Visit: 8/14/2003

Profile Updated by Institution: None

✸✸✸✸✸

Name: Shaw Historical Library at Oregon Institute of Technology

County: Klamath

Mailing Address: Oregon Institute of Technology, 3201 Campus Dr.

> **City:** Klamath Falls   **State:** OR   **Postal Code:** 97601-8801

Street Address: 3201 Campus Dr.

Institution Email: shawlib@oit.edu

Telephone Number: (541) 885-1772   **Fax Number:** (541) 885-1777

Contact Name: Anne Hiller Clark   **Contact Email:** hillerca@oit.edu

Institution Type: Academic Library

Affiliation: Oregon Institute of Technology

Web site URL: http://www.oit.edu/shaw

Hours: M–F 1–5, or by appt.

Staff in Archives: 2p, 1v

Archives Are Handicapped Accessible: Yes

List of Researchers Available: Yes

Review of Facilities: The Shaw Historical Library is located at the Oregon Institute of Technology (OIT) in the Learning Resources Center building. It is a privately founded and funded institution sharing space at the university. There is a computer station and a large polished mahogany conference table. The room is classic and very elegant, as well as functional and well lit. Staff office areas are at one end of the large room, slightly removed from the rest of the library. Strict archival standards are maintained. Only the book collection is stored in the research room, and it is locked in the mahogany glass-fronted bookcases that line the wall. Research collections are stored in an adjacent staff-only area or on another storage floor of the institution.

Vertical Files: Yes   **Vertical Files in Cubic Feet:** 5

  Vertical File Description and Subjects: General subject file

Manuscripts: Yes   **Manuscripts Volume in Cubic Feet:** 115

  Manuscript Types: Business records, organizational records, school records, family papers

  Manuscript Subjects: Logging, local history, education in the county, Jessie Carr and the Modoc War, Klamath River camp at Commission

Photographs: Yes   **Number of Photographs:** 3,500

  Storage of Photographs: Photographs are stored in paper sleeves in archival boxes. Photographs are in the collections, some having item-level descriptions, and others not.

  Photograph Subjects: Alfred "Cap" Collier collection of World War I images and military history.

  Photograph Reproductions Are Available: Yes

    Photographic Prints: Yes   **Digital Prints:** Yes

Books: Yes   **Number of Books in Collection:** 3,000

  Description of Books: Local area history, water supply in the basin, logging; book holdings on computer at OIT and available online

Newspapers: Yes

  Newspapers on Microfilm: Yes

  Microfilm and Dates: Microfilm of local papers available at OIT Learning Resources Center, Klamath Falls Museum, or Klamath County Library

Oral Histories: Yes   **Oral Histories Number:** 30

  Oral Histories Description: Oral history of Winema National Forest; interviews with Klamath Indians, loggers, ranchers, farmers, hunters. and Federal employees, 34 in number. Oral history interviews are listed on the Web site. Transcriptions available.

Maps and Drawings: Yes   **Estimated Number of Maps and Drawings:** 2,000

  Description of Maps and Drawings: Local area history and maps of the Modoc War in Oregon, California, and Nevada

Genealogy Sources: No

Special Collections: Yes

  Special Collections Description: 16 volumes of local annual history magazine *Klamath Echoes* and original research of memoirs or background information with photographs

Indexes: Yes

Manuscript Finding Aids: Photographs and manuscripts have finding aids, some specialized for subject areas.

Online Sources: Finding aids available on Web site. Book titles available in the online book catalog.

Review of Collections: The collections of the Shaw Historical Society Library are significant and professionally maintained. Listings of most collections are included on the Web site. All nonbook collections are arranged by collection name having the images, documents, maps, and oral histories housed with the originating collection. Major subject areas include Klamath area history, lumbering, and the Modoc War.

Museum on Premises: No

Parking: Paved parking lot behind the Learning Resources Building

Lunch: Student Union on campus or a short drive to variety of chain and local restaurants near campus

Lodging: http://klamathcounty.net

Nearest Commercial Airport: Klamath Falls (LMT) [8 miles]

Subjects

Historical Periods: 1800–1865; 1865–1900; 1900–1940; 1940–present

Eras: Indian Wars; World War I; CCC; World War II

Natural Resources: Water; Irrigation; Logging

Transportation: Railroads; Stagecoach/Freight; Ferries

Agriculture: Ranching/Livestock; Vegetable/Truck Crops

Business: Retail

Manufacturing: Sawmills; Wood Products

Government: Tribal

Organizations: Schools; Colleges/Universities; Women's

Ethnic Groups: Native American; Japanese; Czech

Date of Reviewer's Visit: 8/14/2003

Profile Updated by Institution: 11/19/2004

MEDFORD

Name: Southern Oregon Historical Society   **County:** Jackson

Mailing Address: 106 N. Central Ave.

  City: Medford   **State:** OR   **Postal Code:** 97501-5926

Street Address: 106 N. Central Ave.

Institution Email: library1@sohs.org

Telephone Number: (541) 773-6536   **Fax Number:** (541) 776-7994

Contact Name: Carol Harbison Samuelson, Library Manager

Institution Type: Regional Museum

Web site URL: http://www.sohs.org

Hours: Tu–F 1–5

Staff in Archives: 1f 1p 4v

Archives Are Handicapped Accessible: Yes

Cost for Researcher—In-house: $5

Cost for Researcher—Remote: Fee schedule

Review of Facilities: The Southern Oregon Historical Society is located in a former department store in downtown Medford. The research library is just off the main entrance to the museum and has separate hours. A staff desk and counter is just inside the doorway. The room is spacious and airy and has large, well-lit workspaces. The only research materials in the library are card file indexes and browsing periodicals. Other materials are kept in a large storage area behind the research room.

Vertical Files: Yes   **Vertical Files in Cubic Feet:** 36

   Vertical File Description and Subjects: General subject files of Jackson County history. Clipping files.

Manuscripts: Yes   **Manuscripts Volume in Cubic Feet:** 4,000

   Manuscript Types: All manuscript types

   Manuscript Subjects: Southwestern Oregon history, including business records, family papers, organizational records, and architectural drawings

Photographs: Yes   **Number of Photographs:** 1 million

   Storage of Photographs: Photographs are filed in plastic sleeves in archival photo boxes.

   Photograph Subjects: Railroading, gold mining, street scenes

   Photograph Reproductions Are Available: Yes

      Photographic Prints: Yes   **Digital Prints:** Yes

Books: Yes

   Description of Books: Local and regional history, professional collection, genealogy

Newspapers: Yes

   Newspapers in Paper Format: Yes

   Papers and Dates: Local area newspapers from 1850 to the present

Newspapers on Microfilm: Yes

Microfilm and Dates: Microfilm of local papers

Oral Histories: Yes   **Oral Histories Number:** 500

    Oral Histories Description: Local resident oral history interviews. Transcriptions available.

Maps and Drawings: Yes   **Estimated Number of Maps and Drawings:** 500

    Description of Maps and Drawings: Local area maps.

Genealogy Sources: Yes

Special Collections: Yes

    Special Collections Description: A nineteenth-century photograph collection consisting of 10,000 glass plate negatives and prints by pioneer photographer Peter Britt. Britt, best known for taking the first photographs of Crater Lake in 1874, recorded more than half a century of southwestern Oregon history.

Indexes: Card file index of books, manuscripts, maps, newspapers, oral histories, and recordings

    Online Sources: The Web site links to a growing number of documents in PDF form of historical information, including histories of several cemeteries, general historical information, and tours of local history sites.

Review of Collections: The collections of the Southern Oregon Historical Society are diverse and sizable. The photograph collection now numbers close to 1 million images. The collection also includes movie film, newsreels and videos. The collection is professionally maintained. The Southern Oregon Historical Society Web site refers to the archives as a "gold mine of information," an accurate assessment of this collection.

Museum on Premises: Yes

    Museum Hours: W–Su 10–5

    Museum Is Handicapped Accessible: Yes

Parking: Free on-street parallel parking (2-hr. limit)

Lunch: Driving distance to most chain restaurants and a variety of local eateries

Lodging: http://www.visitmedford.org

Nearest Commercial Airport: Rogue Valley International–Medford (MFR) [4 miles]

Subjects

    Historical Periods: 1865–1900; 1900–1940; 1940–present

    Mining: Gold; Copper

    Transportation: Railroads; Stagecoach/Freight

    Agriculture: Dairy; Ranching/Livestock; Grains; Orchards

    Business: Retail; Legal/Medical Services; Hotels/Restaurants; Entertainment/Theaters

Organizations: Schools; Hospitals/Medical Facilities

Ethnic Groups: Native American; African; Pacific Islander; Japanese

Religious Sites and Organizations: Protestant; Catholic; Jewish

Date of Reviewer's Visit: 8/14/2003

Profile Updated by Institution: 11/22/2004

MORO

✳✳✳

Name: Sherman County Historical Society   **County:** Sherman

Mailing Address: PO Box 173

City: Moro   **State:** OR   **Postal Code:** 97039-0000

Street Address: 200 Dewey St.

Institution Email: info@shermanmuseum.org

Telephone Number: (541) 565-3232   **Fax Number:** (541) 565-3080

Contact Name: Elaine Kalista   **Contact Email:** info@shermanmuseum.org

Institution Type: Local Museum

Web site URL: http://www.shermanmuseum.org

Hours: Daily 10–5, May–Oct; by appt. only Nov–Apr

Staff in Archives: 1p; 80v

Archives Are Handicapped Accessible: No

Access Description: Staff will provide access to otherwise inaccessible collections on main floor.

Cost for Researcher—Remote: Fee schedule

Review of Facilities: The Sherman County Museum is located a few blocks from the downtown area, in a park, with a series of buildings constituting the museum complex. The archive materials are separated in two different parts of the building. The genealogy collection and family history documents are located just inside the main entrance. The photograph archive is in another part of the building and will be accessed by staff.

Vertical Files: Yes   **Vertical Files in Cubic Feet:** 4

  Vertical File Description and Subjects: Ephemera collection, county subjects (note family histories under genealogy section)

Manuscripts: Yes   **Manuscripts Volume in Cubic Feet:** 20

  Manuscript Types: Scrapbooks

  Manuscript Subjects: Major subjects are people and events of Sherman County

Photographs: Yes   **Number of Photographs:** 5,000

Storage of Photographs: 16 cu. ft. of photographs and oversize photographs are filed by family names or subject. Filed in folders in file cabinets. There is no index to the photos, but they are arranged by subject matter. They are in the process of scanning the photographs to the PastPerfect system and backing them up on DVD.

Photograph Subjects: Sherman County people, towns, and events are the main focus of the photograph collection

Photograph Reproductions Are Available: Yes

Photographic Prints: Yes

Books: Yes   **Number of Books in Collection:** 100

Description of Books: Local and regional history, family histories, annuals

Newspapers: Yes

Newspapers on Microfilm: Yes

Microfilm and Dates: Have access to microfilm of local papers; inquire at the museum ahead of your visit

Oral Histories: No

Maps and Drawings: No

Genealogy Sources: Yes

Genealogy Sources Description: 12 cu. ft. of genealogy and family history files. Obituary files.

Special Collections: Yes

Special Collections Description: Historical society has published *For the Record* twice yearly since 1983. This local magazine has historical records, family histories, reminiscences, and so forth. These publications are indexed and available for sale for $5 each. They are also a wonderful source of the local history of the area. A second special collection is of World War II stories of county residents with an index.

Indexes: Photographs currently have no indexing separate from the filing system. Likewise, the genealogy collection is filed by surname.

Review of Collections: This collection is well cared for, though breaking it into two distinct parts is a weakness. The family history collection is particularly well developed. The photograph collection will be stronger when they have some better indexing through PastPerfect or some other system. The published history is more extensive than most museums of this size. The staff and volunteers are well versed in the collection and very helpful.

Museum on Premises: Yes

Museum Hours: Daily 10–5, May–Oct; by appt. only Nov–Apr

Cost of Entry to Museum: $3

Museum Is Handicapped Accessible: Yes

Description of Museum: This museum is very well done. The museum is spread out over three buildings (only two connect). The displays are extremely well done, especially considering they are done by a volunteer committee. They have won regional and national awards on their displays.

Parking: Free parking lot; adjacent walkway to museum, has a covered bridge, but is accessible.

Lunch: Local eateries and small store easy walking distance within two blocks

Lodging: http://www.visitcentraloregon.com

Nearest Commercial Airport: Portland International (PDX) [122 miles]; Tri-Cities (Pasco, WA) (PSC) [131 miles]

Subjects

Historical Periods: Pre-1800; 1800–1865; 1865–1900; 1900–1940; 1940–present

Eras: Civil War; Indian Wars; Spanish American War; World War I; World War II; Korean War; Vietnam War

Natural Resources: Dams; Hunting; Logging

Transportation: Railroads; Stagecoach/Freight; Ferries

Agriculture: Ranching/Livestock; Grains; Orchards; Dry Land Farming

Business: Banking; Retail; Legal/Medical services; Hotels/Restaurants; Entertainment/Theaters

Manufacturing: Grist/Flour Mills; Brick Making;

Government: City; County

Organizations: Schools; Civic and Fraternal; Women's

Ethnic Groups: Native American; Chinese

Religious Sites and Organizations: Protestant; Catholic

Date of Reviewer's Visit: 8/12/2003

Profile Updated by Institution: 11/22/2004

NEWPORT

Name: Oregon Coast History Center

Mailing Address: 545 SW Ninth St.

City: Newport   **State:** OR

Street Address: 545 SW Ninth St.

Institution Email: coasthistory@newportnet.com

County: Lincoln

Postal Code: 97365-0000

Telephone Number: (541) 265-7509   **Fax Number:** (541) 265-3992

Contact Name: Jodi Weeber   **Contact Email:** OHCarchivist@newportnet.com

Institution Type: Local Museum

Affiliation: Lincoln County Historical Society

Web site URL: http://www.oregoncoast.history.museum

Hours: Tu–Th 11–4; Tu–Sa 11–4 by appt.

Staff in Archives: 1p

Archives Are Handicapped Accessible: Yes

Cost for Researcher—Remote: Fee schedule

Review of Facilities: The Oregon Coast History Center is located in the old Burrows House near the center of Newport. The research room is in a new addition built to the back of the 1890s house/boarding house. The room, although not large, feels open with two round worktables. Staff work areas, bookcases, cabinets, and historical materials fill out the room.

Vertical Files: Yes

Vertical File Description and Subjects: Biography files, location and general subject files, mostly newspaper clippings

Manuscripts: Yes   **Manuscripts Volume in Cubic Feet:** 70

Manuscript Types: Schools records, business records, organizational records

Manuscript Subjects: Lawyers' offices, hotels, Bank of Newport, nineteenth-century legal records, financial records, tax records, building projects, calling card collection, social clubs, Yaquina Bay Yacht Club

Photographs: Yes   **Number of Photographs:** 8,000

Storage of Photographs: Photographs stored in plastic sleeves in document boxes

Photograph Subjects: Maritime, people, cities in the county; photos are from 1860s to present

Photograph Reproductions Are Available: Yes

Photographic Prints: Yes   **Digital Prints:** Yes

Digital Images on CD or Electronically: Yes

Books: Yes   **Number of Books in Collection:** 800

Description of Books: Native Americans, local interest, telephone directories, annuals

Newspapers: Yes

Newspapers in Paper Format: Yes

Papers and Dates: Have old newspapers, but only microfilmed copies are available for research

Newspapers on Microfilm: Yes

Microfilm and Dates: County papers from 1901 to present from Newport, Waldport, and Delake

Oral Histories: Yes   **Oral Histories Number:** 120

Oral Histories Description: Interviews of local area residents from 1970s to present. A few are on video, most are on audiocassette and have transcriptions.

Maps and Drawings: Yes   **Estimated Number of Maps and Drawings:** 200

Description of Maps and Drawings: County maps of various types, blueprints of local buildings, some maps of Indian reservation

Genealogy Sources: Yes

Genealogy Sources Description: Family histories, biography file

Special Collections: No

Indexes: Vertical file subjects guide listed in notebook and on staff computer.

Review of Collections: The collections of the Lincoln County Historical Society focus on the entirety of the county, although they are stronger in covering the central part of the county. The manuscript collections have papers from numerous businesses, social organizations, and families of the area. The photographs represent the maritime and tourism history of the area. Great smaller historical society.

Museum on Premises: Yes

Museum Hours: Summer Tu–Su 10–5, winter Tu–Su 11–4

Cost of Entry to Museum: Donation

Museum Is Handicapped Accessible: Yes

Parking: Free on-street parallel parking

Lunch: Variety of restaurants a few blocks away in the downtown area

Lodging: http://www.discovernewport.com

Nearest Commercial Airport: Mahlon Sweet Field (Eugene, OR) (EUG) [85 miles]

Subjects

Historical Periods: 1800–1865; 1865–1900; 1900–1940; 1940–present

Eras: Indian Wars; Spanish American War; World War I; WPA; CCC; World War II

Natural Resources: Water; Fishing; Hunting; Shellfish; Logging

Mining: Gold; Coal; Surface Mining; Tunnel Mining

Transportation: Railroads; Stagecoach/Freight; Ships and Shipping; Ferries; Aviation

Agriculture: Dairy; Vegetable/Truck Crops; Orchards

Business: Banking; Retail; Legal/Medical Services; Hotels/Restaurants; Entertainment/Theaters

Manufacturing: Cannery; Brewery; Grist/Flour Mills; Creamery; Sawmills; Wood Products

Government: City; County

Organizations: Schools; Colleges/Universities; Hospitals/Medical Facilities; Charities; Nonreligious Organizations; Civic and Fraternal; Women's; Business; Children's; Labor and Union

Ethnic Groups: Native American; Japanese; Chinese; Danish; English; Finnish; German; Irish; Norwegian; Scottish; Swedish

Religious Sites and Organizations: Protestant; Catholic

Date of Reviewer's Visit: 8/21/2003

Profile Updated by Institution: 11/15/2004

OREGON CITY

Name: Museum of the Oregon Territory   **County:** Clackamas

Mailing Address: 211 Tumwater

  City: Oregon City   **State:** OR   **Postal Code:** 97045-0000

Street Address: 211 Tumwater

Institution Email: museum@orcity.com

Telephone Number: (503) 655-5574   **Fax Number:** (503) 655-0035

Contact Name: Patrick Harris   **Contact Email:** museum@orcity.com

Institution Type: Regional Museum

Affiliation: Clackamas County Historical Society

Web site URL: http://www.orcity.com/museum/

Hours: Tu–W 10–4; 1st and 3d Sa, 12–4

Staff in Archives: 2f; 1p; 5v

Archives Are Handicapped Accessible: Yes

Access Description: The research room has some narrow aisles.

Cost for Researcher—In-house: Donation

Cost for Researcher—Remote: Fee schedule

List of Researchers Available: Yes

Review of Facilities: The library at the Museum of the Oregon Territory is a merger of two library collections. Some material is owned by the Clackamas County Family

History Society and other material by the Clackamas County Historical Society, which runs the museum itself. The library is on the main floor of the museum, through the back of the gift shop. The area is accessible with some limitations of narrow passage areas. The room just isn't very large. One wall is lined with the microfilm/microfiche readers. By the window is a conference table with six chairs. The books are on open stacks and arranged by Dewey number. They had not completed their shifting of the collection at the time of the visit, so some files cabinets and research materials were out of order. Photographs and manuscript materials are housed in a room adjacent to the library area. The library itself is maintained by volunteers from the Clackamas County Family History Society.

Vertical Files: Yes   **Vertical Files in Cubic Feet:** 64

Vertical File Description and Subjects: Biography and general subject clipping and ephemera files

Manuscripts: Yes   **Manuscripts Volume in Cubic Feet:** 60

Manuscript Types: Business and personal papers, some governmental records

Manuscript Subjects: Oregon City Hospital Records from early twentieth century. Tax records, land records. Philip Foster personal papers.

Photographs: Yes   **Number of Photographs:** 150,000

Storage of Photographs: Filed in archival envelopes and plastic sleeves. The photographs are arranged by subject. Listing of photographs is being done on computer.

Photograph Subjects: Clackamas County and Oregon history

Photograph Reproductions Are Available: Yes

Photographic Prints: Yes   **Digital Prints:** Yes

Books: Yes   **Number of Books in Collection:** 1,000

Description of Books: Oregon and area history books, city directories, telephone books, yearbooks, professional collection. Books shelved by Dewey number.

Newspapers: Yes

Newspapers on Microfilm: Yes

Microfilm and Dates: 1846–1975 Oregon city papers

Oral Histories: Yes   **Oral Histories Number:** 20

Oral Histories Description: Audiocassettes, reel-to-reels, and videotapes. None have been transcribed.

Maps and Drawings: No

Genealogy Sources: Yes

Genealogy Sources Description: Cemetery, birth, marriage, and death records. Obituary index on 4 x 6 card files.

Special Collections: No

Indexes: Obituary index (card file), general subject index (card file). Computer index of photo descriptions in process.

Published Guides: Marriage, birth, and cemetery records published and available for sale

Review of Collections: The archival collections at the Museum of the Oregon Territory are large for the size of institution. The genealogy part of the collection is the strongest and since the Clackamas County Family History Society is the main group collecting new material, that is understandable. The photo collection is voluminous and covers most subject areas for the county. The Oregon City Hospital Records are a significant collection. They include over 9 cu. ft. of card files that list patient information, reason for admission, and outcome. They are filed by name and not arranged by date. The comprehensive dates are unclear, but the records cover at least from the 1910s through the 1940s.

Museum on Premises: Yes

Museum Hours: 10–5 M–F, 1–5 Sa–Su

Cost of Entry to Museum: Fee

Museum Is Handicapped Accessible: Yes

Description of Museum: This is a good quality museum of moderate size featuring changing exhibits on Clackamas County people, businesses, and events.

Parking: Free parking lot adjacent to building

Lunch: Variety of restaurants within driving distance

Lodging: http://www.mthoodterritory.com; http://www.traveloregon.com/

Nearest Commercial Airport: Portland International (PDX) [19 miles]

Subjects

Historical Periods: 1800–1865; 1865–1900; 1900–1940; 1940–present

Eras: Fur Trade; Indian Wars; Spanish American War; WPA; CCC; World War II

Natural Resources: Water; Dams; Fishing; Logging

Transportation: Railroads; Stagecoach/Freight; Ferries

Agriculture: Dairy; Vegetable/Truck Crops; Grains; Orchards

Business: Entertainment/Theaters

Manufacturing: Grist/Flour Mills; Creamery; Woolen/Fabric Mills; Brick Making; Boatbuilding/Shipyard; Sawmills

Government: City; County

Organizations: Schools; Hospitals/Medical Facilities; Nonreligious Organizations; Business

Ethnic Groups: Native American; Japanese; Chinese; German; Swedish

Religious Sites and Organizations: Protestant; Catholic; Jewish; Mennonite/ Amish

Date of Reviewer's Visit: 11/4/2003

Profile Updated by Institution: 11/24/2004

PENDLETON

Name: Heritage Station Museum   **County:** Umatilla

Mailing Address: PO Box 253

  City: Pendleton   **State:** OR   **Postal Code:** 97801-0000

Street Address: 108 SW Frazer Ave.

Institution Email: uchs@oregontrail.net

Telephone Number: (541) 276-0012   **Fax Number:** (541) 276-7989

Contact Name: Julie Reese, Director

Institution Type: Local Museum

Affiliation: Umatilla County Historical Society

Web site URL: http://www.umatillahistory.org

Hours: Tu–F 10–4

Staff in Archives: 1p, 6v

Archives Are Handicapped Accessible: Yes

Cost for Researcher—Remote: Fee schedule

Review of Facilities: Heritage Station, the Umatilla County Historical Society Museum is located in a historic (1909) railroad depot that is still on the railroad tracks. A new addition was constructed in 2003 and the staff offices and research materials are located in this area. There is not a separate research area but the museum allows researchers to use the conference room. This room is moderate-sized with a single table in the center. Research collection materials are stored down the hall in the climate-controlled collections storage at the end of the hall. Smaller institution with plenty of potential.

Vertical Files: Yes   **Vertical Files in Cubic Feet:** 30

  Vertical File Description and Subjects: Biographical file

Manuscripts: Yes

  Manuscript Types: School records, government records, personal papers, organizational records

  Manuscript Subjects: Ledgers, county government, school district records from one- and two-room schools, women's clubs, Red Cross, ephemera

Photographs: Yes   **Number of Photographs:** 10,000

> **Storage of Photographs:** Photographs are stored in file folders in file cabinets

> **Photograph Subjects:** Umatilla County and northeastern Oregon. Photographs from 1860 to present.

> **Photograph Reproductions Are Available:** Yes

> **Photographic Prints:** Yes **Digital Prints:** Yes

> **Digital Images on CD or Electronically:** Yes

Books: Yes   **Number of Books in Collection:** 800

> **Description of Books:** Local history, annuals

Newspapers: No

Oral Histories: Yes   **Oral Histories Number:** 41

> **Oral Histories Description:** Local resident interviews on audiotape. They have not been transcribed. All interviews were done since 1974.

Maps and Drawings: Yes   **Estimated Number of Maps and Drawings:** 100

Genealogy Sources: No

Special Collections: No

Indexes: No

Review of Collections: The collections are not well indexed at this institution and there may be far more research content to be revealed. The photographs of Pendleton, Umatilla County, and the surrounding areas are the anchor of the collection. The documents are in various states of processing and not cataloged or indexed in any manner. All materials are stored with staff-access only.

Museum on Premises: Yes

> **Museum Hours:** Tu–Sa 10 to 4

> **Cost of Entry to Museum:** $4

> **Museum Is Handicapped Accessible:** Yes

> **Description of Museum:** Newly remodeled museum in historic depot depicts life of Umatilla County.

Parking: Free parking lot adjacent

Lunch: Variety of restaurants within a short drive

Lodging: http://www.pendleton-oregon.org

Nearest Commercial Airport: Eastern Oregon Regional at Pendleton (PDT) [5 miles]

Subjects

> **Historical Periods:** 1865–1900; 1900–1940; 1940–present

> **Natural Resources:** Irrigation; Logging

> **Transportation:** Railroads; Ferries; Aviation

Agriculture: Dairy; Ranching/Livestock; Vegetable/Truck Crops; Grains; Orchards; Dry Land Farming

Business: Retail; Legal/Medical Services; Hotels/Restaurants; Entertainment/ Theaters

Manufacturing: Grist/Flour Mills; Woolen/Fabric Mills; Sawmills

Organizations: Schools; Hospitals/Medical Facilities; Nonreligious Organizations

Religious Sites and Organizations: Protestant; Catholic

Date of Reviewer's Visit: 9/26/2003

Profile Updated by Institution: 11/19/2004

Name: Tamastslikt Cultural Institute   **County:** Umatilla

Mailing Address: 72789 Hwy 331

   City: Pendleton   **State:** OR   **Postal Code:** 97801-0000

Street Address: 72789 Hwy. 331

Institution Email: tciarch@wildhorseresort.com

Telephone Number: (541) 966-9748   **Fax Number:** (541) 966-9927

Contact Name: Malissa Minthorn   **Contact Email:** malissa.minthorn@tamaslikt.org

Institution Type: Regional Museum

Affiliation: Confederated Tribes of the Umatilla Indian Reservation

Web site URL: http://www.tamastslikt.com

Hours: M–F 9–5; appts. can be scheduled during same hours

Staff in Archives: 1f; 2p

Archives Are Handicapped Accessible: Yes

Review of Facilities: The Tamastslikt Cultural Institute is located four miles outside of Pendleton on Highway 331 on the Confederated Tribes of the Umatilla Indian Reservation. It is located down a road behind the Wild Horse Resort and Casino. The building housing the Cultural Institute was built in 1998 and is gorgeous. Using materials from the reservation, they have incorporated tribal history into a foyer that is visually pleasing and peaceful. The center foyer branches off into several directions. The museum is down one hall and offices and activity rooms are down the other two halls. The archives room is off the hall to the right but all visitors will need to check in at the main desk and be escorted to the archives area. The archives itself is nice but standard. Two large worktables are in the center of this bright, warm room. Bookshelves line one wall and ranges of bookshelves stand off to one side. Many of the bookshelves are still empty, but as the collection grows, will not remain so. The bulk of the collection is stored in an adjoining room with archival shelving and care.

Vertical Files: Yes

> **Vertical File Description and Subjects:** General subject files. Article clipping files in multiple three-ring binders of local and regional papers of interest to the tribes.

Manuscripts: Yes

> **Manuscript Types:** Business records, legal records, archeology reports, family papers, land records

> **Manuscript Subjects:** Fishery research, archeology reports, tribal legal history, Umatilla Indian Reservation, land claims records

Photographs: Yes   **Number of Photographs:** 5,000

> **Storage of Photographs:** Photographs are stored in plastic sleeves in binders.

> **Photograph Subjects:** History of the Cayuse, Umatilla, and Walla Walla peoples

> **Photograph Reproductions Are Available:** Yes

> > **Photographic Prints:** Yes   **Digital Prints:** Yes

Books: Yes   **Number of Books in Collection:** 1,200

> **Description of Books:** Local history, tribal history, professional collection, archeology, and anthropology

Newspapers: Yes

> **Newspapers in Paper Format:** Yes

> **Papers and Dates:** Tribal paper, 1970s to the present

Oral Histories: No

Maps and Drawings: No

Genealogy Sources: Yes

> **Genealogy Sources Description:** Family files, obituary files, cemetery records

Special Collections: No

Indexes: Yes

> **Manuscript Finding Aids:** Finding aids on selected manuscript collections

Review of Collections: The research library at the Tamastslikt Cultural Institute is in its infancy, having started in 1998. For such a recent endeavor, they have done a beautiful job collecting and organizing the materials. The collection is being handled in archival manner from the beginning, something most institutions would envy. The collections are unique to the areas and the peoples they illustrate. The Cayuse, Umatilla, and Walla Walla tribes have lived in the region for 10,000 years, and collecting the early history necessitates archeological and anthropological research, the results of which are also being collected. The museum is a model for tribal museums and this research collection has the potential to be one as well.

Museum on Premises: Yes

Museum Hours: Daily 9–5

Cost of Entry to Museum: $6

Museum Is Handicapped Accessible: Yes

Description of Museum: This museum is beautifully done. Modern museum displays exhibit the history of the Cayuse, Umatilla, and Walla Walla people. Undoubtedly one of the best tribal museums in the country.

Parking: Free paved parking lot adjacent

Lunch: Cafe on the premises serving soup, sandwiches, and so forth. Driving distance to other restaurants.

Lodging: http://www.pendleton-oregon.org

Nearest Commercial Airport: Eastern Oregon Regional at Pendleton (PDT) [12 miles]

Subjects

Historical Periods: 1800–1865; 1865–1900; 1900–1940; 1940–present

Transportation: Railroads

Government: City; Tribal

Ethnic Groups: Native American

Religious Sites and Organizations: Protestant; Catholic

Date of Reviewer's Visit: 9/25/2003

Profile Updated by Institution: 12/3/2004

PHILOMATH

Name: Benton County Historical Museum and Society   **County:** Benton

Mailing Address: PO Box 35

City: Philomath   **State:** OR   **Postal Code:** 97370-0000

Street Address: 1101 Main St.

Institution Email: None

Telephone Number: (541) 929-6230   **Fax Number:** (541) 929-6261

Contact Name: Mary Gallagher   **Contact Email:** gallagher@bentoncounty museum.org

Institution Type: Local Museum

Affiliation: Benton County Historical Society

Web site URL: http://www.bentoncountymuseum.org

Hours: Tu–F 1–4 or by appt.

Staff in Archives: 1f

Archives Are Handicapped Accessible: No

Access Description: There are several steps up to the archives area.

Review of Facilities: The Benton County Historical Society has its headquarters in the former Philomath College building. The center of this three-story brick building was constructed in 1867 with the wings added by 1907. The research room is on the main floor, although at a slightly higher level, necessitating several steps up into the room. The research room is fairly large, with a high ceiling and with book stacks dominating half the room. A worktable is available for researchers, as well as a staff desk, and some workstations for volunteers. Although a significant part of the collection is housed in the research room, the rest is housed upstairs in a staff-only storage area.

Vertical Files: Yes   **Vertical Files in Cubic Feet:** 56

    Vertical File Description and Subjects: Vertical files include local interest subjects and newspaper clippings.

Manuscripts: Yes   **Manuscripts Volume in Cubic Feet:** 170

    Manuscript Types: Business records, organizational records, personal papers, legal records

    Manuscript Subjects: Clubs and civic groups in county, architectural plans, Camp Adair (World War II training camp) family papers, wills and probate records from Benton County, cultural resource survey documents

Photographs: Yes   **Number of Photographs:** 24,000

    Storage of Photographs: Photographs stored in archival sleeves in document boxes. Photograph number includes photo albums and slides.

    Photograph Subjects: Benton County

    Photograph Reproductions Are Available: Yes

      Photographic Prints: Yes   **Digital Prints:** Yes

      Digital Images on CD or Electronically: Yes

Books: Yes   **Number of Books in Collection:** 5,600

    Description of Books: Local history, regional history, professional collection, phone books, city directories, annuals

Newspapers: Yes

    Newspapers in Paper Format: Yes

Papers and Dates: *Corvallis Gazette Times* in bound volumes

Newspapers on Microfilm: Yes

Microfilm and Dates: Microfilm of Corvallis paper from 1865–1979

Oral Histories: No

Maps and Drawings: Yes   **Estimated Number of Maps and Drawings:** 431

Description of Maps and Drawings: Maps of state of Oregon and Benton County, mostly stored flat

Genealogy Sources: Yes

Genealogy Sources Description: Family files, obituary files in binders, cemetery records, marriage records, family histories

Special Collections: No

Indexes: In-house computer index. Each item is on computer, but in varying level of detail, using PastPerfect software.

Review of Collections: The collections of Benton County history are well cared for and indexed to a certain degree. There are over 10,000 records listed on the computer of the archival documents. The Benton County Genealogical Society collection is also housed at this location. The Web site has a number of short historical history facts about certain subjects. One of the main areas is Camp Adair, a World War II training camp that existed for the duration of the war. Overall this is a great collection with a great staff to back it up.

Museum on Premises: Yes

Museum Hours: Tu–Sa 10–4:30

Cost of Entry to Museum: Donation

Museum Is Handicapped Accessible: Yes

Description of Museum: Located in a historic (1867; 1907) building. Displays of local history in permanent and rotating exhibits of history and art.

Parking: Free parking lot adjacent to the museum

Lunch: Driving distance to a variety of local and fast-food chains

Lodging: http://www.visitcorvallis.com

Nearest Commercial Airport: Portland International (PDX) [89 miles]; Mahlon Sweet Field (Eugene) (EUG) [53 miles]

Subjects

Historical Periods: 1800–1865; 1865–1900; 1900–1940; 1940–present

Eras: CCC; World War II

Natural Resources: Logging

Transportation: Railroads

Agriculture: Dairy; Ranching/Livestock; Vegetable/Truck Crops; Grains; Orchards

Business: Entertainment/Theaters

Manufacturing: Cannery; Sawmills

Organizations: Schools; Colleges/Universities; Civic and Fraternal; Women's

Date of Reviewer's Visit: 8/20/2003

Profile Updated by Institution: 11/15/2004

PORTLAND

Name: Lewis and Clark College—Aubrey R. Watzek Library
County: Multnomah

Mailing Address: 0615 SW Palatine Hill Rd.

   City: Portland   **State:** OR   **Postal Code:** 97219-0000

Street Address: 0615 SW Palatine Hill Rd.

Institution Email: refdesk@lclark.edu

Telephone Number: (503) 768-7274   **Fax Number:** (503) 768-7282

Contact Name: Doug M. Erickson   **Contact Email:** dme@lclark.edu

Institution Type: Academic Library

Web site URL: http://library.lclark.edu/

Hours: M–F 1–3 walk in, M–F 9–5 by appt.

Staff in Archives: 2f

Archives Are Handicapped Accessible: Yes

Review of Facilities: The Special Collections of Lewis and Clark College are located in the Heritage Room of the Aubrey R. Watzek Library. The library is located centrally on the campus. The Heritage Room is a limited-access room with glass-fronted locked bookcases on several walls and a large mahogany conference table, surrounded by eight plush chairs in the center of the room. The space is elegant. Staff offices are adjacent to this area. Collections are stored in adjacent areas, or elsewhere in the building.

Vertical Files: No

Manuscripts: Yes   **Manuscripts Volume in Cubic Feet:** 6,160

   Manuscript Types: All manuscript types

   Manuscript Subjects: Lewis and Clark/Albany College history, Lewis and Clark expedition, club records, YWCA Portland, Pacific Northwest Athletic Association, papers related to the professional and literary careers of William Stafford, Vern Rutsala and Erskine Wood College Archives (6,000 cu. ft.); Special Collections(160 cu. ft.)

Photographs: Yes   **Number of Photographs:** 10,000

Storage of Photographs: Photographs are stored in a variety of containers. Selected photographs are being added to an online database.

Photograph Subjects: Lewis and Clark/Albany College historic photos, YWCA of Portland

Photograph Reproductions Are Available: Yes

   Photographic Prints: Yes   **Digital Prints:** Yes

   Digital Images on CD or Electronically: Yes

Books: Yes   **Number of Books in Collection:** 4,500

Description of Books: Regional history, local area history, annuals, professional books, old books

Newspapers: Yes

Newspapers in Paper Format: Yes

   Papers and Dates: Portland Area papers, various titles

   Newspapers on Microfilm: Yes

   Microfilm and Dates: Microfilm of local newspapers

Oral Histories: No

Maps and Drawings: Yes   **Estimated Number of Maps and Drawings:** 100

Description of Maps and Drawings: Maps relating to North American exploration, early maps of the American West, campus and other maps produced for institutional purposes

Genealogy Sources: No

Special Collections: Yes

   Special Collections Description: Lewis and Clark Expedition Collection holds a comprehensive collection of printed materials dealing with the expedition in historic and modern editions. The collection also holds all known editions of the journals, newspapers, and other writings at the time of the expedition in multiple languages, and serials containing articles and maps. There is also a collection of juvenile literature on the expedition.

Indexes: Staff-only computerized index of holdings. Specialized indexes for manuscripts and photographs. Books available.

   Manuscript Finding Aids: Finding aids available for most collections.

   Published Guides: The *Literature of the Lewis and Clark Expedition*, published in 2003, is a bibliography of publications relating to the subject and a guide to collections held at the institution.

Online Sources: Some finding aids available from Web site.

Review of Collections: Lewis and Clark College collections are limited in scope in all areas outside of college history. The historical archives of the college are large. The historical significance of some of the other Special Collections merit this institution's inclusion. The collections of printed materials related to the Lewis and Clark Expedition is one of the most complete in the country. Printed materials of other regional exploration and settlement are also held by the library.

Museum on Premises: No

Parking: Stop at information booth; $3-per-day parking permit required

Lunch: Driving distance to variety of restaurants

Lodging: http://www.travelportland.com

Nearest Commercial Airport: Portland International (PDX) [18 miles]

Subjects

> **Historical Periods:** Pre-1800, 1800–1865; 1865–1900; 1900–1940; 1940–present
>
> **Eras:** Exploration
>
> **Organizations:** Colleges/Universities; Nonreligious Organizations; Civic and Fraternal

Date of Reviewer's Visit: 11/6/2003

Profile Updated by Institution: 11/24/2004

✹✹✹✹

Name: Multnomah County Library—John Wilson Room, Special Collections
County: Multnomah

Mailing Address: 801 SW 10th Ave.

City: Portland   **State:** OR   **Postal Code:** 97212-0000

Street Address: 801 SW 10th Ave.

Institution Email: None

Telephone Number: (503) 988-6287   **Fax Number:** (503) 988-5226

Contact Name: Jim Carmin   **Contact Email:** jimc@multcolib.org

Institution Type: Public Library

Affiliation: Multnomah County

Web site URL: http://www.multcolib.org

Hours: Tu 2:30–5:30, W 3:30–7, F 10–2, Sa 2:30–6

Staff in Archives: 1.5f

Archives Are Handicapped Accessible: Yes

Access Description: Elevator to John Wilson Room is available; ask at library service desk for directions

Review of Facilities: The Central Library of Multnomah County System is located in the heart of downtown Portland in the original 1913 library building (renovation complete 1997). The John Wilson Room houses the rare book collections and other special materials. Access to the John Wilson Room is from the second floor by way of a carved wooden staircase directly up to the room. (An elevator is available if needed.) The room is elegant, with polished wood worktables and decorative glass windows. The tables have adequate lighting. All collections are stored in locked, glass-fronted bookcases and are retrieved by staff upon request.

Vertical Files: No

Manuscripts: Yes   **Manuscripts Volume in Cubic Feet:** 500

    Manuscript Subjects: Lewis and Clark Centennial Exposition (1905) materials, Seaman's Societies lists, register of Metropolis Hotel, contemporary printers' ephemera, Native American literature

Photographs: Yes   **Number of Photographs:** 1,100

    Photograph Subjects: Music and dance touring groups' WPA projects, Timberline Lodge on Mt. Hood

    Photograph Reproductions Are Available: Yes

      Photographic Prints: Yes   **Digital Prints:** No

Books: Yes   **Number of Books in Collection:** 10,000

    Description of Books: Six core collections, including an Oregon and Pacific Northwest collection, natural history collection, children's literature collection, literature collection, Native American literature collection, and books arts/history of the book collection

Newspapers: No

Oral Histories: No

Maps and Drawings: No

Genealogy Sources: No

Special Collections: No

Indexes: All collections indexed in Multnomah County Library computer

    Online Sources: Web page and library catalog

Review of Collections: The collection of the John Wilson Room are listed in the library's catalog with finding aids for manuscripts available on site. There are approximately 10,000 volumes of books, with six major collections. Noteworthy primary collections include large holdings related to the 1905 Lewis and Clark

Centennial Exposition, seventeenth-century travel accounts, and a collection of manuscripts by Native American writers.

Museum on Premises: No

Parking: Metered on-street parallel parking or pay box or attended parking lots within several blocks

Lunch: Street vendors and local and chain restaurants within blocks

Lodging: http://www.travelportland.com; downtown Portland

Nearest Commercial Airport: Portland International (PDX) [13 miles]

Subjects

> **Historical Periods:** Pre-1800; 1800–1865; 1865–1900; 1900–1940; 1940–present
>
> **Eras:** Exploration; WPA
>
> **Transportation:** Aviation
>
> **Agriculture:** Ranching/Livestock
>
> **Business:** Hotels/Restaurants
>
> **Ethnic Groups:** Native American

Date of Reviewer's Visit: 9/27/2002

Profile Updated by Institution: 12/8/2004

✺✺✺✺✺

Name: Oregon Health and Science University Library   **County:** Multnomah

Mailing Address: 3181 SW Sam Jackson Park Rd.

  City: Portland   **State:** OR   **Postal Code:** 97207-0573

Street Address: 3181 SW Sam Jackson Park Rd.

Institution Email: None

Telephone Number: (503) 494-3239   **Fax Number:** (503) 418-0235

Contact Name: Karen Peterson   **Contact Email:** petersk@ohsu.edu

Institution Type: Academic Library

Web site URL: http://www.ohsu.edu/Library/hom

Hours: M–Th 8–4 by appt.

Staff in Archives: 2f

Archives Are Handicapped Accessible: Yes

Access Description: The research room is up a flight of stairs. They could accommodate a researcher in the main library building if necessary.

Cost for Researcher—In-house: Fee schedule

Cost for Researcher—Remote: Fee schedule

Review of Facilities: The research room of the History of Medicine Library is located in the auditorium building and not the main library. It can be hard to find, so it might be wise to get directions when you make the appointment. The room is up a flight of stairs and has an old-fashioned, old world feel. This is despite the state-of-the-art computer system. The room itself is ringed by locked bookcases with equally old books. The research table is a large conference table and the room has a wonderful ambiance. The indexes and finding aids are available in the research room but most nonbook collections are stored on another floor of the same building.

Vertical Files: Yes   **Vertical Files in Cubic Feet:** 34

Vertical File Description and Subjects: Newspaper clipping files of general subjects and biographical information are stored in boxes in storage room.

Manuscripts: Yes   **Manuscripts Volume in Cubic Feet:** 110

Manuscript Types: Transcripts of speeches, organizational papers, general manuscript collections.

Manuscript Subjects: Oregon State Medical Society papers; History of Dentistry Collection; OHSU archives

Photographs: Yes   **Number of Photographs:** 8,000

Storage of Photographs: Photographs are stored in clamshell boxes. Their collection includes photographs, negatives and lantern slides.

Photograph Subjects: Oregon Health and Science University makes up the bulk of the photo collection. The remainder are medical- or dental-related photographs.

Photograph Reproductions Are Available: Yes

Photographic Prints: Yes   **Digital Prints:** Yes

Books: Yes   **Number of Books in Collection:** 4,860

Description of Books: The History of Medicine collection contains books published before 1901 on medical topics and includes some facsimile reprints. The Pacific Northwest Archives has books containing talks to the Medical History Club of the Medical School during the 1920s to the 1940s, publications of the university from its earliest years to the present, annual reports of the Medical Research Foundation of Oregon, and books of local historical documents.

Newspapers: No

Oral Histories: Yes   **Oral Histories Number:** 90

Oral Histories Description: The oral history collection consists of some 90 interviews, all with transcriptions. All have audiocassettes, but some also have a videocassette recording. The interviews are from one to eight hours in length.

Maps and Drawings: No

Genealogy Sources: Yes

    Genealogy Sources Description: Biographical files

Special Collections: Yes

    Special Collections Description: The Medical Museum Collection includes medical artifacts and realia. There are a number of doctor's supplies, surgery kits, and miscellaneous medical equipment. This collection is not listed in the library's online catalog. An incomplete card index to the collection is available in the History of Medicine Library. Cataloged items can now be viewed online, in the OHSU Digital Resources Library.

Indexes: Yes

    Manuscript Finding Aids: All of the Manuscript collections have finding aids of various complexity.

    Online Sources: The Web site gives greater detail on all of the collections. Some finding aids and other resources are available online

Review of Collections: The History of Medicine Library Collection is divided into several distinct collections. The History of Medicine Collection contains medical books published prior to 1901. The Pacific Northwest Archives collection contains books, manuscripts, photographs, and other paper-based materials relating to OHSU or the Pacific Northwest region, some of which are rare or fragile. The Medical Museum Collection has miscellaneous medical artifacts. The manuscript and photograph collections include personal papers and organizational records and photographs of the campus people and various campus activities. Finding aids are available for most of these materials. There is also a History of Dentistry Collection of books, which is housed in the History of Dentistry Room in the main library. The collections are professionally maintained and accessible by appointment only. These collections are historically significant because they represent training for and practice of medicine in the Pacific Northwest region.

Museum on Premises: No

Parking: Stop at the information booth on the way into campus to get a campus map and review your parking options. They sell parking passes and there are some metered parking lots. The meters take only quarters.

Lunch: Many cafeterias on campus

Lodging: http://www.travelportland.com

Nearest Commercial Airport: Portland International (PDX) [12 miles]

Subjects

    Historical Periods: 1865–1900; 1900–1940; 1940–present

    Eras: World War I; World War II

    Business: Legal/Medical Services

Organizations: Colleges/Universities; Hospitals/Medical Facilities; Charities; Nonreligious Organizations

Date of Reviewer's Visit: 11/6/2003

Profile Updated by Institution: 11/12/2004

★★★★★

Name: Oregon Historical Society **County:** Multnomah

Mailing Address: 1200 SW Park Ave.

City: Portland **State:** OR **Postal Code:** 97205-2483

Street Address: 1200 SW Park Ave.

Institution Email: orhist@ohs.org

Telephone Number: (503) 222-1741 **Fax Number:** (503) 221-2035

Contact Name: Shawna Gandy

Institution Type: Historical Society Archives

Web site URL: http://www.ohs.org

Hours: W–S 1–5

Archives Are Handicapped Accessible: Yes

Cost for Researcher—In-house: Museum admission $8

Cost for Researcher—Remote: $60 per hr.; 1/2-hr. minimum

Review of Facilities: The Oregon History Center is located in a large building in the Park District of downtown Portland. The research library of the Oregon History Center is located on the fourth floor of the building. It has a pleasant research room with large tables and adequate lighting. Coin lockers are provided for storage of all items except paper and pencil. Registration is required for all researchers. A reference desk is staffed with professional librarians and archivists. Large banks of card files line one section of the room and contain some of the major indexes to the collection. Most of the materials are stored in closed stacks. A separate large map area is set aside at the back of the large room.

Vertical Files: Yes **Vertical Files in Cubic Feet:** 107

Vertical File Description and Subjects: Large file with 4,000 subjects of Oregon history and culture, including place files. A second collection contains 1,500 files of biographical and genealogical materials. There is an index to the vertical file.

Manuscripts: Yes **Manuscripts Volume in Cubic Feet:** 12,000

Manuscript Types: All manuscript types

Manuscript Subjects: Organizations, shipbuilding, architecture, lumbering, businesses, mining, sheep ranching (mostly Willamette Valley), large collections of manuscript materials dating from the eighteenth century. Personal papers, business files, scrapbooks, diaries, legal records, ships' logbooks, architectural records, and others make up the manuscript collections.

Photographs: Yes   **Number of Photographs:** 2,500,000

Storage of Photographs: Self-indexing photographic files by Portrait, Locations, and Subjects. Only around 40,000 of the photographs are indexed. Aerial photographs are stored in the map collection.

Photograph Subjects: The photographs deal with the people, places, and events in Oregon and the Pacific Northwest from the 1850s to the present. The collection illustrates the growth of agriculture, industries, transportation, and the infrastructure of the development. Also included are the various ethnic groups who helped build the region.

Photograph Reproductions Are Available: Yes

   Photographic Prints: Yes

Books: Yes   **Number of Books in Collection:** 35,000

Description of Books: Oregon history in third floor storage and rare books

Newspapers: Yes

Newspapers in Paper Format: Yes

Papers and Dates: Second largest newspaper collection of state newspapers (University of Oregon has largest collection). Some indexing to the *Portland Oregonian* and *Salem Statesman*.

Newspapers on Microfilm: Yes

Microfilm and Dates: 16,000 reels of microfilm on Oregon, Washington, California, Hawaii, and Panama. Majority of collection is on 100-plus Oregon cities and covers the period from 1846.

Oral Histories: Yes   **Oral Histories Number:** 2,100

Oral Histories Description: Extensive oral history collection with 2,100 individual interviews and over 8,400 hours of tape. Most interviews are on audiocassette, but 400-plus interviews are on reel-to-reel. Many are transcribed. Collection started in 1976. Collection includes agriculture, major industries, religious institutions, state government, and the people and places of Oregon. An alphabetic list of interview subjects is available on the Web site.

Maps and Drawings: Yes   **Estimated Number of Maps and Drawings:** 30,000

Description of Maps and Drawings: Map collection focusing on Western exploration, the Oregon Territory, and the Pacific Northwest region. Thousands of aerial photographs are also part of the map collection.

Genealogy Sources: Yes

Genealogy Sources Description: Large variety of sources of interest to genealogists

Special Collections: Yes

Special Collections Description: Moving Image collection includes 15,000-plus titles of film and videotape. Subjects included are early newsreels, family movies, commercial/industrial films, and television news programs. Earliest films are from 1902.

Indexes: There are separate card indexes for the vertical files, scrapbooks, manuscripts, biography, county historical publication, Overland Journeys Index, Catholic Mission Index, Territorial and Provisional Government Papers Index, and maps.

Manuscript Finding Aids: All processed manuscript collections have at least a register, but others have varying levels of finding aids.

Review of Collections: The Oregon State Historical Society research collections are extensive. Although they focus on "the history and cultural heritage of the State of Oregon, the Oregon Territory, the Old Oregon Country and the Westward Overland Migration," the bulk of the information is from the Willamette Valley area. Few materials are from other parts of the state. Central and eastern Oregon are sparsely covered. This does not diminish the expanse of materials that are available, however. Detailed subject indexes are available on site in the reading room. The majority of the manuscript materials are stored off site, so prior planning is essential.

Museum on Premises: Yes

Museum Hours: Th–Sa 1–5; W 1–5 for OHS members only

Cost of Entry to Museum: $8

Museum Is Handicapped Accessible: Yes

Description of Museum: Accredited by the American Museum Association, this is one of the top historical museums in the region.

Parking: Metered on-street parallel parking or pay box parking lots within blocks

Lunch: Not on site, but various restaurants within blocks

Lodging: Downtown Portland; http://www.travelportland.com

Nearest Commercial Airport: Portland International (PDX) [10 miles]

Subjects

Historical Periods: Pre-1800; 1800–1865; 1865–1900; 1900–1940; 1940–present

Eras: Exploration; Fur Trade; Civil War; Indian Wars; Spanish American War; World War I; WPA; World War II; Korean War; Vietnam War

Natural Resources: Water; Dams; Irrigation; Fishing; Hunting; Whaling; Shellfish; Logging

Mining: Mining

Transportation: Railroads; Stagecoach/Freight; Ships and Shipping; Ferries; Aviation

Agriculture: Dairy; Ranching/Livestock; Vegetable/Truck Crops; Grains; Orchards; Vineyard; Dry Land Farming

Business: Banking; Retail; Legal/Medical services; Hotels/Restaurants; Entertainment/Theaters

Manufacturing: Cannery; Brewery; Grist/Flour Mills; Creamery; Woolen/ Fabric Mills; Boatbuilding/Shipyard; Technology/Computers; Sawmills; Wood Products

Government: City; County; State; Federal

Organizations: Schools; Colleges/Universities; Hospitals/Medical Facilities; Charities; Nonreligious Organizations; Civic and Fraternal; Women's; Business; Children's; Labor and Union

Ethnic Groups: Native American; Latin American; African; Pacific Islander; Japanese; Chinese; Basque; Dutch; English; Finnish; French; German; Irish; Italian; Norwegian; Russian; Scottish; Swedish;

Religious Sites and Organizations: Protestant; Catholic; Jewish; Buddhist; Mennonite/Amish

Date of Reviewer's Visit: 9/26/2002

Profile Updated by Institution: 11/15/2004

✯✯✯✯

Name: Oregon Jewish Museum **County:** Multnomah

Mailing Address: 310 NW Davis St.

City: Portland **State:** OR **Postal Code:** 97209-0000

Street Address: 310 NW Davis St.

Institution Email: museum@ojm.org

Telephone Number: (503) 226-3600 **Fax Number:** (503) 226-1800

Contact Name: Judy Margles

Institution Type: Regional Museum

Web site URL: http://www.ojm.org

Hours: T– F 11–2, Su 1–4 by appt. only

Staff in Archives: 2p 4v

Archives Are Handicapped Accessible: Yes

List of Researchers Available: Yes

Review of Facilities: The Oregon Jewish Museum is located in a storefront building in the midst of Chinatown. The research room is located off the small Jewish Museum exhibit floor. The room is small but well lit, with a research table in the center and manuscripts and books on shelves lining the walls. Space is at a premium for this museum and collection.

Vertical Files: Yes   **Vertical Files in Cubic Feet:** 5

Vertical File Description and Subjects: Subject file regarding Oregon Jewish history

Manuscripts: Yes   **Manuscripts Volume in Cubic Feet:** 60

Manuscript Types: Business records, organizational records, scrapbooks, family papers, diaries

Manuscript Subjects: Jewish cultural and philanthropic organizations (mostly Portland), organization records of 50-plus organized groups, but includes some other Oregon areas. Records of the museum. Collections cover years 1850 to present. The MS collection is indexed.

Photographs: Yes   **Number of Photographs:** 2,000

Storage of Photographs: Photos stored in boxes on site

Photograph Subjects: Oregon Jewish history

Photograph Reproductions Are Available: Yes

Photographic Prints: Yes   **Digital Prints:** Yes

Digital Images on CD or Electronically: Yes

Books: Yes   **Number of Books in Collection:** 500

Description of Books: Jewish-American history, local and regional Jewish history

Newspapers: Yes

Newspapers in Paper Format: Yes

Papers and Dates: *Portland Jewish Review* clipping and partials, incomplete. Journals and local publications.

Oral Histories: Yes   **Oral Histories Number:** 125

Oral Histories Description: Oral history from Oregon Jews taken in 1980. Growing collection of interviews undertaken by active oral history committee.

Maps and Drawings: No

Genealogy Sources: No

Special Collections: No

Indexes: Computer index in house. Index to manuscripts

Manuscript Finding Aids: Finding aids to manuscript collections

Published Guides: Database with key to archives

Online Sources: Web site

Review of Collections: The research collections are maintained by professionally trained staff. Collection scope is limited to Jewish history in the Oregon area. The original collection was gathered by the Jewish Historical Society of Oregon and later moved to the Oregon Jewish Museum. All aspects of Jewish life in Oregon are covered, but the bulk of the collection is on individual organizations.

Museum on Premises: Yes

Museum Hours: Tu–F 11–2, Su 1–4

Museum Is Handicapped Accessible: Yes

Description of Museum: Small but well-done museum featuring changing exhibits of Jewish history in Oregon from the earliest time to present

Parking: Metered on-street parallel parking or pay box parking lots within blocks

Lunch: Variety of restaurants and cafes serving ethnic cuisine within walking distance

Lodging: http://www.travelportland.com; Portland Metro area

Nearest Commercial Airport: Portland International (PDX) [9 miles]

Subjects

Historical Periods: 1800–1865; 1865–1900; 1900–1940; 1940–present

Eras: Indian Wars; World War I; World War II

Mining: Mining

Business: Retail

Manufacturing: Cannery; Grist/Flour Mills; Woolen/Fabric Mills

Government: City; State

Organizations: Women's

Religious Sites and Organizations: Jewish

Date of Reviewer's Visit: 9/27/2002

Profile Updated by Institution: 11/12/2004

Name: Oregon Maritime Museum   **County:** Multnomah

Mailing Address: 115 SW Ash Suite 400 C

City: Portland   **State:** OR   **Postal Code:** 97204-0000

Street Address: On steamer *Portland* at Waterfront Park

Institution Email: info-oregonmar@oregonmaritimemuseum.org

Telephone Number: (503) 224-7724   **Fax Number:** (503) 224-7767

Contact Name: Charles Cardinell

Institution Type: Regional Museum

Web site URL: http://www.oregonmaritimemuseum.org

Hours: F–Su 11–4

Staff in Archives: 1p, v

Archives Are Handicapped Accessible: No

Access Description: Extremely steep ramp onto ship

Cost for Researcher—In-house: Museum admission

Review of Facilities: The Oregon Maritime Museum is located in downtown Portland at the foot of SW Pine St. on the seawall. The museum is on a 1947 historic steam-powered sternwheeler *Portland*. The research area is in the back corner of the boat. The area is sparse, with little room for researchers or storage of materials. A local computer houses some digital images and collection records of materials that are stored offsite.

Vertical Files: Yes

Vertical File Description and Subjects: Files of materials focusing on individual ships that plied the local waters or significant events in maritime history

Manuscripts: Yes

Manuscript Types: Business records, personal papers

Manuscript Subjects: Off-site storage in bank vaults; shipping directories, steamboat records, ships, warships of early 1900s, deep sea trade, trade on Columbia and Snake Rivers

Photographs: Yes   **Number of Photographs:** 20,000

Storage of Photographs: Photographs are stored digitally in PastPerfect at resolution of 150 dpi; 9,300 on computer and an additional 10,000 not cataloged. Originals stored offsite.

Photograph Subjects: Columbia, Willamette, and Snake River systems, barges on Snake River, photos from 1850s onward

Books: Yes

Description of Books: Early shipping, *Lloyd Register of Shipping*

Newspapers: No

Oral Histories: No

Maps and Drawings: No

Genealogy Sources: No

Special Collections: No

Indexes: Card files for manuscript collections; computer index for photographs

Review of Collections: The photo collection is sizable and unique, focusing on the life, activities, and business that occurred on and around the rivers and ocean of the Pacific Northwest. Manuscript materials deal with similar subjects, but most of the records were stored off site and were not examined. Off-site storage is a necessity for this facility.

Museum on Premises: Yes

   Museum Hours: F–Su 11–4

   Cost of Entry to Museum: $5

   Museum Is Handicapped Accessible: No

   Description of Museum: The museum is housed on a steam-powered sternwheeler *Portland* ship being the focus of the exhibit with models and artifacts of early life on the Northwest rivers and coast.

Parking: Pay box parking lots within blocks

Lunch: Short distance to downtown/International District restaurants

Lodging: http://www.travelportland.com

Nearest Commercial Airport: Portland International (PDX) [9 miles]

Subjects

   Historical Periods: 1865–1900; 1900–1940; 1940–present

   Transportation: Ships and Shipping; Ferries

Date of Reviewer's Visit: 9/27/2002

Profile Updated by Institution: 12/9/2004

✳✳✳✳

Name: Washington County Historical Society and Museum Library

County: Washington

Mailing Address: 17677 NW Springville Rd.

   City: Portland   **State:** OR   **Postal Code:** 97229-0000

Street Address: 17677 NW Springville Rd.

Institution Email: wchs@teleport.com

Telephone Number: (503) 645-5353   **Fax Number:** (503) 645-5650

Institution Type: Local Museum

Web site URL: http://www.washingtoncountymuseum.org

Hours: M–Sa 10–4:30; appt. available during same hours

Staff in Archives: 1f 2p 5v

Archives Are Handicapped Accessible: Yes

Access Description: Automatic door to building.

Cost for Researcher—Remote: Fee schedule

Review of Facilities: The Washington County Historical Society is located on the Portland Community College/Rock Creek Campus. This creates some difficulty with the parking situation (see parking section). The archives room is off the main entry area of the museum. The archives room is fairly small and triangularly shaped, but space is well utilized. Worktables are arranged along one wall; microfilm machines, indexes, and map cases are on another wall; while the third is made up with compact shelving, for holding the bulk of the collection. Lighting seemed barely sufficient over the worktable area, but otherwise it is a functional room. Paper and pencils are the only things allowed in the research area. Remaining items such as briefcases and large purses will be held in staff offices. Laptops without cases may be allowed by permission only.

Vertical Files: Yes   **Vertical Files in Cubic Feet:** 22

  Vertical File Description and Subjects: Newspaper clipping files stored in clamshell boxes

Manuscripts: Yes   **Manuscripts Volume in Cubic Feet:** 300

  Manuscript Types: Business records, school records, church records; donation land claim records. Cultural Resource Management files.

  Manuscript Subjects: Orenco City Records (planned corporate town) 1906–1938; school records from 1905–1970, including census, contracts, textbooks used; Tulatin Hotel Register, 1895–1902.

Photographs: Yes   **Number of Photographs:** 22,000

  Storage of Photographs: Photographs stored in acid-free folders in clamshell boxes

  Photograph Subjects: All areas of Washington County history

  Photograph Reproductions Are Available: Yes

    Photographic Prints: Yes

Books: Yes   **Number of Books in Collection:** 600

  Description of Books: Local area history

Newspapers: Yes

  Newspapers on Microfilm: Yes

  Microfilm and Dates: Local papers, 1873–1950s. Not indexed.

Oral Histories: Yes   **Oral Histories Number:** 192

  Oral Histories Description: Local residents recorded on audiotape. Some have transcriptions.

Maps and Drawings: Yes   **Estimated Number of Maps and Drawings:** 1,404

Description of Maps and Drawings: Local area historical maps

Genealogy Sources: Yes

Genealogy Sources Description: Obituary index—incomplete in card files. Marriage index from 1848–1906. Some cemetery records.

Special Collections: No

Indexes: Photograph index was done twice in two separate card files. There are card file indexes for manuscript collections and oral histories.

Online Sources: Some details about the collection, research policies, and reproduction costs are on the Web site.

Review of Collections: The Washington County Historical Society archive/library collection is well maintained and easily accessible. Most of the parts of the collections are indexed on card files. The school records collection is of particular interest. They also have a collection of textbooks that were used in the local schools. Also notable are records from Orenco City, a corporate planned city built for the workers of the Orenco Nursery. Although the archive has some items of interest for genealogists, the collection is not geared to that group. The photograph collection is quite large, well indexed, and includes over 1,000 glass plate negatives.

Museum on Premises: Yes

Museum Hours: M–Sa 10–4

Cost of Entry to Museum: $3

Museum Is Handicapped Accessible: Yes

Description of Museum: This museum is small, but the displays are modern and state-of-the-art. They are fundraising for an expansion to the building, which is greatly needed.

Parking: There are six parking spots reserved for the museum (and two handicapped spots). When entering the museum you will need to ask for a parking pass to be placed in your vehicle. The parking pass is free for the lot adjacent to the building.

Lunch: There are a number of chain and local restaurants at the intersection of NW West Union and 185th.

Lodging: http://www.travelportland.com

Nearest Commercial Airport: Portland International (PDX) [25 miles]

Subjects

Historical Periods: Pre-1800; 1800–1865; 1865–1900; 1900–1940; 1940–present

Natural Resources: Fishing; Logging

Mining: Gold; Silver; Coal

Transportation: Railroads; Stagecoach/Freight; Ships and Shipping; Ferries

Agriculture: Dairy; Ranching/Livestock; Vegetable/Truck Crops; Grains; Orchards; Vineyard; Dry Land Farming

Business: Retail; Legal/Medical Services; Hotels/Restaurants; Entertainment/ Theaters

Manufacturing: Sawmills

Government: City; County

Organizations: Schools; Colleges/Universities; Hospitals/Medical Facilities; Nonreligious Organizations

Ethnic Groups: Native American; Latin American; Pacific Islander; Middle Eastern; Japanese; Chinese; Danish; Dutch; English; Finnish; German; Irish; Italian; Norwegian; Russian; Scottish; Swedish; Armenian

Religious Sites and Organizations: Protestant; Catholic

Date of Reviewer's Visit: 11/6/2003

Profile Updated by Institution: 11/12/2004

PRINEVILLE

Name: Crook County Historical Society/Bowman Memorial Museum
County: Crook

Mailing Address: 246 North Main St.

  City: Prineville   **State:** OR   **Postal Code:** 97754-0000

Street Address: 246 North Main St.

Institution Email: bowmuse@netscape.net

Telephone Number: (541) 447-3715   **Fax Number:** (541) 447-3715

Contact Name: Gordon Gillespie/Vivian Zimmerlee

Institution Type: Local Museum

Affiliation: Crook County Historical Society

Web site URL: http://bowmanmuseum.org/historicalsociety.htm

Hours: Tu, Th 11:30–4

Staff in Archives: 1f, 2p, 14v

Archives Are Handicapped Accessible: No

Access Description: The photographs are stored on the ground floor. The research library itself is on the second floor up a flight and half of stairs.

Review of Facilities: The museum is housed in an old bank building in the downtown area. The building was built in 1910 of stone blocks from a local quarry.

The interior has wonderful wood and marble tellers' windows. Photos are available from binders stored on a narrow table downstairs. The remaining collection on the main floor is in a closed storage vault. The research library itself is located on the second floor. The library has one large worktable and is open and well lit, with the indexes nearby. The book and scrapbook collections flank the walls. The microfilm reader, printer, and film is also located in this room.

Vertical Files: Yes   **Vertical Files in Cubic Feet:** 6

   Vertical File Description and Subjects: Family histories

Manuscripts: Yes   **Manuscripts Volume in Cubic Feet:** 24

   Manuscript Types: Business records, scrapbooks

   Manuscript Subjects: Family history and a collection of scrapbooks from local farm women

Photographs: Yes   **Number of Photographs:** 500

   Storage of Photographs: Photos are displayed in binders with 3 x 5 reproductions of a large percentage of photos in seven large binders. Original photos are stored in file folders in file cabinets in a vault area.

   Photograph Subjects: The timber industry is a major sub-collection of photographs, but they deal with all areas of Crook County history.

   Photograph Reproductions Are Available: Yes

      Photographic Prints: No   **Digital Prints:** Yes

      Digital Images on CD or Electronically: Yes

Books: Yes   **Number of Books in Collection:** 400

   Description of Books: City directories, genealogy collection, high school yearbooks, local history, and professional collection

Newspapers: Yes

   Newspapers on Microfilm: Yes

   Microfilm and Dates: *Prineville Review/Crook County Journal* under various names from 1884 onward

Oral Histories: Yes   **Oral Histories Number:** 100

   Oral Histories Description: Eighty of the oral histories deal with the history of the timber industry in the area. These eighty have written transcriptions.

Maps and Drawings: No

Genealogy Sources: Yes

   Genealogy Sources Description: Family history collections filed in binders. There are a large number of detailed cemetery records from Prineville and adjoining communities and census records of Crook County.

Special Collections: No

Indexes: Obituary index on card file, index to scrapbooks and pamphlets on card file.

Review of Collections: The photograph collection is large and well rounded. The timber industry photos are a particularly strong collection. This collection is maintained by two separate groups: the Historical Society maintains some of the collections, and the Genealogical Society the rest. The division of the collection seems to work and appears more a division of volunteer labor rather than space. One problem may be that the people working in one part of the collection do not have a familiarity with what the collections maintained by the other society contains. Therefore, the researcher should talk to more than one person to find out the collection contents. The genealogy and family history collections have received a great deal of attention from a large group of volunteers.

Museum on Premises: Yes

Museum Hours: Tu–F 10–5, Sa 11–4

Museum Is Handicapped Accessible: No

Description of Museum: Small museum with two floors of Crook County history, City of Prineville, railroad, and timber industry.

Parking: Free on-street parallel parking

Lunch: Local and chain restaurants within driving distance

Lodging: http://www.cityofprineville.com; http://www.prineville-crookcounty.org

Nearest Commercial Airport: Roberts Field (Redmond, OR) (RDM) [19 miles]

Subjects

Historical Periods: 1865–1900; 1900–1940; 1940–present

Natural Resources: Logging

Mining: Gold; Tunnel Mining

Transportation: Railroads; Stagecoach/Freight

Business: Retail

Manufacturing: Sawmills

Government: City

Organizations: Schools

Date of Reviewer's Visit: 8/12/2003

Profile Updated by Institution: 11/18/2004

RICKREALL

Name: Polk County Museum   **County:** Polk

Mailing Address: PO Box 67

City: Monmouth   **State:** OR   **Postal Code:** 97361-0000

Street Address: 650 S. Pacific Hwy., Rickreall, OR

Institution Email: pchs@open.org

Telephone Number: (503) 623-6251

Contact Name: Nancy Noble   **Contact Email:** bn.nn@comcast.net

Institution Type: Local Museum

Affiliation: Polk County Historical Society

Web site URL: http://www.open.org/~pchs/

Hours: M, W–Sa 1–5, appt. times negotiable

Staff in Archives: 5v for archives

Archives Are Handicapped Accessible: Yes

Access Description: Elevator to second floor

Cost for Researcher—In-house: Donation

Cost for Researcher—Remote: Fee schedule

List of Researchers Available: No

Review of Facilities: The Polk County Museum is in a new building and already they have run out of space for both the library and the archival collections. This collection is divided into three distinct parts. The library is on the main floor, three walls contain bookshelves, and the other wall is a large bank of file cabinets that are the general files of the collection. There is a large worktable in the middle of the room. The archival storage is on the second floor but is primarily staff-only. The Collins collections are stored separately on the second floor.

Vertical Files: Yes   **Vertical Files in Cubic Feet:** 84

  Vertical File Description and Subjects: Church, schools, cities, family files, biography, and general subject files of mostly photocopies of clippings, ephemera, and manuscript materials

Manuscripts: Yes   **Manuscripts Volume in Cubic Feet:** 100

  Manuscript Types: School records, land records, legal records, organizational records, government records

  Manuscript Subjects: Schools, legal, property records, cultural and civic groups, and family papers. Polk County records; circuit court, probate records, voters' records, sheriff department records. School district records including teacher contract ledgers; civic organizational records. Seven cu. ft. of scrapbooks of Polk County history.

Photographs: Yes   **Number of Photographs:** 8,000

  Storage of Photographs: Photographs stored in hanging plastic folders in plastic file bins. Many of the photographs have been photocopied and put in the general vertical files.

Photograph Subjects: Schools, families, agriculture, transportation, timber industry, government, communities in Polk County

Photograph Reproductions Are Available: Yes

    Digital Prints: Yes   **Digital Images on CD or Electronically:** Yes

Books: Yes   **Number of Books in Collection:** 500

Description of Books: Family histories, local interest, professional collection, and old books

Newspapers: No

Microfilm and Dates: Polk County newspapers available at public library in Dallas

Oral Histories: Yes   **Oral Histories Number:** 30

Oral Histories Description: Videotapes or audiotaped oral history interviews. Without transcriptions.

Maps and Drawings: Yes   **Estimated Number of Maps and Drawings:** 100

Genealogy Sources: Yes

Genealogy Sources Description: Cemetery, marriage, death records, biographical and family files. Large collection of family histories.

Special Collections: Yes

Special Collections Description: Family papers of James Layton Collins and son Dean Collins. This collection includes correspondence, literary writing, reminiscences from the westward migration, California gold fields of the 1850s, and business and politics of the late nineteenth and early twentieth centuries in Polk County.

Indexes: The vertical files serve as an index to most of the rest of the collection. Copies of significant archives, items, and photographs are filed by subject in the vertical files in the first floor library.

Review of Collections: The Polk County Museum is working hard to collect and maintain their historical documents. The museum is run by volunteers, who are assigned specific duties in helping maintain the collections. The library is designed to be the contact point for researchers. The large bank of 10 file cabinets holds a major part of the collection in the form of photocopies. These are arranged by general subjects and then more specific subjects. The book collections spanning the walls of the library need some attention in the form of collection maintenance and cataloging. The system at Polk County Museum is designed to separate the researcher from the actual documents in the collection: significant documents, photographs, and research materials have been photocopied and placed in the vertical file. For the casual researcher or genealogist, this system would work fine. For the serious historical researcher, the disconnect from the actual documents would not be acceptable. The actual documents can be accessed with permission. The Collins family collection is the most significant untapped collection the reviewer has seen in a small historical society.

Museum on Premises: Yes

> **Museum Hours:** M, W–Sa 1–5
>
> **Cost of Entry to Museum:** $3
>
> **Museum Is Handicapped Accessible:** Yes
>
> **Description of Museum:** This museum opened at this location in 2000. It is a moderate-sized museum focusing primarily on the pioneer history of Polk County.

Parking: Free gravel parking lot in front of museum

Lunch: Variety of restaurants within driving distance

Lodging: http://www.dallasoregon.org, go to "Business Directory" section

Nearest Commercial Airport: Portland International (PDX) [60 miles]

Subjects

> **Historical Periods:** Pre-1800; 1800–1865; 1865–1900; 1900–1940; 1940–present
>
> **Eras:** Indian Wars; World War I; World War II
>
> **Natural Resources:** Logging
>
> **Transportation:** Railroads; Ferries
>
> **Agriculture:** Dairy; Ranching/Livestock; Grains; Orchards
>
> **Business:** Legal/Medical Services; Hotels/Restaurants; Entertainment/Theaters
>
> **Manufacturing:** Cannery; Brewery; Grist/Flour Mills; Sawmills; Wood Products
>
> **Government:** City; County; State
>
> **Organizations:** Schools; Colleges/Universities; Hospitals/Medical Facilities; Civic and Fraternal; Women's; Business; Children's
>
> **Ethnic Groups:** Native American; African; Japanese; English; German; Russian
>
> **Religious Sites and Organizations:** Protestant; Catholic; Mennonite/Amish

Date of Reviewer's Visit: 11/5/2003

Profile Updated by Institution: 11/29/2004

ROSEBURG

Name: Douglas County Museum of History and Natural History

County: Douglas

Mailing Address: 123 Museum Dr.

  City: Roseburg   **State:** OR   **Postal Code:** 97470-0000

Street Address: 123 Museum Dr.

Institution Email: museum@co.douglas.or.us

Telephone Number: (541) 957-7007   **Fax Number:** (541) 957-7017

Contact Name: Karen Bratton, Research Librarian

Contact Email: kabratto@co.douglas.or.us

Institution Type: Local Museum

Affiliation: Douglas County

Web site URL: http://www.co.douglas.or.us/museum/

Hours: M–F 1:00– 4:30; appt. on weekdays

Staff in Archives: 1f, 2p

Archives Are Handicapped Accessible: Yes

Access Description: Marginal access, check in at front desk and ask for directions for alternate entrance

Cost for Researcher—In-house: $3.50

Cost for Researcher—Remote: Fee schedule

Review of Facilities: The Lavola M. Bakken Research Library is located on the lower level of the Douglas County Museum. The museum itself is located outside of town near the fairgrounds. Enter through the main gate. Researchers pay the entrance fee to the museum and go down a long flight of stairs to the research room. The library is medium-sized with only one medium worktable and one study carrel for researchers. Microfilm reader, film, and computer station are in one section. Another section has a row of file cabinets, bookshelves, and staff workspace.

Vertical Files: Yes   **Vertical Files in Cubic Feet:** 14

  Vertical File Description and Subjects: General subject files

Manuscripts: Yes   **Manuscripts Volume in Cubic Feet:** 200

  Manuscript Types: Personal papers, government records, diaries, ledgers, scrapbooks, land records

  Manuscript Subjects: Donation land claims, building surveys, title abstracts, title deeds, personal manuscript collections

Photographs: Yes   **Number of Photographs:** 35,000

  Storage of Photographs: 5 x 7 file copies of photographs are filed by subject for researchers' use. Originals stored archivally elsewhere.

  Photograph Subjects: History of the Umpqua Valley, 1850s to present

  Photograph Reproductions Are Available: Yes

Photographic Prints: Yes   **Digital Prints:** Yes

Books: Yes   **Number of Books in Collection:** 6,000

Description of Books: Local and regional history, Oregon history, professional collection, city directories, yearbooks, and miscellaneous books are arranged on shelves by Dewey Decimal classification. Card files index the book collections.

Newspapers: Yes

Newspapers in Paper Format: Yes

Papers and Dates: Selected papers

Newspapers on Microfilm: Yes

Microfilm and Dates: 1872–1927 microfilm of local papers

Oral Histories: Yes   **Oral Histories Number:** 439

Oral Histories Description: Local area residents, most have transcriptions, will sell duplicate tapes or transcriptions

Maps and Drawings: Yes   **Estimated Number of Maps and Drawings:** 200

Description of Maps and Drawings: Douglas County locations, plat maps, regional history

Genealogy Sources: Yes

Genealogy Sources Description: Family files, (5 cu. ft.), cemetery indexes, 175 genealogies

Special Collections: Yes

Special Collections Description: Collection of 1,500 photographs by Gus Peret—avid photographer who chronicled Douglas County in the 1920s and 1930s—as well as numerous photos of Alaska and Africa

Indexes: "Grey File" is the card index of items in the collection with subject description of photos, manuscripts, maps, and other types of materials. In-house index to photographs on computer using PastPerfect.

Review of Collections: The photograph collection at the Douglas County Museum is one of the largest in the state. It covers all the eras of Douglas County history, with photographs taken from glass-plate negatives, albums, or original photography. The manuscript materials also contain important local area history and information. Natural history of the area is a major subject that is included in this collection. A herbarium collection of Douglas County is one of the specialized collections in this area. Overall, the collections are professionally processed and maintained. The available indexing is much better than average for similar-sized institutions.

Museum on Premises: Yes

Cost of Entry to Museum: $3.50

Museum Is Handicapped Accessible: Yes

Description of Museum: Large museum spread over four wings and two floors with a wide variety of exhibits on natural and social history of Douglas County and area

Parking: Free adjacent parking lot

Lunch: Drive into town (1–2 miles) for a variety of fast-food, chain, and local restaurants

Lodging: http://www.visitroseburg.com

Nearest Commercial Airport: Mahlon Sweet Field (Eugene) (EUG) [71 miles]; Rogue Valley International–Medford (MFR) [98 miles]

Subjects

> **Historical Periods:** 1800–1865; 1865–1900; 1900–1940; 1940–present
>
> **Eras:** Indian Wars; CCC; World War II
>
> **Natural Resources:** Fishing; Hunting; Logging
>
> **Mining:** Gold; Coal; Placer Mining; Surface Mining; Tunnel Mining; Nickel
>
> **Transportation:** Railroads; Stagecoach/Freight; Ferries
>
> **Agriculture:** Dairy; Ranching/Livestock; Vegetable/Truck Crops; Grains; Orchards; Vineyard
>
> **Business:** Banking; Retail; Legal/Medical Services; Hotels/Restaurants; Entertainment/Theaters
>
> **Manufacturing:** Cannery; Brewery; Grist/Flour Mills; Creamery; Brick Making; Sawmills
>
> **Government:** City; County; State; Federal
>
> **Organizations:** Schools; Hospitals/Medical Facilities; Nonreligious Organizations; Civic and Fraternal; Women's; Business; Children's
>
> **Ethnic Groups:** Native American; Pacific Islander
>
> **Religious Sites and Organizations:** Catholic; Jewish

Date of Reviewer's Visit: 8/18/2003

Profile Updated by Institution: 11/15/2004

SALEM

Name: Marion County Historical Society   **County:** Marion

Mailing Address: 260 12th St. SE

  City: Salem   **State:** OR   **Postal Code:** 97301-4101

Street Address: 1313 Mill Street SE

Institution Email: mchs@open.org

Telephone Number: (503) 364-2128   **Fax Number:** (503) 391-5356

Contact Name: Ross Sutherland   **Contact Email:** mchs@open.org

Institution Type: Local Museum

Web site URL: http://www.open.org/mchs

Hours: Tu–F 12–4

Staff in Archives: 1f, 6v

Archives Are Handicapped Accessible: Yes

Cost for Researcher—In-house: Museum admission

Cost for Researcher—Remote: Fee schedule

Review of Facilities: The Marion County Historical Society (MCHS) is located on the grounds of the Mission Mill Museum and is accessible from the Mission Mill parking lot. Researchers should proceed through a metal gate, to the left of the main warehouse building, and walk across the small wooden bridge spanning Mill Creek. The Historical Society is housed in the yellow building, located slightly west of the two-story brick mill building, and contains a modest research area with several library tables.

Vertical Files: Yes   **Vertical Files in Cubic Feet:** 20

  Vertical File Description and Subjects: General subject files of clippings and ephemera. Biographical files with genealogies and obituaries.

Manuscripts: Yes   **Manuscripts Volume in Cubic Feet:** 500

  Manuscript Types: Business and organizational records, family papers

  Manuscript Subjects: The personal and professional records of the Daue Family, David Duniway, Kathryn Gunnell, Renska Swart, and McEwan Photo Studio. MCHS also houses the records of numerous local organizations, along with the records of the Salem-Keizer School District.

Photographs: Yes   **Number of Photographs:** 8,000

  Storage of Photographs: Photocopies of photographs are available in subject-arranged file cabinets. Original photos are stored by accession number in archival folders elsewhere on the premises.

  Photograph Subjects: The photographs document the life and the development of Marion County, Oregon. There are significant numbers of photographs from Kathryn Gunnell and McEwan Photo Studio.

  Photograph Reproductions Are Available: Yes

    Photographic Prints: Yes

Books: Yes   **Number of Books in Collection:** 1,600

  Description of Books: Marion County history, Oregon state history, city directories, telephone books, and annuals of local schools

Newspapers: No

Oral Histories: Yes   **Oral Histories Number:** 50

> **Oral Histories Description:** Audiocassettes or videotapes of interviews of old-timers in the area. Some have reference indexes. Interviews have not been transcribed.

Maps and Drawings: Yes   **Estimated Number of Maps and Drawings:** 50

> **Description of Maps and Drawings:** Printed maps and reproductions of historic maps of Salem and Marion Counties

Genealogy Sources: Yes

> **Genealogy Sources Description:** Large card file "People Index," including obituaries and citations of newspapers articles and some manuscript collection materials. Files from 1850s to the present. Indexes to marriage records, probate records, and local cemeteries.

Special Collections: No

Indexes: Currently there is little indexing of the collection. Vertical files and photo files are arranged by subject.

> **Manuscript Finding Aids:** Finding aids are available for some manuscript collections.

Review of Collections: This collection focuses on the history of Marion County. The photograph collection is large and varied. The manuscript collections are primarily business and organizational papers, though there are numerous collections of family papers as well. Indexes and finding aids are limited, but plans are underway to enhance researcher access to archival and published materials.

Museum on Premises: Yes

> **Museum Hours:** Tu– F 12–4

> **Cost of Entry to Museum:** $3

> **Museum Is Handicapped Accessible:** Yes

> **Description of Museum:** Museum has permanent and temporary exhibits on the history of Marion County and Salem, Oregon's capital.

Parking: Free parking in the Mission Mill Museum lot. For those with mobility problems, contact the staff in advance to park closer to the museum in a restricted area.

Lunch: Cafe in Mission Mill Museum on the property

Lodging: http://www.travelsalem.com

Nearest Commercial Airport: Portland International (PDX) [58 miles]

Subjects

> **Historical Periods:** 1800–1865; 1865–1900; 1900–1940; 1940–present

> **Agriculture:** Vegetable/Truck Crops; Orchards

Business: Retail; Legal/Medical Services; Hotels/Restaurants; Entertainment/ Theaters

Government: City; County; State

Organizations: Schools; Charities; Nonreligious Organizations; Civic and Fraternal; Women's

Date of Reviewer's Visit: 11/4/2003

Profile Updated by Institution: 11/24/2004

✸✸✸✸✸

Name: Oregon State Archives   **County:** Marion

Mailing Address: 800 Summer St. NE

City: Salem   **State:** OR   **Postal Code:** 97310-0000

Street Address: 800 Summer St. NE

Institution Email: reference.archives@state.or.us

Telephone Number: (503) 373-0701   **Fax Number:** (503) 373-0953

Institution Type: Archives

Affiliation: State of Oregon

Web site URL: http://arcweb.sos.state.or.us

Hours: M–F 8 –12 and 1–4:45

Staff in Archives: 6f

Archives Are Handicapped Accessible: Yes

Access Description: ADA-compliant building

Cost for Researcher—In-house: Basic information free; other requests fee schedule

Cost for Researcher—Remote: Fee schedule—see Web site

Review of Facilities: The Oregon State Archives research room is spacious and beautiful. Before entering the research area, each individual is asked to fill out a research request form and receives a Researcher Identification Card, which is valid for up to one year, There is no charge for this, although photo identification is required. Keys to lockers are provided for all personal items except pencil and paper. The research room is large, with ten large worktables, six microfilm reader/printers, several computer stations, and cabinets with microfilm and other research materials. The bulk of the collection is stored elsewhere in the building. A reference desk is staffed all open hours, although appointments are encouraged.

Vertical Files: No

Manuscripts: Yes   **Manuscripts Volume in Cubic Feet:** 30,000

Manuscript Types: All manuscript types

Manuscript Subjects: State, county and local government records from throughout the state of Oregon

Photographs: Yes

Storage of Photographs: Photographs are stored with manuscript collections

Photograph Reproductions Are Available: Yes

Photographic Prints: Yes   **Digital Prints:** Yes

Books: Yes   **Number of Books in Collection:** 200

Description of Books: General reference and some Oregon history

Newspapers: No

Oral Histories: No

Maps and Drawings: Yes

Description of Maps and Drawings: Maps are part of individual collections

Genealogy Sources: No

Special Collections: Yes

Special Collections Description: Provisional and territorial government documents from 1837 to 1859

Indexes: Indexes to the State and Agency Records, Oregon Historical County Records Guide; Provisional and Territorial Government Records Guide, and the Oregon Historical Records Index are all searchable from the Web site.

Online Sources: The Web site provides detailed information about the State Archives and its holdings. Archival holdings indexes and finding aids are searchable from the Web site.

Review of Collections: The collections of the State Archives are divided into three types of records. The first is the State and Agency Records, which are, of course, arranged by the creating agency. The second is the Oregon Historical County Records, which are the records from individual counties in the state. The guide to this collection on the Web site will also do a county-by-county listing of where the records from the individual county can be found, including those not at the State Archives. The third group includes general historical records of Oregon that don't fall into either category above. The Provisional and Territorial Government Records are some of the oldest in this group. The Oregon Historical Records Index allows a surname search into the historical records. Overall, the collection is professionally maintained, and the Web site is the place to start for any research involving the State Archives.

Museum on Premises: No

Parking: Metered parking lot and on-street metered parallel parking. Individual parking spaces have limits of 30 min., 4 hrs., or 10 hrs.

Lunch: Driving distance to variety of restaurants

Lodging: http://www.travelsalem.com

Nearest Commercial Airport: Portland International (PDX) [57 miles]

Subjects

    Historical Periods: 1800–1865; 1865–1900; 1900–1940; 1940–present

    Eras: Civil War; Indian Wars; Spanish American War; World War I; World War II

    Mining: Mining

    Transportation: Railroads

    Business: Legal/Medical Services

    Government: City; County; State

    Organizations: Schools; Hospitals/Medical Facilities

Date of Reviewer's Visit: 11/4/2003

Profile Updated by Institution: 11/10/2004

✻✻✻✻

Name: Oregon State Library   **County:** Marion

Mailing Address: 250 Winter St. NE

    City: Salem   **State:** OR   **Postal Code:** 97301-3950

Street Address: 250 Winter St. NE

Institution Email: None

Telephone Number: (503) 378-4243   **Fax Number:** (503) 588-7119

Contact Name: Merrialyce Blanchard

Contact Email: merrialyce.k.blanchard@state.or.us

Institution Type: Special Library

Affiliation: State of Oregon

Web site URL: http://egov.oregon.gov/OSL

Hours: M–F 10–5

Staff in Archives: 1f

Archives Are Handicapped Accessible: Yes

Review of Facilities: The Oregon State Library is located on the Capital Campus across the street from the state capitol. The white marble building was built in 1939. An oak catalog room on the second floor features built-in card catalogs with hundreds of drawers of information on Oregon history. Two large conference tables provide room for researchers. In the main reference room, the oak paneled décor gives an elegant "old library" feel. Numerous tables, some with computers, line both sides of the room. Large windows stretch from above the bookcases up to their two-storied ceiling. The genealogy room is smaller with oak paneling and furniture, as well. Research collections are stored in staff-only areas in various parts of the building. Hopefully the State of Oregon will give more attention to the historical materials located in this facility.

Vertical Files: Yes   **Vertical Files in Cubic Feet:** 82

   Vertical File Description and Subjects: Oregon history, general information by subject

Manuscripts: Yes

   Manuscript Types: All manuscript types

   Manuscript Subjects: Oregon history, 200 manuscript collections, many not cataloged

Photographs: Yes   **Number of Photographs:** 10,000

   Photograph Subjects: General Oregon history is illustrated in the photograph collection.

   Photograph Reproductions Are Available: Yes

      Photographic Prints: Yes   **Digital Prints:** Yes

Books: Yes   **Number of Books in Collection:** 5,500

   Description of Books: Oregon history, Oregon documents, books by Oregon authors, cataloged using Dewey classification

Newspapers: No

Oral Histories: No

Maps and Drawings: Yes

   Description of Maps and Drawings: 30 drawers of historical maps of Oregon

Genealogy Sources: Yes

   Genealogy Sources Description: The Oregon State Library has a partnership with the Willamette Valley Genealogical Society. Each contributes to the genealogy Resource Center on the second floor of the Oregon State Library.

Special Collections: Yes

   Special Collections Description: WPA Oregon Writers Project for Northern Oregon

Indexes: Card file indexes available include: 200 drawers of Oregon Biography Index and 420 drawers of Oregon Index. Index all aspects of Oregon history from published and unpublished sources. Also, WPA Biography and Manuscripts Indexes.

   Online Sources: Oregon Index to several Oregon newspapers and magazines, 1985– current

Review of Collections: The collections at the Oregon State Library are limited more by accessibility than by availability. The focus of the Oregon State Library is to provide reference to the Oregon state government employees. Historical research is so far down their list of priorities that it is not even mentioned on the Web site. The indexes are so important, however, that they bear mentioning here. The Oregon Biography Index and Oregon (history) Index with respectively 200 and 420 card catalog file drawers record Oregon history from the beginning. The available manuscript and photograph collections require more than 24 hours turnaround time for each request. Indexing is minimal, staffing sparse. The State Library also has a collection of Oregon State documents.

Museum on Premises: No

    Parking: Metered parking for 2-hr. or 10-hr. periods or all-day parking lots within blocks

    Lunch: Variety of restaurants within a short drive or scenic walk

    Lodging: http://www.travelsalem.com

    Nearest Commercial Airport: Portland International (PDX) [58 miles]

Subjects

    Historical Periods: 1800–1865; 1865–1900; 1900–1940; 1940–present

    Organizations: Colleges/Universities

    Ethnic Groups: Native American; Japanese; Chinese; Danish; English; Finnish; German; Irish; Norwegian; Russian; Scottish; Swedish

Date of Reviewer's Visit: 8/20/2003

Profile Updated by Institution: None

✳✳✳

Name: Salem Public Library   **County:** Marion

Mailing Address: PO Box 14810

    City: Salem   **State:** OR   **Postal Code:** 97309-5020

Street Address: 585 Liberty St. SE

Institution Email: library@open.org

Telephone Number: (503) 588-6315   **Fax Number:** (503) 588-6055

Contact Name: Janice Weide

Institution Type: Public Library

Affiliation: City of Salem

Web site URL: http://www.open.org/library

Hours: Su 1–5, Sept–May; by appt. Tu–Th 10–9, F–Sa 10–6

Staff in Archives: 1f

Archives Are Handicapped Accessible: Yes

Review of Facilities: The library is in a modern building. There is a Salem Heritage Room that is beautiful but functions mostly as a study room. The Hugh Morrow Oregon collection of published materials is housed in the main part of the library, in open stacks. The vertical file information is housed by the reference desk. Research materials are limited, and the main strength in the collection is on their Web site.

Vertical Files: Yes   **Vertical Files in Cubic Feet:** 15

  Vertical File Description and Subjects: Subject files of clippings and ephemera on Oregon and Salem area history

Manuscripts: Yes

  Manuscript Types: Scrapbooks, personal papers

  Manuscript Subjects: Scrapbooks, postcards collected by Ben Maxwell, Salem local photo journalist

Photographs: Yes   **Number of Photographs:** 5,000

  Storage of Photographs: Digital access to the photograph collection is available at http://photos.salemhistory.org

Books: Yes

  Description of Books: Hugh Morrow Oregon Collection of books on Oregon topics. Around two-thirds of this collection is circulating, one-third is library-use only.

Newspapers: Yes

  Newspapers on Microfilm: Yes

  Microfilm and Dates: Microfilm of Salem newspapers, 1854 to present.

Oral Histories: No

Maps and Drawings: No

Genealogy Sources: No

Special Collections: No

Indexes: Books are listed in the online library computer catalog.

  Online Sources: Salem Online History is a database of local historical interest. They take an encyclopedia approach to providing access to Salem's history of culture, events, institutions, and people. The Online Historic Photo Collection is at http://photos.salemhistory.org.

Review of Collections: The Salem Online History Web site is the crowning glory of this collection. Skip the visit to the facility and browse the web for the majority of the historical resources offered by Salem Public Library. Much of the information on the Web site is not actually available in the library. The Web site is http://www.salemhistory.net.

Museum on Premises: No

Parking: Parking garage and adjacent lot are both coin-metered

Lunch: Cafe on the lower level of the building

Lodging: http://www.travelsalem.com

Nearest Commercial Airport: Portland International (PDX) [58 miles]

Subjects

    Historical Periods: 1800–1865; 1865–1900; 1900–1940; 1940–present

    Agriculture: Orchards

    Business: Entertainment/Theaters

Date of Reviewer's Visit: 11/4/2003

Profile Updated by Institution: 11/15/2004

SEASIDE

Name: Seaside Museum and Historical Society   **County:** Clatsop

Mailing Address: PO Box 1024

   City: Seaside   **State:** OR   **Postal Code:** 97138-0000

Street Address: 570 Necanicum Dr.

Institution Email: office@seasidemuseum.org

Telephone Number: (503) 738-7065   **Fax Number:** (503) 738-7065

Contact Name: Mark Tolonen, Helen Gaston

Institution Type: Local Museum

Affiliation: Seaside Historical Society

Web site URL: http://www.seasidemuseum.org

Hours: M–F 1–4 or by appt.

Staff in Archives: 1p; 4v

Archives Are Handicapped Accessible: Yes

Review of Facilities: The Seaside Museum and Historical Society is located in a single-story museum building close to downtown Seaside. The library is located in the main building to the right of the entrance. A smaller room, the library contains a medium-sized worktable and bookshelves containing the book collection and other materials. This area also serves as a kitchenette for staff and volunteers. They are in the process of constructing a new storage addition, which will house the bulk of the research materials and collections.

Vertical Files: Yes   **Vertical Files in Cubic Feet:** 2

Vertical File Description and Subjects: General history files. Have photocopies of some of the materials in notebooks in the library.

Manuscripts: Yes   **Manuscripts Volume in Cubic Feet:** 200

Manuscript Types: Organizational records, personal papers, business records

Manuscript Subjects: Donation land grants, personal papers, Women's Club, World War II women serving as coastal monitors, fire department history, men's groups

Photographs: Yes   **Number of Photographs:** 7,000

Storage of Photographs: Archival sleeves in file folders. Arranged by subject. Stored in secure area.

Photograph Subjects: Seaside history, coastal scenes, lighthouses, postcards

Photograph Reproductions Are Available: Yes

   Photographic Prints: Yes   **Digital Prints:** Yes

Books: Yes   **Number of Books in Collection:** 700

Description of Books: Local history, regional history, annuals, professional collection, telephone books, and city directories

Newspapers: No

Oral Histories: Yes   **Oral Histories Number:** 12

Oral Histories Description: Interviews of local residents done 2002–2004. Some are on CD, all on audiocassette. Interviews have transcriptions.

Maps and Drawings: Yes   **Estimated Number of Maps and Drawings:** 6

Description of Maps and Drawings: Sanborn Insurance Map, updated 1963. Clatsop Tree Farm, updated 1956.

Genealogy Sources: Yes

Special Collections: Yes

Special Collections Description: A special collection of research on the south Clatsop County area done by one local resident in the 1940s and 1950s. The collection includes copies of published materials, oral histories, and personal notes and reminiscences.

Indexes: Yes

Online Sources: Searchable photo archive

Review of Collections: The collections of the Seaside Museum are undergoing a transitional phase. Work is being done to evaluate and upgrade both the storage and indexing of the collections. The collections focus on the many aspects of life in Seaside and also the southern part of Clatsop County. Although the collections are moderate in size and scope, they provide some valuable materials that illustrate the history of Seaside and the region.

Museum on Premises: Yes

  Museum Hours: Mon–Fri 10–4

  Cost of Entry to Museum: $2

  Museum Is Handicapped Accessible: Yes

  Description of Museum: Small, local, but very nice museum and historic beach cottage adjacent

Parking: Free gravel parking lot adjacent or on-street parallel parking

Lunch: Less than 1/2 mile to downtown with variety of tourist and local restaurants

Lodging: http://www.seasideor.com

Nearest Commercial Airport: Portland International (PDX) [92 miles]

Subjects

  Historical Periods: Pre-1800; 1800–1865; 1865–1900; 1900–1940; 1940–present

  Natural Resources: Logging

  Transportation: Railroads; Stagecoach/Freight; Ships and Shipping

  Agriculture: Dairy; Vegetable/Truck Crops; Grains

  Business: Retail; Legal/Medical Services; Hotels/Restaurants; Entertainment/Theaters

  Manufacturing: Sawmills

  Government: City

  Organizations: Schools; Hospitals/Medical Facilities

  Ethnic Groups: Native American; Chinese; Danish; Finnish; Norwegian; Swedish

  Religious Sites and Organizations: Protestant; Catholic

Date of Reviewer's Visit: 8/23/2003

Profile Updated by Institution: 11/10/2004

THE DALLES

Name: Columbia Gorge Discovery Center and Wasco County Historical Museum

County: Wasco

Mailing Address: 500 Discover Dr.

  City: The Dalles   **State:** OR   **Postal Code:** 97058-0000

Street Address: 500 Discover Dr.

Institution Email: library@gorgediscovery.org

Telephone Number: (541) 296-8600   **Fax Number:** (954) 298-8660

Contact Name: Timothy Brown

Institution Type: Regional Museum

Web site URL: http://www.gorgediscovery.org

Hours: M, W, Th, and F 11–3

Staff in Archives: 4v

Archives Are Handicapped Accessible: Yes

Review of Facilities: The Columbia Gorge Discovery Center and the Wasco County Historical Museum are housed in opposite wings of an impressive museum complex. The library is located off a side corridor from the main lobby. The library is moderate-sized, with large worktables in the center of the room. It is a very pleasant room with wooden bookshelves lining two sides of the room. A third wall boasts a large three-canvas painting over two computer stations plus file cabinets and a staff workspace. Vertical file materials, books, maps, and some photo collections are housed in the library. Part of the photograph collection is available for viewing from their Web site (or the computers in the library). The library has set research hours. Another department of the museum maintains the remainder of the paper research collections. These include the manuscript materials, scrapbooks, ledgers, county records, and other miscellaneous collections.

Vertical Files: Yes   **Vertical Files in Cubic Feet:** 31

> **Vertical File Description and Subjects:** The vertical files are divided into two parts. One half is a biographical/family/genealogical file and the other half is a subject file. The subject files encompass all aspects of the local area history.

Manuscripts: Yes   **Manuscripts Volume in Cubic Feet:** 50

> **Manuscript Types:** Business records, organizational records, personal papers, legal records

> **Manuscript Subjects:** Limited local area history Prescription records from local drugstore (early twentieth century), county assessment rolls, scrapbooks, Jim Weeks research notes, and materials on the Rajneesh settlement

Photographs: Yes   **Number of Photographs:** 5,000

> **Storage of Photographs:** Nearly 2,000 of the photographic images are searchable from the Web site. Originals are stored in clamshell boxes and filed by accession number.

> **Photograph Subjects:** Wasco County, The Dalles, and surrounding communities of the Columbia River Corridor

> **Photograph Reproductions Are Available:** Yes

> **Photographic Prints:** Yes   **Digital Prints:** Yes

Digital Images on CD or Electronically: Yes

Books: Yes   **Number of Books in Collection:** 2,000

Description of Books: Local and regional history, school curriculum (local area interests), annuals, and city directories make up the bulk of the book collections. A card file indexes the books by author, title, and subject.

Newspapers: No

Oral Histories: No

Maps and Drawings: Yes   **Estimated Number of Maps and Drawings:** 40

Description of Maps and Drawings: Variety of local area maps, primarily covering Wasco County

Genealogy Sources: Yes

Genealogy Sources Description: Large genealogy vertical files (15 cu. ft.)

Special Collections: Yes

Special Collections Description: Forty-four super oversized ledgers of prescription records from the early part of the twentieth century.

Indexes: Books are indexed in catalog card file; vertical file is self-indexed, manuscript collections listed on staff computer using FileMaker Pro software.

Online Sources: A large portion of the photographic collection is available from the Web site.

Review of Collections: The research collections at this institution seem fragmented. By housing parts of the collection in two departments, the demarcation lines are blurred, and understanding of the entirety of the holdings is uncertain. The manuscript collection is more easily noted for what it is missing. Besides general vertical file materials, there is little on local businesses, organizations, or schools. The prescription books are a significant collection, but little else is of wide-ranging importance.

Museum on Premises: Yes

Museum Hours: Daily 9–5

Cost of Entry to Museum: $6.50

Museum Is Handicapped Accessible: Yes

Description of Museum: Large museum with two distinct sections. The Columbia Gorge Discovery Center has 26,100 sq. ft. of exhibit space interpreting the Columbia River Gorge National Scenic area. The second part is a 17,200-sq.-ft. exhibit wing on the history and people of Wasco County.

Parking: Large free paved parking lot

Lunch: Cafe located in the museum.

Lodging: http://www.thedalleschamber.com

Nearest Commercial Airport: Portland International (PDX) [78 miles]
Subjects

 Historical Periods: 1800–1865; 1865–1900; 1900–1940

 Agriculture: Orchards; Dry Land Farming

 Business: Retail; Hotels/Restaurants

 Government: City; County

 Organizations: Schools; Hospitals/Medical Facilities

 Religious Sites and Organizations: Protestant; Catholic

Date of Reviewer's Visit: 3/24/2004

Profile Updated by Institution: 11/17/2004

TILLAMOOK

Name: Tillamook County Pioneer Museum/Research Library
County: Tillamook

Mailing Address: 2106 2nd St.

 City: Tillamook **State:** OR   **Postal Code:** 97141-0000

Street Address: 2106 2nd St.

Institution Email: clb@tcpm.org

Telephone Number: (503) 842-4553 **Fax Number:** (503) 842-4553

Contact Name: Carol Brown, Director

Contact Email: clb@tcpm.org

Institution Type: Local Museum

Affiliation: Tillamook County Pioneer Museum Foundation

Web site URL: http://www.tcpm.org

Hours: M–F 8–5 and weekends by appointment

Staff in Archives: 3f 1p

Archives Are Handicapped Accessible: No

Access Description: There is a full flight of stairs from main entrance. From the 1st St. entrance, there are only 2 stairs at, but narrow there is a narrow doorway.

Cost for Researcher—Remote: Fee Schedule

Review of Facilities: The Tillamook County Pioneer Museum is located in the former county courthouse built in 1905. The research library is on the lower level. The research room is large and divided by bookshelves. There are long worktables, and the book collection surrounds the walls. The vertical file materials, indexes, and books are available for the use of the researcher. There is a microfilm reader in the room as well. Most other research materials are stored in an adjacent room. Manuscript materials are stored elsewhere in the building.

Vertical Files: Yes   **Vertical Files in Cubic Feet:** 36

Vertical File Description and Subjects: The vertical files include family files and general subject files. Much of the subject files are newspaper clippings.

Manuscripts: Yes   **Manuscripts Volume in Cubic Feet:** 10

Manuscript Subjects: Families, Oregon history, pioneer history, college theses

Photographs: Yes   **Number of Photographs:** 10,000

Storage of Photographs: Photographs are stored in document cases in plastic sleeves. The arrangement is topical.

Photograph Subjects: Local history, logging, civic groups, schools, shipping, families, homes, businesses, and scenery

Photograph Reproductions Are Available: Yes

Photographic Prints: Yes   **Digital Prints:** Yes

Digital Images on CD or Electronically: Yes

Books: Yes   **Number of Books in Collection:** 4,000

Description of Books: Local and regional history, genealogy, professional collection, city directories, phone books and annuals

Newspapers: Yes

Newspapers in Paper Format: Yes

Papers and Dates: *Tillamook Herald, Tillamook Headlight, Headlight-Herald, Kilchis Advocate,* and *Oregonian* from 1880s to the present

Newspapers on Microfilm: Yes

Microfilm and Dates: Tillamook papers 1888–1932; Cloverdale papers 1909–1942, and other miscellaneous papers

Oral Histories: Yes   **Oral Histories Number:** 300

Oral Histories Description: Oral history interviews with Tillamook County residents on audiocassette. Some have transcriptions.

Maps and Drawings: Yes

Description of Maps and Drawings: Tillamook County, Tillamook Bay, west coast charts

Genealogy Sources: Yes

Genealogy Sources Description: Family files, obituary files (1961–present), marriage records (1862–1910), cemetery records

Special Collections: No

Indexes: Family file card index listing obituaries, books, and other types of files

Review of Collections: The research collections are well developed in the area of genealogy. Of the book collection, over 20 percent of the material is genealogy-related. The photograph collection is relatively large for similar-sized institutions. The collections illustrate the broad range of history of Tillamook County. Although the museum has been in the present building since 1932, which is unusual for the Pacific Northwest, the research collection materials do not cover the breadth that one would expect for a collection of its age. Apparently most of the collecting was done in the artifact area and in photographs, but collection of paper documentation is a more recent development.

Museum on Premises: Yes

    Museum Hours: Tu–Sa 9–5, Su 11–5

    Cost of Entry to Museum: $3

    Museum Is Handicapped Accessible: No

    Description of Museum: Local museum displaying artifacts of Tillamook County history

Parking: On-street parallel parking or private paid parking lot across street

Lunch: Variety of local cafes within a few blocks

Lodging: http://www.tillamookchamber.org

Nearest Commercial Airport: Portland International (PDX) [86 miles]

Subjects

    Historical Periods: 1865–1900; 1900–1940; 1940–present

    Eras: World War I; CCC; World War II

    Natural Resources: Fishing; Logging

    Transportation: Railroads; Stagecoach/Freight; Ferries

    Agriculture: Dairy; Ranching/Livestock

    Business: Retail; Hotels/Restaurants

    Manufacturing: Cannery; Creamery; Boatbuilding/Shipyard; Sawmills; Wood Products

    Organizations: Schools; Nonreligious Organizations; Civic and Fraternal; Women's

    Ethnic Groups: Native American; Danish; English; German; Irish; Norwegian; Scottish; Swedish; Swiss

    Religious Sites and Organizations: Protestant; Catholic

Date of Reviewer's Visit: 8/22/2003

Profile Updated by Institution: 11/24/2004

VALE

Name: Malheur Historical Project—Stone House Museum   **County:** Malheur

Mailing Address: PO Box 413

  City: Vale   **State:** OR   **Postal Code:** 97918-0000

Street Address: 255 Main St.

Institution Email: None

Telephone Number: (541) 473-2070

Contact Name: Neva Demayo

Institution Type: Historic Site

Affiliation: Malheur County

Web site URL: None

Hours: Tu–Sa 12–4, May–Oct

Staff in Archives: 10v

Archives Are Handicapped Accessible: No

List of Researchers Available: Yes

Review of Facilities: The Malheur Historical Project is housed in the Rhinehart Stone House in Vale, Oregon. The sandstone house is undergoing restoration and functions as a museum. The house does not have a separate research area. The kitchen on the main level has a small table, and some materials are stored in various cabinets. Other materials are stored on the as-yet unrestored second floor in file cabinets in the corner. This room is accessed by a steep outside stairs. The facility is small and so is the collection.

Vertical Files: Yes   **Vertical Files in Cubic Feet:** 4

  Vertical File Description and Subjects: Malheur County subjects, biography, and administrative records

Manuscripts: Yes   **Manuscripts Volume in Cubic Feet:** 6

  Manuscript Types: Business records, personal papers

  Manuscript Subjects: Malheur County history

Photographs: Yes   **Number of Photographs:** 1,000

  Photograph Subjects: Malheur County and communities of Vale, Westfall, and Brogan

  Photograph Reproductions Are Available: Yes

    Photographic Prints: Yes

Books: Yes   **Number of Books in Collection:** 350

  Description of Books: Local history

Newspapers: Yes

Newspapers in Paper Format: Yes

Papers and Dates: 1901 *Malheur Gazette* and miscellaneous local papers

Oral Histories: Yes **Oral Histories Number:** 10

Oral Histories Description: Interviews with local residents

Maps and Drawings: Yes **Estimated Number of Maps and Drawings:** 10

Description of Maps and Drawings: Local area maps

Genealogy Sources: Yes

Genealogy Sources Description: Vertical file consisting of family records and cemetery records

Special Collections: Yes

Special Collections Description: Cyrus and Maria Locey diaries, 1852–1929

Indexes: Collection is being entered on PastPerfect software.

Review of Collections: The collection is not indexed and most is not organized. There may be some important gems in the collection for those trying to research the history of the area, however. Most records are organized by family name. They do include the cemetery records for Malheur County. History is collected for the communities of Vale, Westfall, and Brogan.

Museum on Premises: Yes

Museum Hours: Tu-Sa 12–4, Mar 1–Nov 1

Cost of Entry to Museum: Free

Museum Is Handicapped Accessible: No

Description of Museum: The Rhinehart Stone House, built in 1872 and located on the Oregon Trail, became a wayside stop for travelers as well as a nucleus of the community. Now being restored to its former state, it functions as a historical museum of the early settlement period.

Parking: Free on-street vertical parking

Lunch: Various local eateries and Dairy Queen

Lodging: http://www.valeoregon.com ; Ontario (16 miles away) has most major chain hotels

Nearest Commercial Airport: Boise Air Terminal/Gowen Field (Boise, ID) (BOI) [73 miles]

Subjects

Historical Periods: 1800–1865; 1865–1900; 1900–1940; 1940–present

Eras: Fur Trade; Civil War; Indian Wars; Spanish American War; World War I; World War II

Natural Resources: Water; Dams; Irrigation; Fishing; Hunting

Mining: Gold; Placer Mining; Surface Mining; Tunnel Mining

Transportation: Railroads; Stagecoach/Freight

Agriculture: Ranching/Livestock; Vegetable/Truck Crops; Grains; Orchards; Dry Land Farming

Business: Banking; Retail; Legal/Medical Services; Hotels/Restaurants

Manufacturing: Grist/Flour Mills; Brick Making; Sawmills

Government: City; County; State

Organizations: Schools

Ethnic Groups: Native American; Latin American; Japanese; Chinese; Basque; English; French; German; Irish; Italian; Scottish; Spanish; Hungarian

Religious Sites and Organizations: Protestant; Catholic; LDS (Mormon)

Date of Reviewer's Visit: 7/31/2002

Profile Updated by Institution: 11/24/2004

WALDPORT

Name: Waldport Heritage Museum   **County:** Lincoln

Mailing Address: PO Box 822

City: Waldport   **State:** OR   **Postal Code:** 97394-0000

Street Address: 320 NE Grant

Institution Email: None

Telephone Number: (541) 563-7092

Contact Name: Colleen Nickerson

Contact Email: Colleen@pacificonline.net

Institution Type: Local Museum

Affiliation: Alsi Historical and Genealogical Society and Lincoln County

Web site URL: None

Hours: F 12–4, Sa–Su 10–4, or call (541) 563-2301 for appt.

Staff in Archives: 9v

Archives Are Handicapped Accessible: Yes

Access Description: Ramp on side of building

Cost for Researcher—Remote: Fee schedule

Review of Facilities: The Alsi Historical and Genealogical Society maintains the Waldport Heritage Museum, located just blocks from the center of the town of Waldport. The museum is in a former Civilian Conservation Corps barracks moved to the present location in 1988. The research area is on one end of the museum away from the displays. There are large worktables located in the center of the room. Kitchen-type cabinets surround this area and hold the majority of the research materials. The work area is larger than average among similar-sized institutions, but items can be difficult to locate within the various storage areas.

Vertical Files: Yes   **Vertical Files in Cubic Feet:** 6

  Vertical File Description and Subjects: General subject files, biography, and family history files of local clippings and ephemera

Manuscripts: Yes   **Manuscripts Volume in Cubic Feet:** 6

  Manuscript Types: Scrapbooks, business records

  Manuscript Subjects: Family history

Photographs: Yes   **Number of Photographs:** 1,000

  Storage of Photographs: Photographs are housed in 36-plus binders in plastic sleeves with 2–6 photos per page. Arrangement is by subject.

  Photograph Subjects: Southern Lincoln County, families and life of area

  Photograph Reproductions Are Available: Yes

      Photographic Prints: Yes   **Digital Prints:** Yes

Books: Yes   **Number of Books in Collection:** 700

  Description of Books: Local and regional area history, flora and fauna of area, genealogy, annuals

Newspapers: No

  Microfilm and Dates: Newspapers at Lincoln County Historical Society in Newport, OR

Oral Histories: Yes   **Oral Histories Number:** 13

  Oral Histories Description: Oral history interviews with local area residents on audiocassette with transcriptions

Maps and Drawings: Yes   **Estimated Number of Maps and Drawings:** 77

  Description of Maps and Drawings: South Lincoln County Township maps from 1900 to 1967 with index

Genealogy Sources: Yes

  Genealogy Sources Description: Detailed cemetery indexes, including photographs of headstones. Family history files (birth, obituaries, marriage, military)

Special Collections: No

Indexes: Library holdings list in binder for each type of item in the collection (photos, scrapbooks, books, and so on)

Review of Collections: The Waldport Heritage Museum research collection is relatively small. The museum just opened in 1997, so most of the growth has probably not yet happened. The collection is very much geared to genealogists, an arrangement that will need to be changed to adapt to new donations. The photograph portion is the strongest part of the collection. Despite the sparsity of materials here, they are working hard to make what they have available and are learning as they go. Volunteer-run organization with potential.

Museum on Premises: Yes

Museum Hours: F 12–4, Sa–Su 10– 4

Cost of Entry to Museum: Donation

Museum Is Handicapped Accessible: Yes

Description of Museum: Small museum with single exhibit room of Waldport and area history

Parking: Free paved parking lot adjacent

Lunch: Local restaurants in town 6 blocks away

Lodging: http://www.waldport-chamber.com

Nearest Commercial Airport: Mahlon Sweet Field (Eugene, OR) (EUG) [93 miles]

Subjects

Historical Periods: 1800–1865; 1865–1900; 1900–1940; 1940–present

Eras: World War I; CCC; World War II

Natural Resources: Water; Fishing; Logging

Mining: Gold

Business: Retail; Hotels/Restaurants

Manufacturing: Sawmills

Government: City

Organizations: Schools; Charities; Civic and Fraternal

Ethnic Groups: Native American; Japanese; Chinese

Religious Sites and Organizations: Protestant; Catholic

Date of Reviewer's Visit: 8/21/2003

Profile Updated by Institution: 11/9/2004

6

Washington Profiles

Population (2003 estimate): 6,131,445

Land area: 66,544 square miles

Persons per square mile (2000 estimate): 88.6

ANACORTES

Name: Anacortes Museum   **County:** Skagit

Mailing Address: 1305 8th St.

   City: Anacortes   **State:** WA   **Postal Code:** 98221-0000

Street Address: 1305 8th St.

Institution Email: coa.museum@cityofanacortes.org

Telephone Number: (360) 293-1915   **Fax Number:** (360) 293-1929

Contact Name: Terry Slotemaker

Institution Type: Local Museum

Affiliation: City of Anacortes

Web site URL: http://www.anacorteshistorymuseum.org

Hours: M, Th, and F 1–5 p.m., appt. any weekday

Staff in Archives: 2p, 10v

Archives Are Handicapped Accessible: Yes

Review of Facilities: The Anacortes Museum is housed in a 1909 Carnegie Library Building. The research room is in the daylight basement of the museum. Entrance is flat without stairs or ramps. The research room has numerous large worktables with adequate lighting. Books and research files are on walls surrounding the tables.

The photo collection is stored in an adjoining room. Manuscript collections are in a storage area adjacent to research room.

Vertical Files: Yes   **Vertical Files in Cubic Feet:** 35

   Vertical File Description and Subjects: General research files by subjects

Manuscripts: Yes   **Manuscripts Volume in Cubic Feet:** 432

   Manuscript Types: Business records, personal papers, organizational records

   Manuscript Subjects: Cod fishing, canneries, boat building, lumber and shingle mills, Fidalgo Island Packing Co. records

Photographs: Yes   **Number of Photographs:** 13,000

   Storage of Photographs: Photographs stored in boxes, oversize containers, and in a fire-safe cabinet

   Photograph Subjects: Wallie Funk Collection of 10,000-plus images from 1890s onward, which staff is in process of adding to the collection

   Photograph Reproductions Are Available: Yes

      Digital Prints: Yes

Books: Yes   **Number of Books in Collection:** 950

   Description of Books: Professional collection, local history, city directories, phone books

Newspapers: Yes   **Newspapers in Paper Format:** Yes

   Papers and Dates: 1889–present of *Anacortes American* and other local papers

   Newspapers on Microfilm: No

   Microfilm and Dates: Anacortes Public Library has microfilm of newspapers

Oral Histories: Yes   **Oral Histories Number:** 200

   Oral Histories Description: Interviews with local area residents

Maps and Drawings: Yes

   Description of Maps and Drawings: Large collection of maps and architectural drawings

Genealogy Sources: Yes

   Genealogy Sources Description: Obituary collection

Special Collections: Yes

   Special Collections Description: Preston Collection; map collection mostly of Fidalgo Island, and Anacortes Bowman-Child-Curtis Collection of Anacortes founding families

Indexes: Computerized index to photographs, laser prints in binders arranged by subject or accession number

   Manuscript Finding Aids: Computerized finding aids to manuscripts and photographs

Review of Collections: The Anacortes Museum collection is very impressive for a town of this size. The collection is well rounded, with family and business histories equally well represented. Histories of the fisheries, canneries, boat building, and lumber and shingle mills in the area are included in the manuscript materials, as well as the photographs. The collection is well cared for and maintained and has a significant amount of use. The various computerized finding aids and indexes make the collection accessible.

Museum on Premises: Yes

Museum Hours: Th–M 1–5

Cost of Entry to Museum: Donation

Museum Is Handicapped Accessible: No

Description of Museum: The Carnegie Gallery is located on the upper floors of the Carnegie Building. The exhibits focus on the cultural heritage of the Fidalgo and Guemes Islands.

Parking: Free on-street parallel unmarked parking

Lunch: Numerous local and chain restaurants within a short driving distance

Lodging: http://www.anacortes.org/

Nearest Commercial Airport: Anacortes Airport (74S) [3 miles], Seattle-Tacoma International (SEA) [95 miles]

Subjects

Historical Periods: Pre-1800; 1800–1865; 1865–1900; 1900–1940; 1940–present

Natural Resources: Logging

Mining: Copper; Tunnel Mining; Gravel; Petroleum

Transportation: Railroads; Ships and Shipping; Ferries; Aviation

Agriculture: Dairy; Ranching/Livestock; Vegetable/Truck Crops; Grains; Orchards; Vineyard;

Business: Legal/Medical Services; Hotels/Restaurants; Entertainment/Theaters

Manufacturing: Boatbuilding/Shipyard; Technology/Computers; Sawmills

Government: City

Organizations: Schools; Hospitals/Medical Facilities; Charities; Nonreligious Organizations

Ethnic Groups: Native American; Latin American; Japanese; Chinese; Norwegian; Swedish; Croatian

Religious Sites and Organizations: Protestant; Catholic; LDS (Mormon); Jewish; Jehovah Witness; Indian Shaker; Native American

Date of Reviewer's Visit: 4/24/2003

Profile Updated by Institution: 11/12/2004

AUBURN

Name: White River Valley Museum   **County:** King

Mailing Address: 918 H St. SE

   City: Auburn   **State:** WA   **Postal Code:** 98002-0000

Street Address: 918 H St. SE

Institution Email: None

Telephone Number: (253) 288-7433   **Fax Number:** (253) 931-3098

Contact Name: Alyssa Shirley Morein   **Contact Email:** amorein@auburnwa.gov

Institution Type: Local Museum

Affiliation: City of Auburn and White River Valley Historical Society

Web site URL: http://www.wrvmuseum.org

Hours: W–Su 12–4 by appt. for research

Staff in Archives: 1f 1p 5v

Archives Are Handicapped Accessible: Yes

Cost for Researcher—Remote: Fee schedule

Review of Facilities: The White River Valley Museum is located in the heart of Auburn in Les Gove Park, near the Auburn Public Library and the senior center. The building is a modern one-story structure. The research room of the White River Valley Museum is dominated by the compact shelving. There is a medium-sized worktable, registration table, copy machine, and the shelving. There are also a number of lockers and a coat rack used by museum volunteers. Sections of the compact shelving house the bound newspapers, some of the books, vertical files, copy photo files, and assorted other materials. Most manuscript materials and other research collections are stored at the opposite end of the building in the main collections storage area.

Vertical Files: Yes   **Vertical Files in Cubic Feet:** 10

   Vertical File Description and Subjects: General subject files and newspaper clippings

Manuscripts: Yes   **Manuscripts Volume in Cubic Feet:** 70

   Manuscript Types: Organizational records, personal papers, business records

   Manuscript Subjects: Railroads, family history, correspondence, club records, scrapbooks, city records

Photographs: Yes   **Number of Photographs:** 6,000

   Storage of Photographs: Select browser file of photocopies of photographs filed on shelves in file folders. Originals stored in clamshell boxes in acid-free envelopes. Photograph information only is being added onto PastPerfect.

Photograph Subjects: Auburn, Kent, and White River Valley local historical sites and scenes

Photograph Reproductions Are Available: Yes

    Photographic Prints: Yes   **Digital Prints:** Yes

Books: Yes   **Number of Books in Collection:** 1,300

Description of Books: Regional history, city directories, yearbooks, professional collection, and old books

Newspapers: Yes   **Newspapers in Paper Format:** Yes

Papers and Dates: Auburn newspapers, 1893–1982, in bound volumes; Kent newspapers, 1902–1982, in bound volumes

Newspapers on Microfilm: No

Microfilm and Dates: Auburn Public Library next door has the microfilm

Oral Histories: Yes   **Oral Histories Number:** 70

Oral Histories Description: 45 oral histories of Japanese Americans regarding World War II and internment; interviews with railroaders; Auburn schools, farming, local history. Most have partial or full transcriptions.

Maps and Drawings: Yes   **Estimated Number of Maps and Drawings:** 250

Description of Maps and Drawings: Maps of assorted local interest; town plats, blueprints, and maps of Auburn

Genealogy Sources: No

Special Collections: Yes

Special Collections Description: There is a special collection of Northern Pacific Railroad history; this is housed separately from the other collections. There is a large number of ephemeral items, schedules, and miscellaneous items.

Indexes: Yes

Manuscript Finding Aids: Some collections have non–item-level finding aids.

Online Sources: Oral history interviews listed on Oral History Catalog at the Museum of History and Industry in Seattle.

Review of Collections: The collections of the White River Valley Museum are focused on the cities of Auburn, Kent, and neighboring communities. There is a significant amount of information on the Japanese Americans who settled in the White River Valley, much of which covers the World War II period. There is also a special collection of Northern Pacific Railroad materials, including oral histories, manuscripts, and ephemera. Special collections include photographs of the Northern Clay Company, later Gladding McBean, and an architectural terra cotta manufacturing plant.

Museum on Premises: Yes

Museum Hours: W–Su 12–4

Cost of Entry to Museum: $2

Museum Is Handicapped Accessible: Yes

Description of Museum: The museum has several galleries—some permanent, some rotating—that illustrate the history of Auburn and the White River Valley. The museum displays are professionally designed and well worth a visit.

Parking: Free parking lot adjacent

Lunch: Variety of local and chain restaurants within a short drive

Lodging: http://www.auburnareawa.org/

Nearest Commercial Airport: Seattle-Tacoma International (SEA) [16 miles]

Subjects

Historical Periods: 1865–1900; 1900–1940

Eras: Indian Wars

Transportation: Railroads

Agriculture: Vegetable/Truck Crops

Manufacturing: Cannery

Government: City

Organizations: Schools; Charities; Nonreligious Organizations; Civic and Fraternal; Women's

Ethnic Groups: Native American; Japanese

Religious Sites and Organizations: Buddhist

Date of Reviewer's Visit: 1/16/2004

Profile Updated by Institution: 11/17/2004

BAINBRIDGE ISLAND

Name: Bainbridge Island Historical Museum   **County:** Kitsap

Mailing Address: 215 Ericksen Ave. NE

   City: Bainbridge Island   State: WA   **Postal Code:** 98110-0000

Street Address: 215 Ericksen Ave. NE

Institution Email: bihs@nwinet.com

Telephone Number: (206) 842-2773   **Fax Number:** (206) 842-0914

Contact Name: Erica Varga, Curator

Institution Type: Local Museum

Affiliation: Bainbridge Island Historical Society and Bainbridge Foundation

Web site URL: www.bainbridgehistory.org

Hours: W–F 1–4, Sa 10–4, Su 1–4, call for appt.

Staff in Archives: 2p, 10v

Archives Are Handicapped Accessible: Yes

Review of Facilities: The Bainbridge Island Historical Museum is located within the newly restored 1908 Island Center School and expanded facility in the heart of the downtown area within walking distance from the Seattle/Bainbridge ferry. The institution moved to this location in fall 2004 and was not visited by the reviewer.

Vertical Files: Yes

Vertical File Description and Subjects: General subject and biographical files

Manuscripts: Yes

Manuscript Types: Business records, land records, organizational records, personal papers, diaries

Manuscript Subjects: Island industry records, government agencies, postcards, ferry and steamer schedules, music, census rolls and records of school attendance, post offices, and hotels. Logs and diaries of early explorers and settlers.

Photographs: Yes   **Number of Photographs:** 4,000

Photograph Subjects: All aspects of history and life on Bainbridge Island, 1854 to the present

Books: Yes   **Number of Books in Collection:** 342

Description of Books: Bainbridge Island history, regional history, schoolbooks, atlases, encyclopedias, annuals from 1914 to the present

Newspapers: Yes

Newspapers in Paper Format: Yes

Papers and Dates: Bainbridge Island newspapers

Newspapers on Microfilm: Yes

Microfilm and Dates: Bainbridge Island and regional newspapers from 1902 to the present

Oral Histories: Yes   **Oral Histories Number:** 150

Oral Histories Description: Oral histories on audiocassette

Maps and Drawings: Yes

Description of Maps and Drawings: Charts, maps and surveys from the 1700s to the present. Shipbuilding, industrials drawings, and blueprints.

Genealogy Sources: Yes

Genealogy Sources Description: Biographical files, cemetery records

Special Collections: No

Indexes: Unknown

Review of Collections: The collections at Bainbridge Island Historical Society were in a state of flux because of their recent move. The collections represent a wide variety of subjects throughout the history of the island. Of particular note are some collections on Japanese Americans before and during the internment periods of World War II.

Museum on Premises: Yes

    Museum Hours: Su, W–F 1–4; Sa 10–4

    Cost of Entry to Museum: $2.50

    Description of Museum: Museum moved in 2004 and was not visited.

Parking: Parking available nearby

Lunch: Variety of restaurants within short walk

Lodging: http://www.bainbridgechamber.com/

Nearest Commercial Airport: Seattle-Tacoma International (SEA) [24 miles]

Subjects

    Historical Periods: 1865–1900; 1900–1940; 1940–present

    Eras: World War II

    Natural Resources: Logging

    Transportation: Ships and Shipping; Ferries

    Government: City; County

    Organizations: Schools; Charities; Nonreligious Organizations

    Ethnic Groups: Native American; Japanese; Filipino; Danish; English; Finnish; German; Irish; Norwegian; Scottish; Swedish

    Religious Sites and Organizations: Protestant; Catholic; LDS (Mormon); Jewish

Date of Reviewer's Visit: Not Visited

Profile Updated by Institution: 11/23/2004

BELLEVUE

Name: Eastside Heritage Center   **County:** King

Mailing Address: PO Box 40535

    City: Bellevue   **State:** WA   **Postal Code:** 98015-0000

Street Address: 2102 Bellevue Way SE

Institution Email: director@eastsideheritagecenter.org

Telephone Number: (425) 450-1049

Contact Name: Mike Luis, Director

Institution Type: Historical Society Archives

Web site URL: http://www.eastsideheritagecenter.org

Hours: Tu 10–3

Staff in Archives: 1f, 3p, 5v

Archives Are Handicapped Accessible: Yes

Access Description: Lower level handicapped entrance, narrow walkways in research room

Cost for Researcher—In-house: Dependent upon time needed

Cost for Researcher—Remote: Staff research $25 per hr.

List of Researchers Available: Yes

Review of Facilities: The research collections of the Eastside Heritage Center are divided into two parts and stored in two locations. The Winters House in Bellevue houses the collections that belonged to the Bellevue Historical Society and the Bellevue and Kirkland part of the former Marymoor Museum collection. The remaining Marymoor collections and some others are housed at the McDowell House at 118th and Main in Bellevue. The Winters House is the location visited. This house is at the edge of Bellefield Nature Park. The street out front is a divided roadway with the entrance from the northbound lane. The house is available for rental to the public for social events. It is not a museum. The Heritage Center has offices in the lower level, and that is where the research room is. The room is not very big, and there is one medium-sized work table. File cabinets, bookcases, and locked cabinets surround the room and make the room seem smaller than it is. The overall impression is overstuffed, but intriguing. Additional archival material is stored upstairs in a staff-only area.

Vertical Files: Yes   **Vertical Files in Cubic Feet:** 9

  Vertical File Description and Subjects: Clipping files and general subject files with special sections for schools and people files

Manuscripts: Yes   **Manuscripts Volume in Cubic Feet:** 60

  Manuscript Types: Family papers, organizational records

  Manuscript Subjects: Bellevue Chamber of Commerce papers, miscellaneous Bellevue and area history

Photographs: Yes

  Storage of Photographs: Photographs are stored in two ways, some on cardstock in binders, others as photocopies in subject-arranged file cabinets

  Photograph Reproductions Are Available: Yes

    Photographic Prints: Yes   **Digital Prints:** Yes

    Digital Images on CD or Electronically: Yes

Books: Yes   **Number of Books in Collection:** 200

   Description of Books: Local history, annuals

Newspapers: No

Oral Histories: Yes   **Oral Histories Number:** 100

   Oral Histories Description: Interviews of local residents mostly 1990s or newer. Transcriptions for some.

Maps and Drawings: Yes

   Description of Maps and Drawings: Bellevue History and general Eastside area maps

Genealogy Sources: No

Special Collections: No

Indexes: Card catalog indexes for photographs, slides, and documents

Review of Collections: The collection at the Winters House location of the Eastside Heritage Center is a combination of the former Bellevue Historical Society and part of the collections from the former Marymoor Museum. The Marymoor collection was divided into two parts by the area of the materials. Those dealing with Bellevue and Kirkland were sent to the Winters House, where they are being integrated with the former Bellevue Historical Society collections. Those dealing with Redmond and other east King County areas are currently housed at the McDowell House, another Eastside Heritage Center office. The collection is in process of reevaluation and reprocessing and relabeling.

Museum on Premises: No

Parking: Free parking lot adjacent to building

Lunch: Driving distance to variety of restaurants or bring a lunch and eat on the park grounds

Lodging: http://www.bellevuechamber.org/

Nearest Commercial Airport: Seattle-Tacoma International (SEA) [19 miles]

Subjects

   Historical Periods: Pre-1800; 1800–1865; 1865–1900; 1900–1940; 1940–present

   Natural Resources: Logging; Whaling

   Mining: Gold; Coal

   Transportation: Railroads; Ferries; Aviation

   Agriculture: Dairy; Vegetable/Truck Crops

   Business: Retail; Legal/Medical Services

   Manufacturing: Boatbuilding/Shipyard; Sawmills

   Government: City; County; State

Organizations: Schools; Charities; Women's; Business

Ethnic Groups: Native American; Japanese; Chinese; Dutch; Croatian

Date of Reviewer's Visit: 12/2/2003

Profile Updated by Institution: 12/21/2004

✹✹✹✹✹

Name: Washington State Archives, Puget Sound Region **County:** King

Mailing Address: Pritchard-Fleming Building, 3000 Landerholm Circle SE, MS-N100

City: Bellevue   **State:** WA   **Postal Code:** 98007-6484

Street Address: 3000 Landerholm Circle SE

Institution Email: archives@bcc.ctc.edu

Telephone Number: (425) 564-3940   **Fax Number:** (425) 564-3945

Contact Name: Michael Saunders, Regional Archivist

Contact Email: msaunder@bcc.ctc.edu

Institution Type: Archives

Affiliation: State of Washington

Web site URL: http://www.secstate.wa.gov/archives/archives_puget.aspx

Hours: M–F 8:30–4:30, by appt.

Staff in Archives: 5f

Archives Are Handicapped Accessible: Yes

Cost for Researcher—In-house: No charge

Cost for Researcher—Remote: Limited research available, Payment required in advance

List of Researchers Available: Yes

Review of Facilities: The Washington State Archives, Puget Sound Region is located on the lower level of the Pritchard-Fleming Building on the campus of Bellevue Community College. The lobby has a reception desk where researchers check in. There are lockers for storage of all bags and personal items. Keys are available at the reception desk and only paper, pencils, and laptops are allowed in the research room. The research room has eight narrow tables that can be pulled together for big collection needs. Each table has access to power for laptops. There are separate audiovisual areas for microfilm, slides, video, light tables, and copy stand. The room is well equipped and pleasant. This branch is the busiest of all the regional branches, and so appointments are a necessity. Three days or longer lead time for appointments is important. Because of the volume of requests, leaving email or voice mail messages on the phone or email are the most efficient means of contact.

Vertical Files: No

Manuscripts: Yes   **Manuscripts Volume in Cubic Feet:** 21,000

   Manuscript Types: Government records

   Manuscript Subjects: County records, municipal records, records of special districts of Puget Sound Washington and the counties of King, Kitsap, and Pierce. Spans the early territorial period to the present.

Photographs: Yes   **Number of Photographs:** 600,000

   Storage of Photographs: Some photographs are interfiled with the agency manuscript and record collections

   Photograph Reproductions Are Available: Yes

      Photographic Prints: Yes   **Digital Prints:** Yes

      Digital Images on CD or Electronically: Yes

Books: Yes   **Number of Books in Collection:** 100

   Description of Books: City directories in reading room

Newspapers: No

Oral Histories: No

Maps and Drawings: Yes   **Estimated Number of Maps and Drawings:** 8,381

   Description of Maps and Drawings: Large map collections

Genealogy Sources: Yes

   Genealogy Sources Description: Marriage records, some birth and death records, probate case files, territorial census, school district census.

Special Collections: Yes

   Special Collections Description: Data sheets with photographs of King County buildings

Indexes: Yes

   Manuscript Finding Aids: Some finding aids and inventories

   Online Sources: Online Historical Records Search. Available from http://www.secstate.wa.gov/history/search.aspx for access to selected census, naturalization, birth, marriage, death, prison and other miscellaneous records. For Washington history, see http://www.secstate.wa.gov/history.

Review of Collections: Collections include records from counties, municipalities, and special districts in the three-county region. Although limited to three counties, they are the most populous of the state. The counties are King, Kitsap, and Pierce. The collections include historical information on buildings, businesses, land use, property, education, genealogy, and social and economic issues of the region. A partial list of some records is available from the Web site. All records are public.

Museum on Premises: No

Parking: Free parking spots available adjacent to facility. Other lots require permit.

Lunch: Driving distance to variety of restaurants

Lodging: http://www.bellevuechamber.org/

Nearest Commercial Airport: Seattle-Tacoma International (SEA) [16 miles]

Subjects

    Historical Periods: 1800–1865; 1865–1900; 1900–1940; 1940–present

    Eras: WPA; World War II

    Natural Resources: Dams

    Transportation: Aviation

    Government: City; County

    Organizations: Schools

Date of Reviewer's Visit: 5/5/2004

Profile Updated by Institution: 11/29/2004

BELLINGHAM

✡✡✡✡✡

Name: Center for Pacific Northwest Studies   **County:** Whatcom

Mailing Address: Goltz-Murray Archives Building, Western Washington University

    City: Bellingham   **State:** WA   **Postal Code:** 98225-9123

Street Address: 808 25th St.

Institution Email: cpnws@wwu.edu

Telephone Number: (360) 650-7747   **Fax Number:** (360) 650-3323

Contact Name: Elizabeth Joffrion   **Contact Email:** Elizabeth.Joffrion@wwu.edu

Institution Type: Archives

Affiliation: Western Washington University

Web site URL: http://www.acadweb.wwu.edu/cpnws

Hours: M–F 9–noon and 1:30–4:30

Staff in Archives: 1f 3p

Archives Are Handicapped Accessible: Yes

Cost for Researcher—In-house: No charge

Cost for Researcher—Remote: First hr. free

List of Researchers Available: Yes

Review of Facilities: The Center for Pacific Northwest Studies shares space with the Northwest Regional Branch of the Washington State Archives. The building is located at the edge of the Western Washington Campus. The building is a modern single-story structure. Because the space is shared, when you sign in at the front desk they will connect you with the correct personnel for the collection you are researching. The reading room is limited-access with lockers for personal items. Large research tables are centered in a spacious, airy room. There are some books in the research room, two microfilm readers, and computer terminals available for researchers.

Vertical Files: Yes   **Vertical Files in Cubic Feet:** 53

Vertical File Description and Subjects: Subject arrangement of Center for Pacific Northwest Studies pamphlet collection

Manuscripts: Yes   **Manuscripts Volume in Cubic Feet:** 3,500

Manuscript Types: All manuscript types

Manuscript Subjects: Economic development, cultural and social history of the region, fishing and processing industries, several hundred individual collections

Photographs: Yes   **Number of Photographs:** 10,000

Storage of Photographs: Photographs are sorted archivally

Photograph Subjects: Howard Buswell Collection, Galen Biery Collection, and P. R. Jeffcott Collections.

Photograph Reproductions Are Available: Yes

Photographic Prints: Yes   **Digital Prints:** Yes

Digital Images on CD or Electronically: Yes

Books: Yes   **Number of Books in Collection:** 2,000

Description of Books: Local and regional history, city directories

Newspapers: Yes

Newspapers on Microfilm: Yes

Microfilm and Dates: Bellingham papers, 1873–present, and papers from surrounding counties

Oral Histories: Yes   **Oral Histories Number:** 500

Oral Histories Description: The majority of interviews are on audiocassette. There are fewer video interviews. Topics include Native American tribal history and culture, women's history, and Washington State politics.

Maps and Drawings: Yes   **Estimated Number of Maps and Drawings:** 2,200

Description of Maps and Drawings: Maps and architectural drawings. Many of Bellingham area, but also some late-eighteenth- and nineteenth-century maps of exploration and settlement.

Genealogy Sources: No

Special Collections: No

Indexes: Yes

> **Manuscript Finding Aids:** Most collections have finding aids; 65 percent of the collections have finding aids online.

> **Online Sources:** Online catalog to search the Center for Pacific Northwest Studies manuscript collection. Separate searches in a Map Catalog or Photograph Catalog all available from the Web site. Some images available at this time.

Review of Collections: Collection focuses on the areas of Washington, Oregon, Idaho, Alaska, and British Columbia. The center collects materials that represent significant developments in the region. Although covering a broad area, the collection is richest in the areas of northern Puget Sound and Whatcom, Skagit, and Snohomish Counties. The search capability of the collection is excellent, with a separate photograph and map collection search choice, as well as the collection finders. All parts of online indexes have browse functions as well. Professionally managed and maintained.

Museum on Premises: No

Parking: There is a permit required lot; the permits are available at the staff desk inside the building.

Lunch: Driving distance to a variety of restaurants

Lodging: http://www.bellingham.org

Nearest Commercial Airport: Bellingham International (BLI) [8 miles]

Subjects

> **Historical Periods:** Pre-1800; 1800–1865; 1865–1900; 1900–1940; 1940–present

> **Eras:** CCC

> **Natural Resources:** Fishing

> **Mining:** Coal

> **Transportation:** Railroads; Ships and Shipping

> **Business:** Entertainment/Theaters

> **Manufacturing:** Cannery; Sawmills

> **Government:** City; County; State; Federal

> **Organizations:** Schools; Colleges/Universities; Civic and Fraternal; Women's

> **Ethnic Groups:** Native American; Pacific Islander; Japanese; Chinese; Norwegian

Date of Reviewer's Visit: 4/25/2003

Profile Updated by Institution: 11/15/2004

✺✺✺✺✺

Name: Washington State Archives, Northwest Regional Branch

County: Whatcom

Mailing Address: Western Washington University, MS 9123

  City: Bellingham   **State:** WA   **Postal Code:** 98225-9123

Street Address: 808 25th St.

Institution Email: State.Archives@wwu.edu

Telephone Number: (360) 650-3125   **Fax Number:** (360) 650-3323

Contact Name: Diana Shenk   **Contact Email:** diana.shenk@wwu.edu

Institution Type: Archives

Affiliation: State of Washington

Web site URL: http://www.secstate.wa.gov/archives/

Hours: M–F 8:30–5

Staff in Archives: 3f, 9v

Archives Are Handicapped Accessible: Yes

List of Researchers Available: Yes

Review of Facilities: The Washington State Archives- Northwest Regional Branch is located at the edge of the Western Washington University campus. The building has a secure entrance, lockers for personal belongings, and is a professionally maintained facility. This institution also shares space with the Center for Pacific Northwest Studies (see separate entry). The research room is large with numerous tables, several microfilm readers, and computer terminals for researchers' use. A staff area overlooks the research room. Collection storage is in attached staff-only, climate-controlled storage rooms.

Vertical Files: No

Manuscripts: Yes   **Manuscripts Volume in Cubic Feet:** 25,000

  Manuscript Types: Government records

  Manuscript Subjects: County records, municipal records, special district records. Northwest Washington and the counties of Clallam, Island, Jefferson, San Juan, Skagit, Snohomish, and Whatcom. Spans the early territorial period to present.

Photographs: Yes   **Number of Photographs:** 4,000

  Storage of Photographs: Photographs are interfiled with the agency manuscript and record collections.

  Photograph Reproductions Are Available: Yes

    Photographic Prints: Yes   **Digital Prints:** Yes

    Digital Images on CD or Electronically: Yes

Books: Yes   **Number of Books in Collection:** 2,000

Description of Books: Local and regional history, city directories

Newspapers: No

Oral Histories: No

Maps and Drawings: Yes   **Estimated Number of Maps and Drawings:** 1,000

Description of Maps and Drawings: Variety of types of maps dealing with the region

Genealogy Sources: Yes

Genealogy Sources Description: Birth and death records of Northwest region, territorial court records; working on making online index

Special Collections: No

Indexes: Gencat (online catalog), collections abstract in paper form

Manuscript Finding Aids: On a computerized system, box level for some collections

Online Sources: Online Historical Records Search. Available from http://www.secstate.wa.gov/history/search.aspx for access to selected census, naturalization, birth, marriage, death, prison and other miscellaneous records. For Washington history, see http://www.secstate.wa.gov/history.

Review of Collections: Collections include records from counties, municipalities, and special districts within the region. There are seven counties—Clallam, Island, Jefferson, San Juan, Skagit, Snohomish, and Whatcom—whose records are stored and maintained at this facility. Records of note include birth and death records (1891–1907), marriage records, court records including naturalization records, land records, and educational records. All records are public.

Museum on Premises: No

Parking: There is a permit-required lot; the permits are available at the desk inside. There is handicapped access on the side.

Lunch: Driving distance to a variety of restaurants

Lodging: http://www.bellingham.org

Nearest Commercial Airport: Bellingham International (BLI) [8 miles]

Subjects

Historical Periods: 1865–1900; 1900–1940; 1940–present

Natural Resources: Logging

Mining: Mining

Government: City; County; State

Date of Reviewer's Visit: 4/25/2003

Profile Updated by Institution: 12/1/2004

Name: Whatcom Museum of History and Art   **County:** Whatcom

Mailing Address: 121 Prospect St.

City: Bellingham   **State:** WA   **Postal Code:** 98225-0000

Street Address: 121 Prospect St.

Institution Email: museuminfo@cob.org

Telephone Number: (360) 676-6981   **Fax Number:** (360) 738-7409

Contact Name: Toni Nagel, Photo Archivist/Curator

Contact Email: tnagel@cob.org

Institution Type: Regional Museum

Affiliation: City of Bellingham

Web site URL: http://www.whatcommuseum.org/

Hours: W–F 1–4:45 by appt.

Staff in Archives: 2f

Archives Are Handicapped Accessible: Yes

Access Description: Handicapped entrance is available from the rear of the building. There are elevators to the research room.

Review of Facilities: The Whatcom Museum of History and Art is located in a four-building complex in downtown Bellingham. One of the buildings is a 1892 city hall building that is beautifully restored and a visible landmark of the area. The research facilities are located on the second floor of the Syre Education Building (old fire hall) which adjoins the old City Hall. Collections were relocated after the reviewer's visit to the Syre Building. The research room has several tables available for researchers. Collections are stored in adjoining staff-access-only rooms. The archives require that users store all personal items. Cotton gloves (provided) are required for handling all photographs and archival materials.

Vertical Files: Yes   **Vertical Files in Cubic Feet:** 20

   Vertical File Description and Subjects: Advertising bills, menus, church bulletins, theater playbills; all local area

Manuscripts: No

Photographs: Yes   **Number of Photographs:** 175,000

   Storage of Photographs: Photographs are stored in clamshell boxes

   Photograph Subjects: Mostly Whatcom, Skagit, San Juan, and Island Counties with some Alaska

   Photograph Reproductions Are Available: Yes

   Photographic Prints: Yes   **Digital Prints:** Yes

   Digital Images on CD or Electronically: Yes

Books: Yes   **Number of Books in Collection:** 1,000

  Description of Books: Pacific Northwest history, local history, ethnology, art, museology

Newspapers: No

Oral Histories: Yes   **Oral Histories Number:** 100

  Oral Histories Description: There are oral history interviews within the Darius Kinsey Photography Collection and the H. C. Hanson Naval Architecture Collection.

Maps and Drawings: Yes

  Description of Maps and Drawings: Local, Pacific Northwest

Genealogy Sources: No

Special Collections: Yes

  Special Collections Description: H. C. Hanson Naval Architecture Collection: 11,000 blueprints; 4,200 line drawings; 4,800 photographs; and 32 oral histories on the shipbuilding industry from 1918 to 1970

Indexes: PastPerfect database of images is searchable on computer in the research room. Over 75,000 images are available currently.

  Manuscript Finding Aids: Staff

  Published Guides: Subject guides to various collections

  Online Sources: Few images on Web site

Review of Collections: This collection is almost exclusively photographs, which allows the staff to concentrate on one particular format. The quality of the major photographers is evident in their work. The J. W. Sandison Photography Collection and the Darius Kinsey Photography Collection are only two of the major ones. This is a truly remarkable collection of photographs.

Museum on Premises: Yes

  Museum Hours: Tu–Su 12–5

  Cost of Entry to Museum: $2.50 for children's museum; otherwise free

  Museum Is Handicapped Accessible: Yes

  Description of Museum: Four-building complex featuring contemporary art, regional history, and a children's museum.

Parking: Free parking lot adjacent or metered on-street parking

Lunch: Several restaurants on the same block behind main museum building

Lodging: http://www.bellingham.org

Nearest Commercial Airport: Bellingham International (BLI) [5 miles]

Subjects

  Historical Periods: 1800–1865; 1865–1900; 1900–1940; 1940–present

Eras: World War I; World War II

Natural Resources: Dams; Fishing; Hunting; Whaling; Logging

Mining: Gold; Coal; Placer Mining; Tunnel Mining

Transportation: Railroads; Ships and Shipping; Ferries; Aviation

Agriculture: Dairy; Ranching/Livestock; Grains

Business: Banking; Retail; Legal/Medical Services; Hotels/Restaurants; Entertainment/Theaters

Manufacturing: Cannery; Brewery; Creamery; Boatbuilding/Shipyard; Sawmills; Wood Products

Government: City

Organizations: Schools; Colleges/Universities; Hospitals/Medical Facilities; Nonreligious Organizations; Civic and Fraternal; Women's

Ethnic Groups: Native American; Pacific Islander; Japanese; Chinese; Danish; Dutch; English; Finnish; German; Norwegian; Scottish; Swedish

Religious Sites and Organizations: Protestant; Catholic; LDS (Mormon)

Date of Reviewer's Visit: 4/25/2003

Profile Updated by Institution: 11/29/2004

BREMERTON

Name: Kitsap County Historical Society Museum Library   **County:** Kitsap

Mailing Address: PO Box 903

   City: Bremerton   **State:** WA   **Postal Code:** 98337-0000

Street Address: 280 4th St.

Institution Email: kchsm@telebyte.net

Telephone Number: (360) 479-6226   **Fax Number:** (360) 415-9294

Contact Name: Pamela Kruse-Buckingham

Institution Type: Local Museum

Web site URL: http://www.waynes.net/kchsm/

Hours: 9–5 by appt. only

Staff in Archives: 2f, 1p, 10v

Archives Are Handicapped Accessible: Yes

Access Description: Electric door

Cost for Researcher—Remote: Fee schedule

Review of Facilities: The Kitsap County Historical Society Museum is housed in a former bank building in the downtown Bremerton area, just down the street from city hall. The research room is located on the main floor and doubles as a conference room for museum functions. Along one wall are five large file cabinets that house the vertical file type of materials. Copies of photographs are also housed in this room. One wall has a small percentage of the book collection. A large well lit table is in the center of the room. The research area is large and very pleasant. The bulk of the collection is housed in the basement in modern compact shelving in a staff-only area.

Vertical Files: Yes   **Vertical Files in Cubic Feet:** 45

    Vertical File Description and Subjects: General subjects on Kitsap County history

Manuscripts: Yes   **Manuscripts Volume in Cubic Feet:** 180

    Manuscript Types: Records, scrapbooks, personal papers, business records

    Manuscript Subjects: Bremerton and Kitsap County subjects, land title records without index, Bremerton Housing Authority from World War II

Photographs: Yes   **Number of Photographs:** 30,000

    Storage of Photographs: Photographs have copies stored by photo number in Cardex files. There is a subject guide to the photos on the staff computer system. Originals of photographs are stored in clamshell boxes in Mylar sleeves

    Photograph Subjects: Bremerton and Kitsap County

    Photograph Reproductions Are Available: Yes

       Photographic Prints: Yes   **Digital Prints:** Yes

Books: Yes   **Number of Books in Collection:** 1,000

    Description of Books: Regional history, general history, city directories, yearbooks, old books, and professional collection

Newspapers: No

    Papers and Dates: Newspapers were transferred to University of Washington

Oral Histories: Yes   **Oral Histories Number:** 50

    Oral Histories Description: Interviews of local area residents from 1997 to present. Transcriptions for some.

Maps and Drawings: Yes

    Description of Maps and Drawings: Large collection of maps and large flat documents

Genealogy Sources: Yes

    Genealogy Sources Description: Obituary index on 4 x 6 cards

    Special Collections: No

Indexes: No

Review of Collections: The Kitsap County Museum has a well-stored collection of Bremerton and Kitsap County history. The historical society began collecting in 1948, which makes it older than many in the area. Access to the collection could be improved with finding aids and better indexing. Photo indexing and guides are available only by way of staff searching. The collection is limited in genealogy areas, with an obituary index, some cemetery records, and family histories. The strengths in the collection are in areas of Bremerton history, particularly of the World War II period and immediately after. The Bremerton Housing Authority records of segregated housing are of particular note.

Museum on Premises: Yes

Museum Hours: Tu–Sa 9–5

Cost of Entry to Museum: $2

Museum Is Handicapped Accessible: Yes

Description of Museum: This museum illustrates the history of Kitsap County. The galleries are on two floors and beautifully done. This is a professionally designed museum.

Parking: On-street parallel and diagonal parking free with 2-hr. limit; $5 per day parking garage nearby

Lunch: Numerous restaurants within a few blocks in the downtown area

Lodging: http://www.bremertonwa.com

Nearest Commercial Airport: Seattle-Tacoma International (SEA) [53 miles]

Subjects

Historical Periods: 1800–1865; 1865–1900; 1900–1940; 1940–present

Eras: Spanish American War; World War I; World War II

Natural Resources: Water; Dams; Fishing; Logging

Mining: Gold; Petroleum; Tin

Transportation: Railroads; Ships and Shipping; Ferries; Aviation

Agriculture: Dairy; Ranching/Livestock; Vegetable/Truck Crops; Grains; Orchards; Vineyard

Business: Retail; Legal/Medical Services; Hotels/Restaurants; Entertainment/ Theaters

Manufacturing: Brewery; Creamery; Brick Making; Sawmills; Wood Products

Government: City; County

Organizations: Schools; Colleges/Universities; Hospitals/Medical Facilities; Charities; Nonreligious Organizations; Civic and Fraternal; Women's; Business

Ethnic Groups: Native American; African; Japanese; Chinese; Finnish; German; Norwegian; Swedish

Religious Sites and Organizations: Protestant; Catholic; Muslim

Date of Reviewer's Visit: 1/13/2004

Profile Updated by Institution: 11/22/2004

Name: Naval Memorial Museum of the Pacific   **County:** Kitsap

Mailing Address: 402 Pacific Ave.

   City: Bremerton   **State:** WA   **Postal Code:** 98337-0000

Street Address: 402 Pacific Ave.

Institution Email: bremnavmuseum@aol.com

Telephone Number: (360) 479-7447

Contact Name: Charleen Zettl or Lyle L. Nelson

Institution Type: Local Museum

Web site URL: None

Hours: M–Sa 10–4, Su 1–4;

Staff in Archives: 3v

   Archives Are Handicapped Accessible: No

   Access Description: Archives is up a flight of stairs

Cost for Researcher—Remote: Donation

Review of Facilities: The Naval Memorial Museum of the Pacific is also known as the Bremerton Naval Museum. It is located in a downtown storefront on the corner of Fourth and Pacific. This is temporary housing, as they plan to move to a historic building nearby after renovations are completed. The museum is located on the main floor and basement. The library/archives is located on the second floor. The room is medium-sized and inadequately lit. A medium-sized square worktable is in the center of the room. A second worktable is nearby. The book collections are on shelves that cover two walls of the room. Rare books are in a locked case. Another wall of the room has a large number of framed photographs of all sizes. The photographic collections and vertical file materials are stored in an adjacent staff work area. Some manuscript materials are stored in a basement storage area. Overall, the facility is adequate for a temporary facility, but it is hoped with the new building a better equipped library/archives will follow as well.

Vertical Files: Yes   **Vertical Files in Cubic Feet:** 16

   Vertical File Description and Subjects: General information on naval ships, and history of the Puget Sound Naval Shipyard

Manuscripts: Yes   **Manuscripts Volume in Cubic Feet:** 10

   Manuscript Types: Organizational records, personal papers

   Manuscript Subjects: History of Bremerton and area

Photographs: Yes   **Number of Photographs:** 1,000

   Storage of Photographs: Photographs stored in plastic sleeves or files in file cabinets. Large collection of framed and oversize photographs.

Photograph Subjects: Individuals and ship photographs, naval stations

Photograph Reproductions Are Available: Yes

    Digital Prints: Yes

Books: Yes   **Number of Books in Collection:** 500

Description of Books: Naval nonfiction, ship annuals, technical manuals

Newspapers: No

Oral Histories: No

Maps and Drawings: Yes

    Description of Maps and Drawings: Maps of the surrounding area as well as the city of Bremerton, navigation maps

Genealogy Sources: No

Special Collections: No

Indexes: No

Review of Collections: The collections of the Naval Memorial Museum are not well indexed. The book collection are arranged by general subject. The photograph and vertical file collections are arranged by general subject. The collections deal with the Bremerton Naval Shipyard (est. 1893) and later the Puget Sound Naval Shipyard in Bremerton. The collection also focuses on the various ships that have come through the shipyards from the Spanish American War onward. This collection does not aim to keep track of individuals and their contributions, so it is not a genealogical resource.

Museum on Premises: Yes

    Museum Hours: M–Sa 10–4, Su 1–4

    Cost of Entry to Museum: Donation

    Museum Is Handicapped Accessible: Yes

    Description of Museum: The Naval Memorial Museum displays treasures from the Puget Sound Naval Shipyard and the navy's history. Displays focus on the ships that have visited the shipyard over the years.

Parking: On-street parallel and diagonal parking free with 2-hr. limit; $5-per-day parking garage nearby

Lunch: Several local restaurants within the block

Lodging: http://www.bremertonwa.com

Nearest Commercial Airport: Seattle-Tacoma International (SEA) [54 miles]

Subjects

    Historical Periods: 1865–1900; 1900–1940; 1940–present

    Eras: World War I; World War II

    Transportation: Ships and Shipping

Manufacturing: Boatbuilding/Shipyard

Government: City; Federal

Organizations: Schools; Colleges/Universities; Hospitals/Medical Facilities; Charities; Nonreligious Organizations; Civic and Fraternal; Women's; Business; Children's; Labor and Union

Ethnic Groups: Native American; Japanese; Norwegian; Swedish

Religious Sites and Organizations: Protestant; Catholic; LDS (Mormon); Jewish

Date of Reviewer's Visit: 1/13/2004

Profile Updated by Institution: 11/15/2004

CHEHALIS

✳✳✳

Name: Lewis County Historical Museum Library   **County:** Lewis

Mailing Address: 599 NW Front Way

   City: Chehalis   **State:** WA   **Postal Code:** 98532-0000

Street Address: 599 NW Front Way

Institution Email: lchm@lewiscountymuseum.org

Telephone Number: (360) 748-0831   **Fax Number:** (360) 740-5646

Contact Name: Gary Schmauder, Director

Institution Type: Local Museum

Web site URL: http://www.lewiscountymuseum.org/

Hours: Tu–Sa 9–5, Su 1–5

Staff in Archives: 2f, 3v

Archives Are Handicapped Accessible: Yes

Cost for Researcher—In-house: Museum entrance fee

Review of Facilities: The Lewis County Historical Museum is located in a Northern Pacific 1912 railroad depot on the edge of the Chehalis downtown area. The library is in a moderate-sized room in the middle of the building. Bookshelves line one wall and file cabinets hide two others. Large worktables take up the space in the center of the room. The library is well lit, high-ceilinged, and pleasant. An adjacent room contains numerous file cabinets housing the sizable photograph collections. Oral history interviews are also stored in this area, along with various indexes to the collection. The remainder of the collection is housed in a high-ceiling attic room, with a steep staircase, which is a staff-only area. The Lewis County Genealogical Society is also housed in this museum.

Vertical Files: Yes   **Vertical Files in Cubic Feet:** 66

Vertical File Description and Subjects: Biography, general subject areas, mostly newspaper clippings and ephemera

Manuscripts: Yes   **Manuscripts Volume in Cubic Feet:** 120

Manuscript Types: Organizational records, government records, scrapbooks, family papers

Manuscript Subjects: Chehalis and Lewis County records (and some court records) 1880s–1920s, various church and civic organizations, school records, local families

Photographs: Yes   **Number of Photographs:** 20,000

Storage of Photographs: Photographs are stored in folders in file cabinets by accession number. There is both a shelf list and subject card files to access the photos, as well as a detailed description file.

Photograph Subjects: Photographs focus on Lewis County and local communities. Also included is a large number of oversize photographs.

Photograph Reproductions Are Available: Yes

Photographic Prints: Yes   **Digital Prints:** Yes

Books: Yes   **Number of Books in Collection:** 200

Description of Books: Local history, city directories, professional collection

Newspapers: Yes   **Newspapers in Paper Format:** Yes

Papers and Dates: *Chehalis Bee,* 1884–1964; *People's Advocate, Centralia News-Examiner, Centralia Chronicle, Toledo Messenger,* all of various dates, most prior to 1920

Newspapers on Microfilm: No

Microfilm and Dates: Microfilm available at the Washington State Library

Oral Histories: Yes   **Oral Histories Number:** 400

Oral Histories Description: Local resident interviews, majority from 1970s to 1980s. Transcriptions available for some.

Maps and Drawings: Yes

Description of Maps and Drawings: Various maps of Lewis County, town plat maps, military road maps, Sanborn maps, school district and railroad section maps

Genealogy Sources: Yes

Genealogy Sources Description: Large number of indexes for the aid of genealogists. Obituary files on 5 x 8 cards with the newest information on computerized database. Other sources include clipping file notebooks of births, birthdays, wedding anniversaries, and family reunions.

Special Collections: No

Indexes: Subject card files of photographs, Card and computer index to obituaries. Variety of subject indexes to the local newspapers.

Manuscript Finding Aids: Lists of manuscript collections

Review of Collections: Lewis County Historical Society is blessed with two dedicated volunteers of 25-plus years' tenure, who have been responsible for collecting and maintaining the information in the research collection. They have compiled a number of files to aid the researcher in finding information on specific topics. Many of these sources are of a genealogical nature but are useful for the historical researcher as well. Clipping indexes including obituary files, birth records, birthdays, wedding anniversaries, and articles on family and communities by subject. These are only a few of the various subject notebooks kept by these volunteers. There are abstracts of newspapers prior to 1900. Cemetery records from most of the county and some neighboring areas are also available. Early Lewis County records are compiled in notebooks in the library. Manuscript materials, though not as well described, provide a broad variety of subjects throughout the history of Lewis County. The collection has early city and county records, business and organizational records, family and personal papers, some school records, church and civic club papers, scrapbooks and other records.

Museum on Premises: Yes

Museum Hours: Tu–Sa 9–5 and Su 1–5

Cost of Entry to Museum: $2

Museum Is Handicapped Accessible: Yes

Description of Museum: The museum is housed in a restored 1912 brick railroad depot. They offer four galleries of exhibits that focus on the early days and settlement of Lewis County. The museum has a combination of room vignettes and changeable exhibit spaces.

Parking: Free parking lot adjacent to building

Lunch: Variety of local restaurants one block away in the downtown area

Lodging: http://www.tourlewiscounty.com

Nearest Commercial Airport: Portland International (PDX) [87 miles]

Subjects

Historical Periods: 1800–1865; 1865–1900; 1900–1940; 1940–present

Eras: Fur Trade; Civil War; Indian Wars; Spanish American War; World War I; WPA; CCC; World War II; Vietnam War

Natural Resources: Water; Dams; Fishing; Hunting; Logging

Mining: Gold; Silver; Copper; Coal; Surface Mining; Tunnel Mining

Transportation: Railroads; Stagecoach/Freight; Ferries; Aviation

Agriculture: Dairy; Ranching/Livestock; Vegetable/Truck Crops; Grains; Orchards

Business: Banking; Retail; Legal/Medical Services; Hotels/Restaurants; Entertainment/Theaters

Manufacturing: Cannery; Grist/Flour Mills; Creamery; Woolen/Fabric Mills; Brick Making; Sawmills; Wood Products

Government: City; County

Organizations: Schools; Hospitals/Medical Facilities; Charities; Nonreligious Organizations; Civic and Fraternal; Women's; Business; Children's; Labor and Union

Ethnic Groups: Native American; Japanese; English; Finnish; German; Irish; Norwegian; Swedish

Religious Sites and Organizations: Protestant; Catholic; LDS (Mormon); Jewish

Date of Reviewer's Visit: 1/15/2004

Profile Updated by Institution: 11/15/2004

CHELAN

Name: Lake Chelan Historical Society   **County:** Chelan

Mailing Address: PO Box 1948

   City: Chelan   **State:** WA   **Postal Code:** 98816-0000

Street Address: 204 E Woodin Ave.

Institution Email: museum@chelanmuseum.com

Telephone Number: (509) 682-5644

Contact Name: Linda Martinson, Director

Contact Email: museum@chelanmuseum.com

Institution Type: Local Museum

Web site URL: http://www.chelanvalley.com/history/

Hours: M–Sa 10–4 by appt. only

Staff in Archives: 1p, 10v

Archives Are Handicapped Accessible: No

Access Description: Stairs to museum

Cost for Researcher—In-house: Admission

Cost for Researcher—Remote: Fee schedule

Review of Facilities: The Lake Chelan Historical Society Museum is located in downtown Chelan in a former bank building. The museum has divided their research collections into two parts. A moderate-sized table is located at the front of the museum, with a bookcase holding copies of some research materials that are available during all the museum's open hours. The open research materials include dozens of binders that have photocopies of articles, documents, and photographs arranged by subjects or family names. There are also copies of materials compiled and collected by the local genealogical society. The majority of original materials are stored in the vault and are available only with a research appointment. These materials include the photographs, scrapbooks, and manuscript-type materials.

Vertical Files: Yes   **Vertical Files in Cubic Feet:** 12

 Vertical File Description and Subjects: Vertical file materials are divided into family and general subject files

Manuscripts: Yes   **Manuscripts Volume in Cubic Feet:** 55

 Manuscript Types: Business records, land records, organizational records, scrapbooks

 Manuscript Subjects: Women's clubs, store ledgers

Photographs: Yes   **Number of Photographs:** 1,500

 Storage of Photographs: Photographs are stored in binders by general subject

 Photograph Subjects: Lake Chelan and area history

 Photograph Reproductions Are Available: Yes

  Photographic Prints: Yes   **Digital Prints:** Yes

Books: Yes   **Number of Books in Collection:**

 Description of Books: Local history and annuals

Newspapers: No

 Microfilm and Dates: Microfilm of local papers available at Chelan Community Library

Oral Histories: Yes

 Oral Histories Description: Audiotaped interviews of local residents and collection of video tapes of family histories are both available.

Maps and Drawings: Yes   **Estimated Number of Maps and Drawings:** 80

 Description of Maps and Drawings: Original plats of town, Metskers and miscellaneous maps

Genealogy Sources: Yes

 Genealogy Sources Description: Obituary files in binders, Index to Marriage Records

Special Collections: No

Indexes: No

Review of Collections: The Lake Chelan Historical Society is interesting, with more buried gems than would first appear. As at many institutions, staff has not been able to spend as much time on the research collections as they would like. They do have plans for additional processing, indexing, and so forth to get a better handle on the collections. There may be some interesting retail business records in their intriguing pile of ledgers. Otherwise the collection is rather standard for institutions of this size. In addition to the vertical file materials, photographs, and manuscripts, they also have 48 binders of family names with clippings and photos of each family group.

Museum on Premises: Yes

    Museum Hours: M–Sa 10–, June 1–Oct 1

    Cost of Entry to Museum: $2

    Museum Is Handicapped Accessible: No

    Description of Museum: Two-story local museum features the history of the Chelan area back to earliest settlement

Parking: On-street free diagonal parking (some areas are 2 hrs. only)

Lunch: Variety of local cafes and restaurants in adjoining blocks

Lodging: http://www.lakechelan.com

Nearest Commercial Airport: Pangborn Memorial (East Wenatchee) (EAT) [44 miles]

Subjects

    Historical Periods: 1900–1940; 1940–present

    Natural Resources: Dams; Irrigation; Hunting; Logging

    Mining: Gold; Silver; Copper

    Transportation: Stagecoach/Freight; Ferries

    Agriculture: Dry Land Farming

    Business: Banking; Hotels/Restaurants; Entertainment/Theaters

    Manufacturing: Brewery; Grist/Flour Mills; Boatbuilding/Shipyard; Sawmills

    Government: City

    Organizations: Schools

    Ethnic Groups: Native American

    Religious Sites and Organizations: Protestant; Catholic

Date of Reviewer's Visit: 6/30/2004

Profile Updated by Institution: 11/9/2004

CHENEY

Name: Eastern Washington University   **County:** Spokane

Mailing Address: John F. Kennedy Memorial Library, 816 F St., MS-84

City: Cheney   **State:** WA   **Postal Code:** 99004-2453

Street Address: 816 F St.

Institution Email: None

Telephone Number: (509) 359-2254   **Fax Number:** (509) 359-4840

Contact Name: Charles V. Mutschler   **Contact Email:** cmutschler@ewu.edu

Institution Type: Academic Library

Web site URL: http://www.library.ewu.edu

Hours: 8–5 M–F

Staff in Archives: 2f

Archives Are Handicapped Accessible: Yes

Review of Facilities: The John F. Kennedy Library at Eastern Washington University is located in the center of the campus on the quad. Archives and Special Collections are located on the lower level of the Kennedy Library in the southwest corner. The reading room is beautifully furnished with light wood tables and bookcases. Two large conference tables and four study carrels are in the center of the room and bookcases surround the perimeter. A door connects to the staff work area, where the manuscript research room is located. The research room is smaller, with a desk and a row of carrels. This area has limited access and allows pencils and paper only. The bulk of the collections is stored in a staff-access-only room adjacent to the staff work area.

Vertical Files: Yes   **Vertical Files in Cubic Feet:** 110

Vertical File Description and Subjects: The Deutsch Northwest Clipping and Pamphlet files of Pacific Northwest history consists of 100 boxes of clippings with finding guide; 10 boxes miscellaneous Eastern Washington University history files.

Manuscripts: Yes   **Manuscripts Volume in Cubic Feet:** 2,031

Manuscript Types: Business records, personal papers

Manuscript Subjects: Eastern Washington University archives, some listed on catalog; research materials and papers of professors

Photographs: Yes   **Number of Photographs:** 1,200

Storage of Photographs: Photographs are stored in file folders and arranged by subject

Photograph Subjects: Cheney, Eastern Washington University, aerial views

Photograph Reproductions Are Available: Yes

Photographic Prints: Yes   **Digital Prints:** Yes

Books: Yes

Description of Books: Local and regional history, science fiction collection, regional city directories

Newspapers: Yes

Newspapers in Paper Format: Yes

Papers and Dates: *Easterner, Focus, Cheney Free Press,* Cheney papers. Listings are available on the library catalog.

Newspapers on Microfilm: Yes

Microfilm and Dates: Microfilm of Cheney papers stored in periodicals elsewhere in building

Oral Histories: Yes   **Oral Histories Number:** 160

Oral Histories Description: Women's history, military history, pioneer life, university history

Maps and Drawings: Yes   **Estimated Number of Maps and Drawings:** 500

Description of Maps and Drawings: Topographical maps, geological maps, some county atlas sheets

Genealogy Sources: No

Special Collections: No

Indexes: Archival holdings are listed in the electronic catalog called Griffin.

Manuscript Finding Aids: Finding aids are available in the staff area.

Review of Collections: The archives and special collections at Eastern Washington University have several separate functions. The University Archives consists of the inactive records and history of the institution. The Special Collections includes the books and periodicals of the history and government of the Pacific Northwest. Archival collections also include personal papers and business records of significance to the region. Photographs represent the greater inland Northwest, people, events and scenes.

Museum on Premises: No

Parking: On-street metered parking or parking pass can be obtained at Parking Services

Lunch: Student Union has a cafeteria and some cafes

Lodging: http://www.visitspokane.com

Nearest Commercial Airport: Spokane International (GEG) [12 miles]

Subjects

    Historical Periods: 1800–1865; 1865–1900; 1900–1940; 1940–present

    Eras: World War I; World War II

    Natural Resources: Logging

    Mining: Gold; Silver; Surface Mining; Tunnel Mining

    Transportation: Railroads

    Agriculture: Grains; Dry Land Farming

Business: Banking; Retail

Government: City

Organizations: Schools; Colleges/Universities; Nonreligious Organizations; Civic and Fraternal; Women's

Ethnic Groups: Native American; African

Religious Sites and Organizations: Protestant

Date of Reviewer's Visit: 8/18/2004

Profile Updated by Institution: 12/7/2004

✹✹✹✹✹

Name: Washington State Archives, Eastern Regional Branch   **County:** Spokane

Mailing Address: 960 Washington St.

City: Cheney   **State:** WA   **Postal Code:** 99004-0000

Street Address: 960 Washington St.

Institution Email: era@mail.ewu.edu

Telephone Number: (509) 235-7508   **Fax Number:** (509) 235–7505

Contact Name: Sherry Bays

Institution Type: Archives

Affiliation: State of Washington

Web site URL: http://www.secstate.wa.gov/archives/archives_eastern.aspx

Hours: M–F 8–4:30 (excluding holidays)

Staff in Archives: 3f

Archives Are Handicapped Accessible: Yes

Review of Facilities: The Washington State Archives Eastern Regional Branch is located in a new building (2004) on the outskirts of the Eastern Washington University (EWU) campus. The Eastern Regional Branch covers the 11 counties in eastern Washington. The lobby leading to the research room has lockers for personal items. Keys are available from staff. Only research notes, paper, pencils, and laptops are allowed in the research area. The research room is large, with seven research tables, three microfilm reader/printers, and a long-term project room. "Washington Reports," "War of the Rebellions," and other local regional historical books and publications are available and accessible in the research room. City directories are open-access items in the room. A staff desk with a workroom behind overlooks the reference room. Collections are stored in adjacent, climate-controlled storage rooms. This institution shares a building with the Washington State Digital Archives (see separate entry).

Vertical Files: No

Manuscripts: Yes   **Manuscripts Volume in Cubic Feet:** 6,400

Manuscript Types: Government records

Manuscript Subjects: County records, municipal records, records of special districts of Eastern Washington and the counties of Adams, Asotin, Columbia, Ferry, Garfield, Lincoln, Pend Oreille, Spokane, Stevens, Walla Walla, and Whitman. Spans the early territorial period to the present.

Photographs: Yes   **Number of Photographs:** 10,000

Storage of Photographs: Photographs are interfiled with the agency manuscript and record collections.

Photograph Reproductions Are Available: Yes

   Photographic Prints: Yes   **Digital Prints:** Yes

   Digital Images on CD or Electronically: Yes

Books: Yes   **Number of Books in Collection:** 300

Description of Books: City directories, local history

Newspapers: No

Oral Histories: Yes

Oral Histories Description: Printed copies of oral histories done by State Archives Oral History Program

Maps and Drawings: Yes

Description of Maps and Drawings: Maps are stored with agency records.

Genealogy Sources: Yes

Genealogy Sources Description: Birth, death, cemetery, and marriage records

Special Collections: No

Indexes: Yes

Manuscript Finding Aids: Record series to item level, finding aids in paper and electronic

Published Guides: State Archives Published Guides and *Fronting Justice: Guide to Court Records of Washington Territory 1853–1889*

Online Sources: A guide to the collections held at the Eastern Regional Branch is available at http://www.ewu.edu/era Online Historical Records Search. Available from http://www.secstate.wa.gov/history/search.aspx for access to selected census, naturalization, birth, marriage, death, prison and other miscellaneous records. For Washington history, see http://www.secstate.wa.gov/history.

Review of Collections: Collections include records from county and municipal agencies in the counties of Adams, Asotin, Columbia, Ferry, Garfield, Lincoln, Pend Oreille, Spokane, Stevens, Walla Walla, and Whitman, and also special taxing districts such as fire, schools, or transportation. Collection covers from territorial period to present. Included are school census, tax assessment, court dockets and case files, photographs, maps, plats and engineering drawings. All records are public.

Museum on Premises: No

Parking: Free parking lot adjacent, limited spots, some metered parking on the street or obtain a parking pass from EWU parking authorities

Lunch: Driving distance to a variety of restaurants, moderate hike to student union cafeteria

Lodging: http://www.visitspokane.com

Nearest Commercial Airport: Spokane International (GEG) [12 miles]

Subjects

    Historical Periods: 1800–1865; 1865–1900; 1900–1940; 1940–present

    Eras: World War I

    Natural Resources: Water; Irrigation

    Mining: Mining

    Agriculture: Ranching/Livestock; Dry Land Farming

    Government: City; County; State

    Organizations: Schools; Colleges/Universities

Date of Reviewer's Visit: 8/18/2004

Profile Updated by Institution: 11/10/2004

✳✳✳✳✳

Name: Washington State Digital Archives   **County:** Spokane

Mailing Address: 960 Washington St.

  City: Cheney   **State:** WA   **Postal Code:** 99004-0000

Street Address: 960 Washington St.

Institution Email: digitalarchives@secstate.wa.gov

Telephone Number: (509) 235-7509   **Fax Number:** (509) 235-7504

Contact Name: Adam Jansen   **Contact Email:** Ajansen@secstate.wa.gov

Institution Type: Archives

Affiliation: State of Washington

Web site URL: http://www.digitalarchives.wa.gov/

Hours: M–F 8–4:30 (online research available 24/7)

Staff in Archives: 3f

Archives Are Handicapped Accessible: Yes

Cost for Researcher—In-house: No charge

Cost for Researcher—Remote: After 15 mins., $30 per hr.

Review of Facilities: The Washington State Digital Archives is housed in a new building (2004) on the edge of the Eastern Washington University (EWU) campus. The Washington State Archives–Eastern Regional Branch is on the first floor of the building. The Digital Archives are on the second floor. Although this is a digital archives, they also have a reading room with high-speed computers to access the collections. The room is spacious and pleasant, with large tables holding multiple computer stations. The lobby leading to the research room has lockers for personal items. Keys are available from staff. The computers in the research room utilize the same Web interface available from home.

Vertical Files: No

Manuscripts: Yes

  Manuscript Types: Government records, legal records

  Manuscript Subjects: Vital records from throughout the state of Washington are being digitized and made available online.

Photographs: Yes (online only)

  Photograph Reproductions Are Available: Yes

  Photographic Prints: Yes   **Digital Prints:** Yes

  Digital Images on CD or Electronically: Yes

Books: No

Newspapers: No

Oral Histories: No

Maps and Drawings: No

Genealogy Sources: Yes

  Genealogy Sources Description: Census records, naturalization records, military records, death records, birth records, and marriage records are available for selected counties. Lists of what is available is online and being regularly supplemented.

Special Collections: No

Indexes: There is a search engine on the Web site to search the various records by type and subject.

  Online Sources: Everything at the Washington State Digital Archives is available online.

Review of Collections: The digital archives consists of territorial, early state records, vital and legal records, census records from 1847 through 1892, and various other state and governmental records. Naturalization records are available depending on the county from 1854 to 1988. Institution records contain a listing of inmates serving time at Seatco Prison from 1877–1888 and Walla Walla State Penitentiary from 1887–1914. Military records cover Washington citizens who served in the armed forces. Also available is a listing of residents at several veterans' and soldiers' homes from the 1890s to 1970s. Death records contain listings from cemeteries, death indexes, and burial permits. Birth records are available for certain counties before 1914. Marriage records provide indexing and some images of records from as early as 1900 to the late twentieth century for limited counties. Miscellaneous historical records are collections of records not falling into other categories; currently there are Oaths of Office with the names of nearly 16,000 elected officials who took an oath of office between 1854 and 1978 and a listing of physicians who practiced in Washington State between 1872 through 1938.

Museum on Premises: No

Parking: Free parking lot adjacent, limited spots, some metered parking on the street or obtain a parking pass from EWU parking authorities

Lunch: Driving distance to a variety of restaurants, moderate hike to student union cafeteria

Lodging: http://www.visitspokane.com

Nearest Commercial Airport: Spokane International (GEG) [12 miles]

Subjects

    Historical Periods: 1865–1900; 1900–1940; 1940–present

    Eras: Spanish American War; World War I

    Business: Legal/Medical Services

    Government: City; County; State

    Organizations: Hospitals/Medical Facilities

Date of Reviewer's Visit: 8/18/2004

Profile Updated by Institution: 11/2004

COLVILLE

Name: Keller Heritage Center   **County:** Stevens

Mailing Address: PO Box 25

    City: Colville   **State:** WA   **Postal Code:** 99114-0025

Street Address: 700 N. Wynne St.

Institution Email: museum@plix.com

Telephone Number: (509) 684-5968

Contact Name: Judy Smith

Institution Type: Local Museum

Affiliation: Stevens County Historical Society

Web site URL: http://stevenscountyhistoricalsociety.org

Hours: M–Sa 2–5, Su 1–4

Staff in Archives: 10v

Archives Are Handicapped Accessible: Yes

Access Description: Ramp to enter building with handicap space on left side of building. Large doorsill.

Cost for Researcher—In-house: $5 per hr.

Cost for Researcher—Remote: Fee schedule

List of Researchers Available: Yes

Review of Facilities: The Keller Heritage Center of the Stevens County Historical Society is located on a hillside overlooking town. The museum grounds include the main museum and the Keller House. The research area is located in the main part of the museum. During open research hours there is a side door that opens directly into the room. Otherwise the entry is through the main museum. The research library is housed in one room. Two long tables and two desks are pushed together in the center of the room to provide workspace for researchers and volunteers. The large room is surrounded on two sides by bookcases and two walls with file cabinets, computer station, and staff office entrance. Some materials are stored in an adjoining walk-in closet and in an archival area.

Vertical Files: Yes   **Vertical Files in Cubic Feet:** 14

  Vertical File Description and Subjects: General miscellaneous files divided into people, town, and general subject files

Manuscripts: Yes   **Manuscripts Volume in Cubic Feet:** 30

  Manuscript Types: Scrapbooks, land records

  Manuscript Subjects: Family history scrapbooks, Planning Commission Inventory of Historic Sites

Photographs: Yes   **Number of Photographs:** 2,000

  Storage of Photographs: Photographs are housed in file cabinets and being transferred to archival plastic sleeves. The photos are arranged into location or people files.

  Photograph Subjects: Stevens County scenes and people

  Photograph Reproductions Are Available: Yes

    Photographic Prints: Yes   **Digital Prints:** Yes

Books: Yes   **Number of Books in Collection:** 150

  Description of Books: Local history, family history, professional collection, annuals from Colville and Kettle Falls

Newspapers: Yes   **Newspapers in Paper Format:** Yes

Papers and Dates: Colville and Stevens County newspapers, incomplete, 1893–present

Oral Histories: Yes   **Oral Histories Number:** 65

Oral Histories Description: Interviews of local area pioneers. Most have transcriptions, which are filed in the vertical file people files. Local people over 80 years of age interviewed in 1980–82. Dunning collection of 92 pioneer biographical sketches ca. 1920.

Maps and Drawings: Yes   **Estimated Number of Maps and Drawings:** 200

Description of Maps and Drawings: Maps and plat maps of area. Some old Hudson's Bay-Fort Colville maps from as early as 1857.

Genealogy Sources: Yes

Genealogy Sources Description: Obituary records from 1909 to present. Cemetery records, county birth and death records. Compiled indexes to histories of local area; census records; military records.

Special Collections: No

Indexes: Computer database of indexes. Index to the miscellaneous records of the historical society. Variety of compiled indexes of various subjects.

Review of Collections: The research collections of the Stevens County Historical Society are in the process of being organized. The research room contains an unusually large number of compiled indexes and without the use of the computer, it is hard to understand what the collection contains. Volunteers are available by appointment and are needed to access the materials as they are currently organized. The collections are all housed in one room, including manuscript materials, out-of-print books, legal records of various types, histories of the area, and scrapbooks. The volunteers are pleasant and helpful in the areas with which they are familiar. For locating history of the area or finding information about local people, this collection is very helpful. Attempting to research anything with a broader interest may not be worth the effort.

Museum on Premises: Yes

Museum Hours: May, Sept, 1–4 daily; June–Aug 11–5 daily

Cost of Entry to Museum: $3

Museum Is Handicapped Accessible: Yes

Description of Museum: Local history museum with area vignettes of history and historic Keller House (not reviewed)

Parking: Gravel parking lot in front of building. Some parallel and some vertical parking.

Lunch: Variety of local and chain restaurants within driving distance

Lodging: http://www.colville.com/

Nearest Commercial Airport: Spokane International (GEG) [79 miles]

Subjects

Historical Periods: 1800–1865; 1865–1900; 1900–1940; 1940–present

Eras: Fur Trade; Indian Wars; World War I; CCC; World War II

Natural Resources: Water; Dams; Irrigation; Fishing; Logging

Mining: Gold; Silver; Copper; Placer Mining; Surface Mining; Tunnel Mining

Transportation: Railroads; Stagecoach/Freight

Agriculture: Dairy; Ranching/Livestock; Grains; Orchards; Dry Land Farming

Business: Retail; Legal/Medical Services; Hotels/Restaurants; Entertainment/Theaters

Manufacturing: Grist/Flour Mills; Brick Making; Boatbuilding/Shipyard; Sawmills

Government: City; County; State

Organizations: Schools; Colleges/Universities; Hospitals/Medical Facilities; Civic and Fraternal; Women's; Business; Labor and Union

Ethnic Groups: Native American; Latin American; Chinese; Dutch; English; Finnish; German; Irish; Italian; Norwegian; Russian; Scottish; Swedish

Religious Sites and Organizations: Protestant; Catholic; LDS (Mormon); Mennonite/Amish

Date of Reviewer's Visit: 7/1/2004

Profile Updated by Institution: 11/16/2004

COUPEVILLE

Name: Island County Historical Society and Museum   **County:** Island

Mailing Address: PO Box 305

   City: Coupeville   **State:** WA   **Postal Code:** 98239-0000

Street Address: 908 NW Alexander St.

Institution Email: ichscpvl@whidbey.net

Telephone Number: (360) 678-3310   **Fax Number:** (360) 678-1702

Contact Name: Janet Enzmann

Institution Type: Local Museum

Web site URL: http://www.islandhistory.org/index.htm

Hours: F 10–4, appt. by arrangement

Staff in Archives: 1f, 1p, 6v

Archives Are Handicapped Accessible: Yes

Cost for Researcher—In-house: Free or fee schedule for prolonged research assistance

Cost for Researcher—Remote: Fee schedule

Review of Facilities: The Island County Historical Society and Museum is located at the edge of the historic downtown of Coupeville near the water. A research library and archives are located on the second floor of the museum. Archival storage is in a climate-controlled room. Plans are underway to add a larger archival storage area to accommodate current and future growth. Because of a mix-up at the time of visit, the interior of the building was not seen by the reviewer.

Vertical Files: Yes   **Vertical Files in Cubic Feet:** 12

  Vertical File Description and Subjects: Coupeville history, Island County history

Manuscripts: Yes

  Manuscript Types: Business records, personal papers, organizational records, scrapbooks, diaries

  Manuscript Subjects: Local history of Whidbey Island and Island County, Methodist church, newspaper editor Wally Funk

Photographs: Yes   **Number of Photographs:** 5,000

  Photograph Reproductions Are Available: Yes

    Digital Prints: Yes

    Digital Images on CD or Electronically: Yes

Books: Yes   **Number of Books in Collection:** 350

  Description of Books: Local history, exploration of Northwest, Native Americans of the Puget Sound area, city directories

Newspapers: No

Oral Histories: Yes

  Oral Histories Description: Oral history project in process

Maps and Drawings: Yes   **Estimated Number of Maps and Drawings:** 50

  Description of Maps and Drawings: Local area maps and architectural drawings

Genealogy Sources: Yes

  Genealogy Sources Description: Extensive obituary collection, cemetery records

Special Collections: Yes

Special Collections Description: Methodist Church, newspaper editor Wally Funk

Indexes: No

Review of Collections: The research library and archives collect and maintain a wide variety of manuscripts and documents types from throughout Island County from the earliest times to the present. The materials include personal papers, organizational records, business records, oral histories, scrapbooks, maps, and architectural drawings. The photograph collection is sizable, with a variety of subjects represented. There are also holdings of audio- and videotapes and electronic records. Artwork, ephemera, and miscellaneous materials round out the collection.

Museum on Premises: Yes

    Museum Hours: F, Sa, Su, and M 10–4, Oct.–Apr; daily except Tu 10–5, May–Sept

    Cost of Entry to Museum: $3

    Museum Is Handicapped Accessible: Yes

    Description of Museum: Small local history museum was not visited

Parking: Free diagonal on-street parking and parking lot nearby

Lunch: Several local cafes in historic waterfront district within blocks

Lodging: http://www.whidbey.net/visitor/visitors.html; http://www.centralwhidbeychamber.com; Coupeville Inn adjacent, numerous B&B's

Nearest Commercial Airport: Seattle-Tacoma International (SEA) [117 miles]

Subjects

    Historical Periods: 1800–1865; 1865–1900; 1900–1940; 1940–present

    Eras: Indian Wars; CCC; World War II

    Natural Resources: Logging

    Transportation: Ships and Shipping; Ferries

    Agriculture: Vegetable/Truck Crops; Grains; Orchards; Dry Land Farming

    Business: Retail

    Manufacturing: Sawmills

    Government: County; State

    Organizations: Schools; Hospitals/Medical Facilities; Civic and Fraternal; Women's

    Ethnic Groups: Native American; Chinese; Dutch; Finnish

    Religious Sites and Organizations: Protestant; Catholic

Date of Reviewer's Visit: 4/24/2003

Profile Updated by Institution: 11/15/2004

DAVENPORT

Name: Lake Roosevelt National Recreation Area/Fort Spokane   **County:** Lincoln

Mailing Address: 44303 State Rt. 25 N.

City: Davenport   **State:** WA   **Postal Code:** 99122-0000

Street Address: 44303 State Rt. 25 N.

Institution Email: None

Telephone Number: (509) 633-3836   **Fax Number:** (509) 633-3834

Contact Name: Lynne Brougher   **Contact Email:** lynne_brougher@nps.gov

Institution Type: Historic Site

Affiliation: National Park Service

Web site URL: http://www.nps.gov/laro/

Hours: M–F 8–4 by appt. only

Staff in Archives: 1f

Archives Are Handicapped Accessible: No

Access Description: Archives up flight of stairs. Materials could be brought down to main floor conference room by arrangement.

Review of Facilities: The archive collection of the Lake Roosevelt National Recreation Area is housed in the administrative offices on the Fort Spokane historic site. Although the mailing address is Davenport, it is located nearly 25 miles north. The offices are to the back of the tan metal building. The archives are housed on the second floor accessible by an open staircase from the garage area. There is a small anteroom where researchers can view materials. There is a small desk for research space. This area leads to the large staff-only attic storage room (low ceiling, climate controlled) and unlike most facilities, it is not yet near capacity. Additional table space may be available in the main floor conference room. The facility is open by prearrangement only since the archivists' regular office is in another town 1 1/2 hours away.

Vertical Files: No

Manuscripts: Yes   **Manuscripts Volume in Cubic Feet:** 56

Manuscript Types: Archives, organizational records

Manuscript Subjects: Administrative records of Lake Roosevelt National Recreation Area, historic records of Fort Spokane (about 3 cu. ft.) and Indian Boarding School (1 ft.)

Photographs: Yes   **Number of Photographs:** 3,000

Storage of Photographs: Photographs are stored in acid-free folders in a fireproof safe. Photographs are arranged by subject.

Photograph Subjects: Lake Roosevelt and adjacent areas, mostly pre 1960s, Fort Spokane, Indian Boarding School (Ft. Spokane site), Kettle Falls

Photograph Reproductions Are Available: Yes

Photographic Prints: Yes   **Digital Prints:** Yes

Digital Images on CD or Electronically: Yes

Books: No

Newspapers: Yes

Newspapers on Microfilm: Yes

Microfilm and Dates: *Daily Record* from fort on two reels of microfilm

Oral Histories: Yes

Oral Histories Number: 10

Oral Histories Description: Recollections of Fort Spokane from the period of Indian Boarding School. Taken in 1960s. Transcriptions available.

Maps and Drawings: Yes   **Estimated Number of Maps and Drawings:** 200

Description of Maps and Drawings: Maps and architectural drawings of Lake Roosevelt area. Recent and historic.

Genealogy Sources: No

Special Collections: Yes

Special Collections Description: Films and historical footage of Kettle Falls area

Indexes: Yes

Online Sources: An online tour of the military life at Fort Spokane with historic photographs is available with plans for additional slideshows—see http://www.nps.gov/laro/webdirectory/fortspokane.html

Review of Collections: The archives of the Roosevelt recreation area are limited by the fact that they have only been collecting since 2000. Despite the newness of the collection, they are making impressive progress. The photographs are the most significant part of the collection, but there are other areas of interest on several topics. Although there is little original material from Fort Spokane and the Indian Boarding School, and still less on the tuberculosis facility that followed, the materials are significant to the history of the site, and they are adding materials, as available. Other subjects include the Kettle Falls region and areas now encompassing the Lake Roosevelt National Recreation Area.

Museum on Premises: Yes

Museum Hours: W–Su, mid-June to Labor Day, 12–6

Museum Is Handicapped Accessible: No

Description of Museum: Fort Spokane Historic Site with four original buildings and self-guided interpretive trail. Fort Spokane was a military post from 1880 to 1899 and an Indian Boarding School from 1900–1910.

Parking: Paved unmarked parking lot outside of administration building

Lunch: Casino down the road, local store, or other restaurants 7 to 25 miles away. Picnic areas available.

Lodging: http://www.grandcouleedam.org; http://www.visitspokane.com (1-hr. drive)

Nearest Commercial Airport: Spokane International (GEG) [43 miles]

Subjects

>**Historical Periods:** 1865–1900; 1900–1940; 1940–present

>**Eras:** Fur Trade

>**Natural Resources:** Dams; Irrigation

>**Mining:** Gold; Placer Mining

>**Transportation:** Railroads; Ferries

>**Organizations:** Schools; Hospitals/Medical Facilities

>**Ethnic Groups:** Native American

Date of Reviewer's Visit: 8/26/2004

Profile Updated by Institution: 11/12/2004

EASTSOUND

Name: Orcas Island Historical Society and Museum   **County:** San Juan

Mailing Address: PO Box 134

  City: Eastsound   **State:** WA   **Postal Code:** 98245-0000

Street Address: 181 N. Beach Rd.

Institution Email: orcasmuseum@rockisland.com

Telephone Number: (360) 376-4849   **Fax Number:** (360) 376-2994

Contact Name: Jen Vollmer, Director/Curator

Institution Type: Local Museum

Web site URL: http://www.orcasisland.org/~history/

Hours: Tu–Su 1–4 and F 1–6, end of May–end of Sept, by appt. only.

Staff in Archives: 1f

Archives Are Handicapped Accessible: No

Access Description: Steps between rooms

Cost for Researcher—Remote: Fee schedule

Review of Facilities: The Orcas Island Historical Museum is located in the village of Eastsound on Orcas Island. Eastsound is located eight miles inland from the Orcas ferry dock. The museum is a series of log cabins moved onto the site and merged together. The research area consists of a table in the curator's office. There are file cabinets and some bookshelves in the room. The facility is planning a new building, which will eventually house the research and administrative portions of the museum. The collections are housed either in the curator's office or in a vault nearby.

Vertical Files: Yes   **Vertical Files in Cubic Feet:** 10

Vertical File Description and Subjects: Clipping and ephemera files with some original documents divided into two collections; family files and topical files

Manuscripts: Yes   **Manuscripts Volume in Cubic Feet:** 4

Manuscript Types: School records, land deeds, and miscellaneous small manuscript items

Manuscript Subjects: Orcas Island

Photographs: Yes   **Number of Photographs:** 1,000

Storage of Photographs: Photographs stored in plastic sleeves in archival boxes in a storage vault in the museum

Photograph Subjects: Variety of historical subjects on Orcas Island and some of the surrounding smaller islands

Photograph Reproductions Are Available: Yes

Photographic Prints: Yes   **Digital Prints:** Yes

Books: Yes   **Number of Books in Collection:** 75

Description of Books: Local history subjects, professional collection, phone books, county directories

Newspapers: Yes

Newspapers in Paper Format: Yes

Papers and Dates: Variety of local papers from early 1900 to 1980. Prefer that researchers use the microfilm (see below). Some indexing to the newspapers has been done on the Orcas Island subjects only.

Newspapers on Microfilm: Yes

Microfilm and Dates: Microfilm of all newspapers available at the Orcas Island Public Library where there are microfilm readers and printers. Includes San Juan County 1891 to 2003.

Oral Histories: Yes   **Oral Histories Number:** 100

Oral Histories Description: Oral history interviews of local residents taken from 1970s through the present. About 30 also have transcriptions with photographs illustrating the interview in display notebooks.

Maps and Drawings: Yes   **Estimated Number of Maps and Drawings:** 20

Description of Maps and Drawings: Several original maps of area, some Metsker maps with land owners indicated by plot and name, some cabin layouts

Genealogy Sources: Yes

Genealogy Sources Description: Island family genealogies and obituaries are included in family files listed above.

Special Collections: No

Indexes: Access database on staff computer lists the contents of the collection. Some newspaper indexing has been done on Orcas Island topics.

Review of Collections: The collections of the Orcas Island Historical Society are very small, but unique to the area. The photographs, though numerous, are not really browsable, which is unfortunate. Staff knowledge is the main index to the collections. Some of the images are exceptional in content. Subjects of importance include materials on the salmon fishing industry, including the fish canneries, fish traps, and reef netting. Also have an extensive file of Civilian Conservation Corps(CCC) photos and documents from Moran State Park CCC group. The manuscript collection is small and has very little space to grow larger in the current facility.

Museum on Premises: Yes

Museum Hours: Tu–Su 1–4 and F 1–6, end of May–end of Sept, or by appt.

Museum Is Handicapped Accessible: No

Description of Museum: Charming museum of six log homestead cabins linked together and illustrating various aspects of the history of Orcas Island

Parking: Free on-street parallel parking

Lunch: Variety of small tourist cafes in adjacent blocks

Lodging: http://www.orcasisland.org

Nearest Commercial Airport: William R Fairchild International (Port Angeles) (CLM) [123 miles]; Seattle-Tacoma International (SEA) [123 miles]

Subjects

Historical Periods: Pre-1800; 1800–1865; 1865–1900; 1900–1940; 1940–present

Eras: World War I; CCC; World War II

Natural Resources: Fishing; Hunting; Logging

Mining: Gold

Transportation: Ships and Shipping; Ferries; Aviation

Agriculture: Vegetable/Truck Crops; Orchards

Business: Retail; Legal/Medical Services; Hotels/Restaurants; Entertainment/Theaters

Manufacturing: Cannery; Brick Making; Boatbuilding/Shipyard; Sawmills

Government: County

Organizations: Schools; Hospitals/Medical Facilities; Nonreligious Organizations; Civic and Fraternal; Women's; Business

Ethnic Groups: Native American; Pacific Islander; Chinese; German; Scottish; Swedish

Religious Sites and Organizations: Protestant

Date of Reviewer's Visit: 6/17/2004

Profile Updated by Institution: 11/22/2004

EDMONDS

Name: Edmonds Historical Museum   **County:** Snohomish

Mailing Address: PO Box 52

   City: Edmonds   **State:** WA   **Postal Code:** 98020-0000

Street Address: 118 5th Ave. N.

Institution Email: jonisein@yahoo.com

Telephone Number: (425) 774-0900   **Fax Number:** (425) 774-6507

Contact Name: Joni Sein   **Contact Email:** jonisein@yahoo.com

Institution Type: Local Museum

Affiliation: Edmonds-South Snohomish County and Historical Society

Web site URL: http://www.historicedmonds.org/

Hours: W–Su 1–4

Staff in Archives: 2p 3v

Archives Are Handicapped Accessible: Yes

Access Description: Handicapped entrance at side of building and elevator

Cost for Researcher—Remote: Donation

Review of Facilities: The Edmonds Historical Museum is located in an old Carnegie Library building located one-half block from the center of downtown Edmonds. The library area is adjacent to the entry on the main floor. It is a small room with numerous doors leading to staff offices. There is a medium-sized worktable and bookshelves flank the research area. File cabinets, with the photograph collection and vertical file materials, are in an adjacent office. Manuscript materials are stored in a staff-only room in the lower level.

Vertical Files: No   **Vertical Files in Cubic Feet:** 6

   Vertical File Description and Subjects: Newspaper and general subject files

Manuscripts: Yes   **Manuscripts Volume in Cubic Feet:** 10

Manuscript Types: Organizational records

Manuscript Subjects: Clubs and organizations

Photographs: Yes   **Number of Photographs:** 4,000

Storage of Photographs: Photographs are stored in plastic sleeves in file cabinets and filed by subject numbers.

Photograph Subjects: Marine, schools, churches, docks and waterfront, mills and logging, downtown Edmonds, commercial, rural, dwellings, people, transportation

Photograph Reproductions Are Available: Yes

Photographic Prints: Yes   **Digital Prints:** Yes

Digital Images on CD or Electronically: Yes

Books: Yes   **Number of Books in Collection:** 550

Description of Books: Local history, professional collection, annuals

Newspapers: No

Oral Histories: Yes   **Oral Histories Number:** 28

Oral Histories Description: Local resident interviews on audiocassette taken late 1970s to present. Twenty have transcriptions.

Maps and Drawings: Yes

Description of Maps and Drawings: Plat maps for downtown and greater Edmonds, 1900, 1910, 1940; nautical charts for Puget Sound, Strait of Juan de Fuca, Alaska

Genealogy Sources: No

Special Collections: No

Indexes: Books and archival materials are being entered on PastPerfect, which will function as a computer index.

Review of Collections: The Edmonds Historical Museum is focusing most of their collection efforts on the photography collection. There are currently few manuscript materials, and space problems will limit increasing this type of material in the future. The museum does not collect in the area of genealogy. Researchers with genealogical requests are referred to the Sno-Isle Genealogy Society.

Museum on Premises: Yes

Museum Hours: W–Su 1–4

Cost of Entry to Museum: Donation

Museum Is Handicapped Accessible: Yes

Description of Museum: The Edmonds Historical Museum focuses on the history of Edmonds and South Snohomish County. The upper floor has a changing exhibit gallery. The ground floor has exhibits on various aspects of life in Edmonds throughout its history.

Parking: On-street parallel parking with 3 hr. limit, free public parking lot next block, also 3-hr. limit

Lunch: Ethnic and upscale cafes 1/2 to 2 blocks in downtown boutique shopping area

Lodging: http://www.edmondswa.com

Nearest Commercial Airport: Seattle-Tacoma International (SEA) [31 miles]

Subjects

    Historical Periods: 1865–1900; 1900–1940; 1940–present

    Natural Resources: Logging

    Transportation: Railroads; Ships and Shipping; Ferries

    Business: Retail

    Organizations: Schools; Nonreligious Organizations

Date of Reviewer's Visit: 12/3/2003

Profile Updated by Institution: 11/12/2004

ELLENSBURG

Name: Ellensburg Public Library   **County:** Kittitas

Mailing Address: 209 N. Ruby

  City: Ellensburg   **State:** WA   **Postal Code:** 98926-3338

Street Address: 209 N. Ruby

Institution Email: None

Telephone Number: (509) 962-7250   **Fax Number:** (509) 962-7295

Contact Name: Milton Wagy   **Contact Email:** wagyml@ellensburglibrary.org

Institution Type: Public Library

Web site URL: http://www.ellensburglibrary.org

Hours: M–Th 10–8; F 10–6; Sa–Su 1–5

Staff in Archives: 1p 6v

Archives Are Handicapped Accessible: Yes

Review of Facilities: The Ellensburg Public Library is in a newly expanded and remodeled building. A small local history room on the main floor contains bookshelves on two walls with the local history reference collection books and a microfilm reader and microfilmed newspapers in the room. The room also has several worktables for researchers. Circulating local history collection books are in the main reference room. Map cases and some other local history materials and files are also outside the local history room but in an adjoining area. The manuscript and other collections are located in a staff-only area in the basement. Although the book collection is open when the library is open, special appointments are required to use the manuscript and photograph collections.

Vertical Files: Yes   **Vertical Files in Cubic Feet:** 17

Vertical File Description and Subjects: General local history subjects. Also 500 files of people and families (see under genealogy).

Manuscripts: Yes   **Manuscripts Volume in Cubic Feet:** 100

Manuscript Types: Organizational records, family papers, and archives

Manuscript Subjects: 15 different women's club papers and professional club papers (not indexed or arranged)

Photographs: Yes   **Number of Photographs:** 8,500

Storage of Photographs: Digitization project underway with some images available on the Web site. Originals stored in file cabinets in staff storage area. Many images have negatives only.

Photograph Subjects: 2,000 photographs in the Breckon Collection of Ellensburg people from 1942–1962. General area history.

Photograph Reproductions Are Available: Yes

Photographic Prints: Yes   **Digital Prints:** Yes

Digital Images on CD or Electronically: Yes

Books: Yes   **Number of Books in Collection:** 1,000

Description of Books: Local and regional history resources, city directories, telephone books, annuals

Newspapers: Yes

Newspapers in Paper Format: Yes

Papers and Dates: Indexing of newspapers from 1970–present

Newspapers on Microfilm: Yes

Microfilm and Dates: Microfilm of local Ellensburg papers from 1888 to present

Oral Histories: Yes   **Oral Histories Number:** 300

Oral Histories Description: Oral histories of local area residents (children of pioneer families) done in the late 1970s to early 1980s on CD. About two-thirds have transcriptions. Also have paper copies of WPA interviews from the county.

Maps and Drawings: Yes   **Estimated Number of Maps and Drawings:** 75

Description of Maps and Drawings: Local area maps

Genealogy Sources: Yes

> **Genealogy Sources Description:** 500 files of local area people and family histories (8 cu. ft.)

Special Collections: No

Indexes: The Oral History Interviews Index, Historical Subject Files Index, Newspaper Index, and Breckon Photo Collection Index are all on card files.

> **Online Sources:** "Through Open Eyes: 95 years of Roslyn's Black Mining History" (see http://www.ellensburglibrary.org/Roslyn/openeyes.html) is an online exhibit of the history of nearby Roslyn. There is also an online photograph collection on Kittitas Count, including images of the towns of Ellensburg, Cle Elum and Roslyn(see http://www.ellensburglibrary.org/lhimages/index.html).

Review of Collections: The collections at the Ellensburg Public Library are diverse and interesting. At the time of the visit, the library was in the process of moving, so collections were stored in various places. There are a number of great little collections including papers, scrapbooks, and memorabilia from about 15 different women's clubs in Ellensburg history. These collections are not indexed but provide a glimpse at the history of women's organizations in this small college city. General business and organizational history of the region is represented. Family and biographical sources are also available. Sample images of the photograph collection are available from the Web site. Indexing to many parts of the collection is better than that of most similar-sized institutions. Finding aids to the manuscript collections would be a valuable addition to the information available to researchers.

Museum on Premises: No

Parking: 2-hr. free parallel street parking. Parking lot close by.

Lunch: 3–5 blocks to a variety of local and ethnic restaurants. Driving distance to most chain and fast-food restaurants.

Lodging: http://www.ellensburg-chamber.com

Nearest Commercial Airport: Yakima Air Terminal/McAllister Field (YKM) [39 miles]

Subjects

> **Historical Periods:** 1800–1865; 1865–1900; 1900–1940; 1940–present
>
> **Eras:** Indian Wars; WPA
>
> **Natural Resources:** Water; Dams; Irrigation
>
> **Mining:** Gold; Copper; Coal
>
> **Transportation:** Railroads; Stagecoach/Freight
>
> **Agriculture:** Dairy; Ranching/Livestock; Grains
>
> **Business:** Legal/Medical Services; Entertainment/Theaters
>
> **Manufacturing:** Grist/Flour Mills; Creamery; Brick Making; Sawmills

Government: City; County

Organizations: Schools; Colleges/Universities; Charities; Nonreligious Organizations; Business

Ethnic Groups: Native American; African

Religious Sites and Organizations: Protestant; Catholic

Date of Reviewer's Visit: 3/26/2004

Profile Updated by Institution: 12/2/2004

✴✴✴✴✴

Name: Washington State Archives, Central Regional Branch   **County:** Kittitas

Mailing Address: Bledsoe-Washington Archives Bldg., Central Washington University, MS 7547

City: Ellensburg   **State:** WA   **Postal Code:** 98926-7547

Street Address: 215 E. 14th St.

Institution Email: archives@cwu.edu

Telephone Number: (509) 963-2136   **Fax Number:** (509) 963-1753

Institution Type: Archives

Affiliation: State of Washington

Web site URL: http://www.cwu.edu/~archives

Hours: M–F 8:30–4:30 (closed holidays)

Staff in Archives: 3f, 2v

Archives Are Handicapped Accessible: Yes

Cost for Researcher—Remote: Fee schedule

Review of Facilities: The Washington State Archives Central Regional Branch is located in a new building at the edge of the Central Washington University campus. The Central Regional Branch covers the nine counties that make up central Washington. The research room has a secure entrance from the lobby. Secure lockers are available for storage of personal items at no charge. Only pencils and papers are permitted in the research room. Laptops and scanners require special permission. The research room is spacious with four large research tables and low bookshelves under the windows on one long wall. Large historic maps are stored under glass on the tabletops for easy reference. There is a computer station available to researchers, and three media carrels with microfilm, audio, and viewing equipment. Collections are stored adjacent to the research room, in a secure climate-controlled area.

Vertical Files: No

Manuscripts: Yes   **Manuscripts Volume in Cubic Feet:** 15,000

Manuscript Types: Government records

Manuscript Subjects: County records, municipal records, records of special districts. Covers central Washington and the counties of Benton, Chelan, Douglas, Franklin, Grant, Kittitas, Klickitat, Okanogan, and Yakima. Spans the early territorial period to the present.

Photographs: Yes

Storage of Photographs: Photographs are interfiled with the agency manuscript and record collections.

Photograph Reproductions Are Available: Yes

Photographic Prints: Yes   **Digital Prints:** Yes

Books: No

Newspapers: No

Microfilm and Dates: Central Washington University Library has some microfilm of newspapers.

Oral Histories: No

Maps and Drawings: Yes

Description of Maps and Drawings: Maps are available, but stored with records.

Genealogy Sources: Yes

Genealogy Sources Description: Vital records prior to 1907, marriage, and naturalization. Naturalization records have indexes

Special Collections: No

Indexes: Yes

Online Sources: Guides to collections and holdings at the Central Regional Branch are available online at http://www.cwu.edu/~archives. Online Historical Records Search. Available from http://www.secstate.wa.gov/history/search.aspx for access to selected census, naturalization, birth, marriage, death, prison and other miscellaneous records. For Washington history, see http://www.secstate.wa.gov/history.

Review of Collections: Collections include records from public entities, counties, cities, and towns of the nine counties in the region. The counties are Benton, Chelan, Douglas, Franklin, Grant, Kittitas, Klickitat, Okanogan, and Yakima. Major subject areas include land use/property records, education, genealogy, and power. The Central Regional Branch also holds records from Yakima Valley Community College and the Washington Public Power Supply System (Energy Northwest).

Museum on Premises: No

Parking: Two spaces in lot or on-street parallel parking, free parking lot down the street (no permit needed), pay lot across the street

Lunch: Driving distance to a variety of local and chain restaurants

Lodging: http://www.ellensburg-chamber.com

Nearest Commercial Airport: Yakima Air Terminal/McAllister Field (YKM) [41 miles]

Subjects

>   **Historical Periods:** Pre-1800; 1800–1865; 1865–1900; 1900–1940; 1940–present

>   **Natural Resources:** Logging

>   **Mining:** Mining

>   **Government:** City; County; State

>   **Organizations:** Schools

Date of Reviewer's Visit: 3/26/2004

Profile Updated by Institution: 11/9/2004

EVERETT

✹✹✹✹

Name: Everett Public Library **County:** Snohomish

Mailing Address: 2707 Hoyt Ave.

   City: Everett   **State:** WA   **Postal Code:** 98201-3556

Street Address: 2707 Hoyt Ave.

Institution Email: libweb@ci.everett.wa.us

Telephone Number: (425) 257-8005   **Fax Number:** (425) 257-8016

Contact Name: David Dilgard

Institution Type: Public Library

Affiliation: City of Everett

Web site URL: http://www.epls.org

Hours: M–F 10–6

Staff in Archives: 2f, 1p Northwest room only

Archives Are Handicapped Accessible: Yes

Access Description: Ramps, electric doors, elevators

Review of Facilities: The Northwest Room of the Everett Public Library is on the second floor of a modern library building. There is a large beautiful reading room with several well-lit worktables. Comfortable chairs in reading groups and plants make the room warm and friendly. Books surround the room. Vertical files and some photo collections housed in reading room. The bulk of the collections is housed in a storage area in the basement of the building.

Vertical Files: Yes   **Vertical Files in Cubic Feet:** 20

   Vertical File Description and Subjects: General Northwest Subjects

Manuscripts: Yes

   Manuscript Types: Family papers, organizational records

   Manuscript Subjects: WPA writers' project for Snohomish County

Photographs: Yes   **Number of Photographs:** 15,000

   Storage of Photographs: Browsing collection mounted on cardboard in reading room filed by accession number

   Photograph Subjects: Labor history, logging, some early movie footage

   Photograph Reproductions Are Available: Yes

      Photographic Prints: Yes

Books: Yes

   Description of Books: Large historical collection, annuals, city directories

Newspapers: Yes

   Newspapers on Microfilm: Yes

   Microfilm and Dates: *Everett Daily Herald,* 1891–present

Oral Histories: Yes   **Oral Histories Number:** 120

   Oral Histories Description: Most with transcriptions

Maps and Drawings: No

Genealogy Sources: No

   Genealogy Sources Description: Biography and family history collection

Special Collections: Yes

   Special Collections Description: J. A. Juleen Studio photo collection ranging from 1909–1940, 5,000 photos and negatives; Sumner Iron Works—series of 500 glass plate negatives

Indexes: Paper list of photographs, staff card file for manuscripts, some photographs online, some books in library catalog online

   Manuscript Finding Aids: Staff has resources available

   Online Sources: 3,000 photographs in computer database, many are being put on the Web site

Review of Collections: Sizeable photograph collections, many that are searchable in computer in reading room. Collections are well rounded and deal with mainly Snohomish County subjects. Special collections include the City of Everett and a sizable Pacific Northwest collection.

Museum on Premises: No

Parking: Free underground parking garage off Rucker Ave.

Lunch: Local and chain restaurants within a short driving distance

Lodging: http://www.snohomish.org/; http://www.everettchamber.com

Nearest Commercial Airport: Seattle-Tacoma International (SEA) [43 miles]

Subjects

    Historical Periods: 1865–1900; 1900–1940; 1940–present

    Natural Resources: Logging

    Mining: Gold; Silver

    Manufacturing: Sawmills

    Ethnic Groups: English; German; Norwegian; Swedish

Date of Reviewer's Visit: 4/23/2003

Profile Updated by Institution: None

Name: Museum of Snohomish County History   **County:** Snohomish

Mailing Address: PO Box 5556

   City: Everett   **State:** WA   **Postal Code:** 98206-0000

Street Address: 1913 Hewitt Ave.

Institution Email: info@SnoCoMuseum.org

Telephone Number: (425) 259-2022   **Fax Number:** (425) 258-5402

Contact Name: Eric Taylor   **Contact Email:** jerictaylor@att.net

Institution Type: Local Museum

Affiliation: Snohomish County Museum and Historical Association

Web site URL: http://www.SnoCoMuseum.org

Hours: W–Sa 1–4 walk-in; appts. available W–Sa 9–4

Staff in Archives: 1p, 12v

Archives Are Handicapped Accessible: Yes

Cost for Researcher—In-house: Donation

Cost for Researcher—Remote: Donation

Review of Facilities: The Museum of Snohomish County History is currently located in a storefront on Hewitt Avenue in downtown Everett. The building is considered temporary quarters and the archives area is small and cramped. The workspace consists primarily of card tables in a narrow room with file cabinets/materials on both sides and a staff desk at the end. They desperately need an expanded area and/or a new building.

Vertical Files: Yes   **Vertical Files in Cubic Feet:** 10

  Vertical File Description and Subjects: Biography, community histories, businesses

Manuscripts: Yes   **Manuscripts Volume in Cubic Feet:** 2,000

  Manuscript Types: All manuscript types

  Manuscript Subjects: Property histories, Agnew Hardware financials, 1900–1925

Photographs: Yes   **Number of Photographs:** 5,000

  Storage of Photographs: Original photos and copies in file cabinets filed by accession numbers. Photocopies in subject binders.

  Photograph Subjects: Snohomish County and Everett history, Stone and Webster photos of construction of interurban railroad, oversize photos

  Photograph Reproductions Are Available: Yes

    Photographic Prints: Yes

Books: Yes   **Number of Books in Collection:** 250

  Description of Books: Local history, city directories, annuals, professional collection

Newspapers: Yes

  Newspapers in Paper Format: Yes

  Papers and Dates: Bound volumes of Everett and some Snohomish city papers

Oral Histories: Yes   **Oral Histories Number:** 100

  Oral Histories Description: Everett area residents interviewed around 1992

Maps and Drawings: Yes   **Estimated Number of Maps and Drawings:** 50

  Description of Maps and Drawings: County and city plat maps, transportation routes, bird's eye views

Genealogy Sources: Yes

  Genealogy Sources Description: Cemetery records, biographical files

Special Collections: No

Indexes: Binders of photocopies of photos arranged by subject

Review of Collections: This moderate-sized collection is out of space, a fact that limits much that is being done with and for the collection. The photographs cover all subjects of interest in Snohomish County, and Everett particularly. The collection also includes histories of all the communities in the county.

Museum on Premises: Yes

  Museum Hours: W–Sa 1–4

  Cost of Entry to Museum: Donation

Museum Is Handicapped Accessible: Yes

Description of Museum: Small museum with rotating displays

Parking: Free parallel on-street parking

Lunch: Fast-food chains within blocks

Lodging: http://www.everettchamber.com

Nearest Commercial Airport: Seattle-Tacoma International (SEA) [42 miles]

Subjects

    Historical Periods: 1865–1900; 1900–1940; 1940–present

    Eras: Civil War; World War I

    Natural Resources: Logging

    Mining: Silver; Copper

    Transportation: Railroads; Aviation

    Agriculture: Dairy; Ranching/Livestock; Vegetable/Truck Crops

    Business: Retail; Legal/Medical Services; Hotels/Restaurants; Entertainment/Theaters

    Manufacturing: Boatbuilding/Shipyard; Sawmills; Wood Products

    Government: City; County

    Organizations: Schools; Colleges/Universities; Hospitals/Medical Facilities; Charities; Nonreligious Organizations

    Ethnic Groups: Native American; Japanese; Chinese; Danish; English; German; Irish; Italian; Norwegian; Swedish; Greek; Slavic

    Religious Sites and Organizations: Protestant; Catholic; Jewish

Date of Reviewer's Visit: 4/23/2003

Profile Updated by Institution: 11/15/2004

GIG HARBOR

Name: Gig Harbor Peninsula Historical Society and Museum   **County:** Pierce

Mailing Address: PO Box 744

  City: Gig Harbor   **State:** WA   **Postal Code:** 98335-0000

Street Address: 4218 Harborview Dr.

Institution Email: info@gigharbormuseum.org

Telephone Number: (253) 858-6722   **Fax Number:** (253) 853-4211

Contact Name: Victoria Blackwell   **Contact Email:** vicki@gigharbormuseum.org

Institution Type: Local Museum

Web site URL: http://www.gigharbormuseum.org

Hours: Tu–Sa 10–4 and by appt.

Staff in Archives: 2f, 2p, 10v

Archives Are Handicapped Accessible: Yes

Cost for Researcher—In-house: free

Cost for Researcher—Remote: fee schedule

Review of Facilities: The Gig Harbor Peninsula Historical Society Museum is located in a log house off the main road 400 feet. Currently the archives are housed in a small room with the archives materials stored against the walls. File cabinets, bookcases, and map cases fight for space with a single long table. The room is stuffed, but workable. Lighting is adequate. The society is in the process of constructing a new museum complex, which will include a historic schoolhouse, a dry-docked commercial fishing purse seiner, and a modern new building. A larger archives/library area is planned for the new building.

Vertical Files: Yes   **Vertical Files in Cubic Feet:** 18

  Vertical File Description and Subjects: Biography files, schools, newspaper clippings and general files

Manuscripts: Yes   **Manuscripts Volume in Cubic Feet:** 35

  Manuscript Types: Scrapbooks, family papers, business papers, organizational records

  Manuscript Subjects: Tacoma Narrows bridge construction and history

Photographs: Yes   **Number of Photographs:** 5,000

  Storage of Photographs: Subject binders of photocopies of the images are available for researchers. Originals are stored with Mylar sleeves/folders in flat boxes by subject in the research room. Images are being digitized, as resources allow. There are also a large number of slides with a separate index.

  Photograph Subjects: History of the Gig Harbor Peninsula, Tacoma Narrows bridge

  Photograph Reproductions Are Available: Yes

    Photographic Prints: Yes   **Digital Prints:** Yes

    Digital Images on CD or Electronically: Yes

Books: Yes   **Number of Books in Collection:** 200

  Description of Books: Regional history, city directories, annuals, and professional collection, all filed by Dewey number and having a card catalog.

Newspapers: No

  Papers and Dates: Papers are available at the local newspaper office only *(Peninsula Gateway)*

Oral Histories: Yes   **Oral Histories Number:** 55

Oral Histories Description: Interviews from early 1980s through present. Interviews of local residents. Some have transcriptions. Some have a video, as well as an audiotape.

Maps and Drawings: Yes   **Estimated Number of Maps and Drawings:** 100

Description of Maps and Drawings: Variety of local maps and regional oversize documents

Genealogy Sources: Yes

Genealogy Sources Description: Obituary files on 3 x 5 cards, which are kept current. Cemetery records.

Special Collections: Yes

Special Collections Description: Tacoma Narrows Bridge collection of documents and photographs. Binders of photographic images of the building of the bridge.

Indexes: Card catalog for books, slide index, obituary index

Manuscript Finding Aids: Manuscripts are described in PastPerfect.

Review of Collections: This collection is small but growing. They have an active group of volunteers, who are processing new materials. Indexing is kept current. The photo collection is easily accessible, as is the rest of the collection. The main problem is limited space, which will be solved by the new building. The collection focuses on the Gig Harbor Peninsula and goes back to the earliest settlement. The manuscript collection has 4,000 pieces. The photographs number 5,000. On the whole this is a nice little collection that shows great promise.

Museum on Premises: Yes

Museum Hours: Tu–Sa 10–4

Cost of Entry to Museum: $2

Museum Is Handicapped Accessible: Yes

Description of Museum: The museum is currently small, with two changing galleries. New plans for a large multibuilding complex are progressing.

Parking: Small parking lot adjacent to building

Lunch: Driving distance to a variety of restaurants and cafes along the waterfront

Lodging: http://www.gigharborchamber.com

Nearest Commercial Airport: Seattle-Tacoma International (SEA) [32 miles]

Subjects

  Historical Periods: 1865–1900; 1900–1940; 1940–present

  Eras: Civil War; World War II

  Natural Resources: Fishing; Logging

  Transportation: Ships and Shipping; Ferries

Agriculture: Vegetable/Truck Crops; Orchards

Business: Banking; Retail; Hotels/Restaurants

Manufacturing: Sawmills

Government: City

Organizations: Schools; Nonreligious Organizations; Women's

Ethnic Groups: Croatian; Scandinavian

Religious Sites and Organizations: Protestant

Date of Reviewer's Visit: 1/14/2004

Profile Updated by Institution: 12/6/2004

GOLDENDALE

Name: Klickitat County Historical Society   **County:** Klickitat

Mailing Address: PO Box 86

   City: Goldendale   **State:** WA   **Postal Code:** 98620-0086

Street Address: 127 W. Broadway

Institution Email: None

Telephone Number: (509) 773-4303

Contact Name: Bonnie Beeks   **Contact Email:** beeks@gorge.net

Institution Type: Local Museum

Affiliation: Presby Mansion Museum

Web site URL: http://www.ohwy.com/wa/k/klickchm.htm

Hours: Daily 9–5, Apr 1–Oct 31; other times by appt.

Staff in Archives: 1f, 2p, 12v

Archives Are Handicapped Accessible: Yes

Access Description: Lift on side of building to reach porch. Doorjambs are raised slightly.

Cost for Researcher—Remote: Fee schedule

List of Researchers Available: Yes

Review of Facilities: The Klickitat County Historical Society is located in the Presby Museum in a Victorian mansion a block from downtown. The library and research area is a series of rooms on the main floor. The main room has a large worktable, staff offices, and bookcases holding part of the book collection and the photograph collection. The room is also used as the lunchroom/kitchen. Despite the multipurpose feel of the room, it is pleasant and usable. An adjoining room houses the bulk of the local history paper materials.

Vertical Files: No

Manuscripts: Yes   **Manuscripts Volume in Cubic Feet:** 25

Manuscript Types: Scrapbooks, ledgers, business and organizational records

Manuscript Subjects: Schools, fraternal organizations, post office records, hotel register from 1900s

Photographs: Yes   **Number of Photographs:** 4,000

Storage of Photographs: Original photographs are stored in flat file boxes and arranged by subject. Photos are indexed by a card file and are being added to inventory using Microsoft Access.

Photograph Subjects: Local history, but strong in agriculture and schools

Photograph Reproductions Are Available: Yes

Photographic Prints: Yes   **Digital Prints:** Yes

Books: Yes   **Number of Books in Collection:** 200

Description of Books: Local history, annuals, telephone books, old books

Newspapers: Yes

Newspapers in Paper Format: Yes

Papers and Dates: Bound Goldendale newspapers 1879 to present (various titles); incomplete

Oral Histories: No

Maps and Drawings: No

Genealogy Sources: Yes

Genealogy Sources Description: Collection of family histories of county residents, cemetery records

Special Collections: No

Indexes: Inventory available on staff computer. Some indexing to photo collections on card file.

Review of Collections: The research collections of the Klickitat County Historical Society consist of a little of everything. Instead of developing vertical files of subject materials, they have filed some information in binders. Clipping files of specific locales in the county are thus organized. Besides the newspaper collections (some in extremely fragile condition), there is an assortment of community and family history materials. Local fraternal organizations and some business and family histories are spread throughout the scrapbook and manuscript collection. The photo collection is well rounded in subject, but strongest in the earlier years (late nineteenth and early twentieth centuries).

Museum on Premises: Yes

Museum Hours: Daily 9–5 Apr 1–Oct 31

Cost of Entry to Museum: $4.50

Museum Is Handicapped Accessible: Yes

Description of Museum: This is a combination historic house and local history museum. Some rooms are devoted to changing or permanent displays; others are set as the family home. Somehow their designer makes it work and beautifully. Don't miss the frontier cabin in the attic.

Parking: 2-hr. free parallel street parking

Lunch: Variety of local restaurants in downtown area within a few blocks

Lodging: http://www.klickitatcounty.org/Tourism/

Nearest Commercial Airport: Yakima Air Terminal/McAllister Field (YKM) [71 miles]; Portland International (PDX) [100 miles]; Tri-Cities (Pasco) (PSC) [128 miles]

Subjects

Historical Periods:1800–1865; 1865–1900; 1900–1940; 1940–present

Natural Resources: Dams; Logging

Transportation: Railroads; Ferries

Agriculture: Ranching/Livestock; Grains; Orchards; Dry Land Farming

Business: Entertainment/Theaters

Manufacturing: Sawmills

Government: City; County

Organizations: Schools; Hospitals/Medical Facilities; Civic and Fraternal; Women's

Ethnic Groups: Native American; Finnish

Religious Sites and Organizations: Protestant; Catholic

Date of Reviewer's Visit: 3/25/2004

Profile Updated by Institution: 12/13/2004

Name: Maryhill Museum of Art   **County:** Klickitat

Mailing Address: 35 Maryhill Museum Dr.

  City: Goldendale   **State:** WA   **Postal Code:** 98620-0000

Street Address: 35 Maryhill Museum Dr.

Institution Email: maryhill@maryhillmuseum.org

Telephone Number: (509) 773-3733   **Fax Number:** (509) 773-6138

Contact Name: Betty Long-Schleif, Collections Manager

Contact Email: betty@maryhillmuseum.org

Institution Type: Historic Site

Web site URL: http://www.maryhillmuseum.org

Hours: M–F 9–5, Mar 15–Nov 15; M–F 10–4:30, year-round by appt.

Staff in Archives: 6f, 4v

Archives Are Handicapped Accessible: Yes

Review of Facilities: Maryhill Museum is located in a grand mansion overlooking the Columbia River Gorge in a remote location, approximately 100 miles east of the Portland, OR/Vancouver, WA, metro area. It is an art museum of national repute. It also has some interesting photograph and document collections. The library is located on the lower level and doubles for a conference/multipurpose room. This room houses the book collections and four long worktables grouped in the center of the room. Vertical files and other research materials are housed in an adjoining office. The manuscript collections, original photographs, and other materials are stored in a variety of storage rooms on the same floor. The collection is professionally cared for and stored.

Vertical Files: Yes　　　**Vertical Files in Cubic Feet:** 12

　Vertical File Description and Subjects: General historical information and extensive biographical files of artists, particularly those of Boston or American classical realism.

Manuscripts: Yes　　　**Manuscripts Volume in Cubic Feet:** 50

　Manuscript Types: Personal papers, archives

　Manuscript Subjects: Local history subjects such as sheep raising, vineyards, building of the Columbia Gorge Highway, and records of the Maryhill Ranch and Museum. Loie Fuller, Alma Spreckels, artists' correspondence, Gammell, Hunter, Lack. History resources on early modern dance, Northwest road history. Business and personal correspondence of Sam Hill, correspondence of Queen Marie of Romania, documentation of artifacts held by the museum.

Photographs: Yes　　　**Number of Photographs:** 3,800

　Storage of Photographs: Original photographs are stored in clamshell boxes in plastic sleeves or acid-free folders

　Photograph Subjects: J. W. Thompson Collection of slides (1952–1957) of life on Washington and Oregon Indian reservations. Local historical photographs by Fanny Van Dyne and local area interest. Photographs by Albert H. Barmes of the Pacific Northwest, especially of roads and highways, sites of interest such as Columbia River Gorge, Mt. Rainer, Crater Lake, Mt. Hood, and others.

　Photograph Reproductions Are Available: Yes

　　Photographic Prints: Yes　　　**Digital Prints:** Yes

Digital Images on CD or Electronically: Yes

Books: Yes   **Number of Books in Collection:** 2,000

Description of Books: The book collection is divided into two parts: one is primarily a general art reference collection with some local history book included, and the second is an approximately 1,000-book collection from the personal library of founder Sam Hill. Books are cataloged and listed in a local card file.

Newspapers: No

Oral Histories: Yes   **Oral Histories Number:** 10

Oral Histories Description: Oral history interviews done in 1990s and relating to Queen Marie's visit in 1926 for the dedication of the museum

Maps and Drawings: No

Genealogy Sources: No

Special Collections: Yes

Special Collections Description: Road and road building of the Northwest, national and world, ca. 1910–1920. Tourism subjects of Pacific Northwest— Crater Lake, Mt. Rainer.

Indexes: Manuscript collections are inventoried in an in-house computer program. The Sam Hill papers also have a card file index, as well as a file of photocopies of the original materials.

Review of Collections: The research collections at the Maryhill Museum are eclectic in nature but intentional in acquisition. Materials relating to the four founders are collected. These represent a wide diversity of individual interests and each adds an interesting piece to this unique collection: Sam Hill with his various business pursuits; Loie Fuller on the French theater; Queen Marie of Romania with her royal regalia, and Alma de Bretteville Spreckels with her art collection. The collections themselves are professionally processed and handled.

Museum on Premises: Yes

Museum Hours: Daily 9–5, Mar 15–Nov 15

Cost of Entry to Museum: $7

Museum Is Handicapped Accessible: Yes

Description of Museum: An art museum with an interesting history and an impressive view. The quality of the displays and collections rivals any fine art museum in the country.

Parking: Free parking lot adjacent to the museum

Lunch: Maryhill Museum features a cafe on the premises

Lodging: http://www.klickitatcounty.org/Tourism/

Nearest Commercial Airport: Yakima Air Terminal/McAllister Field (YKM) [71 miles]; Tri-Cities (Pasco) (PSC) [128 miles]

Subjects

> **Historical Periods:** Pre-1800; 1800–1865; 1865–1900; 1900–1940; 1940–present
>
> **Transportation:** Railroads; Ferries
>
> **Agriculture:** Ranching/Livestock; Vegetable/Truck Crops; Orchards; Vineyard
>
> **Organizations:** Colleges/Universities
>
> **Ethnic Groups:** Native American; Dutch; English; French; Romanian
>
> **Religious Sites and Organizations:** Quaker

Date of Reviewer's Visit: 3/24/2004

Profile Updated by Institution: 11/12/2004

✸✸ HOQUIAM

Name: Polson Park and Museum Historical Society   **County:** Grays Harbor

Mailing Address: PO Box 432

   City: Hoquiam   **State:** WA   **Postal Code:** 98550-0000

Street Address: 1611 Riverside Ave.

Institution Email: jbl@polsonmuseum.org

Telephone Number: (360) 533-5862   **Fax Number:** (360) 533-5862

Contact Name: John Larson, Director

Institution Type: Local Museum

Web site URL: http://www.polsonmuseum.org/

Hours: W–Sa 11–4, Su 12–4, Apr 1–Dec 23; Sa 11–4, Su 12–4, and weekdays by appt. rest of the year

Staff in Archives: 1f, 3v

Archives Are Handicapped Accessible: No

Review of Facilities: Polson Park and Museum is located in a historic house museum at the edge of Hoquiam. On the main floor is a library with bookshelves in three corners and an antique writing desk as the only work surface. The room is part museum display, part research library. Some materials are stored on bookshelves. Photographs and some other materials are stored in the directors' offices and storage rooms on the second floor. The remainder of the research collections is stored in the attic. The attic provides volunteer and staff workspace.

Vertical Files: Yes   **Vertical Files in Cubic Feet:** 28

   Vertical File Description and Subjects: Arranged by city, then subject

Manuscripts: Yes   **Manuscripts Volume in Cubic Feet:** 44

Manuscript Types: Organizational records, business records, scrapbooks, personal papers

Manuscript Subjects: Promotional materials, Polson Logging Company payroll ledgers, logging, sawmills, Hoquiam YMCA, Ladies Clubs, abstracts of titles, county census records, ledgers, business records, county records

Photographs: Yes   **Number of Photographs:** 20,000

Storage of Photographs: Arranged by geography and then subject in file folders in file cabinets, 500 postcards, 3,000 glass plates, 5,000 prints, 500 nitrates

Photograph Subjects: Shipping, logging, 1977–1982 aerial photos of Rayonier, images of logging camps, 1909–1915. Various subjects for cities within Grays Harbor. Particular emphasis on Hoquiam and Aberdeen.

Photograph Reproductions Are Available: Yes

   Photographic Prints: Yes   **Digital Prints:** Yes

   Digital Images on CD or Electronically: Yes

Books: Yes   **Number of Books in Collection:** 500

Description of Books: City directories, phone books, biographies, local history, old books, Aberdeen and Hoquiam annuals

Newspapers: Yes

   Newspapers in Paper Format: Yes

   Papers and Dates: Hoquiam, Grays Harbor County papers

   Newspapers on Microfilm: No

   Microfilm and Dates: Hoquiam papers on microfilm at Hoquiam Library

Oral Histories: Yes   **Oral Histories Number:** 40

   Oral Histories Description: Interviews of local residents done in the early 1980s (many of the recordings are of poor quality), done by ninth-grade honor students

Maps and Drawings: Yes

   Estimated Number of Maps and Drawings: 300

   Description of Maps and Drawings: 10 x 25 county and city; logging, plats, Metskers, Sanborn maps

Genealogy Sources: No

Special Collections: No

Indexes: No

Review of Collections: This collection has a great deal of potential. The manuscript and other research materials have inadequate indexing and processing, but the institution has plans to remedy the situation. The Polson Logging Company materials and Rayonier Company materials are the most significant research components, although there are some good organizational records as well. Photograph collection is large for the size of the institution.

Museum on Premises: Yes

Museum Hours: W–Sa 11–4, Su 12–4

Cost of Entry to Museum: $4

Museum Is Handicapped Accessible: No

Description of Museum: Polson Park features a historic home with subject displays on several floors.

Parking: Free paved parking lot adjacent

Lunch: Driving distance to a variety of restaurants

Lodging: http://www.ci.hoquiam.wa.us/

Nearest Commercial Airport: Olympia Municipal Airport (OLM) [53 miles]; Seattle-Tacoma (SEA) [110 miles]

Subjects

Historical Periods: 1800–1865; 1865–1900; 1900–1940; 1940–present

Eras: World War I; WPA; World War II

Natural Resources: Water; Fishing; Hunting; Whaling; Logging

Transportation: Railroads; Ships and Shipping; Aviation

Business: Retail; Legal/Medical Services; Hotels/Restaurants; Entertainment/Theaters

Manufacturing: Cannery; Brewery; Boatbuilding/Shipyard; Sawmills; Wood Products

Government: City; County

Organizations: Schools; Hospitals/Medical Facilities; Nonreligious Organizations; Civic and Fraternal; Women's; Labor and Union

Ethnic Groups: Native American; Chinese; Danish; Dutch; English; Finnish; French; German; Irish; Italian; Norwegian; Russian; Scottish; Spanish; Swedish

Religious Sites and Organizations: Protestant; Catholic

Date of Reviewer's Visit: 7/30/2004

Profile Updated by Institution: 11/15/2004

ILWACO

Name: Ilwaco Heritage Museum

County: Pacific

Mailing Address: PO Box 153

City: Ilwaco   **State:** WA

Postal Code: 98624-0000

Street Address: 115 S.E. Lake St.

Institution Email: ihm@ilwacoheritagemuseum.org

Telephone Number: (360) 642-3446   **Fax Number:** (360) 462-4615

Contact Name: Joan Mann, Volunteer Research Librarian

Institution Type: Local Museum

Affiliation: Ilwaco Heritage Foundation

Web site URL: http://www.ilwacoheritagemuseum.org/

Hours: Tu and F 10–12, 1–3

Staff in Archives: 3v

Archives Are Handicapped Accessible: No

Access Description: Lift chair available to go to second floor

Cost for Researcher—In-house: $5 or $15 per hr. after 2 hrs.

Cost for Researcher—Remote: $5and postage

Review of Facilities: The Ilwaco Heritage Museum is located in a former telephone utilities building in the small downtown area of Ilwaco. The research room is on the second floor. A chair lift provides handicapped access. The research room is moderate-sized with a range of wooden bookshelves in the center of the room and additional bookshelves, file cabinets, tables, and map cases hugging the walls. There is a staff desk near the door and a small round table for the use of researchers. The research room leads to an adjacent storage area consisting of two rooms. The storage area is large and has sufficient space for a collection many times larger than the one housed.

Vertical Files: Yes   **Vertical Files in Cubic Feet:** 24

   Vertical File Description and Subjects: The vertical files have a variety of materials types, including some accessioned archival material.

Manuscripts: Yes   **Manuscripts Volume in Cubic Feet:** 40

   Manuscript Types: Ledgers, business records, organizational records

   Manuscript Subjects: Chinook-Colbert Herrold, Troeh-Davis Collection, Joe Knowles Collection, Emory Neale files

Photographs: Yes   **Number of Photographs:** 5,000

   Storage of Photographs: Photocopies of photographs are available to researchers in subject binders. Original photographs are stored in document boxes.

   Photograph Subjects: Aerials, Columbia River industries, logging, Coast Guard, shipping, local towns

   Photograph Reproductions Are Available: Yes

     Digital Prints: Yes

Books: Yes   **Number of Books in Collection:** 900

Description of Books: Local history, regional history, old books, reference books of various subjects, annuals. Arranged by Dewey number.

Newspapers: Yes

Newspapers in Paper Format: Yes

Papers and Dates: Scattered issues

Newspapers on Microfilm: Yes

Microfilm and Dates: *South Bend Journal,* 1889–1967; *Ilwaco News,* 1933–1979

Oral Histories: Yes   **Oral Histories Number:** 40

Oral Histories Description: Interviews done from the mid-1980s to the present; all have transcriptions. Tapes are stored with transcriptions.

Maps and Drawings: Yes   **Estimated Number of Maps and Drawings:** 200

Description of Maps and Drawings: Long Beach Peninsula and Columbia Pacific region

Genealogy Sources: Yes

Genealogy Sources Description: Family files, obituaries, cemetery records

Special Collections: No

Indexes: Rely on institutional knowledge

Manuscript Finding Aids: Troeh Davis Collection finding aid

Review of Collections: The collections of the museum focus on the Columbia River's north shore, Willapa Bay, south Pacific County, and Ilwaco. The collection is strong in the photographs, with a large number of images dealing with all the industries important to the area. The major drawback to the collection is the lack of finding aids, indexes, or other helps to locate specific material. The institution hopes to move to PastPerfect to provide general indexing to the holdings. There is more there than institutional memory can account for. Small institution and small budget, but room to grow.

Museum on Premises: Yes

Museum Hours: Winter, Mon–Sat 10–4; summer: Mon–Sat 9–5, Sun 12–4

Cost of Entry to Museum: $3

Museum Is Handicapped Accessible: Yes

Description of Museum: Small local museum

Parking: On-street free parallel parking

Lunch: Variety of cafes one block away in downtown or several blocks to harbor for seafood restaurant

Lodging: http://funbeach.com/lodging/; Heidi's Inn, AAA

Nearest Commercial Airport: Portland International (PDX) [114 miles]

Subjects

　　Historical Periods: 1865–1900; 1900–1940; 1940–present

　　Eras: World War II

　　Natural Resources: Fishing; Shellfish

　　Transportation: Railroads; Ferries

　　Manufacturing: Cannery; Boatbuilding/Shipyard; Sawmills

　　Government: City

　　Organizations: Schools;   Hospitals/Medical   Facilities;   Nonreligious
　　Organizations; Civic and Fraternal; Women's

　　Ethnic Groups: Native American; Japanese; Finnish

　　Religious Sites and Organizations: Protestant; Catholic

Date of Reviewer's Visit: 7/29/2004

Profile Updated by Institution: 11/12/2004

ISSAQUAH

Name: Gilman Town Hall Museum　　　　　　　**County:** King

Mailing Address: PO Box 695

　　City: Issaquah　　　　**State:** WA　　　　**Postal Code:** 98027-0000

Street Address: 165 SE Andrews St.

Institution Email: info@issaquahhistory.org

Telephone Number: (425) 392-3500　　**Fax Number:** (425) 392-3500

Contact Name: Erica S. Maniez, Museum Director

Institution Type: Local Museum

Affiliation: Issaquah Historical Society

Web site URL: http://www.issaquahhistory.org

Hours: Th–Sa 11–3, other times by appt.

Staff in Archives: 1f, 1p

Archives Are Handicapped Accessible: Yes

Access Description: Ramp to front door

Cost for Researcher—Remote: no charge for first 1/2 hr.; fee schedule thereafter

Review of Facilities: The research collections of the Issaquah Historical Society are housed in the historic Gilman Town Hall. The building is located a few blocks from the downtown area of Issaquah. The David J. Horrocks Memorial Research Area is a grand name for a simple room housing the historical collections. It is located on the ground floor of the town hall building. The room holds a moderate-sized table, bookcases, file cabinets, computer station, and copy machine. Manuscript collections are stored in an upstairs staff-access-only room.

Vertical Files: Yes   **Vertical Files in Cubic Feet:** 6

Vertical File Description and Subjects: Reference files consisting of general subject files and family files

Manuscripts: Yes   **Manuscripts Volume in Cubic Feet:** 20

Manuscript Types: Organization records, personal papers, scrapbooks

Manuscript Subjects: World War I correspondence, railroad ephemera

Photographs: Yes   **Number of Photographs:** 4,000

Storage of Photographs: Photographs are stored in acid-free folders in file cabinets, using a subject arrangement. Subject binders of copies of popular photographs are available for researcher browsing as well. The photographs are listed on local staff computer on PastPerfect.

Photograph Subjects: Logging, schools, local area history

Photograph Reproductions Are Available: Yes

   Photographic Prints: Yes   **Digital Prints:** Yes

   Digital Images on CD or Electronically: Yes

Books: Yes   **Number of Books in Collection:** 100

Description of Books: Local history, trains, professional collection

Newspapers: Yes

Newspapers on Microfilm: Yes

Microfilm and Dates: *Issaquah Press* through 1978. The facility has a reader, but no printer. Microfilm also available at Issaquah Library, which has reader/printer.

Oral Histories: Yes   **Oral Histories Number:** 26

Oral Histories Description: Small oral history project from 1970s yielded around 15 interviews, but with no transcriptions. There is a written history project available through the Web site.

Maps and Drawings: Yes

Description of Maps and Drawings: Coal mine maps, township maps

Genealogy Sources: Yes

Genealogy Sources Description: Copies of Issaquah census, 1900, 1910, 1920

Special Collections: No

Indexes: Yes

Online Sources: Oral history interviews listed on Oral History Catalog at Museum of History and Industry, Seattle

Review of Collections: The collections of the Issaquah Historical Museum focus on the Issaquah (formerly called Gilman) area. The photograph collection is impressive, particularly in the area of the logging industry. Other subjects of note are the local mining, farming, and railroad activities. The bookshelves seem to be in a chaotic arrangement. Manuscript collections are limited and located out of the research area. Collections are in the process of being inventoried and added to the local PastPerfect database.

Museum on Premises: Yes

    Museum Hours: Th–Sa 11–3

    Cost of Entry to Museum: Donation

    Museum Is Handicapped Accessible: Yes

Parking: Free on-street parallel parking on gravel shoulders of street

Lunch: Variety of ethnic and local restaurants 2–4 blocks or full range of restaurants within a short driving distance

Lodging: http://www.issaquahchamber.com

Nearest Commercial Airport: Seattle-Tacoma International (SEA) [22 miles]

Subjects

    Historical Periods: 1865–1900; 1900–1940; 1940–present

    Eras: World War I

    Natural Resources: Logging

    Mining: Mining

    Transportation: Railroads

    Business: Retail

    Manufacturing: Sawmills

    Organizations: Schools; Nonreligious Organizations

Date of Reviewer's Visit: 5/5/2004

Profile Updated by Institution: 11/15/2004

KELSO

Name: Cowlitz County Historical Museum   **County:** Cowlitz

Mailing Address: 405 Allen St.

    City: Kelso   **State:** WA   **Postal Code:** 98626-0000

Street Address: 405 Allen St.

Institution Email: None

Telephone Number: (360) 577-3119   **Fax Number:** (360) 423-9987

Contact Name: David Freece   **Contact Email:** freeced@co.cowlitz.wa.us

Institution Type: Local Museum

Affiliation: Cowlitz County Historical Society and Cowlitz County

Web site URL: http://www.cowlitzcounty.org/museum

Hours: T–Sa 9–5, Su 1–5.

Staff in Archives: 2f, 1p, 6v

Archives Are Handicapped Accessible: No

Access Description: Ramp in back from parking lot

Cost for Researcher—In-house: Free

Review of Facilities: The Cowlitz County Historical Museum is located in the center of Kelso. The newly renovated one-story building is practical and attractive. The research room is located down a hall from the main entrance. Check in at the main desk first. The fairly large room has two long worktables and metal shelving around several walls. File cabinets and map cases and rolled map storage fill out the remaining walls. The materials are stacked to the high ceiling in both the research room and adjacent storage areas. Some of the materials stored in the research room are for browsing and others are staff-mediated-use only. The research room is functional and designed for storage more than for researchers. The adjacent storage areas could use some compact shelving and reorganization. Great institution, helpful staff, and great collection.

Vertical Files: Yes   **Vertical Files in Cubic Feet:** 16

   Vertical File Description and Subjects: General subject files, mostly clippings, family histories.

Manuscripts: Yes   **Manuscripts Volume in Cubic Feet:** 200

   Manuscript Types: Organizational records, scrapbooks, ledgers, business records

   Manuscript Subjects: Collection of research files from the local newspaper, chamber records, fire department records, Longview Women's club

Photographs: Yes   **Number of Photographs:** 12,000

   Storage of Photographs: Photos are stored in plastic sleeves in file cabinets by subject, some originals are stored in document cases. Computerized cataloging is ongoing.

   Photograph Subjects: Cowlitz County, southwest Washington

   Photograph Reproductions Are Available: Yes

      Photographic Prints: Yes

Books: Yes   **Number of Books in Collection:** 400

   Description of Books: Local history, regional history, professional collection, city directories

Newspapers: Yes

> **Newspapers in Paper Format:** Yes
>
> **Papers and Dates:** Kelso papers, 1906–1950, *Longview Daily News,* 1926–1952
>
> **Newspapers on Microfilm:** No
>
> **Microfilm and Dates:** Microfilm at Longview Public Library in nearby Longview

Oral Histories: Yes   **Oral Histories Number:** 75

> **Oral Histories Description:** Oral history interviews with local area residents from the 1960s–1990s. Some deal with the history of the churches from the early 1990s. Some interviews have transcriptions. Most interviews are audiocassette, but some are reel-to-reel; the museum may have player.

Maps and Drawings: Yes   **Estimated Number of Maps and Drawings:** 450

> **Description of Maps and Drawings:** General maps, blueprints

Genealogy Sources: No

Special Collections: No

Indexes: The collection is indexed on a local computer.

> **Manuscript Finding Aids:** Processed manuscripts have basic finding aids

Review of Collections: Currently collections at this institution suffer more from their storage arrangement than anything else. Although they are well stored, they are hard to locate because of their arrangement. The collection is fairly large with more hiding than is perhaps realized. The photograph collection is accessible to researchers by subject and represents a good cross-section of the county history. The manuscript collection needs more attention, although processed collections have basic finding aids. There is a large number of materials that are totally unprocessed or inadequately processed. The institution is utilizing IO Museum Software to organize their computer listing of the collections. Great potential for hidden research gems.

Museum on Premises: Yes

> **Museum Hours:** Tu–Sa 9–5, Su 1–5
>
> **Cost of Entry to Museum:** Donation
>
> **Museum Is Handicapped Accessible:** Yes
>
> **Description of Museum:** The museum exhibits the history of Cowlitz County with permanent and traveling exhibits.

Parking: Free parking lot at the side of the building

Lunch: Short drive to a variety of restaurants

Lodging: http://www.co.cowlitz.wa.us/tourism/; http://kelsolongviewchamber.org/

Nearest Commercial Airport: Portland International (PDX) [48 miles]

Subjects

Historical Periods:1800–1865; 1865–1900; 1900–1940; 1940–present

Eras: Fur Trade; WPA

Natural Resources: Fishing; Logging

Mining: Coal

Transportation: Railroads; Ferries

Agriculture: Dairy; Ranching/Livestock; Vegetable/Truck Crops; Grains; Orchards

Business: Banking; Retail; Legal/Medical Services; Hotels/Restaurants; Entertainment/Theaters

Manufacturing: Cannery; Brewery; Sawmills; Wood Products

Government: City; County

Organizations: Schools; Hospitals/Medical Facilities; Charities; Civic and Fraternal; Women's

Ethnic Groups: Native American; Japanese; Finnish; Norwegian; Scottish; Swedish

Religious Sites and Organizations: Protestant; Catholic

Date of Reviewer's Visit: 7/28/2004

Profile Updated by Institution: 11/19/2004

KENNEWICK

✸✸✸

Name: East Benton County Historical Society and Museum   **County:** Benton

Mailing Address: PO Box 6964

City: Kennewick   **State:** WA   **Postal Code:** 99336-0602

Street Address: 205 Keewaydin Dr.

Institution Email: ebchs@gte.net

Telephone Number: (509) 582-7704

Contact Name: Corene Hulse, Administrator

Institution Type: Local Museum

Web site URL: http://www.owt.com/ebchs/

Hours: Tu–Sa 12–4

Staff in Archives: 1f, 1p

Archives Are Handicapped Accessible: Yes

Cost for Researcher—In-house: Museum admission

Cost for Researcher—Remote: Fee schedule

Review of Facilities: The East Benton County Historical Society Museum is located at the edge of Keewaydin Park, not far from the downtown area and adjacent to other city buildings. The museum is a single-level building built in 1982. The research room is located off the main museum room, with some materials on a high counter outside the room itself. The room boasts a large conference table in the center with bookshelves, file cabinets, and assorted materials ringing the room. The lighting is dim, but the research area is functional and pleasant.

Vertical Files: Yes   **Vertical Files in Cubic Feet:** 27

   Vertical File Description and Subjects: Local historical information and newspaper clipping files arranged by general subject

Manuscripts: Yes   **Manuscripts Volume in Cubic Feet:** 25

   Manuscript Types: Organizational records

   Manuscript Subjects: Memorabilia and ephemera from various local organizations and events: fairs, rodeos, school history

Photographs: Yes   **Number of Photographs:** 5,000

   Storage of Photographs: Photograph files are accessible only through staff. Originals are filed in folders in file cabinets and arranged by accession number.

   Photograph Subjects: Local area history, people and events

   Photograph Reproductions Are Available: Yes

      Photographic Prints: Yes   **Digital Prints:** Yes

Books: Yes   **Number of Books in Collection:** 500

   Description of Books: Local history books, city directories, high school annuals, collection of bird books from the Audubon Society

Newspapers: No

Oral Histories: Yes   **Oral Histories Number:** 200

   Oral Histories Description: Local resident interviews. A few have partial transcriptions.

Maps and Drawings: No

Genealogy Sources: Yes

   Genealogy Sources Description: Over 50 binders of obituary files started in 1982. Large file cabinet of files on local families. They also have an online obituary file.

Special Collections: Yes

   Special Collections Description: The museum boasts a large record collection donated by a local radio station when they went off the air in 2002. The majority of the collection is 33 1/3 LP's but there is also a significant number of 45's. There is a wide variety of music, mostly popular, but spread over many decades. The collection currently does not have a listing or finding aid to identify individual pieces.

Indexes: There are card file indexes of the photograph and book collections

Online Sources: Alphabetical obituary listing is available from the Web site. The 1910 census for Benton County is also available at the Web site.

Review of Collections: The research collections of the East Benton County Historical Society and Museum deal with all aspects of the history of the area. The collection holds items from the pioneer era forward. The collection focuses on the history of the towns of Kennewick and Richland and surrounding communities. Although the collections are not large they cover a broad range of local subjects. The photography collection is tightly controlled by staff. Most of the rest of the collection is open to browsers.

Muscum on Premises: Yes

Museum Hours: Tu–Sa 12–4

Cost of Entry to Museum: $2

Museum Is Handicapped Accessible: Yes

Parking: Free parking lot adjacent

Lunch: Driving distance to a variety of local and chain restaurants

Lodging: http://www.visittri-cities.com

Nearest Commercial Airport: Tri-Cities (Pasco) (PSC) [6 miles]

Subjects

Historical Periods: 1800–1865; 1865–1900; 1900–1940; 1940–present

Eras: Indian Wars; Spanish American War; World War I; Korean War; Gulf War

Natural Resources: Water; Dams; Irrigation; Logging

Transportation: Railroads; Ferries; Aviation

Agriculture: Dairy; Ranching/Livestock; Vegetable/Truck Crops; Grains; Orchards; Vineyard; Dry Land Farming

Business: Retail; Legal/Medical Services; Hotels/Restaurants; Entertainment/ Theaters

Government: City; County

Organizations: Schools; Colleges/Universities; Hospitals/Medical Facilities; Charities; Nonreligious Organizations; Civic and Fraternal; Women's; Business; Children's

Ethnic Groups: Native American

Religious Sites and Organizations: Protestant; Catholic

Date of Reviewer's Visit: 10/10/2003

Profile Updated by Institution: 11/18/2004

KENT

Name: Greater Kent Historical Society   **County:** King

Mailing Address: 855 E. Smith St.

   City: Kent   **State:** WA   **Postal Code:** 98032-4623

Street Address: 220 4th Ave S.

Institution Email: cityofknt@msn.com

Telephone Number: (253) 856-5785   **Fax Number:** (253) 859-0979

Contact Name: John Mergens   **Contact Email:** jpmergens@msn.com

Institution Type: Local Museum

Web site URL: http://www.cyberkent.com/kenthistoric/museum

Hours: W–Sa 11–3

Staff in Archives: 2p 4 v

Archives Are Handicapped Accessible: Yes

Access Description: The entrance has a handicap ramp up to the porch but there are some raised doorjambs.

Review of Facilities: The Greater Kent Historical Society is located in the historic Bereiter house in a predominately residential area outside the main downtown area in Kent. The small research room is on the first floor in a former office or bedroom. Archival collections are stacked along the walls in bookcases and file cabinets. Research table space is extremely limited. The lighting in the room is adequate. Most of the collections are stored in the research room or a nearby storage room.

Vertical Files: No

Manuscripts: Yes   **Manuscripts Volume in Cubic Feet:** 32

   Manuscript Types: Family papers, personal papers, organizational papers, scrapbooks

   Manuscript Subjects: Kent area families, school records, civic/fraternal club records

Photographs: Yes   **Number of Photographs:** 500

   Storage of Photographs: Browsing collection of photographs is stored in file cabinet in a nearby storage area

Photograph Subjects: Kent area history

Photograph Reproductions Are Available: Yes

Photographic Prints: Yes   **Digital Prints:** Yes

Digital Images on CD or Electronically: Yes

Books: Yes   **Number of Books in Collection:** 80

Description of Books: Local and regional history, annuals, city directories

Newspapers: Yes

Newspapers in Paper Format: Yes

Papers and Dates: Kent area papers, 1930–1990

Oral Histories: Yes   **Oral Histories Number:** 5

Oral Histories Description: Oral history interviews with local area residents. Four are on videotape. Interviews done 1980, 1985, and 2003.

Maps and Drawings: Yes   **Estimated Number of Maps and Drawings:** 6

Description of Maps and Drawings: City streets and businesses

Genealogy Sources: Yes

Genealogy Sources Description: Death records, marriage records, obituary files

Special Collections: No

Indexes: Card file and PastPerfect database with listing of photographs and manuscript materials

Review of Collections: The collection of the Greater Kent Historical Society is small for the size of community. Although the collections are limited they still provide valuable insight into the history of the city of Kent. Particularly interesting are some of the items on the Japanese-American truck farms that were in the valley pre-World War II. Otherwise the collection focuses on a wide variety of businesses, organizations, and ethnic groups but has little information on any one topic.

Museum on Premises: Yes

Museum Hours: W–Sa 11–3

Cost of Entry to Museum: Donation

Museum Is Handicapped Accessible: Yes

Description of Museum: Historic house with displays in various rooms and some period rooms

Parking: Free parking lot behind museum

Lunch: Driving distance to a variety of restaurants

Lodging: http://www.kentchamber.com

Nearest Commercial Airport: Seattle-Tacoma International (SEA) [8 miles]

Subjects

> **Historical Periods:** 1940–present
>
> **Eras:** Civil War; World War I; World War II
>
> **Natural Resources:** Fishing; Logging
>
> **Transportation:** Railroads; Ships and Shipping; Aviation
>
> **Agriculture:** Dairy; Ranching/Livestock; Vegetable/Truck Crops; Orchards
>
> **Business:** Banking; Retail; Legal/Medical Services; Hotels/Restaurants; Entertainment/Theaters
>
> **Manufacturing:** Cannery; Creamery; Sawmills
>
> **Government:** City
>
> **Organizations:** Schools; Hospitals/Medical Facilities; Charities; Nonreligious Organizations; Civic and Fraternal; Women's; Business; Children's
>
> **Ethnic Groups:** Native American; Latin American; African; Japanese; Danish; Finnish; Irish; Russian; Spanish; Swedish
>
> **Religious Sites and Organizations:** Protestant; Catholic; LDS (Mormon); Jewish; Buddhist

Date of Reviewer's Visit: 7/19/2002

Profile Updated by Institution: 11/29/2004

LA CONNER

Name: Skagit County Historical Society and Museum Library   **County:** Skagit

Mailing Address: PO Box 818

  City: La Conner   **State:** WA   **Postal Code:** 98257-0818

Street Address: 501 S. 4th St.

Institution Email: Museum@co.skagit.wa.us

Telephone Number: (360) 466-1611

Contact Name: Karen Marshall, Director

Contact Email: karenm@co.skagit.wa.us

Institution Type: Local Museum

Affiliation: Skagit County Historical Society/Skagit County

Web site URL: http://www.skagitcounty.net/museum

Hours: Tu–Su 11–5 by appt. only

Staff in Archives: 2p

Archives Are Handicapped Accessible: Yes

Access Description: Ramp and handicapped parking

Review of Facilities: The Skagit County Historical Museum is located on "top of the hill" in historic La Conner. The museum is in one building and the research library is in another next door. The research library building is a former house that was renovated to hold the museum offices and library. The research room is on the main floor and is well lit. The room is spartan but functional, with plenty of table space. Although a small institution, the policies and procedures for research are well defined: pencils only, registration form required, and all research materials accessible by staff only. Finding aids are staff-only use as well. Most research materials are stored on the second floor, in less than spacious quarters.

Vertical Files: No

Manuscripts: Yes   **Manuscripts Volume in Cubic Feet:** 20

  Manuscript Types: Business records, organizational records

  Manuscript Subjects: Skagit County places or people, business ledgers and scrapbooks of businesses and organizations

Photographs: Yes   **Number of Photographs:** 15,000

  Storage of Photographs: The photographs are filed in archival sleeves and arranged by accession number

  Photograph Subjects: Skagit County people and places; includes a postcard collection

  Photograph Reproductions Are Available: Yes

    Photographic Prints: Yes

Books: Yes   **Number of Books in Collection:** 2,100

  Description of Books: Local and regional history, professional collection, city directories

Newspapers: Yes

  Newspapers in Paper Format: Yes

  Papers and Dates: *Mount Vernon Argus,* 1899–1940s

  Newspapers on Microfilm: Yes

  Microfilm and Dates: Microfilm of *Puget Sound Mail* (La Conner)

Oral Histories: Yes   **Oral Histories Number:** 300

  Oral Histories Description: Interviews of local area residents

Maps and Drawings: Yes   **Estimated Number of Maps and Drawings:** 201

  Description of Maps and Drawings: Skagit Valley, La Conner, and surrounding area maps

Genealogy Sources: Yes

  Genealogy Sources Description: Obituary files, cemetery records

Special Collections: No

Indexes: Any indexes to the collection are available to staff only.

Review of Collections: The research collection is locally based, covering the Skagit County area, including La Conner. The manuscript materials are basic local business and organizational records. The photograph collection is large and covers all aspects of life in the Skagit Valley area. The collection is very staff-dependent at all levels of research, which necessitates staff intervention. The collection is well stored and maintained. The staff is moving to incorporate the collection onto PastPerfect, so the access problems will be minimized.

Museum on Premises: Yes

> **Museum Hours:** Tu–Su 11–5
>
> **Cost of Entry to Museum:** $4
>
> **Museum Is Handicapped Accessible:** Yes
>
> **Description of Museum:** Two moderate-sized permanent galleries display Skagit Valley history, another gallery hosts temporary exhibits on local, state, and national subjects. An interactive gallery and a video room round out the museum's educational opportunities.

Parking: Free vertical on-street parking in front of building

Lunch: Variety of restaurants within a few block in the downtown historic district

Lodging: http://www.laconnerchamber.com

Nearest Commercial Airport: William R Fairchild International (Port Angeles) (CLM) [91 miles]

Subjects

> **Historical Periods:** 1865–1900; 1900–1940; 1940–present
>
> **Eras:** CCC; World War II
>
> **Natural Resources:** Irrigation; Fishing; Logging
>
> **Mining:** Surface Mining
>
> **Transportation:** Railroads; Ships and Shipping; Ferries
>
> **Agriculture:** Dairy; Ranching/Livestock; Vegetable/Truck Crops
>
> **Business:** Retail; Legal/Medical Services; Entertainment/Theaters
>
> **Manufacturing:** Cannery; Boatbuilding/Shipyard; Sawmills
>
> **Organizations:** Schools; Hospitals/Medical Facilities; Nonreligious Organizations; Women's; Business
>
> **Ethnic Groups:** Native American; Norwegian; Swedish

Date of Reviewer's Visit: 4/24/2003

Profile Updated by Institution: 11/29/2004

LACEY

Name: Lacey Museum   **County:** Thurston

Mailing Address: 829 1/2 Lacey St.

  City: Lacey   **State:** WA   **Postal Code:** 98503-0000

Street Address: 829 1/2 Lacey St.

Institution Email: museum@ci.lacey.wa.us

Telephone Number: (360) 438-0209   **Fax Number:** (360) 438-2669

Contact Name: Andrea Taylor, Curator

Institution Type: Local Museum

Affiliation: City of Lacey

Web site URL: None

Hours: Th–F 12–4, Sa 10–4

Staff in Archives: 2p

Archives Are Handicapped Accessible: No

Access Description: Building is not accessible. Four stairs at entrance and large doorjamb.

Review of Facilities: The Lacey Museum is located in an old house off the street in the historic district of town. The white frame building now contains some smallish exhibit rooms on the first floor and offices and storage on the second floor. The stairway to the second floor is steep, although it is a staff-only area. The research table is in the front room and it is a large conference table against one wall. The research materials are all stored on the second floor in offices and closets.

Vertical Files: Yes   **Vertical Files in Cubic Feet:** 10

  Vertical File Description and Subjects: Copies and original documents by subject or family name

Manuscripts: Yes   **Manuscripts Volume in Cubic Feet:** 30

  Manuscript Types: Business records, organizational records

  Manuscript Subjects: Men's clubs, business records

Photographs: Yes   **Number of Photographs:** 2,000

  Storage of Photographs: Photographs are stored in plastic sleeves in file cabinets and arranged by accession number

  Photograph Subjects: Photographs are collected of all phases of life in the city of Lacey and the surrounding area.

  Photograph Reproductions Are Available: Yes

Photographic Prints: Yes   **Digital Prints:** Yes

Books: Yes   **Number of Books in Collection:** 100

Description of Books: Local history, annuals, professional collection

Newspapers: Yes

Newspapers in Paper Format: Yes

Papers and Dates: Complete run of the *Lacey Leader*

Newspapers on Microfilm: Yes

Microfilm and Dates: *Lacey Leader* newspaper, 1967–1981; 6 rolls at Lacey City Hall vault can be viewed by request.

Oral Histories: Yes   **Oral Histories Number:** 18

Oral Histories Description: Oral history interviews done of local Lacey residents from 1983–1995. Seven have been transcribed.

Maps and Drawings: Yes   **Estimated Number of Maps and Drawings:**

Description of Maps and Drawings: Copies of Metsker maps, 1929, 1948, 1962; Original of Thurston County Metsker for Thurston County 1973

Genealogy Sources: Yes

Genealogy Sources Description: Family history files of pioneer families, cemetery records

Special Collections: No

Indexes: In-house computerized list of subjects and vertical file list

Review of Collections: Lacey Museum collects historical research materials about the city of Lacey and surrounding areas. Materials are held on all aspects of the life and occupations of Lacey and area residents from the pioneer days forward. There are a number of collections on businesses of the area, including some retail, some manufacturing, and some agriculture. There are also some city and county records. Organizational records include those from women's clubs, children's clubs, and other civic and fraternal organizations. The collection is a combination of copies and original materials.

Museum on Premises: Yes

Museum Hours: Th–F 12–4 and Sa 10–4

Cost of Entry to Museum: Free

Museum Is Handicapped Accessible: No

Description of Museum: This is a small museum with an educational focus primarily outside the building. The exhibit area is extremely small for the size of the city.

Parking: Free gravel parking lot in front

Lunch: Variety of restaurants within driving distance

Lodging: http://www.visitolympia.com/

Nearest Commercial Airport: Seattle-Tacoma International (SEA) [45 miles]

Subjects

> **Historical Periods:** 1800–1865; 1865–1900; 1900–1940; 1940–present
>
> **Eras:** Indian Wars; World War I; World War II
>
> **Natural Resources:** Water; Irrigation; Fishing; Hunting; Shellfish; Logging
>
> **Transportation:** Railroads; Ships and Shipping; Ferries; Aviation
>
> **Agriculture:** Dairy; Ranching/Livestock; Vegetable/Truck Crops; Grains; Orchards; Dry Land Farming
>
> **Business:** Retail; Legal/Medical Services; Hotels/Restaurants; Entertainment/ Theaters
>
> **Manufacturing:** Cannery; Woolen/Fabric Mills; Sawmills
>
> **Government:** City; County; State
>
> **Organizations:** Schools; Colleges/Universities; Hospitals/Medical Facilities; Charities; Nonreligious Organizations; Civic and Fraternal; Women's; Business; Children's
>
> **Ethnic Groups:** Native American; Pacific Islander; Japanese; Chinese; German; Swedish
>
> **Religious Sites and Organizations:** Protestant; Catholic

Date of Reviewer's Visit: 1/15/2004

Profile Updated by Institution: 11/17/2004

LONGVIEW

Name: Longview Public Library

County: Cowlitz

Mailing Address: 1600 Louisiana St.

City: Longview   **State:** WA

Postal Code: 98632-2993

Street Address: 1600 Louisiana St.

Institution Email: None

Telephone Number: (360) 442-5307   **Fax Number:** (360) 442-5954

Contact Name: Karen Dennis

Contact Email: karen.dennis@ci.longview.wa.us

Institution Type: Public Library

Affiliation: City of Longview

Web site URL: http://www.longviewlibrary.org/

Hours: W 3–5

Staff in Archives: 1f

Archives Are Handicapped Accessible: Yes

Review of Facilities: The Longview Public Library is housed in a 1926 two-story building and a two-plus-story addition off the back. The first floor has a grand front entrance with a flight of stairs. The addition has a ground floor entrance off the parking lot. An elevator goes directly up from this entrance to the Longview Room on the mezzanine, but any visit outside of open hours would require stopping at the first floor reference desk. The Longview Room is a moderate-sized L-shaped room with one wall holding 15 file cabinets and a map case. The opposite wall has 2 bookcases. Another bookcase is at the end, dividing off a staff work/storage area. Two round antique tables provide seating/workspace for researchers. Although they have four chairs apiece, it would be difficult for more than one or two serious researchers to utilize each table. Five of the file cabinets are the vertical file materials, ten house the manuscript collections, and the map case houses oversize photographs and materials. The research room gives an "old library" feel although it is in the newer unadorned building.

Vertical Files: Yes   **Vertical Files in Cubic Feet:** 30

Vertical File Description and Subjects: General subject files with ephemera, small document collections

Manuscripts: Yes   **Manuscripts Volume in Cubic Feet:** 60

Manuscript Types: Business records, scrapbooks, government records

Manuscript Subjects: Long-Bell Lumber Company records including all the planning records for the town of Longview

Photographs: Yes   **Number of Photographs:** 2,500

Storage of Photographs: Photocopies of photographs are available in binders by general subjects for research use. Originals housed archivally elsewhere in file cabinet.

Photograph Subjects: Longview history, Long-Bell Lumber Company photographs

Photograph Reproductions Are Available: Yes

Photographic Prints: Yes

Books: Yes   **Number of Books in Collection:** 676

Description of Books: Local history, regional history, city directories, annuals. Approximately half the book collection circulates.

Newspapers: Yes

Newspapers in Paper Format: Yes

Papers and Dates: Longview *(Daily News)*

Newspapers on Microfilm: Yes

Microfilm and Dates: Longview papers, 1923 to present. Kelso papers, 1888–1889, 1906–1926.

Oral Histories: No

Maps and Drawings: Yes   **Estimated Number of Maps and Drawings:** 120

Description of Maps and Drawings: Maps and architectural drawings are primarily rolled. Original maps and plans from the building of Longview.

Genealogy Sources: No

Special Collections: No

Indexes: Yes

Manuscript Finding Aids: Folder-level finding aid to the records of the Long-Bell Lumber Company

Review of Collections: The collections of the Longview Public Library–Longview Room deal with all aspects of Longview history. The majority of the manuscript collections consists of the transfer files of the Long-Bell Lumber Company, the planners and founders of Longview. These records deal with everything from the development of the planned community to advertising, schools, sewers, rental houses, and much more. The finding aid to this collection is 18 pages in length with just a folder listing. The vertical file collections contain small manuscript collections of many areas of Longview history.

Museum on Premises: No

Parking: Free parking lot to the back, on-street parallel 1-hr. parking in front

Lunch: Number of fast-food chains within 2 blocks

Lodging: http://kelsolongviewchamber.org/

Nearest Commercial Airport: Portland International (PDX) [50 miles]

Subjects

Historical Periods: 1900–1940

Natural Resources: Logging

Transportation: Ships and Shipping; Ferries

Business: Banking; Retail; Legal/Medical Services; Hotels/Restaurants; Entertainment/Theaters

Manufacturing: Sawmills; Wood Products

Date of Reviewer's Visit: 7/27/2004

Profile Updated by Institution: 11/22/2004

LOPEZ ISLAND

Name: Lopez Island Historical Museum   **County:** San Juan

Mailing Address: PO Box 163

   City: Lopez Island   **State:** WA   **Postal Code:** 98261-0000

Street Address: 28 Washburn Place

Institution Email: lopezmuseum@rockisland.com

Telephone Number: (360) 468-2049

Contact Name: Mark Thompson-Klein, Director

Institution Type: Local Museum

Affiliation: Lopez Island Historical Society

Web site URL: http://www.rockisland.com/~lopezmuseum/

Hours: F–Su 12–4, May–June and Sept; W–Su 12–4, July–Aug

Staff in Archives: 1p, 10v

Archives Are Handicapped Accessible: Yes

Access Description: Gravel walkway

Cost for Researcher—In-house: Fee schedule

Cost for Researcher—Remote: Fee schedule

Review of Facilities: The Lopez Island Historical Museum is located in the heart of Lopez Village. The museum is in a new structure designed to look like old buildings. The museum is one large room with an office area in the back that is partitioned off. The research workspace is a large tile table in the front and center of the museum with four chairs. A volunteer was scanning collections at the time of the visit. The research collections are stored either in the office in the back or in a storage room adjacent. Some seldom-used collections are stored in neighboring building on the property.

Vertical Files: Yes   **Vertical Files in Cubic Feet:** 24

   Vertical File Description and Subjects: The vertical files are divided into two sections: family files and topical files. Mostly newspaper clippings, but also primary documents, ephemera, and miscellaneous.

Manuscripts: Yes   **Manuscripts Volume in Cubic Feet:** 20

   Manuscript Types: Business records, organizational records

   Manuscript Subjects: Local school records, set of diaries from 1860s from woman in first white family in area, other diaries from 1920s describing life in area. Richardson Store records, other local business records.

Photographs: Yes   **Number of Photographs:** 2,000

   Storage of Photographs: Photos are stored in folders in file cabinet (not archival), slides stored in slide boxes. Most images are in slides.

Photograph Subjects: Port Stanley School, collection of slides taken from originals of local family photographs covering all aspects of Lopez Island history

Photograph Reproductions Are Available: Yes

Photographic Prints: Yes   **Digital Prints:** Yes

Books: Yes   **Number of Books in Collection:** 150

Description of Books: Local history, phone books, professional collection

Newspapers: Yes

Newspapers in Paper Format: Yes

Papers and Dates: *Island Record* from the 1970s and 1980s

Oral Histories: Yes   **Oral Histories Number:** 20

Oral Histories Description: Interviews from 1985 of local residents, some have partial transcriptions. New oral history project being undertaken.

Maps and Drawings: No

Genealogy Sources: Yes

Genealogy Sources Description: Family files listed above

Special Collections: No

Indexes: Local computer index on PastPerfect being developed. Old card file index to the slide collection.

Review of Collections: The collections at the Lopez Island Museum are small but have some significant items of interest. The history of Lopez is primarily of a working community (as opposed to a tourist island), and the collections reflect this reality. There are papers of several local businesses, including the store in Richardson, one of the towns on the island. A notable item in the collection are the diaries of a young woman from the Davis family, who were the earliest white settlers on the island. The museum is in the process of digitally photographing these diaries dating from the 1860s.

Museum on Premises: Yes

Museum Hours: Fri–Sun 12–4, May–June and Sept; Wed–Sun. 12–4, July–Aug

Cost of Entry to Museum: $2

Museum Is Handicapped Accessible: Yes

Description of Museum: Small museum with a historical timeline along one wall and a changeable exhibit of local history on the other. Focus is on the interpretation of the various aspects of the history of Lopez Island.

Parking: Free on-street parallel parking on shoulder, gravel parking lot behind building

Lunch: Variety of local restaurants within blocks

Lodging: http://www.lopezisland.com

Nearest Commercial Airport: Lopez Airport (S31) [3 miles], Anacortes Airport (74S) [18 miles], Seattle-Tacoma International (SEA) [115 miles]

Subjects

    Historical Periods: Pre-1800; 1800–1865; 1865–1900; 1900–1940; 1940–present

    Natural Resources: Logging

    Mining: Gold; Lime

    Transportation: Ships and Shipping; Ferries; Aviation

    Agriculture: Dairy; Ranching/Livestock; Vegetable/Truck Crops; Grains; Orchards; Vineyard

    Business: Retail; Legal/Medical Services; Hotels/Restaurants; Entertainment/Theaters

    Manufacturing: Sawmills

    Government: City; County

    Organizations: Schools; Nonreligious Organizations

    Ethnic Groups: Native American; Chinese; English; Finnish; Irish

    Religious Sites and Organizations: Protestant; Catholic

Date of Reviewer's Visit: 6/18/2004

Profile Updated by Institution: 11/12/2004

LYNDEN

Name: Lynden Pioneer Museum   **County:** Whatcom

Mailing Address: 217 W. Front St.

  City: Lynden   **State:** WA   **Postal Code:** 98264-0000

Street Address: 217 W Front St.

Institution Email: infor@lyndenpioneermuseum.com

Telephone Number: (360) 354-3675

Contact Name: Troy Luginbill

Contact Email: troy@lyndenpioneermuseum.com

Institution Type: Local Museum

Affiliation: Lynden Heritage Foundation

Web site URL: http://www.lyndenpioneermuseum.com/

Hours: M–Sa 10– 4

Staff in Archives: 2f, 4p, 10v

Archives Are Handicapped Accessible: No

Access Description: Archive is upstairs

Review of Facilities: The Lynden Pioneer Museum is located in a storefront building on the main street of the business district. The museum is located on the first floor of the building. There is a research space in the attic of the museum. It shares space with staff offices. The area for researchers consists of a worktable with the subject guides on a shelf above the table. The materials are stored nearby with the museum collections. The stairway up is very steep and very narrow and at the top the ceiling is low.

Vertical Files: Yes   **Vertical Files in Cubic Feet:** 4

    Vertical File Description and Subjects: Vertical file arranged by community and geographic area, then by broad subject, then by individual or business

Manuscripts: Yes   **Manuscripts Volume in Cubic Feet:** 350

    Manuscript Types: Personal papers, business papers, school records, organizational records, government records, scrapbooks

    Manuscript Subjects: Whatcom County business and individual personal papers, some church records, city records

Photographs: Yes   **Number of Photographs:** 4,500

    Storage of Photographs: Original photographs are stored in document boxes elsewhere in the building. A browsing collection of photographs is available through a computer database and subject notebooks hold copies of photographs for research use.

    Photograph Subjects: Whatcom County and Lynden, military photos of Whatcom County veterans from the Civil War to the present

    Photograph Reproductions Are Available: Yes

    Photographic Prints: Yes

Books: Yes   **Number of Books in Collection:** 60

    Description of Books: Local history, city directories, miscellaneous

Newspapers: Yes

    Newspapers in Paper Format: Yes

    Papers and Dates: Various Whatcom County titles from 1896– 1982

Oral Histories: Yes   **Oral Histories Number:** 33

    Oral Histories Description: Oral history interviews of local area residents. Interviews done from 1990–2003. Some are on audiotape and others on videotape. Most have transcriptions.

Maps and Drawings: Yes   **Estimated Number of Maps and Drawings:** 45

    Description of Maps and Drawings: Maps of local communities and regions; many are copies of originals and are stored rolled

Genealogy Sources: No

Special Collections: No

Indexes: Guide to vertical file. Rebuilding a computer index to collections.

Published Guides: Copies of photographs in subject notebooks

Review of Collections: The collection at Lynden Pioneer Museum is out of space. This fact limits the usability of the collection that they have and prevents them from growing the collection in future years. The collection covers the town of Lynden and surrounding areas. This is one of the few institutions visited that limit their collecting to the earliest years of the pioneer era. Only the history of the first 75 years of the town is recorded at this location. This makes the entire collection pre-1966.

Museum on Premises: Yes

Museum Hours: M–Sa 10–4, Su 1:30–4

Cost of Entry to Museum: $5

Museum Is Handicapped Accessible: Yes

Description of Museum: This is an amazingly well executed museum. The heart of the museum is a large street scene reproduction with 16 separate buildings of a pioneer town. They have some wonderful photos on their Web site.

Parking: Free diagonal on-street parking

Lunch: Numerous wonderful eateries in the nearby blocks. Many are Dutch.

Lodging: http://www.lynden.org; Dutch Village Inn in Lynden or Bellingham 12 miles south

Nearest Commercial Airport: Bellingham International (BLI) [15 miles]

Subjects

Historical Periods: 1865–1900; 1900–1940; 1940–present

Eras: Fur Trade; Civil War; World War I; World War II

Natural Resources: Water; Dams; Fishing; Hunting; Logging

Mining: Tunnel Mining

Transportation: Railroads

Agriculture: Dairy; Vegetable/Truck Crops; Grains

Business: Banking; Retail; Legal/Medical Services; Hotels/Restaurants; Entertainment/Theaters

Manufacturing: Cannery; Creamery; Sawmills

Government: City

Organizations: Schools; Nonreligious Organizations; Civic and Fraternal

Ethnic Groups: Native American; Latin American; Chinese; Dutch; English; German; Irish; Norwegian; Swedish

Religious Sites and Organizations: Methodist

Date of Reviewer's Visit: 4/25/2003
Profile Updated by Institution: 11/10/2004

MARBLEMOUNT

Name: North Cascades National Park Service Complex   **County:** Skagit
Mailing Address: 7280 Ranger Station Rd.

   City: Marblemount   **State:** WA   **Postal Code:** 98267-0000
Street Address: 7280 Ranger Station Rd.
Institution Email: None
Telephone Number: (360) 873-4590   **Fax Number:** (360) 873-4590
Contact Name: Museum Curator, North Cascades National Park
Contact Email: jesse_kennedy@nps.gov
Institution Type: Historic Site
Affiliation: National Park Service
Web site URL: http://www.nps.gov/noca
Hours: By Appt only, 9–3 , M–F
Staff in Archives: 1f, 1v
Archives Are Handicapped Accessible: Yes
Cost for Researcher—Remote: Depends on nature of inquiry

Review of Facilities: Note: The North Cascades National Park Service Complex was not visited by the reviewer. The following information was provided by National Park Service staff and independently verified by the reviewer.

The North Cascades National Park Service Complex is located two miles outside the town of Marblemount. The Marblemount Curation Facility, built in 1993, is a single-story depository with staff offices, administrative research areas, two laboratories, and two storage rooms. Research area includes a conference table and a computer station for the National Park Service database. The Curation Facility deals with collections from North Cascades National Park, San Juan Island National Park, and Ebey's Landing National Historical Reserve.

Vertical Files: Yes   **Vertical Files in Cubic Feet:** 100
   Vertical File Description and Subjects: General vertical file materials arranged by topic and accession numbers
Manuscripts: Yes   **Manuscripts Volume in Cubic Feet:** 200
   Manuscript Types: Archives, business records, land records, personal papers, family papers

Manuscript Subjects: General park history and public land management and commerce

Photographs: Yes   **Number of Photographs:** 1,000

Storage of Photographs: Photographs are stored in boxes or binders in a staff-only storage area. Some images are available in a computer database.

Photograph Subjects: Photograph subjects include transportation, mining, trapping, and government in the North Cascades National Park Service Complex.

Photograph Reproductions Are Available: Yes

> **Digital Prints:** Yes
>
> **Digital Images on CD or Electronically:** Yes

Books: No

Newspapers: No

Oral Histories: Yes

> **Oral Histories Number:** 50
>
> **Oral Histories Description:** Oral history interviews of pioneers of the North Cascades area done from 1968 to 1999. Interviews are on audiocassette and some have been transcribed.

Maps and Drawings: Yes   **Estimated Number of Maps and Drawings:** 100

> **Description of Maps and Drawings:** USGS Quads and Forest Service maps

Genealogy Sources: No

Special Collections: No

Indexes: Computer index of collections available on staff and research room computer

> **Manuscript Finding Aids:** Manuscript finding aids are available on in-house computer system and also in printed form in binders on the premises.

Review of Collections: The collections of the Marblemount Curation Facility encompass the records of three National Park Service facilities in northwestern Washington state. The history and records of the North Cascades National Park represent only a portion of the available resources at this facility. Research collections from the San Juan Island National Historic Park (located on San Juan Island) and Ebey's Landing National Historic Reserve (located on Whidbey Island near Coupeville) are also archived at this facility.

Museum on Premises: No

Parking: Free parking lot adjacent

Lunch: Restaurants in the town of Marblemount 2 miles away

Lodging: http://www.marblemount.com or http://www.nps.gov/noca/accomm.htm

Nearest Commercial Airport: Seattle-Tacoma International (SEA) [125 miles]

Subjects

    Historical Periods:1900–1940; 1940–present

    Natural Resources: Dams; Logging

    Mining: Gold; Silver; Copper; Placer Mining; Tunnel Mining

    Government: City; Federal

Date of Reviewer's Visit: Not Visited

Profile Updated by Institution: 12/1/2004

NEAH BAY

Name: Makah Cultural and Research Center   **County:** Clallam

Mailing Address: PO Box 160

    City: Neah Bay   **State:** WA   **Postal Code:** 98357-0000

Street Address: 1880 Bayview Ave.

Institution Email: makahmuseum@centurytel.net

Telephone Number: (360) 645-2711   **Fax Number:** (360) 645-2656

Contact Name: Keely Parker   **Contact Email:** mcrckeeley@centurytel.net

Institution Type: Local Museum

Affiliation: Makah Tribe

Web site URL: http://www.makah.com/mcrchome.htm

Hours: By appt.

Staff in Archives: 1f

Archives Are Handicapped Accessible: Yes

Cost for Researcher—In-house: Museum admission

Review of Facilities: The Makah Cultural and Resource Center is located outside the small village of Neah Bay. There is not a dedicated research area. Staff may have researchers use a classroom on the main floor off the entrance area. The classroom has two long tables in a very large room. There is also a small computer room nearby with internet terminals. The collections themselves are stored on the second floor in the administrative offices area. Everything except the books are in a locked archive room. This collection is specialized and has restrictions on use of many of the materials. The archivist and executive director are the only people on the staff to determine use of the collections. Appointments are essential at this institution.

Vertical Files: Yes   **Vertical Files in Cubic Feet:** 25

Manuscripts: Yes   **Manuscripts Volume in Cubic Feet:** 150

Manuscript Types: Family papers, personal papers, business records

Manuscript Subjects: Northwest Coast Indians with concentration on Makah

Photographs: Yes   **Number of Photographs:** 30 cu. ft. of photographs

Photograph Subjects: Northwest Coast Indians, fishing, Makah

Photograph Reproductions Are Available: Yes

   Photographic Prints: Yes

Books: Yes   **Number of Books in Collection:** 400

Description of Books: Local history, tribal history

Newspapers: Yes

   Newspapers on Microfilm: Yes

   Microfilm and Dates: Local papers on microfilm, 1885–1935

Oral Histories: No

Maps and Drawings: No

Genealogy Sources: No

Special Collections: No

Indexes: No

Review of Collections: The collecting focus of the Makah Cultural and Research Center is Makah culture and the Neah Bay community. Tracing the history of the Makah from the earliest times to the present, the research collection consists of paper documents and historical artifacts. The photograph collection is large at about 30 cubic feet. Manuscript collections include information on the Northwest Coast Indians with a special focus on the Makah.

Museum on Premises: Yes

   Museum Hours: Daily 10–5, June–Sept; W–Su 10–5 rest of year

   Cost of Entry to Museum: $5

   Museum Is Handicapped Accessible: Yes

   Description of Museum: The Makah Cultural and Research Center is large and very beautifully done. The interpretation is almost exclusively of the precontact Makah way of life. Displays include four types of canoes, tools, baskets, and a full-size longhouse.

Parking: A free paved parking lot is adjacent

Lunch: There are a number of small cafes in Neah Bay.

Lodging: http://www.clallambay.com; http://www.northwestsecretplaces.com/

Nearest Commercial Airport: William R. Fairchild International (Port Angeles) (CLM) [69 miles]

Subjects

    Historical Periods: Pre-1800; 1800–1865

    Eras: Exploration; Fur Trade

    Natural Resources: Fishing; Hunting; Whaling; Shellfish; Logging

    Government: Tribal

    Ethnic Groups: Native American

Date of Reviewer's Visit: 6/23/2004

Profile Updated by Institution: 11/24/2004

NEWPORT

Name: Pend Oreille County Historical Society   **County:** Pend Oreille

Mailing Address: PO Box 1409

   City: Newport   **State:** WA   **Postal Code:** 99156-1409

Street Address: 402 S. Washington Ave.

Institution Email: geau@povn.com

Telephone Number: (208) 447-5388

Contact Name: Faith McClenny   **Contact Email:** faith@povn.com

Institution Type: Local Museum

Web site URL: None

Hours: M and W by appt. only

Staff in Archives: 3v

Archives Are Handicapped Accessible: Yes

Access Description: Ramp to building with library, some parts of museum have stairs

Cost for Researcher—Remote: fee schedule

Review of Facilities: The Pend Oreille Historical Society Museum is located on the main highway on the edge of the downtown area. The original museum is a 1908 railroad depot. The library/research room is located in a 1994 building next to the depot up an ADA ramp. The front of the building opens to an exhibit area and to the rear is a door that leads to the library area. The library/research room is actually two smaller rooms with a connecting door. The first room contains two walls of bookcases holding the book collections, scrapbooks, and bound newspapers. A copy machine and computer are against the wall and a medium-sized table and card table are pushed against the bookcases to provide research space. The adjoining room has a medium worktable in the center of the room, a row of file cabinets, and a large wooden case, where the manuscript materials are stored. The area is well lit, but small, and at the time of the visit crowded with volunteers and researchers.

Vertical Files: Yes   **Vertical Files in Cubic Feet:** 12

Vertical File Description and Subjects: Vertical file materials are divided into biography and general reference subject files of clippings, art, and original documents.

Manuscripts: Yes   **Manuscripts Volume in Cubic Feet:** 36

Manuscript Types: School records, organizational papers, scrapbooks

Manuscript Subjects: Newport school files from 1911 to 1925, fraternal organizations, 42 scrapbooks of various types

Photographs: Yes   **Number of Photographs:** 5,000

Storage of Photographs: Photographs are stored in file cabinets arranged by subject, some stored in plastic sleeves.

Photograph Subjects: Pend Oreille County subjects, particularly logging. Most photos with better-than-average identification. Agriculture, businesses, steamboats, early mining communities.

Photograph Reproductions Are Available: Yes

   Photographic Prints: Yes

Books: Yes   **Number of Books in Collection:** 100

Description of Books: Local history, annuals

Newspapers: Yes

   Newspapers in Paper Format: Yes

   Papers and Dates: Newport newspapers from 1897–1978

   Newspapers on Microfilm: No

   Microfilm and Dates: Newport Public Library, about three blocks from the museum, has microfilm of local newspapers.

Oral Histories: Yes   **Oral Histories Number:** 22

Oral Histories Description: Audiocassette tapes of local family interviews, some with transcriptions from the 1970s.

Maps and Drawings: Yes   **Estimated Number of Maps and Drawings:** 30

Description of Maps and Drawings: Homestead maps, local area history

Genealogy Sources: Yes

Genealogy Sources Description: Obituary index late 1970s to present, biography files, some birth and marriage records

Special Collections: No

Indexes: Photos and vertical files are arranged in alphabetical order. Obituary index in binders, indexes of the scrapbook collection contents

Online Sources: Plan to be online late 2005.

Review of Collections: Pend Oreille County Historical Society's main purpose is to preserve the history of Pend Oreille County in the northeast corner of Washington. The collections of the Pend Oreille Historical Society are adequately, if not professionally processed. The collection's strong points are the photo collection and the school history materials. The limited staff of volunteers is working at processing new materials, as well as identifying the older materials. The photograph collection is particularly strong in logging history of the county.

Museum on Premises: Yes

Museum Hours: Daily 10–4 mid-May to Oct

Cost of Entry to Museum: Donation

Description of Museum: The museum consists of the historic depot now used as a gift shop/exhibit area, numerous historic buildings moved to the site, railroad cars, and machinery sheds.

Parking: Free paved parking lot adjacent

Lunch: Walking distance to several local restaurants

Lodging: http://www.newportoldtownchamber.org/

Nearest Commercial Airport: Spokane International (GEG) [55 miles]

Subjects

Historical Periods: 1865–1900; 1900–1940; 1940–present

Eras: Fur Trade; CCC; World War II

Natural Resources: Water; Dams; Fishing; Hunting; Logging

Mining: Gold; Silver; Copper; Placer Mining; Tunnel Mining; Lead; Zinc; Cement

Transportation: Railroads; Stagecoach/Freight; Ferries

Agriculture: Ranching/Livestock; Grains; Dry Land Farming

Business: Banking; Retail; Hotels/Restaurants; Entertainment/Theaters

Manufacturing: Creamery; Brick Making; Boatbuilding/Shipyard; Sawmills; Wood Products

Government: County

Organizations: Schools; Hospitals/Medical Facilities; Nonreligious Organizations; Civic and Fraternal; Women's; Business; Children's; Labor and Union

Ethnic Groups: Native American; Japanese; Chinese

Religious Sites and Organizations: Protestant; Catholic; Mennonite/Amish

Date of Reviewer's Visit: 8/25/2004

Profile Updated by Institution: 11/16/2004

OKANOGAN

Name: Okanogan County Historical Society   **County:** Okanogan

Mailing Address: PO Box 258

   City: Okanogan   **State:** WA   **Postal Code:** 98840-0000

Street Address: 1410 2nd St.

Institution Email: ochs@ncidata.com

Telephone Number: (509) 422-2825

Contact Name: Marilynn Moses

Institution Type: Historical Society Archives

Web site URL: http://www.omakchronicle.com/ochs/

Hours: M–W and F 8–12, Th 8–3

Staff in Archives: 1p, 2v

Archives Are Handicapped Accessible: Yes

Cost for Researcher—Remote: Fee Schedule

Review of Facilities: The Okanogan County Historical Society is located at the northern edge of the town of Okanogan. This is a multibuilding complex with numerous historic and reproduced buildings. The Wilson Research Center is located to the right of the museum in a newly constructed building and has a separate entrance. The research center is one large room, off which the director's office is located. The room has bookshelves ranging along one wall, file cabinets on another, and in the back there are desks for volunteer workers and the collections of the Okanogan County Genealogical Society, which share the space. Worktables are in the center of the room. The room is open, well lit, and pleasant.

Vertical Files: Yes   **Vertical Files in Cubic Feet:** 9

   Vertical File Description and Subjects: Biography and general subject files.

Manuscripts: Yes   **Manuscripts Volume in Cubic Feet:** 130

   Manuscript Types: School records, business records, title abstracts, scrapbooks and organizational records

   Manuscript Subjects: Okanogan County organizations, Okanogan Civic League, Omak Chamber of Commerce, Brewster Triangle Club, school histories, hotel registers, and bank business records. Land title company records account for nearly 64 cubic feet of the collection.

Photographs: Yes   **Number of Photographs:** 20,000

Storage of Photographs: Copies of photos are filed in binders by accession number. Originals are stored in acid-free folders in file cabinets. Photos are indexed by subject in card files. Computer indexing is in progress.

Photograph Subjects: Okanogan area history is available in the general collection, and of special note is the Frank Matsura photo collection from the early 1900s (description below). A large collection of negatives from George B. Ladd from 1903 to 1946 with documentation of the events, places, and people of the area. A less well known but very significant photo collection of early county buildings, by Ed Valentine, rounds out the subject area.

Photograph Reproductions Are Available: Yes

Photographic Prints: Yes   **Digital Prints:** Yes

Books: Yes   **Number of Books in Collection:** 750

Description of Books: Local history, family histories, fur trade, professional collection. Arranged on shelves by general subject.

Newspapers: Yes   **Newspapers in Paper Format:** Yes

Papers and Dates: *Omak Chronicle,* 1910–2004, and other Okanogan County newspapers

Newspapers on Microfilm: Yes

Microfilm and Dates: *Okanogan Independent* on microfilm with reader available

Oral Histories: Yes   **Oral Histories Number:** 175

Oral Histories Description: Local resident "Pioneer Interviews" done since 1970s. Some tapes are audio recordings of diaries of early settlers. Some transcriptions available.

Maps and Drawings: Yes   **Estimated Number of Maps and Drawings:** 200

Description of Maps and Drawings: Old area maps, Metsker maps, assorted regional maps, some flat and some rolled.

Genealogy Sources: Yes

Genealogy Sources Description: Surname index, cemetery records (5 cu. ft.), vital statistics records, and others, some part of the genealogy society collection, but available to all researchers. Administered by Okanogan County Genealogy Society.

Special Collections: Yes

Special Collections Description: The Frank Matsura Photograph Collection is based on a nitrate and glass-plate negative collection of a young Japanese immigrant who recorded the history of the greater Okanogan area from 1903 to 1913. Matsura is respected as one of the great photographers of the Northwest. A second photograph collection that is less well known, but significant, is the nearly 1,000 Ed Valentine photos of buildings from 1900 to the 1950s. The collection records primarily houses from the largest to the crudest shacks from the towns, villages, and rural areas of Okanogan County and includes the legal property description to mark the location.

Indexes: Subject card indexes are available for the photograph collection. Also there is a large card index for the contents of the society newsletter, books in the collection, and other local information of interest. There are indexes of the Chamber of Commerce and businesses of the area as well. Computer indexing is complete for all items except photographs—scanning and computer indexing of photos is in progress.

> **Published Guides:** Frank Matsura photographs available in the books *Images of Okanogan County as Photographed by Frank S. Matsura* or *Frank Matsura, Frontier Photographer.*

> **Online Sources:** The Matsura collection is partly archived at OCHS (about 2,000 images) and at Washington State University. The portion of the collection at WSU is available online at http://www.wsulibs.wSuedu/holland/masc/xmatsura.html.

Review of Collections: This collection covers the broad and diverse areas of Okanogan County. From their coverage of larger towns to the small settlements , the materials seem equally divided among numerous communities and areas. With the exception of the land title documents, some newspapers, and some unprocessed smaller collections, everything is housed in the research library. The majority of manuscript materials is housed either in file cabinets or interfiled on the bookshelves. For the researcher, some of the indexing and filing methods are obscure, but the materials are cared for and available. The photo collections are exceptionally strong because of the quality photographs of the three major photographers of the county, Frank S. Matsura, George B. Ladd, and Ed Valentine.

Museum on Premises: Yes

> **Museum Hours:** Daily 10–4 May–Sept

> **Museum Is Handicapped Accessible:** Yes

> **Description of Museum:** The museum portrays the varied history of Okanogan County using a variety of display methods, including an outdoor old west town with original and reproduction buildings in a living history setting. Not reviewed.

Parking: Free off-street parallel parking

Lunch: Variety of local cafes to the south in downtown Okanogan or to the north in Omak, including a variety of fast-food chains

Lodging: http://www.visitokanogancountry.com Also check Omak, which is only a few miles away.

Nearest Commercial Airport: Pangborn Memorial (East Wenatchee) (EAT) [95 miles]

Subjects

> **Historical Periods:** 1800–1865; 1865–1900; 1900–1940; 1940–present

Eras: Fur Trade

Natural Resources: Water; Dams; Irrigation; Fishing; Hunting; Logging

Mining: Gold; Silver; Copper; Placer Mining; Tunnel Mining

Transportation: Railroads; Stagecoach/Freight; Ferries; Aviation

Agriculture: Dairy; Ranching/Livestock; Vegetable/Truck Crops; Orchards; Vineyard; Dry Land Farming

Business: Banking; Retail; Legal/Medical Services; Hotels/Restaurants; Entertainment/Theaters

Manufacturing: Manufacturing: Grist/Flour Mills; Brick Making; Sawmills; Wood Products

Government: City; County

Date of Reviewer's Visit: 7/1/2004

Profile Updated by Institution: 11/19/2004

OLYMPIA

✶✶✶✶✶

Name: Washington State Archives, Southwest Regional Branch
County: Thurston

Mailing Address: PO Box 40238

City: Olympia **State:** WA **Postal Code:** 98504-0238

Street Address: 1129 Washington St. SE

Institution Email: Southwest@secstate.wa.gov

Telephone Number: (360) 753-1684 **Fax Number:** (360) 664-2803

Contact Name: Lanny Weaver **Contact Email:** lweaver@secstate.wa.gov

Institution Type: Archives

Affiliation: State of Washington

Web site URL: http://www.secstate.wa.gov/archives/archives_southwest.aspx

Hours: M–F 8:30–4:30 (excluding holidays)

Staff in Archives: 2f 2p 5v

Archives Are Handicapped Accessible: Yes

List of Researchers Available: Yes

Review of Facilities: The Southwest Regional Archives is located on the Washington State Capitol Campus. The Southwest Region shares a reading room with the state government archives, although the collections are maintained separately by different staffs. The entrance to the archives has a reception room where glass cases display some items of Washington history. There is a buzzer on the wall to contact the staff inside. Researchers are then buzzed into another anteroom where there is a reception desk, lockers for belongings, and a doorway that leads to the reading room. All bags, purses, computer cases and so forth need to be locked up. The keys are held by staff members. Only paper, pencil, and laptop (sans case) are allowed past this point. The reading room itself is extremely pleasant with an "old museum" feel. There are four extremely long, old, dark, wood worktables. The room is ringed with low bookcases containing museum artifacts, such as old lantern slide projectors. Several small cubicle rooms are in the rear with the sound, VHS, and other audiovisual equipment. A microfilm reader printer is also available.

Vertical Files: No

Manuscripts: Yes   **Manuscripts Volume in Cubic Feet:** 20,000

  Manuscript Types: Government records

  Manuscript Subjects: County records, municipal records, records of special districts of southwest Washington and the counties of Clark, Cowlitz, Grays Harbor, Lewis, Mason, Pacific, Skamania, Thurston, and Wahkiakum. Spans the early territorial period to the present.

Photographs: Yes   **Number of Photographs:** 10,000

  Storage of Photographs: Photographs are interfiled with the agency manuscript and record collections.

  Photograph Subjects: Assessor's house photographs, mug shots, aerials

  Photograph Reproductions Are Available: Yes

    Photographic Prints: Yes **Digital Prints:** Yes

    Digital Images on CD or Electronically: Yes

Books: Yes   **Number of Books in Collection:** 500

  Description of Books: Local history, city directories

Newspapers: No

Oral Histories: Yes   **Oral Histories Number:** 15

  Oral Histories Description: Audiocassettes, most transcribed

Maps and Drawings: Yes

  Description of Maps and Drawings: Maps are interfiled with agency records.

Genealogy Sources: No

Special Collections: No

Indexes: Yes

  Manuscript Finding Aids: Finding aids vary by record group and originating agency. Some collections have inventories, other have ledger indexes.

  Online Sources: Online Historical Records Search. Available from http://www. secstate.wa.gov/history/search.aspx for access to selected census, naturalization, birth, marriage, death, prison and other miscellaneous records. For Washington history, see http://www.secstate.wa.gov/history.

Review of Collections: The collections of the Southwest Regional Archives cover the records of public entities, counties, towns, and cities of the nine counties in the region. The counties are Clark, Cowlitz, Grays Harbor, Lewis, Mason, Pacific, Skamania, Thurston, and Wahkiakum. Records are included from county offices such as the Auditor, the Clerk, the Treasurer, the Board of Commissioners, and from municipalities, school districts, and other service districts. All records are public.

Museum on Premises: No

Parking: Three free spaces in front of building or visitor parking lot across the street. Pay box will dispense tickets at the rate of 50 cents per hr.

Lunch: Walking distance to a variety of restaurants

Lodging: http://www.thurstonchamber.com

Nearest Commercial Airport: Seattle-Tacoma International (SEA) [49 miles]

Subjects

    Historical Periods: 1865–1900; 1940–present

    Eras: WPA

    Natural Resources: Water; Dams; Fishing; Logging

    Mining: Mining

    Transportation: Railroads; Stagecoach/Freight; Ferries

    Government: City; County; State

    Organizations: Schools; Colleges/Universities; Hospitals/Medical Facilities

Date of Reviewer's Visit: 5/7/2004

Profile Updated by Institution: 11/15/2004

✳✳✳✳✳

Name: Washington State Government Archives **County:** Thurston

Mailing Address: PO Box 40238

    City: Olympia   **State:** WA   **Postal Code:** 98504-0238

Street Address: 129 Washington St. SE

Institution Email: research@secstate.wa.gov

Telephone Number: (360) 586-1492   **Fax Number:** (360) 650-3323

Contact Name: Dave Hasting   **Contact Email:** dhastings@secstate.wa.gov

Institution Type: Archives

Affiliation: State of Washington

Web site URL: http://www.secstate.wa.gov

Hours: M–F 8:30–4:30 (excluding holidays)

Staff in Archives: 4f 1p 3v

Archives Are Handicapped Accessible: Yes

List of Researchers Available: Yes

Review of Facilities: The Washington State Government Archives currently shares a research room facility with Southwest Regional Archives. Both are located on the Washington State Capitol Campus. Although the two departments share a reading room, the collections are maintained separately by different staffs. The entrance to the archives has a reception room where glass cases display some items of Washington history. There is a buzzer on the wall to contact the staff inside. This leads to another anteroom where there is a reception desk, lockers for belongings, and a doorway that leads to the reading room. All bags, purses, computer cases, and so forth need to be locked up. There is no charge for the lockers and the keys are held by staff members. Only paper, pencil, and laptop are allowed into the reading room. The research room has a mixture of new and old. There are four extremely long, old, dark, wood worktables. The room is ringed with low bookcases containing museum artifacts. Several small cubicle rooms are in the rear with the sound, VHS, and other audiovisual equipment. A microfilm reader printer is also available. Overall it is a pleasant, well lit space. Collections are stored in secure areas adjacent to the reading room.

Vertical Files: No

Manuscripts: Yes   **Manuscripts Volume in Cubic Feet:** 62,000

    Manuscript Types: State government records

    Manuscript Subjects: Governors' papers, state agencies, legislative, state history, state constitution, state lands, and environmental issues

Photographs: Yes   **Number of Photographs:** 400,000

    Storage of Photographs: Photographs are interfiled with the agency manuscript and record collections.

    Photograph Reproductions Are Available: Yes

      Photographic Prints: Yes   **Digital Prints:** Yes

Books: No

Newspapers: No

Oral Histories: No

Maps and Drawings: Yes   **Estimated Number of Maps and Drawings:** 5,000

    Description of Maps and Drawings: State and local maps from 1889–1990

Genealogy Sources: No

Special Collections: No

Indexes: Yes

Manuscript Finding Aids: Paper and online finding aids to collections

Online Sources: Online Historical Records Search. Available from http://www.
secstate.wa.gov/history/search.aspx for access to selected census, naturalization,
birth, marriage, death, prison and other miscellaneous records. For Washington
history, see http://www.secstate.wa.gov/history.

Review of Collections: The State Records Collections at the State Archives provide
an account of public government at the state level from the early territorial period of
Washington (1853) to the present. Included are papers from each governor, legislative
records, state court records, records from all state agencies, and all official records of
the state. Professionally managed, this collection is open to the public for research
under the Public Disclosure Act.

Museum on Premises: No

Parking: Visitor parking lot across the street; pay box will dispense tickets at the rate
of 50 cents per hr.

Lunch: Driving distance to variety of restaurants

Lodging: http://www.thurstonchamber.com

Nearest Commercial Airport: Seattle-Tacoma International (SEA) [49 miles]

Subjects

Historical Periods: 1800–1865; 1865–1900; 1900–1940; 1940–present

Eras: Civil War; Indian Wars; Spanish American War; World War I; WPA;
CCC; World War II; Korean War; Vietnam War

Natural Resources: Water; Dams; Irrigation; Fishing; Hunting; Shellfish;
Logging

Mining: Gold; Coal; Placer Mining; Surface Mining; Tunnel Mining

Transportation: Railroads; Ships and Shipping; Ferries; Aviation

Agriculture: Dairy; Ranching/Livestock; Vegetable/Truck Crops; Grains;
Orchards; Vineyard; Dry Land Farming

Business: Banking

Manufacturing: Sawmills

Government: City; County; State

Organizations: Schools; Colleges/Universities; Hospitals/Medical Facilities;
Labor and Union

Ethnic Groups: Native American; Japanese; Chinese; Finnish; Norwegian;
Swedish

Date of Reviewer's Visit: 5/7/2004

Profile Updated by Institution: 11/12/2004

Name: Washington State Library   **County:** Thurston

Mailing Address: PO Box 42460

   City: Olympia   **State:** WA   **Postal Code:** 98504-2460

Street Address: 6880 Capitol Blvd. S., Tumwater

Institution Email: refq@secstate.wa.gov

Telephone Number: (360) 704-5221   **Fax Number:** (360) 704-7831

Contact Name: Shirley Lewis or Kathryn Hamilton-Wang

Institution Type: Special Library

Affiliation: State of Washington

Web site URL: http://www.secstate.wa.gov/library

Hours: M–F 8–5 (excluding holidays)

Archives Are Handicapped Accessible: Yes

Cost for Researcher—Remote: Only limited research services offered

Review of Facilities: The Washington State Library is located in a modern office building in an office park in Tumwater, not far from the Olympia Airport. This is south of the main capitol area. The research and reference room is located on the second floor. The Pacific Northwest Book Collection is housed in open stacks. The microfilmed collection of newspapers are also housed here. In the main library there are large worktables, computer stations, microfilm reader/printers, and other facilities for doing research. Since this building was built as office space, some areas are rather chopped up, with rooms and walls in awkward locations One room has nothing except telephone books and city directories from most cities in the state. Some collections, such as the federal documents, are stored on staff-only-access floors. The entirety of the manuscript collections are housed off site, and the library requires 24-hour-notice to retrieve materials from the storage facility.

Vertical Files: Yes   **Vertical Files in Cubic Feet:** 80

   Vertical File Description and Subjects: The vertical files are divided into Indians and general subjects

Manuscripts: Yes   **Manuscripts Volume in Cubic Feet:** 420

   Manuscript Types: Personal papers, government documents

   Manuscript Subjects: Emma Smith Devoe collection; Conte Papers

Photographs: No

Books: Yes   **Number of Books in Collection:** 10,000

   Description of Books: Pacific Northwest history, city directories, phone books, professional collection, reference books

Newspapers: Yes

Newspapers in Paper Format: Yes

Papers and Dates: Paper copies of state newspapers are collected and held only until they can be microfilmed.

Newspapers on Microfilm: Yes

Microfilm and Dates: 40,000 reels of microfilm mostly of Washington state newspapers. Can search on Web site by city and county for holdings; newspaper holdings are also listed in the electronic catalog. Holdings also available on WorldCat and available to libraries through Interlibrary Loan.

Oral Histories: No

Maps and Drawings: Yes

Description of Maps and Drawings: A few scattered maps

Genealogy Sources: Yes

Genealogy Sources Description: Washington State census, county genealogy society newsletters from throughout the state, State of Washington Death Index from 1907–2001

Special Collections: No

Indexes: Electronic catalog lists the book and microfilm holdings. Northwest Index, a large card file, indexes the newspaper and magazine articles, primarily 1965–1987, through the name file and general subject files. Card files list the manuscript materials as well.

Manuscript Finding Aids: Card file to the manuscript materials.

Online Sources: Electronic library catalog available through the Web site and also through WorldCat.

Review of Collections: The collections of the Washington State Library are heavy on the published materials. The Pacific Northwest Book Collection is extensive at about 10,000 volumes. The city directory collection is probably the largest in the state. Likewise the microfilmed newspaper collection is expansive and represents all areas of the state. The manuscript collections have some unique and valuable materials, but because they are housed off site, prior planning is necessary in order to use them.

Museum on Premises: No

Parking: Free parking lot adjacent

Lunch: Small restaurant across street, coffee place in adjacent building, and a variety of restaurants a short driving distance north

Lodging: http://www.thurstonchamber.com

Nearest Commercial Airport: Seattle-Tacoma International (SEA) [49 miles]

Subjects

Historical Periods: 1865–1900; 1900–1940; 1940–present;

Detailed subjects not provided by institution.

Date of Reviewer's Visit: 1/15/2004

Profile Updated by Institution: 11/10/2004

PASCO

Name: Franklin County Historical Museum   **County:** Franklin

Mailing Address: 305 N. 4th

   City: Pasco   **State:** WA   **Postal Code:** 99301-0000

Street Address: 305 N. 4th

Institution Email: museum@franklincountyhistoricalsociety.org

Telephone Number: (509) 547-3714   **Fax Number:** (509) 545-2168

Contact Name: Gabriele Sperling

Institution Type: Local Museum

Web site URL: http://franklincountyhistoricalsociety.org

Hours: T–Sa 12–4 or by appt.

Staff in Archives: 1p, 5v

Archives Are Handicapped Accessible: Yes

Access Description: Handicapped entrance on side of building through gate, down ramp and buzzer at door into basement, elevator to museum level

Cost for Researcher—In-house: 15 minutes free, then fee schedule

Cost for Researcher—Remote: Fee schedule

Review of Facilities: The Franklin County Historical Society and Museum is located in an old Carnegie Library in downtown Pasco. The research area is located on the lower level in several connecting rooms. The research room is small with a small table (four chairs) and wooden shelves stacked floor to ceiling with books, boxes, and historical materials. The room, though full, appears well organized. A staff desk and computer is in one corner of the room and file cabinets adorn the last open wall space. A doorway leads to an adjacent room where more file cabinets and shelves house more materials. Space for researchers is in short supply, but the materials are well cared for.

Vertical Files: Yes   **Vertical Files in Cubic Feet:** 9

   Vertical File Description and Subjects: Newspaper clippings, subject information, ephemera

Manuscripts: Yes   **Manuscripts Volume in Cubic Feet:** 110

   Manuscript Types: Business records, organizational records, personal papers, government records, scrapbooks

Manuscript Subjects: General subjects, personal papers, women's clubs, Ladies Auxiliary to the Brotherhood of Railroad Trainmen, Pasco Business and Professional Women, old treasurers' books from county, Pasco Naval Air Station, aviation

Photographs: Yes   **Number of Photographs:** 5,000

Storage of Photographs: Photographs arranged by subject in file folders in fire-proof file cabinets, some stored in plastic sleeves. Photographs are indexed on staff computer in Filemaker Pro.

Photograph Subjects: Pasco, Franklin County, and surrounding area

Photograph Reproductions Are Available: Yes

   Photographic Prints: Yes   **Digital Prints:** Yes

   Digital Images on CD or Electronically: Yes

Books: Yes   **Number of Books in Collection:** 400

Description of Books: Local and regional history, city directories, old books, phone books, annuals

Newspapers: Yes

   Newspapers in Paper Format: Yes

   Papers and Dates: Pasco newspapers from 1911–1950s

Oral Histories: Yes   **Oral Histories Number:** 3

   Oral Histories Description: Franklin County pioneers

Maps and Drawings: Yes   **Estimated Number of Maps and Drawings:** 100

   Description of Maps and Drawings: Maps and architectural drawings pertaining to Franklin County are stored rolled

Genealogy Sources: Yes

   Genealogy Sources Description: People file, cemetery records

Special Collections: No

Indexes: Indexes to photographs and manuscripts available on staff computer

Review of Collections: The collections of this institution are fairly standard for the size of institution. The strengths lie in the variety of manuscript-type materials from various women's clubs and associations, including scrapbooks, meeting minutes, and so forth for a wide variety of organizations for women in the twentieth century. Pasco has the oldest history of the three Tri-Cities and has the distinction of being the only one of the three in Franklin County. The history of Pasco has been significantly different from its neighbors, although there are commonalities as well. The settlement and development of Franklin County and the Hanford area are reflected in this collection.

Museum on Premises: Yes

Museum Hours: Tu–Sat 12–4

Museum Is Handicapped Accessible: Yes

Parking: On-street parallel parking, on-street diagonal parking

Lunch: Driving distance to a variety of restaurants.

Lodging: http://www.visittri-cities.com

Nearest Commercial Airport: Tri-Cities (Pasco) (PSC) [3 miles]

Subjects

> **Historical Periods:** 1865–1900; 1900–1940; 1940–present
>
> **Eras:** World War I; CCC; World War II
>
> **Natural Resources:** Water; Dams; Irrigation
>
> **Transportation:** Railroads; Stagecoach/Freight; Ships and Shipping; Ferries; Aviation
>
> **Agriculture:** Dairy; Ranching/Livestock; Grains; Vineyard; Dry Land Farming
>
> **Business:** Retail; Hotels/Restaurants; Entertainment/Theaters
>
> **Manufacturing:** Grist/Flour Mills
>
> **Government:** City; County
>
> **Organizations:** Schools; Colleges/Universities; Hospitals/Medical Facilities; Charities; Nonreligious Organizations; Civic and Fraternal; Women's; Business
>
> **Ethnic Groups:** Native American; African; Japanese; Chinese; Southeast Asian
>
> **Religious Sites and Organizations:** Protestant; Catholic; LDS (Mormon); Mennonite/Amish

Date of Reviewer's Visit: 9/26/2003

Profile Updated by Institution: 11/19/2004

POMEROY

Name: Garfield County Historical Association　　**County:** Garfield

Mailing Address: PO Box 854

　City: Pomeroy　　　　　**State:** WA　　　　**Postal Code:** 99347-0000

Street Address: 708 Columbia

Institution Email: None

Telephone Number: (509) 843-3925

Contact Name: Margret Wolf

Institution Type: Local Museum

Web site URL: None

Hours: F 1–5; after May 1, six days a week; appt by arrangement

Staff in Archives: 6v

Archives Are Handicapped Accessible: Yes

Cost for Researcher—Remote: Donation

Review of Facilities: The Garfield County Historical Museum is located in a single-story building constructed in the 1970s for that purpose. It is located one block off the main street in a business area. The research area is located in the staff office area to the right of the main entrance. The room is moderate-sized but has a small table for researchers. Most of the research materials are stored in file cabinets or on bookshelves nearby. The institution is small and the collection is small, but growing.

Vertical Files: Yes   **Vertical Files in Cubic Feet:** 16

    Vertical File Description and Subjects: Vertical file with variety of clippings, ephemera, and miscellaneous history filed by subjects

Manuscripts: Yes   **Manuscripts Volume in Cubic Feet:** 10

    Manuscript Types: Business records, school records, family papers

    Manuscript Subjects: Hotel registry, school records

Photographs: Yes   **Number of Photographs:** 1,000

    Storage of Photographs: Photographs are stored in folders in file drawers and arranged by subject; 8 cu. ft.

    Photograph Subjects: Garfield County history and people

    Photograph Reproductions Are Available: Yes

        Photographic Prints: Yes   **Digital Prints:** Yes

Books: Yes   **Number of Books in Collection:** 200

    Description of Books: Local and regional history, annuals

Newspapers: Yes

    Newspapers in Paper Format: Yes

    Papers and Dates: Local area newspapers bound from 1929

    Newspapers on Microfilm: Yes

    Microfilm and Dates: Microfilm of newspapers from 1882

Oral Histories: Yes   **Oral Histories Number:** 60

    Oral Histories Description: Oral history interviews on audiocassettes of local area residents. There are no transcriptions. Some family histories have been recorded on VHS videotape.

Maps and Drawings: No

Genealogy Sources: Yes

    Genealogy Sources Description: Family histories, obituaries, cemetery records

Special Collections: No

Indexes: No

Review of Collections: The collections of this institution are limited. The manuscript portion is particularly weak. The research collections are not a main focus of this small historical association. What collections there are deal with Garfield County, with some information on communities from an extended area. The collection has a great deal of growth potential, but useful only for local history at this time.

Museum on Premises: Yes

Parking: On-street unmarked free parallel parking, small gravel lot in back

Lunch: Local restaurants one block

Lodging: http://www.clickpomeroy.com

Nearest Commercial Airport: Lewiston-Nez Perce County (Lewiston, ID) (LWS) [34 miles]

Subjects

    Historical Periods:1865–1900; 1900–1940; 1940–present

    Natural Resources: Logging

    Transportation: Railroads; Stagecoach/Freight; Ships and Shipping

    Agriculture: Grains; Orchards

    Business: Retail; Legal/Medical Services; Hotels/Restaurants

    Manufacturing: Sawmills

    Government: City; County; State

    Organizations: Schools; Hospitals/Medical Facilities

    Ethnic Groups: Native American; Chinese; English; German; Irish; Scottish

    Religious Sites and Organizations: Protestant; Catholic

Date of Reviewer's Visit: 9/12/2003

Profile Updated by Institution: 11/15/2004

PORT ANGELES

Name: Museum of Clallam County Historical Society   **County:** Clallam

Mailing Address: PO Box 1327

   City: Port Angeles   **State:** WA   **Postal Code:** 98362-0000

Street Address: 933 W. 9th

Institution Email: artifact@olypen.com

Telephone Number: (360) 452-2662   **Fax Number:** (360) 452-2662

Contact Name: Kathy Monds

Institution Type: Local Museum

Affiliation: Clallam County Historical Society

Web site URL: http://www.olympus.net/arts/ccmuseum/

Hours: Research library Tu 9–3 or by appt.

Staff in Archives: 1f, 6v

Archives Are Handicapped Accessible: No

Access Description: Gravel parking lot, uneven ground, ramp to building

Review of Facilities: The Clallam County Historical Society research room is located not at the museum, but in the administration building adjacent to the old Lincoln School building (eventually to be a museum as well). Plans are to move the historical society research area into the school after it is renovated. It is currently sharing quarters (an old school portable) with the Clallam County Genealogical Society, with the Genealogical Society having the front part of the room, and the Historical Society having the back. Some of the materials are stored on shelves surrounding several worktables. Many of the materials are stored in an adjacent building that is climate controlled.

Vertical Files: Yes   **Vertical Files in Cubic Feet:** 18

Vertical File Description and Subjects: General subject files of clippings and ephemera

Manuscripts: Yes   **Manuscripts Volume in Cubic Feet:** 250

Manuscript Types: Personal papers, organizational papers, school records, local government records

Manuscript Subjects: Women's Relief Corps of the Grand Army of the Republic (GAR) papers, lumber mills, Port Angeles School records

Photographs: Yes   **Number of Photographs:** 6,000

Storage of Photographs: Copies of photographs are filed in albums by subject and available in the research room. Originals are stored in clamshell boxes in a nearby climate-controlled building.

Photograph Subjects: Port Angeles and other communities in Clallam County

Photograph Reproductions Are Available: Yes

Photographic Prints: Yes

Books: Yes   **Number of Books in Collection:** 250

Description of Books: Local history, city directories, yearbooks, professional collection, and old books

Newspapers: Yes

Newspapers in Paper Format: Yes

Papers and Dates: Clallam County papers, 1886–1960s

Newspapers on Microfilm: No

Microfilm and Dates: Microfilm available at local library (see North Olympic Library System entry)

Oral Histories: Yes   **Oral Histories Number:** 200

Oral Histories Description: Oral histories of local pioneer families, experiences during World War II, taken 1970s to the present. Some with transcriptions. Most on audiotape, but 51 are videotaped histories. There is a card file index to the interviews.

Maps and Drawings: Yes   **Estimated Number of Maps and Drawings:** 200

Description of Maps and Drawings: Early Clallam County, many rolled maps in storage building

Genealogy Sources: Yes

Genealogy Sources Description: Obituary index from Clallam County, cemetery records, family files

Special Collections: No

Indexes: Vertical file card index, book card catalog and card index to maps by township range. Local computer listing of manuscript holdings in Access database. Researchers can use printouts of database.

Review of Collections: The research collections at the Clallam County Historical Society were larger than expected. The materials are maintained and stored in an archival manner by a group of dedicated volunteers. Subjects cover all aspects of life in Port Angeles and Clallam County. There is a large number of personal papers; they also have club and organizational records from youth organizations (Boy Scouts and Campfire) women's clubs, and business organizations. They have the papers of several lumber mills in the area, as well as other local businesses. One of the most diverse collections seen in this project.

Museum on Premises: No

Parking: Gravel parking lot adjacent and slightly uphill from the building

Lunch: Driving distance to a variety of local and chain restaurants

Lodging: http://www.portangeles.org; http://www.northwestsecretplaces.com/

Nearest Commercial Airport: William R Fairchild International (Port Angeles) (CLM) [2 miles]

Subjects

    Historical Periods: 1865–1900; 1900–1940; 1940–present

    Eras: World War I; WPA; CCC; World War II

    Natural Resources: Water; Dams; Irrigation; Fishing; Logging

Mining: Mining

Transportation: Railroads; Ships and Shipping; Ferries; Aviation

Agriculture: Dairy

Business: Banking; Retail; Legal/Medical Services; Hotels/Restaurants; Entertainment/Theaters

Manufacturing: Cannery; Brewery; Creamery; Sawmills; Wood Products

Government: City; County

Organizations: Schools; Hospitals/Medical Facilities; Charities; Nonreligious Organizations; Civic and Fraternal; Women's; Business

Ethnic Groups: Native American

Date of Reviewer's Visit: 6/22/2004

Profile Updated by Institution: 11/15/2004

✷✷✷

Name: North Olympic Library System   **County:** Clallam

Mailing Address: 2210 S. Peabody

   City: Port Angeles   **State:** WA   **Postal Code:** 98362-2581

Street Address: 2210 S. Peabody

Institution Email: None

Telephone Number: (360) 417-8501   **Fax Number:** (360) 457-2581

Contact Name: Genie DeVine   **Contact Email:** gdevine@nols.org

Institution Type: Public Library

Affiliation: Library District

Web site URL: http://www.nols.org/

Hours: M, W 12–8; Tu, Th, F, and Sa 10–5

Staff in Archives: 2f, 2p

Archives Are Handicapped Accessible: Yes

Review of Facilities: The Port Angeles Branch of the North Olympic Library System is several miles south of the downtown area. The building is new and with wide open central areas. The archives room is off the main library and is kept locked. The library reference staff provides access to the room. The public area outside the archives room houses a large vertical file on both local and regional history. This file is reference only, but open to everyone during library hours. The archives room is moderately sized with a large worktable and five chairs. There are bookshelves on the perimeter of the room. The reference copies of regional and local history books are housed here, as well as the photo collection, maps, and some documents.

Vertical Files: Yes   **Vertical Files in Cubic Feet:** 24

Vertical File Description and Subjects: Vertical file of clippings, bits of history, some documents; about half on Port Angeles and half on the rest of Clallam County. Reference file but open to general public in library.

Manuscripts: No

Photographs: Yes   **Number of Photographs:** 5,400

Storage of Photographs: Copies of the photographs are filed in notebooks by general subject.

Photograph Subjects: Bert Kellogg gathered photographs from the community, made negatives, and donated the to the library. These are all Clallam County subjects.

Photograph Reproductions Are Available: Yes

   Photographic Prints: Yes

Books: Yes   **Number of Books in Collection:** 800

Description of Books: Local and regional history, city directories, phone books, annuals. Books are listed in the online library catalog but are not listed in WorldCat.

Newspapers: Yes

Newspapers on Microfilm: Yes

Microfilm and Dates: 1916 to current *Peninsula Daily News;* earliest newspapers have been digitized

Oral Histories: Yes   **Oral Histories Number:** 70

Oral Histories Description: Interviews with local residents from 1970s to early 1980s on audiocassette and CD. Oral history tapes are indexed in card files. Some interviews may overlap with those at the Clallam County Historical Society.

Maps and Drawings: Yes   **Estimated Number of Maps and Drawings:** 50

Description of Maps and Drawings: Aerials and old maps of Clallam County

Genealogy Sources: Yes

Genealogy Sources Description: Obituary index in card files and on online catalog

Special Collections: No

Indexes: Card file of Newspaper Index prior to 1993. Obituary Index. Books listed in library catalog.

Review of Collections: The primary documents and local history research collections of the North Olympic Library System are relatively small. The Kellogg photograph collection has numerous wonderful images of Clallam County scenes, people, and activities. Although there are extensive vertical files, they are all in an open-access area. There are collections of local interest, including the Transmountain Low Point project and the Northern Tier Pipeline documents. Also have copies of the Port of Port Angeles minutes and documents.

Museum on Premises: No

Parking: Free paved parking lot adjacent

Lunch: Driving distance to variety of chain and local restaurants

Lodging: http://www.portangeles.org : http://www.northwestsecretplaces.com/

Nearest Commercial Airport: William R Fairchild International (Port Angeles) (CLM) [4 miles]

Subjects

> **Historical Periods:** 1865–1900; 1900–1940; 1940–present
>
> **Natural Resources:** Fishing; Whaling; Logging
>
> **Ethnic Groups:** Native American

Date of Reviewer's Visit: 6/22/2004

Profile Updated by Institution: 11/12/2004

PORT TOWNSEND

✳✳✳

Name: Jefferson County Historical Society History Research Center
County: Jefferson

Mailing Address: 540 Water St.

> **City:** Port Townsend   **State:** WA   **Postal Code:** 98368-5725

Street Address: 13692 Airport Cutoff Road

Institution Email: jchsrescntr@olympus.net

Telephone Number: (360) 379-6730

Contact Name: Marge Samuelson

Institution Type: Historical Society Archives

Web site URL: http://www.jchsmuseum.org

Hours: Tu–Sa 11–4

Staff in Archives: 1p 10v

Archives Are Handicapped Accessible: Yes

Access Description: Gravel parking lot with cement apron to door

Cost for Researcher—In-house: $4

Cost for Researcher—Remote: Fee schedule

Review of Facilities: The Jefferson County Historical Society History Research Center is located outside of town near the airport. The area is wooded and fairly secluded. The facility is shared by the historical society and the local genealogical society. Most of the staffing is provided by the genealogical society volunteers. The facility itself is new, moderate-sized, and almost full. The research room takes up two-thirds of the building. There are three medium-sized research tables, all well lit. There are two staff work areas and ranges of bookshelves, file cabinets, map cases, microfilm reader printers, and assorted other research and staff equipment. The remaining part of the building consists of the lunchroom and storage rooms. Overall this is one of the best county research facilities visited.

Vertical Files: Yes   **Vertical Files in Cubic Feet:** 16

Vertical File Description and Subjects: Vertical files are divided into name files and general subject indexes.

Manuscripts: Yes   **Manuscripts Volume in Cubic Feet:** 160

Manuscript Types: Business records, government records, court records, scrapbooks, family papers, organizational records, school records

Manuscript Subjects: Lumber industry, archives of several paper mills (Washington Mill Co.), local and regional business records, maritime collections, Jefferson County Schools

Photographs: Yes   **Number of Photographs:** 15,000

Storage of Photographs: Binders have copies of photographs arranged by general subject for research use. Originals stored elsewhere, in document boxes with acid-free sleeves.

Photograph Subjects: Jefferson County area and people

Photograph Reproductions Are Available: Yes

Photographic Prints: Yes   **Digital Prints:** Yes

Digital Images on CD or Electronically: Yes

Books: Yes   **Number of Books in Collection:** 750

Description of Books: Local and regional history, professional collection, annuals, city directories (1887 to present, incomplete)

Newspapers: Yes

Newspapers in Paper Format: Yes

Papers and Dates: Port Townsend papers, 1870s to present

Newspapers on Microfilm: Yes

Microfilm and Dates: Papers available on microfilm; have reader/printer available

Oral Histories: Yes   **Oral Histories Number:** 60

Oral Histories Description: Oral history interviews of local residents taken from 1987 to 1998. Most have transcriptions.

Maps and Drawings: Yes   **Estimated Number of Maps and Drawings:** 450

Description of Maps and Drawings: Local area maps, shipping maps, Sanborn Fire maps (six 1884 to 1945); plat maps, Metsker maps

Genealogy Sources: Yes

Genealogy Sources Description: Birth records (1892–1926), death records, marriage records, family histories, cemetery records

Special Collections: No

Indexes: Computerized book index, card files of subject and portrait for the photograph collection. Staff computer indexing.

Manuscript Finding Aids: In-house computer system of finding aids. Printouts available in binders.

Review of Collections: The collections of the History Research Center are diverse and cover the main areas of interest in the history of the county. Maritime, logging, and business records are well represented. Information on Forts Casey, Flagler, Townsend, and Worden are also held in the collection. The center has some items on the history of the Chinese in Port Townsend, as well as on the Olympic Peninsula native tribes. The photograph collection is large and well rounded. Unprocessed negatives in the collection would double the number of images. The collections are archivally processed and stored.

Museum on Premises: No

Parking: Free gravel parking lot adjacent

Lunch: Driving distance to restaurants. Could bring lunch to eat in staff lunchroom or outside.

Lodging: http://www.ptguide.com

Nearest Commercial Airport: William R Fairchild Intl (Port Angeles) (CLM) [47 miles]; Seattle-Tacoma International (SEA) [100 miles]

Subjects

Historical Periods: 1800–1865; 1865–1900; 1900–1940; 1940–present

Eras: Spanish American War; World War I; CCC; World War II

Natural Resources: Logging

Mining: Mining

Transportation: Railroads; Ships and Shipping; Ferries

Agriculture: Dairy

Business: Retail; Hotels/Restaurants

Manufacturing: Cannery; Brewery; Creamery; Brick Making; Boatbuilding/Shipyard; Sawmills; Wood Products

Government: City; County

Organizations: Schools; Hospitals/Medical Facilities; Charities; Nonreligious Organizations; Civic and Fraternal; Women's; Business

Ethnic Groups: Native American; Japanese; Chinese; English; German

Religious Sites and Organizations: Protestant; Catholic

Date of Reviewer's Visit: 6/17/2004

Profile Updated by Institution: 11/15/2004

PULLMAN

Name: Washington State University—Manuscripts, Archives, and Special Collections
County: Whitman

Mailing Address: PO Box 64510

   City: Pullman   **State:** WA   **Postal Code:** 99164-5610

Street Address: Holland Library

Institution Email: libweb@wsu.edu

Telephone Number: (509) 335-9671   **Fax Number:** (509) 335-6721

Contact Name: Laila Miletic-Vejzovic, Head of MASC

Contact Email: Specific personnel listed on Web site

Institution Type: Academic Library

Affiliation: Washington State University

 URL: http://www.wsulibs.wsu.edu

Hours: M–F 8:30–5

Staff in Archives: 3f, 4p

Archives Are Handicapped Accessible: Yes

List of Researchers Available: Yes

Review of Facilities: The Manuscripts, Archives, and Special Collections (MASC) is located in the lower level of Holland Library, in the center of Washington State University campus. Coat racks and lockers are available for personal items; locker keys are obtainable at MASC reception desk. All users must register and have valid ID. Pencil, paper, and laptop are all that may be taken into the reference room. The entry to the MASC suite has space for some art displays, waiting area, and reception area. The research room is spacious, with six research tables. Bookshelves line one wall. There is a small audiovisual room off the main room with the various equipment necessary for hearing, viewing, and/or scanning items. The majority of the collections are housed in a sub-basement in a staff-only area.

Vertical Files: Yes   **Vertical Files in Cubic Feet:** 30

Vertical File Description and Subjects: Variety of vertical file materials, most items will eventually be cataloged

Manuscripts: Yes   **Manuscripts Volume in Cubic Feet:** 15,000

Manuscript Types: All manuscript types

Manuscript Subjects: DeSmet Papers, McWhorter Collection (Nez Perce and Yakimas), William Inman (judge) and Tom Foley; congressional papers are among the many types of materials available. The Westin Hotel and Resorts Archives are one of the business records collections (500 ft.).

Photographs: Yes   **Number of Photographs:** 250,000

Storage of Photographs: Copies of photos in 6 x 8 cards in file cabinets, originals in boxes in acid-free envelopes

Photograph Reproductions Are Available: Yes

Photographic Prints: Yes   **Digital Prints:** Yes

Books: Yes   **Number of Books in Collection:** 38,000

Description of Books: Local and regional history, city directories, professional collection, annuals, outdoor recreation

Newspapers: No

Microfilm and Dates: Newspapers are in the periodicals department of the library

Oral Histories: Yes   **Oral Histories Number:** 700

Oral Histories Description: Donations only, some transcriptions, radio and broadcasting

Maps and Drawings: Yes   **Estimated Number of Maps and Drawings:** 1,000

Genealogy Sources: No

Special Collections: No

Indexes: Paper copies of finding aids are available in the research room.

Manuscript Finding Aids: Available online at http://www.wsulibs.wSuedu/ holland/masc/masc.htm

Online Sources: Library catalog lists most manuscript materials using the location indicator "MASC."

Review of Collections: The Manuscripts, Archives, and Special Collections are large and cross-disciplinary. One-third of the holdings are the Washington State University Archives. The remaining two-thirds are manuscripts and records of various subject areas. The collection includes manuscripts, photographs, audio and video tapes, films, books, maps, and ephemera. The scope of collecting for primary sources is the Pacific Northwest, Eastern Washington culture and history, and twentieth-century European and American music. The collection is primarily nineteenth and twentieth century.

Museum on Premises: No

Parking: Parking permit obtainable from parking services near center of campus

Lunch: Variety of cafes and eating venues next door in Student Union building

Lodging: http://www.pullmanchamber.com

Nearest Commercial Airport: Pullman/Moscow Regional (Pullman) (PUW) [3 miles]

Subjects

    Historical Periods: Pre-1800; 1800–1865; 1865–1900; 1900–1940; 1940– present

    Eras: Fur Trade; Indian Wars; WPA; World War II

    Natural Resources: Water; Dams; Irrigation; Fishing; Hunting; Logging

    Mining: Mining

    Transportation: Railroads

    Agriculture: Ranching/Livestock; Vegetable/Truck Crops; Grains; Dry Land Farming

    Business: Hotels/Restaurants

    Government: City; County; State; Federal

    Organizations: Colleges/Universities; Women's

    Ethnic Groups: Native American; Pacific Islander; Chinese; English; German; Russian

Date of Reviewer's Visit: 1/29/2004

Profile Updated by Institution: 12/6/2004

Name: Whitman County Historical Society   **County:** Whitman

Mailing Address: PO Box 67

    City: Colfax   **State:** WA   **Postal Code:** 99111-0000

Street Address: 115 W. Main, Pullman, Washington

Institution Email: None

Telephone Number: (509) 397-2555

Contact Name: Edwin Garretson, Jr.   **Contact Email:** epgjr@wsu.edu

Institution Type: Historical Society Archives

Web site URL: http://www.wsu.edu/~sarek/wchs-archives.html

Hours: W 9–12 by appt.

Staff in Archives: 5v

Archives Are Handicapped Accessible: Yes

Cost for Researcher—Remote: Fee schedule

List of Researchers Available: Yes

Review of Facilities: The Whitman County Historical Society research collections are housed in the Gladish Community Center building in Pullman, Washington. The corresponding museum is in Colfax. The community center is located in an old school building and the research room is in room 103 past the Montessori school. The room is pleasant and has large old legal cabinets stretching to the high ceiling along two walls. Four long tables in pairs are arranged in the middle of the room. Bookcases, other storage areas, and volunteer work areas cover the remaining walls. An open doorway in the rear forms an L with additional storage areas. The majority of the manuscript collections are housed in the secondary room. The facility is moderate-sized, volunteer-staffed, and functional.

Vertical Files: No

Manuscripts: Yes   **Manuscripts Volume in Cubic Feet:** 102

    Manuscript Types: Business records, personal papers, organizational records

    Manuscript Subjects: Whitman county history, 400 collections

Photographs: Yes   **Number of Photographs:** 5,000

    Storage of Photographs: Photographs are filed by accession number; photocopies of the photographs serve as an index, organized by locale and topics.

    Photograph Subjects: Originals stored in archival envelopes in large document cases

    Photograph Reproductions Are Available: Yes

        Digital Prints: Yes

        Digital Images on CD or Electronically: Yes

Books: Yes   **Number of Books in Collection:** 300

    Description of Books: Local and regional history, MA theses and PhD dissertations from Washington State University from 1909, phonebooks, city directories

Newspapers: Yes

    Newspapers in Paper Format: Yes

    Papers and Dates: Pullman paper, 1888–1989

Oral Histories: Yes   **Oral Histories Number:** 93

    Oral Histories Description: Interviews done from 1973–1980 of local residents on Whitman County history. Several interviews have up to six tapes.

Maps and Drawings: Yes   **Estimated Number of Maps and Drawings:** 100

    Description of Maps and Drawings: Historical maps of Whitman County

Genealogy Sources: Yes

Genealogy Sources Description: 7 1/2 cu. ft. of genealogy files, full obituary files, cemetery records, tombstone records. Older birth records, marriage, and death records.

Special Collections: Yes

Special Collections Description: Esther Pond Smith Collection of photos, newspaper clippings, and various aspects of Pullman history. Consists of research for a history of Pullman that was never published. Don Clarke clipping file, eight archive boxes on Whitman County, fully indexed.

Indexes: Basic index to the contents of 54 local history books and publications

Manuscript Finding Aids: Manuscript collections have summaries and are computer searchable

Review of Collections: Across town from the large professionally managed Washington State University Archives and Special Collections, this institution is like a polar extreme. Both institutions compete for the acquisition of new materials of the area. Despite the disparity of economics and other resources, Whitman County Historical Society is holding its own. With support from the community and several WSU faculty, the collections are growing and being well cared for. The collections content is fairly standard for a rural community. However, as the education level in the county is higher than average, the collection has a more academic tone than that of most comparable institutions.

Museum on Premises: No

Parking: Free parking lot available on State Street but involves more than one flight of stairs

Lunch: Short drive or downhill walk to a variety of restaurants in downtown or outlying neighborhoods

Lodging: http://www.pullmanchamber.com

Nearest Commercial Airport: Pullman/Moscow Regional (Pullman) (PUW) [21 miles]

Subjects

Historical Periods: 1865–1900; 1900–1940; 1940–present

Natural Resources: Logging

Transportation: Railroads; Stagecoach/Freight; Ferries

Agriculture: Ranching/Livestock; Grains; Orchards

Business: Retail

Manufacturing: Grist/Flour Mills; Brick Making; Sawmills

Government: City; County

Organizations: Schools; Colleges/Universities; Hospitals/Medical Facilities; Charities; Nonreligious Organizations; Civic and Fraternal; Women's

Ethnic Groups: Native American; Chinese; English; German; Norwegian

Religious Sites and Organizations: Protestant; Catholic

Date of Reviewer's Visit: 1/28/2004

Profile Updated by Institution: 11/15/2004

RENTON

Name: Renton Historical Museum   **County:** King

Mailing Address: 235 Mill Ave S.

  City: Renton   **State:** WA   **Postal Code:** 98055-2133

Street Address: 235 Mill Ave S.

Institution Email: saanderson@ci.renton.wa.us

Telephone Number: (425) 255-2330   **Fax Number:** (425) 255-1570

Contact Name: Steve Anderson, Director

Contact Email: saanderson@ci.renton.wa.us

Institution Type: Local Museum

Affiliation: City of Renton and Renton Historical Society

Web site URL: http://www.ci.renton.wa.us/commserv/museum

Hours: Tu–F 12–4 by appt.

Staff in Archives: 1f 4p 5 v

Archives Are Handicapped Accessible: Yes

Cost for Researcher—In-house: donations

Review of Facilities: The Renton Historical Museum is located in a WPA-built art deco fire station. The building is all on one level. The research room is located past most of the exhibits, to the back of the museum. The research room is simple with a large worktable and historical items surrounding on several walls. The collection of books and map/large documents is stored in bookcases and oversize map cases in the same room. Photographs, other manuscript materials, as well as the indexes are stored in the staff offices in another part of the building.

Vertical Files: Yes   **Vertical Files in Cubic Feet:** 6

  Vertical File Description and Subjects: Family files

Manuscripts: Yes   **Manuscripts Volume in Cubic Feet:** 6

  Manuscript Types: Business records, organizational records, scrapbooks

  Manuscript Subjects: History of businesses, organizations, and people of Renton

Photographs: Yes   **Number of Photographs:** 13,000

   Storage of Photographs: Photographs are stored in file cabinets

   Photograph Subjects: Renton area history and people, agricultural, logging, business, transportation. Photographs from the mid-1850s to the present.

   Photograph Reproductions Are Available: Yes

      Photographic Prints: Yes   **Digital Prints:** Yes

      Digital Images on CD or Electronically: Yes

Books: Yes   **Number of Books in Collection:** 500

   Description of Books: Local history, city directories, annuals

Newspapers: Yes

   Newspapers In Paper Format: Yes

   Papers and Dates: Renton Public Library has paper copies of Renton papers from 1931–1977.

Oral Histories: Yes   **Oral Histories Number:** 50

   Oral Histories Description: Oral history interviews are on family and Renton historical subjects. Interviews are on audiocassette and some have transcriptions. From 1975 to 2004.

Maps and Drawings: No

Genealogy Sources: Yes

   Genealogy Sources Description: Genealogy files, cemetery records, obituary files on computer

Special Collections: No

Indexes: Photo, manuscript, genealogy information on card files. Listing of maps.

   Manuscript Finding Aids: PastPerfect Software is used.

   Online Sources: Oral history interviews listed on Oral History Catalog at Museum of History and Industry. The collection of photographs (currently 500) is searchable and viewable through the Renton Historical Society Web site or see listing for King County Snapshots in chapter 7..

Review of Collections: The collections at the Renton Museum are divided into several distinct pieces. The bulk of the research materials is stored in the offices of the Renton Historical Society at the opposite end of the building from the research room. The photograph collection is moderate in size, and images are cataloged and some listed on card files by general subject heading. There are nearly 500 images on the Web site of the historical society, and they are keyword searchable. The collections span from mid-nineteenth century to the present.

Museum on Premises: Yes

Museum Hours: Tu–Sa 10–4

Cost of Entry to Museum: $3

Museum Is Handicapped Accessible: Yes

Description of Museum: Moderate-sized local history museum housed in a former fire department building

Parking: Free parking lot across the street

Lunch: Various restaurants within three blocks in the downtown area

Lodging: http://www.gorenton.com

Nearest Commercial Airport: Seattle-Tacoma International (SEA) [8 miles]

Subjects

    Historical Periods:1800–1865; 1865–1900; 1900–1940; 1940–present

    Eras: Fur Trade; World War I; World War II

    Natural Resources: Logging

    Mining: Coal

    Transportation: Railroads; Ferries; Aviation

    Agriculture: Dairy; Ranching/Livestock; Vegetable/Truck Crops; Vineyard

    Business: Retail; Legal/Medical Services; Hotels/Restaurants; Entertainment/ Theaters

    Manufacturing: Brick Making; Sawmills; Wood Products

    Government: City

    Organizations: Schools; Hospitals/Medical Facilities; Charities; Nonreligious Organizations; Civic and Fraternal; Women's; Business; Children's; Labor and Union

    Ethnic Groups: Native American; Latin American; African; Japanese; Chinese; Danish; Dutch; English; Finnish; French; German; Irish; Italian; Norwegian; Russian; Scottish; Spanish; Swedish

    Religious Sites and Organizations: Protestant; Catholic; Hindu

Date of Reviewer's Visit: 7/19/2002

Profile Updated by Institution: 11/19/2004

RICHLAND

�֎֎֎

Name: Columbia River Exhibition of History, Science and Technology (CREHST)
County: Benton

Mailing Address: 95 Lee Blvd.

City: Richland   **State:** WA   **Postal Code:** 99352-4222

Street Address: 95 Lee Blvd.

Institution Email: None

Telephone Number: (509) 943-9000   **Fax Number:** (509) 943-1770

Contact Name: Connie Estep, Curator   **Contact Email:** cestep@crehst.org

Institution Type: Local Museum

Affiliation: Environmental Science and Technology Foundation

Web site URL: http://www.crehst.org

Hours: M–F 9–4 by appt. only

Staff in Archives: 2f,1v

Archives Are Handicapped Accessible: Yes

Access Description: To enter the lower level there is a handicapped entrance at the back of the building.

Review of Facilities: The Columbia River Exhibition of History Science and Technology is located in a two-story building near the downtown area. Museum displays are on the main floor. The archives are located on the lower level along with staff offices. There are current plans for a new building, which hopefully will provide a library, or archives. The current research facilities are poor for the size of institution. There are some worktables available in a workshop area, or in a kitchen/ staff room. The shop area is large, but noisy. The staff is pleasant and helpful, however, and the collection has some unique materials that may make it worth a visit for some researchers.

Vertical Files: Yes   **Vertical Files in Cubic Feet:** 3

   Vertical File Description and Subjects: General subject files of early townspeople and some family histories

Manuscripts: Yes   **Manuscripts Volume in Cubic Feet:** 6

   Manuscript Types: Personal papers, scrapbooks

   Manuscript Subjects: Collections of Hanford Nuclear Reservation records from employees. Some local area history, Hanford records. Personal papers of W. E. B. Johnson, former manager at Hanford. Also papers of Norm Dresser, a draftsman/ engineer. Three scrapbooks of activities and calendars of the Hanford Reach, listing programs for both white and "colored" employees. Only a small percentage is processed.

Photographs: Yes   **Number of Photographs:** 3,500

   Storage of Photographs: Photographs are stored in plastic sleeves to be housed in file boxes.

   Photograph Subjects: De-classified original government photos of Hanford and surrounding areas

Photograph Reproductions Are Available: Yes

    Photographic Prints: Yes   **Digital Prints:** Yes

Books: Yes   **Number of Books in Collection:** 70

    Description of Books: Reports of Hanford, engineering books for era, telephone directories, miscellaneous books

Newspapers: Yes

    Newspapers in Paper Format: Yes

    Papers and Dates: *Hanford Research News* from 1947–1987 and 1990–2002 (official Hanford site newspaper)

Oral Histories: Yes   **Oral Histories Number:** 40

    Oral Histories Description: 20 oral histories with transcripts of interviews done with B reactor employees of Hanford. There are also 15-plus videotaped oral histories.

Maps and Drawings: Yes

    Description of Maps and Drawings: A few maps of Richland town site from the 1940s to 1960

Genealogy Sources: No

Special Collections: No

Indexes: Photograph index is currently a simple contents list but is moving to local computer system.

    Manuscript Finding Aids: Basic finding aids to the manuscript materials are on local computer.

Review of Collections: The archival and manuscript holdings at the CREHST museum are divided into two separate collections. The museum has a contract to curate the materials for the Hanford site; these materials are on loan and not owned by the museum. The remainder of the collection is owned by the museum, and includes some early history of the area. There are some museum materials covering the earliest history and geography of the area; the archival and photograph collection is focused on the World War II growth and aftermath. The collections are limited in scope and subject matter. For researchers studying Hanford, or even World War II community growth, the collection would be helpful. For history of the agriculture, social, or business growth in the area, the researcher would be better served at either the Kennewick or Pasco museums.

Museum on Premises: Yes

    Museum Hours: M–Sa 10–5, Su 12–5

    Cost of Entry to Museum: $3.50

    Museum Is Handicapped Accessible: Yes

Description of Museum: Moderate-sized museum exploring the history and geology of the Columbia River Basin. Includes the history of the Hanford Nuclear Reservation and area agriculture.

Parking: Free parking lot in front of building

Lunch: A sports bar within half a block, located in park by river, with picnic area

Lodging: http://www.visittri-cities.com

Nearest Commercial Airport: Tri-Cities (Pasco) (PSC) [10 miles]

Subjects

> **Historical Periods:**1900–1940; 1940–present
>
> **Eras:** World War II
>
> **Manufacturing:** Technology/Computers
>
> **Government:** Federal

Date of Reviewer's Visit: 10/10/2003

Profile Updated by Institution: 11/16/2004

RITZVILLE

Name: Ritzville Library District #2   **County:** Adams

Mailing Address: 302 W. Main

   City: Ritzville   **State:** WA   **Postal Code:** 99169-0000

Street Address: 302 W. Main

Institution Email: ritzlib@ritzcom.net

Telephone Number: (509) 659-1222   **Fax Number:** (509) 659-1222

Contact Name: Sandra Fitch, Director

Institution Type: Public Library

Affiliation: Library taxing district

Web site URL: http://www.ritzcom.net/ritzlib/

Hours: M, W 2–5, 7–9; Tu and Th 11–5, 7–9; F 2–5, Sa 10–1

Staff in Archives: 1f 1p 3v

Archives Are Handicapped Accessible: Yes

Access Description: Flight of stairs at entrance

Cost for Researcher—Remote: Fee Schedule

Review of Facilities: The Ritzville Library District #2 is located in an old Carnegie Library building in the downtown area. The reading room is upstairs with an oval worktable and chairs in the front corner of the library. The published books and local historical information notebooks are stored in this area and in the office. Photographs and miscellaneous manuscripts are stored downstairs in a locked staff-only area. There are some large worktables in the basement meeting room, where some of the scrapbooks and other local history materials are stored. (The Wagon Train Descendants' Association have their Heritage Research Center in a corner of this room. Their mailing address is 1003 S. Jackson, Ritzville, WA 99169 [509] 659-0237.)

Vertical Files: Yes   **Vertical Files in Cubic Feet:** 2

Vertical File Description and Subjects: Clippings by subject, miscellaneous ephemera

Manuscripts: Yes   **Manuscripts Volume in Cubic Feet:** 37

Manuscript Types: School records, organizational records

Manuscript Subjects: History of schools, classes

Photographs: Yes   **Number of Photographs:** 10,000

Storage of Photographs: Photographs are stored in document cases

Photograph Subjects: Big Bend region, Ritzville, agriculture

Photograph Reproductions Are Available: Yes

   Photographic Prints: No   **Digital Prints:** Yes

Books: Yes   **Number of Books in Collection:** 68

Description of Books: Adams County, Pacific Northwest history, Polk directories, high school annuals, 1958–2002

Newspapers: Yes

Newspapers in Paper Format: Yes

Papers and Dates: Bound newspapers of Ritzville area, 1965–2004

Newspapers on Microfilm: Yes

Microfilm and Dates: Microfilm of 1898–present of Ritzville, *Lind Leader*, and *Othello* newspapers

Oral Histories: Yes

Oral Histories Description: Oral history transcriptions of 1935 (school class project), 1978 (freshman English class project)

Maps and Drawings: Yes

Description of Maps and Drawings: Local area maps, fire insurance maps of various years between 1891 and 1912

Genealogy Sources: Yes

Genealogy Sources Description: Obituaries, family histories, cemetery files

Special Collections: Yes

Special Collections Description: A notable photography collection is the A. M. Bert Kendrick Collection at the Ritzville Public Library. The collection spans the years from 1935 to 1976, when Mr. Kendrick was the area's main portrait and studio photographer. There are over 10,000 negatives in the collection, some dating as far back as 1911, but demonstrating the depth of his interest in a variety of topics. Some of the photographs are available for viewing from the Web site.

Indexes: Yes

Published Guides: Six-page "Ritzville Library District #2 Sources for Genealogical Research 2004," updated as of July 15, 2004

Online Sources: Cemetery records and obituaries are available on the Web site. Selected images from the Kendrick collection are available online as well.

Review of Collections: The Ritzville Public Library collects history of Adams County, particularly the Ritzville area and some old Whitman County history. The collections are small and narrowly focused, but notable. The manuscript collection's strength lies in the Ritzville School District historical records and materials. These records date back to 1900. The Kendrick photo collection is a significant part of the research materials (see above). Portions of the photograph collection are available on the Web site.

Museum on Premises: No

Parking: Free on-street parallel parking

Lunch: Coffee shop and restaurant in next block, variety of local cafes within a few blocks, chain restaurants at freeway exit from Spokane

Lodging: http://www.ritzville.com/Chamber/

Nearest Commercial Airport: Spokane International (GEG) [56 miles]

Subjects

> **Historical Periods:** 1865–1900; 1900–1940; 1940–present
>
> **Eras:** Civil War; Indian Wars; World War I; World War II; Vietnam War
>
> **Natural Resources:** Irrigation; Logging
>
> **Transportation:** Railroads
>
> **Agriculture:** Ranching/Livestock; Grains; Dry Land Farming
>
> **Business:** Banking; Retail; Hotels/Restaurants; Entertainment/Theaters
>
> **Manufacturing:** Grist/Flour Mills; Creamery
>
> **Government:** City; County
>
> **Organizations:** Schools; Hospitals/Medical Facilities; Nonreligious Organizations; Civic and Fraternal; Women's; Children's
>
> **Ethnic Groups:** Native American; English; German; Irish; Russian; Scottish; Spanish
>
> **Religious Sites and Organizations:** Protestant; Catholic; LDS (Mormon); Jewish; Mennonite/Amish; Hutterites

Date of Reviewer's Visit: 3/26/2004
Profile Updated by Institution: 11/24/2004

SEAHURST

✳✳✳

Name: Highline Historical Society   **County:** King
Mailing Address: PO Box 317
  City: Seahurst   **State:** WA   **Postal Code:** 98062-0000
  Street Address: 160th and 6th Ave.
  Institution Email: editor@highlinehistory.org
  Telephone Number: (206) 246-6354   **Fax Number:** (206) 241-5786
Contact Name: Cyndi Upthegrove   **Contact Email:** cyndiu@netquest.net
Institution Type: Historical Society Archives
Web site URL: http://www.highlinehistory.org
Hours: Tu 9–12
Staff in Archives: 1p 8v
Archives Are Handicapped Accessible: No
Access Description: Archives is not accessible
Cost for Researcher—Remote: First 1/2 hr. free, then fee schedule
Review of Facilities: The collections of the Highline Historical Society are stored in the gymnasium of an abandoned school. The building is at the edge of a park but in a primarily residential area. The facilities are temporary, until the funds can be raised and a new museum built. There is not a museum currently, just the storage area of some artifacts and archival materials. The collections are arranged in various parts of the large room by types of materials for the convenience of the volunteers. Researchers are allowed, but the primary function of the facility is preservation and cataloging of the collections. There are worktables spread throughout for volunteer and researchers to use. The facility is open limited hours and run by volunteers. An archivist has been hired to work with the collections three days per month.
Vertical Files: Yes   **Vertical Files in Cubic Feet:** 32
  Vertical File Description and Subjects: School histories of all schools in the Highline District—files with many original documents as well as copies, clippings, and so forth
Manuscripts: Yes   **Manuscripts Volume in Cubic Feet:** 136
  Manuscript Types: School records, personal papers, some business records
  Manuscript Subjects: School district subjects and community history

Photographs: Yes   **Number of Photographs:** 60,000

Storage of Photographs: There is a subject file of photocopies of a select group of the photographs. The originals of the photographs are stored in clamshell boxes in acid-free sleeves/folders.

Photograph Subjects: The photograph collection includes the negative archives from the *Highline Times* newspaper. These negatives number 45,000. In addition, the collection includes both the community photographs from the Highline area and a large number of photographs on the schools.

Photograph Reproductions Are Available: Yes

  Photographic Prints: Yes   **Digital Prints:** Yes

Books: Yes   **Number of Books in Collection:** 1,500

Description of Books: Book collections include large numbers of textbooks that were used in the local schools. These books are presently boxed and stored rather than being on open shelving. There are some professional collection books, regional history, and some on Native Americans.

Newspapers: Yes

  Newspapers in Paper Format: Yes

  Papers and Dates: Bound volumes of the *Highline Times* from 1943

  Newspapers on Microfilm: Yes

  Microfilm and Dates: *Highline Times,* 25 years

Oral Histories: Yes   **Oral Histories Number:** 140

  Oral Histories Description: Project collected oral histories from Burien area residents. Interviews done 1996 to present. All have transcriptions and are indexed

Maps and Drawings: Yes   **Estimated Number of Maps and Drawings:** 15

  Description of Maps and Drawings: Early King County plats

Genealogy Sources: Yes

  Genealogy Sources Description: History of pioneer families of the area

Special Collections: Yes

  Special Collections Description: Collection of materials from Camp Waskowitz, a summer camp run by the school district from the mid-twentieth century, a former Civilian Conservation Corps camp.

Indexes: Oral histories are indexed.

  Published Guides: *Highline School District Chronicle,* written by Carl Jensen

Review of Collections: The collections of the Highline Historical Society are unique in that 60–70 percent of the materials deal with all aspects of school history.

The earliest school started in 1878, and the Highline District consolidated the various local school districts in 1924. The general history coverage of the local areas includes Burien, Seatac, Normandy Park, and some Federal Way and White Center. The collection is growing rapidly and will continue to do so, as the building plans progress. The collections are being professionally processed and stored. A project to scan the photographs is being started. Subject access to the collection is being expanded to include more photographs and documents.

Museum on Premises: No

Parking: Dirt off-street vertical parking on 6th Ave.

Lunch: Variety of chain and local restaurants within driving distance

Lodging: http://www.seattlesouthside.com

Nearest Commercial Airport: Seattle-Tacoma International (SEA) [5 miles]

Subjects

    Historical Periods: 1865–1900; 1900–1940; 1940–present

    Eras: World War I; World War II

    Transportation: Ferries; Aviation

    Agriculture: Vegetable/Truck Crops

    Business: Banking; Retail; Legal/Medical Services

    Government: City; County

    Organizations: Schools; Charities; Nonreligious Organizations; Civic and Fraternal

    Ethnic Groups: Latin American

Date of Reviewer's Visit: 1/13/2004

Profile Updated by Institution: 11/12/2004

SEATTLE

Name: Black Heritage Society of Washington State, Inc. **County:** King

Mailing Address: PO Box 22961

    City: Seattle   **State:** WA   **Postal Code:** 98122-0961

Street Address: 2700 24th Ave. East

Institution Email: None

Telephone Number: (206) 723-5035

Contact Name: Phyllis R. Beaumonte, President

Contact Email: rabeaucon@aol.com

Institution Type: Historical Society Archives

Affiliation: Black Heritage Society of Washington State, Inc.

Web site URL: http://blackheritagewa.org

Hours: By appt.

Staff in Archives: 14v

Archives Are Handicapped Accessible: Yes

Review of Facilities: The collections of the Black Heritage Society of Washington State are housed physically in the archives of the Museum of History and Industry (MOHAI) in McCurdy Park. The collection, though housed in the MOHAI facility, is a completely different entity, and MOHAI staff are unable to assist researchers in the Black Heritage Society collection. Appointments to view the collections must be made directly with the Black Heritage Society. The reading room from this collection shares space with MOHAI archives and the Puget Sound Maritime Research Library.

Vertical Files: Yes   **Vertical Files in Cubic Feet:** 6

   Vertical File Description and Subjects: Ephemera and some original documents are arranged alphabetically

Manuscripts: Yes

   Manuscript Types: Personal papers, organizational records, school records, business records, scrapbooks

   Manuscript Subjects: African American Pioneers dating as far back as 1850

Photographs: Yes   **Number of Photographs:** 2,500

   Storage of Photographs: Photographs are stored in boxes or photo albums or digitally in a computer database. Originals are stored in a nearby storage room.

   Photograph Subjects: Political, businesses, military, education, entertainment, religion, family, civil rights

   Photograph Reproductions Are Available: Yes

   Photographic Prints: Yes   **Digital Prints:** Yes

   Digital Images on CD or Electronically: Yes

Books: Yes   **Number of Books in Collection:** 25

   Description of Books: Books by local African American authors

Newspapers: Yes

   Newspapers in Paper Format: Yes

   Papers and Dates: Selected papers form 1910 to present, but not extensive

Oral Histories: Yes   **Oral Histories Number:** 42

Oral Histories Description: Oral history interviews with African Americans done on audiocassette (2 on videocassette) from the years 1990 to present. The interviews have been transcribed.

Maps and Drawings: No

Genealogy Sources: Yes

Genealogy Sources Description: Obituaries; biographies; funeral programs; birth, marriage and cemetery records

Special Collections: No

Indexes: Staff computer index using Access for books, vertical files, photographs. Card file index of photographs.

Manuscript Finding Aids: Finding aids of manuscript collections available on staff computer.

Review of Collections: The collections of the Black Heritage Society focus on the history of African Americans in Washington State. The collection is strongest in Puget Sound region people and topics. Materials date back to 1850. The photograph collection, though not large, focuses on the business, cultural, and religious lives of African Americans in the state.

Museum on Premises: No

Parking: Free parking lots adjacent

Lunch: Driving distance to variety of restaurants

Lodging: http://www.seeseattle.org/; Best Western University Tower Hotel closest to campus

Nearest Commercial Airport: Seattle-Tacoma International (SEA) [15 miles]

Subjects

Historical Periods: 1865–1900; 1900–1940; 1940–present

Mining: Coal

Transportation: Railroads

Business: Retail; Legal/Medical Services; Hotels/Restaurants; Entertainment/ Theaters

Manufacturing: Sawmills

Government: County; State

Organizations: Colleges/Universities

Ethnic Groups: African

Religious Sites and Organizations: Catholic

Date of Reviewer's Visit: 12/4/2003

Profile Updated by Institution: 11/17/2004

Name: Coast Guard Museum Northwest   **County:** King

Mailing Address: 1519 Alaskan Way S.

City: Seattle   **State:** WA   **Postal Code:** 98134-0000

Street Address: 1519 Alaskan Way S.

Institution Email: None

Telephone Number: (206) 217-6993   **Fax Number:**

Contact Name: Capt. Davis (ret.)

Institution Type: Regional Museum

Web site URL: http://www.uscg.mil/mlcpac/iscseattle/museum/museum.htm

Hours: M, W, and F 9–3

Staff in Archives: 3p, 8v

Archives Are Handicapped Accessible: Yes

Review of Facilities: The Coast Guard Museum is housed in a building on the Coast Guard compound on the Seattle waterfront. Visitors must check in at the main gate to the facility. At the time of the visit there was no parking on the complex, so the reviewer had to park outside and walk into the facility then walk over to the museum. The museum is very nice and the research collections are excellent. The library was a pleasant surprise. The room is large and L-shaped, with two medium-sized worktables. One wall is covered with file cabinets, one wall has the computer system, and the remaining walls are filled with the sizable book collection. Additional research materials are stored in the basement in a staff-only area. Probably one-third of the museum building space is devoted to the library and archival collections. It is a good indication of the value the museum places on the research collections.

Vertical Files: Yes   **Vertical Files in Cubic Feet:** 25

  Vertical File Description and Subjects: Clipping files

Manuscripts: Yes   **Manuscripts Volume in Cubic Feet:** 35

  Manuscript Types: Personal papers, business records, organizational records

  Manuscript Subjects: Lifesaving Service, Coast Guard, memoirs and personal papers of former service people, Douglas Munro Papers. 4,000 documents filed in cabinets and listed in staff database. Variety of types of documents, from official reports to personal papers. Documents from the 1870s through the present.

Photographs: Yes   **Number of Photographs:** 15,000

  Photograph Subjects: Coast Guard, naval, and maritime history, particularly of the Pacific coastal area

  Photograph Reproductions Are Available: Yes

    Photographic Prints: Yes   **Digital Prints:** Yes

Digital Images on CD or Electronically: Yes

Books: Yes   **Number of Books in Collection:** 3,000

Description of Books: Coast Guard, naval, and maritime history and local history; Coast Guard reports; Light lists; yearbooks from Coast Guard Academy; Coast Guard and lighthouse fiction; professional collection

Newspapers: No

Oral Histories: Yes   **Oral Histories Number:** 11

Oral Histories Description: Interviews mostly on Coast Guard in World War II . Transcriptions for all.

Maps and Drawings: Yes   **Estimated Number of Maps and Drawings:** 200

Description of Maps and Drawings: Lighthouse plans, plans for 60 Coast Guard ships

Genealogy Sources: Yes

Genealogy Sources Description: Service lists and some records for Coast Guard service people only

Special Collections: No

Indexes: In-house index on Microsoft Works for staff use only

Online Sources: Oral history interviews listed on Oral History Catalog at MOHAI Web site (see chapter 7)

Review of Collections: The collections at the Coast Guard Museum Northwest were a surprise. It is broader-based in focus and more significant for researchers than the reviewer first imagined. The volunteers, who maintain this collection, value it highly and spend a large amount of time and effort to maintain it in a professional manner. For subjects of maritime history on the Pacific Coast all the way up to Alaska, Artic expeditions, and even some Atlantic seaboard subjects, this is a must-check collection. Although Coast Guard history is the major focus, the collections also contain significant materials on lighthouses, naval affairs, the World Wars, and any issues dealing with the Pacific Coast.

Museum on Premises: Yes

Museum Hours: M,W, and F 9–3

Museum Is Handicapped Accessible: Yes

Description of Museum: The museum consists of one large room for displays. The history of the Coast Guard and related subjects are portrayed. The subject is limited, but the displays are well done and interesting.

Parking: Parking on the compound possibly, otherwise free vertical parking on unpaved area across Alaska Way from the compound.

Lunch: Driving distance to a variety of cafes on the waterfront, Pioneer Square, or Pikes Place market

Lodging: http://www.seattlesouthside.com, http://www.seeseattle.org/

Nearest Commercial Airport: Seattle-Tacoma International (SEA) [13 miles]

Subjects

> **Historical Periods:**1865–1900; 1900–1940; 1940–present
>
> **Eras:** Civil War; Spanish American War; World War I; World War II
>
> **Natural Resources:** Fishing; Whaling
>
> **Transportation:** Ships and Shipping; Ferries
>
> **Organizations:** Nonreligious Organizations

Date of Reviewer's Visit: 12/5/2003

Profile Updated by Institution: 11/15/2004

Name: Loghouse Museum   **County:** King

Mailing Address: 3003 61 SW Ave.

  City: Seattle   **State:** WA   **Postal Code:** 98116-0000

Street Address: 3003 61 SW Ave.

Institution Email: loghousemuseum@comcast.net

Telephone Number: (206) 938-5293

Contact Name: Andrea Mercado

Institution Type: Local Museum

Affiliation: Southwest Seattle Historical Society

Web site URL: http://www.loghousemuseum.org/

Hours: Th 12–6 F–Su 12–3

Staff in Archives: 2p 4v

Archives Are Handicapped Accessible: No

Access Description: Flight of stairs up to archives room

Review of Facilities: The Southwest Seattle Historical Society archival collections are housed in the Loghouse Museum. The museum is in a primarily residential neighborhood with narrow streets. The building was originally a carriage house that was connected to a large estate. The upstairs bears little resemblance to the hayloft it was purported to be at one time. Up a restored wooden staircase is where the archival collections are housed. The area is primarily a staff work area. There is a large worktable under the dormer windows for researchers to use. Most of the documents and photographs are stored in a nearby closet or in adjoining offices. They are discussing moving some of the research materials downstairs to a corner of the exhibit room. Upstairs the room is well lit and pleasant, with the clutter typical of an institution without adequate space.

Vertical Files: Yes   **Vertical Files in Cubic Feet:** 2

    Vertical File Description and Subjects: General clipping files

Manuscripts: Yes   **Manuscripts Volume in Cubic Feet:** 10

    Manuscript Types: Family papers

Photographs: Yes   **Number of Photographs:** 1,200

    Storage of Photographs: Photographs stored in plastic sleeves in binders and then in boxes. Photos filed by photo number with no good cross-referencing. Photos being added to PastPerfect, which will provide the indexing needed. Originals will then be stored off site.

    Photograph Reproductions Are Available: Yes

        Photographic Prints: Yes   **Digital Prints:** Yes

        Digital Images on CD or Electronically: Yes

Books: Yes   **Number of Books in Collection:** 150

    Description of Books: Local history, city directories

Newspapers: Yes

    Newspapers in Paper Format: Yes

    Papers and Dates: Scattered issues only

Oral Histories: Yes   **Oral Histories Number:** 300

    Oral Histories Description: The oral histories were taken between 1998 and 2001 and include interviews of southwest Seattle residents. Most have transcriptions.

Maps and Drawings: No

Genealogy Sources: No

Special Collections: Yes

    Special Collections Description: Clay Eals research and notes from the book entitled *West Side Story*, a history of the west Seattle area based on historic newspaper articles

Indexes: PastPerfect will serve as an index to the collections.

Review of Collections: The collections of the Southwest Seattle Historical Society are small. The collections focus on the photographs and some documentary materials of the area. Little to no information is available for genealogists and they would be advised to look elsewhere. Otherwise the collection deals with the areas of Alki, Dell Ridge, Fauntleroy, White Center, and High Point and the rest of the Duwamish Peninsula.

Museum on Premises: Yes

Museum Hours: Th 12–6 and weekends 12–3

Cost of Entry to Museum: Free

Museum Is Handicapped Accessible: Yes

Description of Museum: The displays are very well done but the museum is small. There are two rooms that hold displays, one for permanent exhibits and one rotating. Southwest Seattle history is the focus of the museum.

Parking: Free on-street parallel parking

Lunch: Upscale eateries and restaurants one block further on Alki Way and overlooking the sound

Lodging: http://www.seeseattle.org/

Nearest Commercial Airport: Seattle-Tacoma International (SEA) [16 miles]

Subjects

Historical Periods:1865–1900; 1900–1940; 1940–present

Natural Resources: Fishing; Logging

Transportation: Railroads; Ships and Shipping; Ferries

Business: Retail; Legal/Medical Services; Hotels/Restaurants

Organizations: Schools; Nonreligious Organizations

Religious Sites and Organizations: Protestant

Date of Reviewer's Visit: 12/5/2003

Profile Updated by Institution: None

✯✯✯✯

Name: Museum of Flight **County:** King

Mailing Address: 9404 E. Marginal Way South

City: Seattle **State:** WA **Postal Code:** 98108-4097

Street Address: 9404 E. Marginal Way South

Institution Email: archives@museumofflight.org

Telephone Number: (206) 764-5720 **Fax Number:** (206) 764-5707

Contact Name: Janice Baker

Contact Email: jbaker@museumofflight

Institution Type: Regional Museum

Web site URL: http://www.museumofflight.org

Hours: M–F 1–5

Staff in Archives: 2f 1p 15v

Archives Are Handicapped Accessible: Yes

Cost for Researcher—Remote: $30 per hr. plus copying and postage

Review of Facilities: The research collections of the Museum of Flight are in temporary quarters for a number of years. The current location is across the street from the museum but will eventually be moved into a wing of the museum. The library is currently housed in an old manufacturing building of the Boeing Company, and it is not a practical space for library and archives. The library portion is large, with the book stacks dominating the area. Most of the research collections are in storage rooms attached, but some at great distance, from the library proper. The storage areas are staff-only. There is a large worktable in the front of the library. Lighting is adequate. The entire library is overfull and due to the temporary nature of the location, the impression is rather chaotic. The collections are the strong element of this facility.

Vertical Files: Yes   **Vertical Files in Cubic Feet:** 38

    Vertical File Description and Subjects: General assorted subject files

Manuscripts: Yes   **Manuscripts Volume in Cubic Feet:** 4,000

    Manuscript Types: Business records, personal papers, organizational records

    Manuscript Subjects: All aspects of aviation and aerospace. Technical manuals, annual reports, promotional materials, business documents, ephemera.

Photographs: Yes   **Number of Photographs:** 21,0000

    Storage of Photographs: Photographs are stored in file cabinets in plastic sleeves. Most manuscript collections also have photographs.

    Photograph Reproductions Are Available: Yes

        Photographic Prints: Yes   **Digital Prints:** Yes

        Digital Images on CD or Electronically: Yes

Books: Yes   **Number of Books in Collection:** 23,000

    Description of Books: Aviation and aerospace and all related fields. Collection also includes 1,000 periodical titles.

Newspapers: No

Oral Histories: Yes   **Oral Histories Number:** 30

    Oral Histories Description: Oral history interviews on the subject of aviation

Maps and Drawings: No

    Description of Maps and Drawings: Aeronautical charts

Genealogy Sources: No

Special Collections: Yes

    Special Collections Description: The Hatfield Collection is the life's·work of aviation historian and collector David Hatfield, documenting the history of aviation in California and beyond. This collection is 1200 cu. ft. of materials of all types.

Indexes: Yes

    Manuscript Finding Aids: Collections have finding aids in varying degree of detail.

Review of Collections: The Museum of Flight's archival collections are tremendous in their scope and content. Notable collections include those from John McDonnell on the McDonnell Aircraft Company; the Lear Collection of original documents of the Lear Aircraft Company; the Parker Space Collection on the Apollo Space Program; the Donald Douglas Collection of company records from the Douglas Aircraft Company; the Elrey B. Jeppesen Collection—the personal and professional papers of the inventor of the Jeppesen aerial navigation maps—and the Hatfield Collection of aviation history. The museum also owns the original papers from the Wright Airplane Company. Researchers wishing to use the Wright Papers need to request special permissions and appointments.

Museum on Premises: Yes

    Museum Hours: Daily 10–5; first Thurs. of month, 10–9:00

    Cost of Entry to Museum: $11

    Museum Is Handicapped Accessible: Yes

    Description of Museum: Large professionally curated museum on the history of aviation

Parking: Free parking lot next to building

Lunch: Café in museum across the road

Lodging: http://www.seattlesouthside.com, http://www.seeseattle.org/

Nearest Commercial Airport: Seattle-Tacoma International (SEA) [7 miles]

Subjects

    Historical Periods:1900–1940; 1940–present

    Eras: World War I; World War II

    Transportation: Aviation

    Business: Legal/Medical Services

    Manufacturing: Technology/Computers

    Organizations: Nonreligious Organizations

Date of Reviewer's Visit: 12/5/2003

Profile Updated by Institution: 12/15/2004

✵✵✵✵

Name: Museum of History and Industry (MOHAI) **County:** King

Mailing Address: 2700 24th Ave E.

City: Seattle **State:** WA **Postal Code:** 98112–0000

Street Address: 2700 24th Ave E.

Institution Email: library@seattlehistory.org

Telephone Number: (206) 324-1126 **Fax Number:** (206) 324-1346

Contact Name: Carolyn Marr

Contact Email: carolyn.marr@seattlehistory.org

Institution Type: Regional Museum

Web site URL: http://www.seattlehistory.org

Hours: M–W 1–5 by appt.

Staff in Archives: 2f 10v

Archives Are Handicapped Accessible: Yes

Cost for Researcher—In-house: No charge with appt.

Cost for Researcher—Remote: First 1/2 hr. free, then $35 per hr.

Review of Facilities: The research library is on the lower level of the Museum of History and Industry. Enter through the main door and ask for directions. For researchers just using the library, and who have an appointment, there is no fee for admission. The library itself is a very pleasant room with the research tables in the center and large glass walls dividing the reading room from the collections on either side. Several rows of compact shelving are to the right, while staff offices, workspace, and some collections are on the left. Only paper and pencils are allowed in the research area. Storage areas are staff-only. There are small unlocked lockers behind the staff desk for researcher's personal belongings. The facility is modern and professional. The facility shares space with the Puget Sound Maritime Historical Society, which has a separate listing, since their collections are maintained separately.

Vertical Files: Yes **Vertical Files in Cubic Feet:** 500

Vertical File Description and Subjects: Seattle area subjects, clippings, brochures, papers

Manuscripts: Yes **Manuscripts Volume in Cubic Feet:** 300

Manuscript Types: Business records, personal papers, organizational records

Manuscript Subjects: Seattle area families and history

Photographs: Yes **Number of Photographs:** 1,500,000

Storage of Photographs: Some of the photographs are in file cabinets in the research room. Photos are mounted or have plastic sleeves. Filed by subject. Over 5,500 images available online through the Web site.

Photograph Subjects: Variety of Seattle area images, collection of commercial photographs from the Webster & Stevens studio

Photograph Reproductions Are Available: Yes

Photographic Prints: Yes   **Digital Prints:** No

Digital Images on CD or Electronically: Yes

Books: Yes   **Number of Books in Collection:** 10,000

Description of Books: Local and regional history, Seattle, Northwest, and Alaska, city directories; books filed by Dewey numbers

Newspapers: Yes

Newspapers in Paper Format: Yes

Papers and Dates: Selected Seattle area papers only, 1880s–1960s

Newspapers on Microfilm: Yes

Microfilm and Dates: *Seattle Times* on microfilm, 1897–1954

Oral Histories: Yes   **Oral Histories Number:** 115

Oral Histories Description: Tech industry interviews 2002, also other Seattle history interviews

Maps and Drawings: Yes   **Estimated Number of Maps and Drawings:** 1,000

Description of Maps and Drawings: Local and regional maps, in-house database indexes and describes the maps

Genealogy Sources: No

Special Collections: No

Indexes: In-house databases, which list most items in the collections.

Online Sources: Web site has an index to photographs, oral history interviews, and some online historical content

Review of Collections: Although the museum is entitled Museum of History and Industry, the research collections do not have a significant industry component. The research collections focus on the various aspects of Seattle area history. The strongest part of the collection is the photographs, which now number 1.5 million. Most are indexed in databases available on site. About 5,500 are available with images on the Web site. The collection is particularly weak in the area of genealogy. The map collection is fairly large, with a thousand or so maps. There are also 100 films and 500 sound recordings in the collection. There is also a searchable computer database of the *Seattle Post-Intelligencer;* negatives inventory is from the 1920s to 1972.

Museum on Premises: Yes

Museum Hours: Daily 10–5

Cost of Entry to Museum: $7

Museum Is Handicapped Accessible: Yes

Description of Museum: Large modern museum displaying the many facets of Seattle history and offering large galleries with rotating exhibits

Parking: Free parking lots adjacent

Lunch: Driving distance to variety of restaurants

Lodging: http://www.seeseattle.org/

Nearest Commercial Airport: Seattle-Tacoma International (SEA) [17 miles]

Subjects

Historical Periods: 1865–1900; 1900–1940; 1940–present

Eras: World War II

Natural Resources: Fishing; Logging

Mining: Silver; Coal

Transportation: Railroads; Ships and Shipping; Ferries; Aviation

Business: Retail; Legal/Medical Services; Hotels/Restaurants; Entertainment/ Theaters

Manufacturing: Boatbuilding/Shipyard; Sawmills; Wood Products

Organizations: Schools; Hospitals/Medical Facilities; Charities; Nonreligious Organizations; Women's

Ethnic Groups: Native American; Japanese; Chinese; Italian; Norwegian

Date of Reviewer's Visit: 12/4/2003

Profile Updated by Institution: 11/10/2004

✳✳✳✳✳

Name: National Archives and Records Administration Pacific and Alaska Region

County: King

Mailing Address: Pacific Alaska Region (Seattle), 6125 Sand Point Way NE

City: Seattle   **State:** WA   **Postal Code:** 98115-7999

Street Address: 6125 Sand Point Way NE

Institution Email: seattle.archives@nara.gov

Telephone Number: (206) 336-5115   **Fax Number:** (206) 336-5112

Institution Type: Archives

Affiliation: Federal Government

Web site URL: http://www.archives.gov/facilities/wa/seattle.html

Hours: M–F 7:45–4:15; call for evening and Sa hrs.

Staff in Archives: 6p, 40v

Archives Are Handicapped Accessible: Yes

Cost for Researcher—In-house: No charge

Cost for Researcher—Remote: Limited to 1 hr. staff time

Review of Facilities: The National Archives and Records Administration (NARA) Pacific Alaska Region is one of the regional federal archives repositories. The research room of the facility is divided into two sections. The first and largest area is the microfilm reading room, with 35 microfilm reading machines and two reader printers. The second smaller area is the Textual Research Room. All researchers need to check in at the desk and register (picture ID and proof of address is needed) . Lockers are provided to store belongings without fee. Coat racks are also available. Only paper and pencil are allowed in the Textual Research Room. Laptops without the case may be allowed with permission. The Textual Research Room is good-sized, with four large worktables. Each table has an electrical outlet. The room is spartan, but functional. Documents are housed in huge staff-only storage rooms in the building, and requests to pull materials may take up to an hour.

Vertical Files: No

Manuscripts: Yes   **Manuscripts Volume in Cubic Feet:** 33,000

   Manuscript Types: Government records

   Manuscript Subjects: Federal records, textual documents, photographs, maps, architectural drawings. Documents from the federal courts and 60 federal agencies in Idaho, Oregon, and Washington from the 1850s to the 1980s (noncurrent records)

Photographs: Yes

   Photograph Subjects: Photographs are interfiled with archival records collections

   Photograph Reproductions Are Available: Yes

   Photographic Prints: Yes   **Digital Prints:** Yes

   Digital Images on CD or Electronically: Yes

Books: Yes

   Description of Books: genealogy and local historical interest. Available for on-site use only.

Newspapers: No

Oral Histories: No

Maps and Drawings: Yes

   Description of Maps and Drawings: Interfiled with archival collections

Genealogy Sources: Yes

   Genealogy Sources Description: Federal census from all states, 1790–1930; some immigration and naturalization records: military records from Revolutionary War onward all on microfilm; records on the Five Civilized Tribes, Bureau of Indian Affairs, Bureau of Refugees.

Special Collections: Yes

Special Collections Description: 1790–1906. The region has a large collection of microfilm of State Department records held in Washington, D.C., relating to consular activities around the world, especially from Pacific Rim countries.

Indexes: Yes

Manuscript Finding Aids: Finding aids and record group descriptions are available in varying detail for all collections.

Online Sources: NARA's Online Locator will list the microfilm holdings of the Seattle facility accessible from the Web site. Selected Finding Aids and Guide to Archival Holdings are also viewable from the Web site: http://www.archives.gov/facilities/wa/seattle.html. The region currently has over 50 percent of its holdings described at the series level online in the Archival Research Catalog (ARC). ARC is searchable through the main NARA Web site.

Review of Collections: The holdings of the NARA Pacific Alaska Region, Seattle office, are difficult to describe. There are records created by over 60 federal agencies in the states of Idaho, Oregon, and Washington. (Most Alaska records are in that state.) The holdings are over 33,000 cubic feet in size and growing daily. The microfilm records are of significant importance to genealogists, but also to historical researchers, since they make certain records available at a regional level, instead of just in Washington, D.C. The Web site is well designed and full of content to describe the various types of services and collections available to researchers. Records of particular note include those dealing with the subjects of Chinese Exclusion, the home front during World War II, the work of the Army Corps of Engineers, Native Americans, the merchant marine service, and smuggling. Check out the Web site to find other gems.

Museum on Premises: No

Parking: Free parking lot in front

Lunch: Variety of restaurants in U Village driving distance

Lodging: http://www.seeseattle.org/

Nearest Commercial Airport: Seattle-Tacoma International (SEA) [21 miles]

Subjects

Historical Periods: Pre-1800; 1800–1865; 1865–1900; 1900–1940; 1940–present

Eras: Exploration, World War I; WPA; CCC; World War II

Natural Resources: Water; Dams; Fishing; Logging

Mining: Mining

Transportation: Railroads; Ships and Shipping; Aviation

Government: Federal

Organizations: Schools

Ethnic Groups: Native American; Chinese

Date of Reviewer's Visit: 12/3/2003

Profile Updated by Institution: 11/12/2004

✼✼✼

Name: Nordic Heritage Museum   **County:** King

Mailing Address: 3014 NW 67th St.

  City: Seattle   **State:** WA   **Postal Code:** 98117-0000

Street Address: 3014 NW 67th St.

Institution Email: nordic@nordicmuseum.org

Telephone Number: (206) 789-5707   **Fax Number:** (206) 789-3271

Contact Name: Lisa Hill-Festa, Marianne Forssblad

Contact Email: lisah@nordicmuseum.org; mariannef@nordicmuseum.org

Institution Type: Regional Museum

Web site URL: http://www.nordicmuseum.com

Hours: Tu–Sa 10–4, Su 12–4

Staff in Archives: 2f, 1p, 10v

Archives Are Handicapped Accessible: No

Access Description: Library portion is up a flight of stairs. Archives area is accessible.

Cost for Researcher—In-house: $5 plus museum admission

Cost for Researcher—Remote: Fee schedule

Review of Facilities: The Nordic Heritage Museum is in an old school building in a residential neighborhood. The archives area is on the third floor and is accessible by elevator. The archival materials are stored in a staff-only area on the third floor. Materials can be viewed at a long research table in the wide hallway of the third floor, directly outside the collections offices. The research library is located up a flight of stairs from the second floor display area and is not accessible. This area consists of one long room with worktables and bookshelves on two walls. The books in this room are English language titles that deal with all aspects of Scandinavian-American life and history. Two rooms open off this main area that also hold the library collections that are in the five languages Norwegian, Swedish, Finnish, Icelandic, and Danish. The area has been divided out with some staff work areas intermingled with the research area. The Gordon Ekvail Tracie Music Archives of Scandinavian Folk Music with sound recordings, sheet music, and musical instruments is also housed in this area. The separation of the archival collections from those of the library is unfortunate, as is the stairs to access the library.

Vertical Files: Yes   **Vertical Files in Cubic Feet:** 30

Vertical File Description and Subjects: General subjects and clipping files

Manuscripts: Yes   **Manuscripts Volume in Cubic Feet:** 100

Manuscript Types: Family papers, organizational records, business records

Manuscript Subjects: Organizations, people, and businesses from the Nordic communities primarily in Western Washington

Photographs: Yes

Storage of Photographs: Photographs are stored in archival folders in clamshell boxes in the archives. Some photos have photocopies available in binders for researchers to browse. The photo collection is being added to PastPerfect and will be searchable in that format.

Photograph Reproductions Are Available: Yes

Photographic Prints: Yes   **Digital Prints:** Yes

Digital Images on CD or Electronically: Yes

Books: Yes   **Number of Books in Collection:** 15,000

Description of Books: Books in all five Nordic languages on all subjects; English-language books about all five groups; English translations of books from the original languages; local history and professional collection books

Newspapers: No

Oral Histories: Yes   **Oral Histories Number:** 150

Oral Histories Description: Over 100 are from a Vanishing Generations project of elderly immigrants (2000–). A dozen or so interviews are from Danes who immigrated post–World War II. Some have transcriptions. Some are on videotape, but most are audiocassette.

Maps and Drawings: No

Genealogy Sources: Yes

Genealogy Sources Description: Norwegian Bygd books—(detailed parish books, not a complete set)

Special Collections: Yes

Special Collections Description: Gordon Ekvail Tracie Music Collection

Indexes: Photographs and manuscript materials are to be indexed using PastPerfect.

Manuscript Finding Aids: Finding aids are in process.

Review of Collections: This collection is still young (under 25 years), and space is a major issue. The photograph collection is large and well cared for. The book collection is diverse and popping at the seams. The manuscript materials were smaller than the reviewer expected given the size of both the photograph and library collections. The archival materials are well housed in a professional manner and staff were in the process of changing the arrangement and labeling to make it more user friendly. The current system of filing by accession number made specific items hard to browse. The Gordon Ekvail Tracie music collection is remarkable in it size and breadth, but still limited to a very specific topic of Scandinavian folk music and dance.

Museum on Premises: Yes

    Museum Hours: Tu–Sa 10–, Su 12–4

    Cost of Entry to Museum: $5

    Museum Is Handicapped Accessible: Yes

    Description of Museum: The museum is divided into several distinct parts. One section explores the Nordic-American experience and history of the area. Another area is divided into the five cultural groups, each with a display room to showcase their individual experiences.

Parking: Free parking lot adjacent to museum

Lunch: Driving distance to downtown Ballard and numerous local and chain restaurants

Lodging: http://www.seeseattle.org/

Nearest Commercial Airport: Seattle-Tacoma International (SEA) [20 miles]

Subjects

    Historical Periods: 1865–1900; 1900–1940; 1940–present

    Eras: World War II

    Business: Retail; Legal/Medical Services; Hotels/Restaurants

    Organizations: Hospitals/Medical   Facilities;   Charities;   Nonreligious Organizations

    Ethnic Groups: Danish; Finnish; Norwegian; Swedish; Icelandic

    Religious Sites and Organizations: Protestant

Date of Reviewer's Visit: 12/3/2003

Profile Updated by Institution: 12/6/2004

✳✳✳✳

Name: Providence Archives   **County:** King

Mailing Address: 4800 37th Ave. SW

    City: Seattle   **State:** WA   **Postal Code:** 98126-2793

Street Address: 4800 37th Ave. SW

Institution Email: archives@providence.org

Telephone Number: (206) 937-4600   **Fax Number:** (206) 923-4001

Contact Name: Loretta Zwolak Greene

Contact Email: loretta.greene@providence.org

Institution Type: Archives

Affiliation: Sisters of Providence, Roman Catholic Church

Web site URL: http://www.providence.org/phs/archives/

Hours: M–F 10–3 by appt.

Staff in Archives: 3f, 1v

Archives Are Handicapped Accessible: Yes

Cost for Researcher—In-house: none

Cost for Researcher—Remote: none

Review of Facilities: The Providence Archives are located in a religious community residence in West Seattle. The Archives are down the hall from the entrance on the main level. The reading room is well lit and has large tables. The collections are housed in compact shelving in a room nearby. The collections are professionally cataloged, stored, and maintained.

Vertical Files: No

Manuscripts: Yes   **Manuscripts Volume in Cubic Feet:** 2,700

   Manuscript Types: Administrative records, hospital records, school records, organizational records, personal papers, letters, diaries, ephemera

   Manuscript Subjects:, Hospitals, schools, healthcare, nursing, correspondence, social services, religious life.

Photographs: Yes   **Number of Photographs:** 50,000

   Storage of Photographs: Document boxes digitally. In-house database that will soon be accessible through the Archives' Web site.

   Photograph Subjects: Providence Health System, Providence services, hospitals, personnel, educational institutions, schools of nursing, and religious life of the sisters of Providence. Photographs from 1850s to the present.

   Photograph Reproductions Are Available: Yes

   Photographic Prints: Yes   **Digital Prints:** Yes

   Digital Images on CD or Electronically: Yes

Books: Yes   **Number of Books in Collection:** 3,000

   Description of Books: Regional histories, religious life, general works on the Roman Catholic Church

Newspapers: Yes

   Newspapers in Paper Format: Yes

Papers and Dates: Select issues

Oral Histories: Yes

Oral Histories Description: Cassette tapes for oral histories of 50 Sisters of Providence done in the 1990s. Some have transcriptions.

Maps and Drawings: No

Genealogy Sources: Yes

Genealogy Sources Description: Early ledgers related to Providence ministries

Special Collections: Yes

Special Collections Description: The personal papers of Mother Joseph of the Sacred Heart (Esther Pariseau), founder of the Sisters of Providence in the West, who lived from 1823–1902, are a significant record of the early years of service of the Sisters of Providence in the Pacific Northwest. This collection also includes documents about the installation of her statue in the National Statuary Hall in Washington, D.C., in 1980.

Indexes: In-house database for visual materials and artifacts.

Manuscript Finding Aids: Collection inventories on site.

Online Sources: Collection inventories available from Web site.

Review of Collections: The Sisters of Providence ministries are found in Washington, Oregon, California, Alaska, Montana, and Idaho, and this collection records that geographically broad history of their activities and the Providence Health System and Providence Services that were born from it. The collections date from the mid-nineteenth century and contain the administrative records of the religious community, as well as personal papers of Mother Joseph of the Sacred Heart and other members of the religious order. Some of the administrative records are confidential and access is restricted. Although limited in scope, this collection provides insight in the early missions to the Native American peoples as well as the development of large numbers of schools, hospitals, and social services throughout the region.

Museum on Premises: No

Parking: Free parking lot adjacent

Lunch: Cafeteria next door at Mount St. Vincents; other restaurants in West Seattle

Lodging: http://www.seeseattle.org/

Nearest Commercial Airport: Seattle-Tacoma International (SEA) [15 miles]

Subjects

> **Historical Periods:** 1800–1865; 1865–1900; 1900–1940; 1940–present
>
> **Business:** Retail; Legal/Medical Services
>
> **Organizations:** Schools; Colleges/Universities; Hospitals/Medical Facilities; Charities
>
> **Ethnic Groups:** French Canadian

Religious Sites and Organizations: Catholic

Date of Reviewer's Visit: 7/19/2002

Profile Updated by Institution: 11/22/2004

✴✴✴

Name: Puget Sound Maritime Historical Society   **County:** King

Mailing Address: 2700 24th Ave. E.

  City: Seattle   **State:** WA   **Postal Code:** 98112-2099

Street Address: MOHAI 2700 24th Ave. E.

Institution Email: None

Telephone Number: (206) 324-1126   **Fax Number:** (206) 324-1346

Contact Name: John S. Carrer, Jr   **Contact Email:** jscnan@aol.com

Institution Type: Historical Society Archives

Affiliation: MOHAI (Museum of History and Industry)

Web site URL: http://www.pugetmaritime.org/

Hours: Th 10–5, Sa 9:30–12:30 by appt.

Staff in Archives: 1p, 3v

Archives Are Handicapped Accessible: Yes

Review of Facilities: The research library is on the lower level of the Museum of History and Industry (MOHAI). Enter through the main door and ask for directions. For researchers just using the library, and who have an appointment, there is no fee for admission. The library itself is a very pleasant room with the research tables in the center and large glass walls dividing the reading room from the collections on either side. Several rows of compact shelving is to the right while staff offices, workspace, and some collections are to the left. Only paper and pencils are allowed in the research area. Storage areas are staff-only. There are small unlocked lockers behind the staff desk for researchers' personal belongings. The facility is modern and professional. The facility shares space with the MOHAI collection, which has a separate listing since their collections are maintained separately.

Vertical Files: Yes   **Vertical Files in Cubic Feet:** 63

  Vertical File Description and Subjects: General subjects by country and subject. Filed in boxes on shelves out of research room. Some manuscript material is housed here as well. Histories of U.S. and foreign ships and shipping companies. Histories of vessels from the 1880s to present.

Manuscripts: No

Photographs: Yes   **Number of Photographs:** 55,000

Storage of Photographs: Photographs are stored in boxes in storage area. Subject-arranged binders of photocopies of images are available to researchers to browse.

Photograph Subjects: Maritime history of the Puget Sound area

Photograph Reproductions Are Available: Yes

Photographic Prints: Yes

Books: Yes   **Number of Books in Collection:** 4,500

Description of Books: Variety of books on Maritime subjects and local history; American, British, and German navies; whaling; Northwest exploration; and seaman narratives. 100 different maritime periodicals as well. There is a card catalog of books, which are interfiled with those owned by MOHAI.

Newspapers: No

Oral Histories: No

Maps and Drawings: Yes   **Estimated Number of Maps and Drawings:** 6,000

Description of Maps and Drawings: Collection of boat and ship drawings from all types and sizes of vessels. Most built or operated out of the Puget Sound area. Also have navigation charts of U.S. and foreign waters.

Genealogy Sources: No

Special Collections: Yes

Special Collections Description: Photograph collection of boats in the Mosquito Fleet.

Indexes: 18 volumes of binders with photocopied images arranged by general subject.

Review of Collections: The collections of the Puget Sound Maritime Historical Society focus on the documentation of the shipping and exploration vessels that plied the northwest waters. Although ostensibly a Northwest collection, there is information on shipping lines throughout the world. The photographs are a strong part of the collection, but the general subject files is where the meat of the collection is stored. This is listed under Vertical File instead of Manuscript Collections, because of the artificial arrangement of the collection. The materials came from a myriad of sources. The collection is notable for the information on shipping companies, shipyards, vessels and biographies of individuals involved in all aspects of the shipping business. The collection also includes a database of arrivals and departures of commercial sailing ships from Port Blakely, Washington during the nineteenth century and details about the cargo, ships, and captains.

Museum on Premises: Yes

Description of Museum: See listing for Museum of History and Industry

Parking: Free parking lots adjacent

Lunch: Variety of restaurants within driving distance

Lodging: http://www.seeseattle.org/

Nearest Commercial Airport: Seattle-Tacoma International (SEA) [16 miles]

Subjects

    Historical Periods: Pre-1800; 1800–1865; 1865–1900; 1900–1940; 1940–present

    Eras: World War I; World War II

    Natural Resources: Fishing; Whaling; Shellfish; Logging

    Transportation: Railroads; Ships and Shipping; Ferries

    Manufacturing: Cannery; Boatbuilding/Shipyard

    Organizations: Nonreligious Organizations

Date of Reviewer's Visit: 12/4/2003

Profile Updated by Institution: 12/9/2004

✴✴✴✴

Name: Seattle Municipal Archives   **County:** King

Mailing Address: PO Box 94728

  City: Seattle   **State:** WA   **Postal Code:** 98124-4728

Street Address: 600 Fourth Ave., Third Floor

Institution Email: archives@seattle.gov

Telephone Number: (206) 233-7807   **Fax Number:** (206) 386-9025

Contact Name: Scott Cline, City Archivist

Contact Email: scott.cline@seattle.gov

Institution Type: Archives

Affiliation: City of Seattle

Web site URL: http://www.cityofseattle.net/CityArchives/

Hours: M–F 8–4:45

Staff in Archives: 2f

Archives Are Handicapped Accessible: Yes

Review of Facilities: The Seattle Municipal Archives is located on the third floor of Seattle's City Hall. It is best entered from the Fifth Avenue entrance. Standard archival rules apply when using the Archives. The Seattle Municipal Archives provides a 650-sq.-ft. research room with two 8-ft. worktables, three microfilm/microfiche reader/printers, two microfilm/microfiche readers/only, one reference computer with printer, and electrical hookups for laptop computers. The research room includes a small collection of reference books and publications. The room is handicapped accessible.

Vertical Files: No

Manuscripts: Yes   **Manuscripts Volume in Cubic Feet:** 6,000

   Manuscript Types: City government records

   Manuscript Subjects: 1,000 records groups, city council records, mayor records, city clerk records, Pike Place Market Urban Renewal projects, the Great Fire

Photographs: Yes   **Number of Photographs:** 1,500,000

   Storage of Photographs: 50,000 of the photographic images are indexed and digitized and available from the Web site.

   Photograph Subjects: City projects, city personnel, engineering department, parks department, water department, *Seattle City Light*, covering the years 1890–1970s

   Photograph Reproductions Are Available: Yes

   Photographic Prints: Yes   **Digital Prints:** Yes

   Digital Images on CD or Electronically: Yes

Books: No

Newspapers: No

Oral Histories: No

Maps and Drawings: Yes   **Estimated Number of Maps and Drawings:** 3,000

   Description of Maps and Drawings: City of Seattle maps from 1890s–1990s. Index and selected images are available from the Web site.

Genealogy Sources: No

Special Collections: Yes

   Special Collections Description: 3,000 audiotapes, 1,000 videotapes, and reels of motion picture film of city projects and people

Indexes: Computerized indexing is available for a large portion of the collection.

   Manuscript Finding Aids: Record entries are available through the online indexes to the collection.

   Published Guides: *A Guide to the Archives of the City of Seattle*, 1988.

   Online Sources: Extensive photography collection is available from the Web site along with a search engine to locate specific topics. In addition, online search resources include Seattle Municipal Archives Guide, Subject File Index, General File Index, Map Index, Photograph Index, and City Documents Index. Online exhibits are also available.

Review of Collections: The Archives holds the public records of the City of Seattle, including the records of the city council, mayor's office, and the various city departments. Some records date back to 1874. The online search capabilities of the collection allow a researcher to locate information without visiting the facility.

Museum on Premises: No

Parking: Street or nearby pay lots

Lunch: Variety of restaurants

Lodging: http://www.seeseattle.org/

Nearest Commercial Airport: Seattle-Tacoma International (SEA) [14 miles]

Subjects

    Historical Periods: 1865–1900; 1900–1940; 1940–present

    Government: City

Date of Reviewer's Visit: Not Visited

Profile Updated by Institution: 12/13/2004

✴✴✴✴

Name: Seattle Public Library **County:** King

Mailing Address: 1000 Fourth Ave.

   City: Seattle   **State:** WA   **Postal Code:** 98104-1193

Street Address: 1000 Fourth Ave.

Institution Email: infospl@spl.org

Telephone Number: (206) 386-4610   **Fax Number:** (206) 386-4119

Contact Name: Jodee Fenton   **Contact Email:** jodee.fenton@spl.org

Institution Type: Public Library

Affiliation: City of Seattle

Web site URL: http://www.spl.org/

Hours: M 1–8, Tu–F 1–5, by appt.

Staff in Archives: 1f

Archives Are Handicapped Accessible: Yes

Access Description: ADA-compliant

Review of Facilities: The new Seattle Public Library is located in the heart of the downtown area. This newly built (2004) glass and steel structure is an architectural marvel. It is the type of building someone either likes or dislikes. The Hugh and Jane Ferguson Seattle Room is located on the tenth level of the building. The "Seattle Room" is a misnomer since there really is not a room involved. Instead there is a section of the floor devoted to the collection and a research area. The collections are stored in a glass-walled room on several levels adjacent to the research area. The research area has numerous tables that are moderate-sized with electrical outlets but not sufficiently large for a serious researcher to spread materials out on. The atmosphere is glass and gray but at least the historical collections are alive and well cared for.

Vertical Files: Yes　　　　　　**Vertical Files in Cubic Feet:** 306

Vertical File Description and Subjects: Regional history, biography, local history subjects, institutional histories, Native American history

Manuscripts: Yes　　　　　　**Manuscripts Volume in Cubic Feet:** 60

Manuscript Types: Scrapbooks, personal papers

Manuscript Subjects: Seattle schools, transportation, early metropolitan development, Century 21, architecture, poetry

Photographs: Yes　　　　　　**Number of Photographs:** 30,000

Storage of Photographs: Photographs are stored in filing cabinets and archival boxes and some collections are bound. At least 8,000 of the photographs are uncataloged. Formats include prints, negatives, slides, glass negatives, panoramic prints, lantern slides, and postcards.

Photograph Subjects: Seattle historic photographs, Werner Lenggenhager Photographs (1945–1980), Pillsbury Panoramic Photograph Collection, Thompson Collection of Native American Subjects, Edward S. Curtis North American Indian, Camerawork, Kunishige Photographs.

Photograph Reproductions Are Available: Yes

　Photographic Prints: Yes　　　　　　**Digital Prints:** Yes

　Digital Images on CD or Electronically: Yes

Books: Yes　　　　　　**Number of Books in Collection:** 35,000

Description of Books: Regional and local history, City of Seattle documents collection, city directories. Holdings in library online catalog.

Newspapers: Yes

Newspapers on Microfilm: Yes

Microfilm and Dates: Variety of titles of Seattle area newspapers from the 1860s to the present. Indexing for the newspapers varies by title, including *Puget Sound Courier* (1860s–1870s), *Seattle Post-Intelligencer* (1900–1919, 1969–1992), and *Seattle Times* (1920–1992).

Oral Histories: Yes

Oral Histories Description: Notable Seattle people from the second half of the twentieth century. Washington State Oral History Project.

Maps and Drawings: Yes　　　**Estimated Number of Maps and Drawings:** 300

Description of Maps and Drawings: Early exploration of the Northwest, Seattle street maps, topographic maps, transportation maps, bird's eye maps. Sanborn Fire Insurance Atlases, Kroll Plat Atlases, and Metskers Atlases. Additional maps of the region stored in the library's Martiz Map Room.

Genealogy Sources: Yes

> **Genealogy Sources Description:** City directories, federal censuses, Washington death index, obituaries

Special Collections: Yes

> **Special Collections Description:** Special collections include: Seattle Public Art Collection; Aviation Collection; Balch Autograph Collection; World War I and World War II Posters Collection and Washington Authors Collection.

Indexes: The Northwest Index is a citation index to local newspapers, magazines, and books about Seattle and regional history. The Ship Index includes citations about marine vessels in Puget Sound from early settlement to the late twentieth century.

> **Online Sources:** Books are cataloged in the Seattle Public Library electronic catalog, which is available online.

Review of Collections: The collections at the Seattle Public Library are diverse and well maintained. The book collection is particularly strong, with a variety of published materials from throughout the region. The 35,000-volume collection is expected to increase as they bring more titles from the general collections. Although the collection now focuses on Seattle area history, in the early years of collecting there was a wider base of interest. The vertical file of miscellaneous materials and the photograph collections are sizable. Manuscript collections are not large but significant.

Museum on Premises: No

Parking: The library has an underground parking garage with staffed pay booth.

Lunch: Variety of restaurants in adjoining blocks

Lodging: http://www.seeseattle.org/

Nearest Commercial Airport: Seattle-Tacoma International (SEA) [14 miles]

Subjects

> **Historical Periods:** 1865–1900; 1900–1940; 1940–present
>
> **Eras:** World War I; World War II
>
> **Transportation:** Ships and Shipping; Aviation
>
> **Business:** Banking; Retail; Legal/Medical Services; Hotels/Restaurants; Entertainment/Theaters
>
> **Government:** City
>
> **Organizations:** Schools
>
> **Ethnic Groups:** Native American

Date of Reviewer's Visit: 6/17/2004

Profile Updated by Institution: 12/7/2004

Name: Seattle Public Schools Archives   **County:** King

Mailing Address: MS 21–345, PO Box 34165

City: Seattle   **State:** WA   **Postal Code:** 98124-1165

Street Address: 2445 3rd Ave. South

Institution Email: None

Telephone Number: (206) 252-0795   **Fax Number:** (206) 252-0796

Contact Name: Eleanor Toews, Archivist

Contact Email: etoews@seattleschools.org

Institution Type: Archives

Affiliation: Seattle School District

Web site URL: http://www.seattleschools.org/area/archives

Hours: M, Th, and F 9–12 and 1–4, by appt. only

Staff in Archives: 1f

Archives Are Handicapped Accessible: Yes

Cost for Researcher—Remote: $25 per hr.

List of Researchers Available: Yes

Review of Facilities: The Seattle Public Schools Archives is located in the John Stanford Center for Educational Excellence. The research room has moderate-sized worktables, good lighting, and personal assistance. This institution was a late entry and was not visited.

Vertical Files: Yes   **Vertical Files in Cubic Feet:** 40

  Vertical File Description and Subjects: Newspaper clipping file of news dealing with the Seattle School District from 1927 to the present (incomplete some years)

Manuscripts: Yes   **Manuscripts Volume in Cubic Feet:** 1,000

  Manuscript Types: School records, scrapbooks, administrative records, superintendent records

  Manuscript Subjects: District relations publications, annual reports, financial statements, final budgets, school board meeting minutes, superintendent files dating back to 1901, racial distribution reports, planning, research and evaluation reports, school histories in 1951, 1961 and 1974, permanent record cards, building dedication programs. District newsletters and papers from 1913 to the present.

Photographs: Yes   **Number of Photographs:** 25,000

  Storage of Photographs: Photographs are organized according to school and other subjects in acid-free folders.

Photograph Subjects: Black and white pictures of classes, teams and safety patrol groups, 1874 to present. Also includes Seattle Public Schools alumni, school buildings, student activities, school board, athletics, and Asahel Curtis photographs.

Photograph Reproductions Are Available: Yes

Photographic Prints: Yes   **Digital Prints:** Yes

Digital Images on CD or Electronically: Yes

Books: Yes   **Number of Books in Collection:** 21,200

Description of Books: High school annuals 1904–1996, textbooks, mostly administrative reports

Newspapers: Yes

Newspapers in Paper Format: Yes

Papers and Dates: *Seattle Times, Seattle-Post Intelligencer,* and *Seattle Star,* 1927– present. High school student newspapers from 1891–present.

Newspapers on Microfilm: Yes

Microfilm and Dates: Lincoln and Queen Anne school newspapers are available on microfilm at University of Washington.

Oral Histories: No

Maps and Drawings: Yes   **Estimated Number of Maps and Drawings:** 500

Description of Maps and Drawings: Architectural drawings, attendance areas, director districts

Genealogy Sources: No

Special Collections: Yes

Special Collections Description: Artifacts, three-dimensional objects, banners, trophies, athletic uniforms, cheerleader outfits

Indexes: Microsoft Access catalog to publications. Printouts of Access database, transmittals, school board indexes, and newspaper indexes.

Online Sources: Some information available through the Web site.

Review of Collections: The collections of the Seattle Public Schools Archives focus on all aspects of school history from the formation of the district to the present day. Histories of individual schools and their various buildings, activities, and people are included. The collection is narrowly focused on the school district's history, people, and events and includes the official archive of the district and supplementary collections on the same subject from other sources. This collection is specialized but strong.

Museum on Premises: No

Parking: Visitor parking lots on Lander St., 3rd Ave. South, and large lot just north of Stanford Center (enter off 3rd Ave. South)

Lunch: Cafeteria on site that is open to the public

Lodging: http://www.seeseattle.org/

Nearest Commercial Airport: Seattle-Tacoma International (SEA) [12 miles]

Subjects

    Historical Periods: 1865–1900; 1900–1940; 1940–present

    Organizations: Schools; Children's

Date of Reviewer's Visit: Not Visited

Profile Updated by Institution: 12/16/2004

✳✳✳✳✳

Name: University of Washington Libraries, Special Collections **County:** King

Mailing Address: Allen Library Room B81, Box 352900

    City: Seattle   **State:** WA   **Postal Code:** 98195-2900

Street Address: Allen Library Room B81, Benton Lane

Institution Email: speccoll@u.washington.edu

Telephone Number: (206) 543-1929   **Fax Number:** (206) 543-1931

Institution Type: Academic Library

Affiliation: University of Washington

Web site URL: http://www.lib.washington.edu/

Hours: M, Tu, Th, and F 10–4:45; W 10–7:45; Sa 1–4:45 limited

Staff in Archives: 17f, 3p

Archives Are Handicapped Accessible: Yes

Review of Facilities: The Special Collections Division is located in the basement of Allen Library South. Upon entering the research area, the researcher is asked to relinquish all items except for loose paper and pencil. Personal items are placed in a storage area by the staff and you are given a number that corresponds with your belongings. Registration is also necessary. The numbers assigned are used throughout the visit to identify the individual researcher and to aid in collection retrieval. The reading room is a modern and pleasant space. The main room has over a dozen separate worktables, the reference desk and computer, microfilm and audiovisual equipment stations. The adjoining room has more tables with better lighting, locked bookcases, and locked photo files. The room also has a lighted drafting table for using the architectural records. All materials in this room are locked up. Manuscript collections are stored elsewhere in the building and off site.

Vertical Files: No

Manuscripts: Yes   **Manuscripts Volume in Cubic Feet:** 41,200

Manuscript Types: All manuscript types

Manuscript Subjects: Regional architecture; Pacific Northwest history; organizational records and personal papers; travel and exploration, and the University of Washington Archives

Photographs: Yes   **Number of Photographs:** 829,000

Storage of Photographs: Most photos are stored in archival boxes. Some are available through the Web site.

Photograph Subjects: Western Washington, Alaska and the Yukon, Native Americans, logging, fishing, Klondike gold rush

Photograph Reproductions Are Available: Yes

Photographic Prints: Yes   **Digital Prints:** No

Digital Images on CD or Electronically: Yes

Books: Yes   **Number of Books in Collection:** 104,000

Description of Books: "History of the book," artists' books, regional history, local city directories, plat atlases, University of Washington information and preservation collection. Literary collections include published works of nineteenth- and twentieth-century American and English Authors and seventeenth- to twentieth-century children's books.

Newspapers: Yes

Microfilm and Dates: Historic and current newspapers are housed in the Microfilm and Newspapers Department. See general library catalog for specific holdings.

Oral Histories: No

Maps and Drawings: Yes   **Estimated Number of Maps and Drawings:** 4,660

Description of Maps and Drawings: Historical map collection from sixteenth-century world to nineteenth, and early-twentieth-century Pacific Northwest maps

Genealogy Sources: No

Special Collections: Yes

Special Collections Description: Pacific Northwest history, historic photos, artists' books, travel and exploration, architectural drawings and plans by Pacific Northwest architects and landscape architects, particularly of the Puget Sound region

Indexes: Yes

Manuscript Finding Aids: Manuscript collections have finding aids of various level of detail.

Online Sources: Some photographs are available through the Web site at http://www.lib.washington.edu/specialcoll/collections/photographs/search.html.

The digital collections page gives access to thousands of documents in a digital format at http://content.lib.washington.edu/all-collections.html. The Pacific Northwest Regional Newspaper and Periodical Index is also available online at http://db.lib.washington.edu/pnw/.

Review of Collections: The scope of the University of Washington Special Collections is huge. The University of Washington Archives and the personal papers and organizational records, which deal with university people and issues, make up half the total volume of the manuscripts collection. The Pacific Northwest portion covers the three-state region, Alaska, and western Canada and includes the political, cultural, environmental, and social heritage of the region. The manuscripts include primary textual materials that document the history and culture of Seattle and the Pacific Northwest. Pioneer settlers, citizen activists, civic leaders, forest products industry, labor and environmental, ethnic and special communities, and major cultural figures are all included in the collections.

Museum on Premises: No

Parking: For on-campus parking stop at booth when entering campus. $8 per day.

Lunch: Variety of food services at Student Union on campus and variety of restaurants in university district

Lodging: http://www.seeseattle.org/; Best Western University Tower Hotel closest to campus

Nearest Commercial Airport: Seattle-Tacoma International (SEA) [19 miles]

Subjects

> **Historical Periods:** Pre-1800; 1800–1865; 1865–1900; 1900–1940; 1940–present
>
> **Natural Resources:** Fishing; Whaling; Logging
>
> **Mining:** Gold; Placer Mining
>
> **Transportation:** Railroads
>
> **Business:** Entertainment/Theaters
>
> **Manufacturing:** Sawmills
>
> **Organizations:** Nonreligious Organizations; Civic and Fraternal; Business; Labor and Union
>
> **Ethnic Groups:** Native American; Pacific Islander

Date of Reviewer's Visit: 12/4/2003

Profile Updated by Institution: 11/22/2004

✳✳✳✳

Name: Washington State Jewish Historical Society   **County:** King

Mailing Address: SCMA, Box 352900

City: Seattle   **State:** WA   **Postal Code:** 98195-0000

Street Address: Allen Library, University of Washington

Institution Email: winthropnw@hotmail.com

Telephone Number: (206) 543-1895   **Fax Number:** (206) 685-8049

Contact Name: Steve Wright, Archivist

Contact Email: winthropnw@hotmail.com

Institution Type: Historical Society Archives

Affiliation: University of Washington

Web site URL: http://www.wsjhs.org/

Hours: M–F 10–5; Tu 8–5 by appt.

Staff in Archives: 1p

Archives Are Handicapped Accessible: Yes

Review of Facilities: The Washington State Jewish Historical Society collection is housed at the University of Washington in the Special Collections department. This is located in the basement of Allen Library South. Upon entering the research area you are asked to relinquish all items except for loose paper and pencil. Personal items are placed in storage area by the staff and you are given a number that corresponds with your belongings. Registration is also necessary. The numbers assigned are used throughout the visit to identify the individual researcher and to aid in collection retrieval. The reading room is a modern and pleasant space. The main room has over a dozen separate worktables, the reference desk and computer, microfilm and audiovisual equipment stations. Manuscript collections are stored elsewhere in the building. Appointments to view the materials should be made through the Washington State Jewish Historical Society archivist and not the University of Washington Archives staff.

Vertical Files: No

Manuscripts: Yes   **Manuscripts Volume in Cubic Feet:** 75

   Manuscript Types: Business records, organizational records, and personal papers

   Manuscript Subjects: Manuscripts include holdings regarding nearly two dozen congregations in Washington State. Organizations include Jewish women's, youth, and social service programs.

Photographs: Yes   **Number of Photographs:** 4,000

   Storage of Photographs: Photographs are stored in document boxes in secure storage area.

   Photograph Subjects: Jewish life in Washington State, including individuals, families, events, buildings, and businesses

   Photograph Reproductions Are Available: Yes

Photographic Prints: Yes   **Digital Prints:** Yes

Digital Images on CD or Electronically: Yes

Books: No

Newspapers: No

Oral Histories: Yes   **Oral Histories Number:** 300

Oral Histories Description: Audiotaped interviews with Washington State Jewish residents, many with transcriptions; 118 are cataloged and a listing is available online.

Maps and Drawings: No

Genealogy Sources: No

Special Collections: No

Indexes: Yes

Published Guides: Last published guide to collection in 1980, currently working on an update. Developing guide for both photographs and manuscripts.

Online Sources: Oral interviews: http://catalog.lib.washington.edu/search/a?SEARCH=jewish+archives

Review of Collections: Information from and about Jewish congregations from throughout Washington State are represented in this collection. Jewish organizations: political, social, educational, and cultural are represented as well. The majority of the materials are from the western part of the state. The photograph collection is sizable and highlights Jewish life in Washington State, including individuals, businesses, and events. All aspects of Jewish life—community, business, law, and religion—have some materials represented in this collection.

Museum on Premises: No

Parking: For on-campus parking stop at booth when entering campus. $8 per day.

Lunch: Variety of food services at Student Union on campus and variety of restaurants in university district

Lodging: http://www.seeseattle.org/. Best Western University Tower Hotel closest to campus.

Nearest Commercial Airport: Seattle-Tacoma International (SEA) [19 miles]

Subjects

Historical Periods: 1865–1900; 1900–1940; 1940–present

Religious Sites and Organizations: Jewish

Date of Reviewer's Visit: 12/4/2003

Profile Updated by Institution: 12/2/2004

Name: Wing Luke Asian Museum   **County:** King

Mailing Address: 407 7th Ave. S

  City: Seattle   **State:** WA   **Postal Code:** 98104-0000

Street Address: 407 7th Ave. S

Institution Email: folks@wingluke.org

Telephone Number: (206) 623-5124   **Fax Number:** (206) 623-4559

Contact Name: Robert Fisher   **Contact Email:** bfisher@wingluke.org

Institution Type: Regional Museum

Web site URL: http://www.wingluke.org

Hours: Tu–Su 1–4; M–F 8–4 by appt.

Staff in Archives: 1f

Archives Are Handicapped Accessible: No

Access Description: Stairs to research area

Cost for Researcher—Remote: First 1/2 hr. free, then fee schedule

Review of Facilities: The Wing Luke Asian Museum is located in the heart of the Chinatown-International District of Seattle. The storefront building is unremarkable from an architectural standpoint. The research area is located in the back of the museum and up a half-flight of stairs. Small, cramped, and stuffed are the adjectives that come to mind when viewing the research area. The book collections are stored in shelves to one side. A single worktable is diminished by the computer station, also living there. File cabinets house some materials, while others are shelved with the rest of the museum collections behind a wall of shelves and boxes. Overhead lighting is poor everywhere, except for directly over the worktable. The museum is planning a move by 2007, so the status of the research room should be improving at that time.

Vertical Files: Yes   **Vertical Files in Cubic Feet:** 16

  Vertical File Description and Subjects: General clipping and subject files

Manuscripts: Yes   **Manuscripts Volume in Cubic Feet:** 24

  Manuscript Types: Business records, personal papers

  Manuscript Subjects: Wing Luke papers, Chinese immigration records, 1898–1912

Photographs: Yes   **Number of Photographs:** 3,500

  Storage of Photographs: Filed in plastic sleeves in binders on the shelf. Photos also on PastPerfect on in-house computer.

  Photograph Subjects: Asian Pacific Americans and some nineteenth- and twentieth-century photos of home countries of immigrants

Photograph Reproductions Are Available: Yes

    Photographic Prints: Yes   **Digital Prints:** Yes

    Digital Images on CD or Electronically: Yes

Books: Yes   **Number of Books in Collection:** 1,500

Description of Books: Asian American history, Asian American literature, professional collection, personal reading materials from immigrants

Newspapers: Yes

    Newspapers in Paper Format: Yes

    Papers and Dates: *International Examiner* (from local area), 1975 to present

Oral Histories: Yes   **Oral Histories Number:** 320

Oral Histories Description: Chinese-American biography, garment workers, Chinatown and international district history, also Asian Pacific American veterans. Most have transcriptions. Interviews done from 1975 to 2000.

Maps and Drawings: No

Genealogy Sources: No

Special Collections: No

Indexes: PastPerfect is used for indexing the photographs

    Online Sources: Wing Luke Web site database at http://www.wingluke.org/ CHC. Oral history interviews listed on Oral History Catalog at MOHAI.

Review of Collections: The collections of the Wing Luke Museum deal with immigrants from all the Asian Pacific cultures. The strongest area of the collections is on the Chinese Americans in the Seattle area. The collections themselves are small, but specialized. The oral histories are one of the strong areas of the collections. The collections are valuable, because some of the materials are difficult to find in the research collection.

Museum on Premises: Yes

    Museum Hours: Tu–F 11–4:30, Sa–Su noon–4

    Cost of Entry to Museum: $4

    Museum Is Handicapped Accessible: Yes

    Description of Museum: The Wing Luke Museum explores the Asian Pacific–American experience relating to history, art, and culture. The history of the Chinatown-International District of Seattle is also displayed.

Parking: On-street metered parking (2-hr.)—ask museum about all-day parking

Lunch: Every type of Asian cuisine available within a few blocks. Non-Asian restaurants 4 blocks' walk (40 restaurants in international district)

Lodging: http://www.seeseattle.org/

Nearest Commercial Airport: Seattle-Tacoma International (SEA) [14 miles]

Subjects

    Historical Periods: 1865–1900; 1900–1940; 1940–present

    Eras: World War II

    Mining: Gold

    Transportation: Railroads

    Agriculture: Vegetable/Truck Crops

    Business: Retail; Hotels/Restaurants; Entertainment/Theaters

    Manufacturing: Cannery; Sawmills

    Organizations: Schools; Nonreligious Organizations

    Ethnic Groups: Pacific Islander; Japanese; Chinese; Korean

    Religious Sites and Organizations: Protestant; Buddhist

Date of Reviewer's Visit: 12/5/2003

Profile Updated by Institution: 11/12/2004

SEQUIM

✹✹✹

Name: Museum and Arts Center in the Sequim-Dungeness Valley

County: Clallam

Mailing Address: 175 West Cedar St.

    City: Sequim   **State:** WA   **Postal Code:** 98382-0000

Street Address: 544 N. Sequim Ave.

Institution Email: info@museumandartscenter.org

Telephone Number: (360) 681-2257   **Fax Number:** (360) 683-8364

Contact Name: Randy Sturgis, Executive Director

Contact Email: info@museumandartscenter.org

Institution Type: Historical Society Archives

Web site URL: http://www.museumandartscenter.org

Hours: Tu–F 1–3

Staff in Archives: 1f, 3p, 8v

Archives Are Handicapped Accessible: Yes

Review of Facilities: The research facilities of the Museum and Arts Center in the Sequim-Dungeness Valley are located in the Dewitt Building, separate from the exhibit space in downtown Sequim. The DeWitt Building is set far back off the road, behind the future site for the new museum building. The research room/library is a large library with multiple rows of bookcases covering half the room, two large worktables, microfiche reader, database, a u-shaped resource area with vertical files, and a map cabinet. The photo archives collection is housed in a small room across the hall from the library. There is a separate storage and registration area. Most materials are housed in these areas, although there are numerous in-process and rare items in the registrar's office as well.

Vertical Files: Yes   **Vertical Files in Cubic Feet:** 14

Vertical File Description and Subjects: Vertical file materials are divided into general files and family files.

Manuscripts: Yes   **Manuscripts Volume in Cubic Feet:** 30

Manuscript Types: Business records, organizational records, school records, scrapbooks, family papers, ledgers

Manuscript Subjects: Dungeness Mercantile Company records, school district records, family and organizational scrapbooks, copies and research from early records of area from other facilities, Irrigation Festival from 1896 to the present

Photographs: Yes   **Number of Photographs:** 7,200

Storage of Photographs: Some copies of photos stored in binders arranged by subject. Originals stored in clamshell boxes in the photo room.

Photograph Subjects: Olympic Peninsula, Sequim, the Dungeness Valley, and the Eastern part of Clallam County; timber industry, early Native American photos

Photograph Reproductions Are Available: Yes

Photographic Prints: Yes

Books: Yes   **Number of Books in Collection:** 2,021

Description of Books: Local history, marine history of Pacific Northwest, professional collections, yearbooks, phone books (1931–present), and some old books. Antique guides, farming journals, and technical pamphlets.

Newspapers: Yes

Newspapers in Paper Format: Yes

Papers and Dates: Local papers from 1911 to present, but incomplete. *Sequim Press,* 1911–1989, and *Sequim Gazette*

Oral Histories: Yes   **Oral Histories Number:** 350

Oral Histories Description: Interviews of local residents on videotape and CD

Maps and Drawings: Yes   **Estimated Number of Maps and Drawings:** 250

Description of Maps and Drawings: Local area maps, Metskers (from 1925), recreation maps from Olympic Peninsula, fire map, natural resource maps, nautical charts, coastal survey maps, biological survey, old city maps

Genealogy Sources: Yes

Genealogy Sources Description: Family files, obituary index (1892 to present) of Sequim-Dungeness area in three-ring binders

Special Collections: Yes

Special Collections Description: Motion picture promotional posters from Sequim theater with "classic" films represented. Also, 258 phonograph records of "old" classics, 870 booklets, 243 sets of sheet music, and 488 old greeting cards.

Indexes: Indexes to books, annuals, and so forth on database. Photograph index on database. Photographs are being digitized for access through local computer.

Manuscript Finding Aids: PastPerfect software

Review of Collections: The collections housed at the Museum and Arts Center are fairly standard, as they currently reflect, but the institution is actively collecting new materials to strengthen and broaden the base. The new facilities allow them space to grow. The collection gathers materials from all over the Sequim-Dungeness Valley, including all the tiny settlements of the area. There are some business records of note. Information on the Irrigation Festival dates back to its beginning in 1896. School records, pioneer family papers, and scrapbooks (many from World War II) round out the collection. The photograph collection covers a slightly larger region than the paper collections, including the Olympic Peninsula area and significant early photographs of the environs.

Museum on Premises: No

Parking: Free paved parking lot adjacent

Lunch: Variety of restaurants within driving distance

Lodging: http://www.visitsun.com; http://www.northwestsecretplaces.com/

Nearest Commercial Airport: William R. Fairchild International (Port Angeles) (CLM) [21 miles]

Subjects

Historical Periods: 1865–1900; 1900–1940; 1940–present

Eras: World War I; World War II; Korean War

Natural Resources: Irrigation; Hunting; Shellfish; Logging

Transportation: Railroads; Ships and Shipping

Agriculture: Dairy; Vegetable/Truck Crops; Grains; Dry Land Farming

Business: Banking; Retail; Legal/Medical Services; Entertainment/Theaters

Manufacturing: Grist/Flour Mills; Creamery; Sawmills; Wood Products

Government: County

Organizations: Schools; Charities; Nonreligious Organizations; Civic and Fraternal; Women's; Business

Ethnic Groups: Native American; German; Irish; Scottish

Date of Reviewer's Visit: 6/22/2004
Profile Updated by Institution: 11/29/2004

SHORELINE

Name: Shoreline Historical Museum   **County:** King
Mailing Address: PO Box 55594
   City: Shoreline   **State:** WA   **Postal Code:** 98155-0000
Street Address: 749 N. 175th
Institution Email: shm@shorelinehistoricalmuseum.org
Telephone Number: (206) 542-7111
Contact Name: Victoria Stiles, Director
Institution Type: Local Museum
Web site URL: http://www.shorelinehistoricalmuseum.org/
Hours: W 10–2; Tu–F 10–4 by appt. with 1-week notice
Staff in Archives: 1f, 9v
Archives Are Handicapped Accessible: Yes
Access Description: Handicapped parking and entrance in back of building
Review of Facilities: The Shoreline Historical Museum is housed in an old schoolhouse. The research room is in the basement. The room is fairly large with high ceilings and the ever-present pipes overhead. Two large worktables are under the windows. To combat the inadequate lighting, the museum has provided a number of desk and archival lamps that can be used by individual researchers to illuminate their reading. The room also houses four and one-half units of compact shelving, where the book and manuscript collections are housed. Photographs are stored in file cabinets at one side of the room, as are the vertical file materials. The museum requires users to register, and pencils only are allowed in the research area with the materials.
Vertical Files: Yes   **Vertical Files in Cubic Feet:** 6
   Vertical File Description and Subjects: General subject and clipping files
Manuscripts: Yes   **Manuscripts Volume in Cubic Feet:** 80
   Manuscript Types: Scrapbooks, organizational records, school records
   Manuscript Subjects: Shoreline and northern King County history
Photographs: Yes   **Number of Photographs:** 8,000
   Storage of Photographs: Photographs are arranged by accession number in file folders in file cabinets, in the research room. A subject card file is available to locate individual photographs. The museum is moving the indexing to PastPerfect.

Photograph Subjects: Shoreline and northern King County

Photograph Reproductions Are Available: Yes

Photographic Prints: Yes   **Digital Prints:** Yes

Books: Yes   **Number of Books in Collection:** 400

Description of Books: Local history, professional collection, some old books

Newspapers: Yes

Newspapers in Paper Format: Yes

Papers and Dates: Local papers 1916 to present

Newspapers on Microfilm: Yes

Microfilm and Dates: *Richmond Beach Herald,* 1920–1928, however, no reader at museum

Oral Histories: Yes   **Oral Histories Number:** 100

Oral Histories Description: Local residents interviewed; some recordings, as early as 1970s, about half have transcriptions

Maps and Drawings: No

Genealogy Sources: Yes

Genealogy Sources Description: Pioneer and family files and obituary index

Special Collections: No

Indexes: Card indexes to manuscript materials, photographs, newspaper content, by holding and subject

Review of Collections: The Shoreline Historical Museum collection is well cared for. The compact shelving was a wise addition, since the collection would have barely fit in the space without it. The collection contains photographs and documentary records, including local community events, school records, businesses, property records, and other documentation of the people who helped shape the community of Shoreline and the surrounding areas. They have a small collection of history from a local amusement park "Playland," from the mid-twentieth century. The collection may be unnoteworthy outside of the area, but they are doing a good job collecting and maintaining the history of Shoreline. Pleasant people, better than average organization, and busy research room on the day of the visit.

Museum on Premises: Yes

Cost of Entry to Museum: Free

Museum Is Handicapped Accessible: Yes

Description of Museum: The Shoreline Historical Museum focuses on the history of Shoreline and the surrounding area. The museum uses a variety of museum styles to tell the history of the area.

Parking: Free paved parking lot adjacent

Lunch: Variety of restaurants along Aurora Ave. N., driving distance

Lodging: http://www.seeseattle.org/

Nearest Commercial Airport: Seattle-Tacoma International (SEA) [26 miles]

Subjects

    Historical Periods: 1865–1900; 1900–1940; 1940–present

    Natural Resources: Fishing; Logging

    Mining: Mining

    Transportation: Railroads; Ships and Shipping; Ferries

    Agriculture: Dairy; Ranching/Livestock; Orchards

    Business: Retail; Legal/Medical Services; Hotels/Restaurants; Entertainment/ Theaters

    Manufacturing: Brick Making; Boatbuilding/Shipyard; Sawmills

    Government: City; County

    Organizations: Schools; Colleges/Universities; Hospitals/Medical Facilities; Charities; Nonreligious Organizations; Civic and Fraternal

    Ethnic Groups: Native American; Japanese; English; German; Norwegian; Scottish; Filipino

    Religious Sites and Organizations: Protestant; Jewish

Date of Reviewer's Visit: 12/3/2003

Profile Updated by Institution: 11/22/2004

SOUTH BEND

Name: Pacific County Historical Society and Museum   **County:** Pacific

Mailing Address: PO Box P

  City: South Bend   **State:** WA   **Postal Code:** 98586-0039

Street Address: 1008 W Robert Bush Dr.

Institution Email: Museum@willapabay.org

Telephone Number: (360) 875-5224   **Fax Number:** (360) 872-5224

Contact Name: Bruce Weilepp

Institution Type: Local Museum

Affiliation: Pacific County Historical Society and Museum Foundation

Web site URL: http://www.pacificcohistory.org

Hours: Daily 11–4

Staff in Archives: 1f

Archives Are Handicapped Accessible: Yes

Cost for Researcher—Remote: Fee schedule

Review of Facilities: The Pacific County Museum is located on the highway in the center of the town of South Bend. The museum is housed in a single-story storefront with inadequate space for displays or collection storage. There is a table in the main room near the entrance that has many of the indexes to the research collection, the indexes are available anytime the museum is open. There is little space for a researcher to work. The indexes are available for walk-in, but all other materials require an appointment with the museum director. The research collections are stored in several back rooms and the curator's office. Small museum with larger-than-expected collection for the size of the area.

Vertical Files: Yes   **Vertical Files in Cubic Feet:** 24

> **Vertical File Description and Subjects:** Subject based vertical files stored in file cabinets

Manuscripts: Yes   **Manuscripts Volume in Cubic Feet:** 500

> **Manuscript Types:** Business records, organizational records, county records, personal papers

> **Manuscript Subjects:** Natural resources, oyster farming, assorted history, county assessor's office records, Chamber of Commerce

Photographs: Yes   **Number of Photographs:** 25,000

> **Storage of Photographs:** Subject binders of copy photos for researchers

> **Photograph Subjects:** Pacific County, mostly northern Raymond, Willipa

> **Photograph Reproductions Are Available:** Yes

> > **Photographic Prints:** Yes   **Digital Prints:** Yes

> > **Digital Images on CD or Electronically:** Yes

Books: Yes   **Number of Books in Collection:** 600

> **Description of Books:** Local history, professional collection, annuals, city directories

Newspapers: Yes

> **Newspapers in Paper Format:** Yes

> **Papers and Dates:** South Bend papers, 1904–1943; *Harbor Pilot; Willipa Harbor Herald,* 1981–1994

> **Newspapers on Microfilm:** Yes

> **Microfilm and Dates:** Some at the library at Raymond, University of Washington, and the Washington State Library

Oral Histories: Yes   **Oral Histories Number:** 120

Oral Histories Description: 1970s local area residents, reel-to-reel and audiotapes, some have transcriptions

Maps and Drawings: Yes   **Estimated Number of Maps and Drawings:** 800

Description of Maps and Drawings: Plat maps, county maps, Oysterland maps

Genealogy Sources: Yes

Genealogy Sources Description: Census index

Special Collections: No

Indexes: Newspaper Indexes

Manuscript Finding Aids: Inventory of map materials

Online Sources: Index to the society's publication, *The Sou'wester,* 1966 and 1999, Shoreline chronology, recent *Sou'wester* issues

Review of Collections: This institution probably has more history here than even they realize. The storage facilities are inadequate to maintain a collection of this size, as is the staffing. The photo collection, large for a museum this size, covers a broad range of the county history. The manuscript collection has information on the oyster farming industry of the area as well as other agricultural pursuits of the region. Business records, organizational records, and histories of the natural resources topics of the area round out the collections. There is also a strong vertical file collection. The indexing to the collection is weak and relies on staff memory for locating items. Needs some serious rearrangement and more space and staffing but certainly has some wonderful history.

Museum on Premises: Yes

Museum Hours: Daily 11–4

Museum Is Handicapped Accessible: Yes

Description of Museum: The oyster and cranberry industries are the focus of this small local museum.

Parking: Free on-street parallel parking

Lunch: Several local restaurants within a few blocks

Lodging: http://www.funbeach.com

Nearest Commercial Airport: Portland International (PDX) [141 miles]

Subjects

Historical Periods: Pre-1800; 1800–1865; 1865–1900; 1900–1940; 1940–present

Eras: World War I

Natural Resources: Water; Dams; Hunting; Whaling; Shellfish; Logging

Mining: Surface Mining; Gravel

Transportation: Railroads; Stagecoach/Freight; Ships and Shipping; Ferries

Agriculture: Dairy; Ranching/Livestock; Orchards

Business: Retail; Legal/Medical Services; Hotels/Restaurants; Entertainment/Theaters

Manufacturing: Cannery; Boatbuilding/Shipyard; Sawmills; Wood Products

Government: City; County

Organizations: Schools; Hospitals/Medical Facilities; Charities; Nonreligious Organizations; Civic and Fraternal; Women's; Business; Labor and Union

Ethnic Groups: Native American; Latin American; African; Japanese; Chinese; Danish; English; Finnish; French; German; Irish; Italian; Norwegian; Russian; Scottish; Spanish; Swedish

Religious Sites and Organizations: Protestant; Catholic

Date of Reviewer's Visit: 7/30/2004

Profile Updated by Institution: 11/12/2004

SPOKANE

✷✷✷✷

Name: Gonzaga University Special Collections   **County:** Spokane

Mailing Address: Foley Center, Gonzaga University

   City: Spokane   **State:** WA   **Postal Code:** 99258-0000

Street Address: Foley Center, Gonzaga University

Institution Email: None

Telephone Number: (509) 323-3847   **Fax Number:** (509) 323-5904

Contact Name: Stephanie Plowman   **Contact Email:** plowman@gonzaga.edu

Institution Type: Academic Library

Web site URL: http://www.foley.gonzaga.edu/spcoll/

Hours: M–F 8:30–12, 1–4:30

Staff in Archives: 2f

Archives Are Handicapped Accessible: Yes

Cost for Researcher—In-house: None

Cost for Researcher—Remote: None

Review of Facilities: The Special Collections department of Gonzaga University is located on the third floor of the Foley Library in the center of the campus. The reading room is circular, with a half-circle devoted to windows overlooking the Spokane River. The furnishings are elegant, with warm wood and upholstered chairs in the center and numbers of polished wood tables and chairs under the windows. The area is spacious and luxurious. Materials are stored in an adjacent staff-only area.

Vertical Files: Yes   **Vertical Files in Cubic Feet:** 48

  Vertical File Description and Subjects: Gonzaga University

Manuscripts: Yes   **Manuscripts Volume in Cubic Feet:** 357

  Manuscript Types: Personal papers, organizational records

  Manuscript Subjects: Grand Coulee Dam, James O'Sullivan papers, Verne Ray papers, Gonzaga University

Photographs: Yes   **Number of Photographs:** 72

  Storage of Photographs: Document boxes

  Photograph Subjects: Gonzaga University

  Photograph Reproductions Are Available: Yes

    Photographic Prints: Yes   **Digital Prints:** Yes

    Digital Images on CD or Electronically: Yes

Books: Yes   **Number of Books in Collection:** 2,046

  Description of Books: Spokane, Northwest history, Gonzaga University

Newspapers: Yes

  Newspapers in Paper Format: Yes

  Papers and Dates: *Gonzaga University Bulletin* (student newspaper), 1927–present

  Newspapers on Microfilm: Yes

  Microfilm and Dates: *Gonzaga University Bulletin* (student newspaper), 1927–1995.

Oral Histories: No

Maps and Drawings: Yes   **Estimated Number of Maps and Drawings:** 20

  Description of Maps and Drawings: Northwest states

Genealogy Sources: No

Special Collections: No

Indexes: Yes

  Manuscript Finding Aids: Finding aids for manuscript collections are available through the Web site.

Review of Collections: Gonzaga University Special Collections are divided into several separate units. (The Jesuit Oregon Province Archives, which share space here, are covered in a separate entry.) The manuscript collections include the Hanford Health Information Archive regarding the health effects of the various projects at Hanford facilities. Also included is the Bing Crosby Collection of papers and memorabilia from the entertainer. The Jay Fox Papers are from an anarchist and labor radical from Home Colony, Washington. The James O'Sullivan Papers record building of Grand Coulee Dam by way of the personal collection and writings of an engineer of the project. The University Archives are also maintained through this department.

Museum on Premises: No

Parking: On-street free parking is limited. Parking permits can be obtained from campus security.

Lunch: Several blocks to some restaurants, student cafeteria in nearby building

Lodging: http://www.visitspokane.com

Nearest Commercial Airport: Spokane International (GEG) [9 miles]

Subjects

> **Historical Periods:** 1900–1940; 1940–present
>
> **Natural Resources:** Water; Dams; Irrigation
>
> **Organizations:** Colleges/Universities
>
> **Ethnic Groups:** Native American

Date of Reviewer's Visit: 12/9/2003

Profile Updated by Institution: 11/16/2004

✹✹✹✹

Name: Jesuit Oregon Province Archives **County:** Spokane

Mailing Address: Foley Center Library, Gonzaga University

  City: Spokane   **State:** WA   **Postal Code:** 99258-0000

Street Address: Foley Center Library, Gonzaga University

Institution Email: jopa@Foley.gonzaga.edu

Telephone Number: (509) 323-3814   **Fax Number:** (509) 324-5904

Contact Name: David Kingma   **Contact Email:** kingma@gonzaga.edu

Institution Type: Academic Library

Affiliation: Gonzaga University

Web site URL: http://www.Foley.gonzaga.edu/spcoll/jopa.html

Hours: M–F 8:30–12 and 1–4

Staff in Archives: 1f, 1v

Archives Are Handicapped Accessible: Yes

Review of Facilities: The Jesuit Oregon Province Archives are housed in the Special Collections department of Gonzaga University. The Special Collections department of Gonzaga University is located on the third floor of the Foley Library in the center of the campus. The reading room is circular, with a half-circle devoted to windows overlooking the Spokane River. The furnishings are elegant, with warm wood and upholstered chairs in the center and numbers of polished wood tables and chairs under the windows. The area is spacious and luxurious. Materials are stored in an adjacent staff-only area.

Vertical Files: Yes   **Vertical Files in Cubic Feet:** 140

Vertical File Description and Subjects: Miscellaneous files, including individual Jesuits' files and Northwest Catholic history. Some clipping files housed with manuscripts as separate collections by subject.

Manuscripts: Yes   **Manuscripts Volume in Cubic Feet:** 1,950

Manuscript Types: Archives, organizational records, personal papers, diaries, scrapbooks

Manuscript Subjects: Jesuit missions, church histories, individual Jesuits

Photographs: Yes   **Number of Photographs:** 85,000

Storage of Photographs: Photographs are integrated with the manuscript collections.

Photograph Subjects: Photos date from 1880s onward.

Photograph Reproductions Are Available: Yes

  Photographic Prints: Yes   **Digital Prints:** Yes

  Digital Images on CD or Electronically: Yes

Books: Yes   **Number of Books in Collection:** 2,250

Description of Books: Mission history in the Northwest and also in Alaska and California, general Jesuit history, biographies, Native Americans, Catholic history, annuals of Jesuit institutions

Newspapers: No

Oral Histories: Yes   **Oral Histories Number:** 90

Oral Histories Description: Oral history interviews of individuals in the Jesuit Oregon Province

Maps and Drawings: Yes   **Estimated Number of Maps and Drawings:** 350

Description of Maps and Drawings: Maps and oversize items collection from 1840 to present. Maps artwork, architectural plans. 134 cu. ft.

Genealogy Sources: Yes

Genealogy Sources Description: Baptism, marriage and burial records, mission school attendance records, sacramental census records

Special Collections: Yes

Special Collections Description: On microfilm, the Pacific Northwest Missions Collection of the Oregon Province Archives of the Society of Jesus, 1853–1960 (34 rolls), the Alaska Mission Collection of the Oregon Province Archives of the Society of Jesus, 1886–1968 (42 rolls), the Alaska Indian Language Collection of the Oregon Province Archives of the Society of Jesus, 1886–1968 (28 rolls), the Pacific Northwest Tribes Indian Language Collection of the Oregon Province Archives of the Society of Jesus, 1853–1948 (21 rolls). The Jesuit Oregon Province Archives also has a collection of Northwest and Alaska Catholic Dioceses periodicals.

Indexes: Yes

Manuscript Finding Aids: Most collections have some level of finding aids. Some are being added to the Web site.

Online Sources: Digital Collection of Language of the Kalispel, http://guweb2. gonzaga.edu/kalispel, with dictionary, grammars, and study of the Kalispel language. (New 2004)

Review of Collections: The Jesuit Oregon Province Archives is the designated repository for materials on the corporate history of the Oregon Province of the Society of Jesus, and a depository of individuals' papers related to the society. The collection covers the areas included in Washington, Oregon, Idaho, Alaska, Montana, and some of California and a variety of subjects dealing with the Jesuits, their missions, and the Native American peoples with whom they came in contact and to whom they ministered. The collection began in the 1920s.

Museum on Premises: No

Parking: On-street free parking is limited. Parking permits can be obtained from campus security.

Lunch: Several blocks to some restaurants, student cafeteria in nearby building

Lodging: http://www.visitspokane.com

Nearest Commercial Airport: Spokane International (GEG) [9 miles]

Subjects

> **Historical Periods:** 1865–1900; 1900–1940; 1940–present
>
> **Eras:** Indian Wars; World War II
>
> **Transportation:** Railroads
>
> **Agriculture:** Ranching/Livestock
>
> **Business:** Banking
>
> **Manufacturing:** Cannery; Grist/Flour Mills
>
> **Government:** Federal
>
> **Organizations:** Schools; Colleges/Universities; Hospitals/Medical Facilities; Charities
>
> **Ethnic Groups:** Native American; Dutch; English; French; German; Irish; Italian; Belgian

Religious Sites and Organizations: Catholic

Date of Reviewer's Visit: 12/9/2003

Profile Updated by Institution: 12/6/2004

✱✱✱✱✱

Name: Northwest Museum of Arts and Culture **County:** Spokane

Mailing Address: 2316 W 1st Ave.

City: Spokane **State:** WA **Postal Code:** 99204-0000

Street Address: 2316 W 1st Ave.

Institution Email: None

Telephone Number: (509) 456-3931 **Fax Number:** (509) 363-5303

Contact Name: Rose Krause, curator of Special Collections

Institution Type: Regional Museum

Affiliation: Eastern Washington State Historical Society and Washington state

Web site URL: http://www.northwestmuseum.org

Hours: T, W, and Th 11–5 or by appt.

Staff in Archives: 1f 1p 20v

Archives Are Handicapped Accessible: Yes

Cost for Researcher—In-house: Museum admission

Cost for Researcher—Remote: Fee schedule

List of Researchers Available: Yes

Review of Facilities: The Northwest Museum of Arts and Culture is located to the west of downtown Spokane in the historic Browne's Addition. The multibuilding complex consists of the museum, the Joel E. Ferris Research Library and Archives, and a historic mansion/museum. The research area is newly renovated with worktables against one wall of windows. Two of the four large worktables have computer stations. Bookshelves and file cabinets fill out one side of the large and open room. The archival materials are stored in a sizable vault room adjacent. Compact shelving and rows of map cases and file cabinets store the large collection of the research library. The library is well organized and well managed.

Vertical Files: Yes **Vertical Files in Cubic Feet:** 254

Vertical File Description and Subjects: The large vertical file consists mostly of clippings mounted on cardstock. The areas are divided by general subject, for example, Indians, Spokane, Biographies.

Manuscripts: Yes **Manuscripts Volume in Cubic Feet:** 1,000

Manuscript Types: Business records, organizational records, personal papers

Manuscript Subjects: Funeral home records, research papers, 600 separate collections

Photographs: Yes   **Number of Photographs:** 100,000

Storage of Photographs: Photocopies of photographs in plastic sleeves are stored in file cabinets in the main reference room, originals are stored in a climate-controlled vault.

Photograph Subjects: Photographs are divided by Indians, biography, Spokane area, and general Subjects

Photograph Reproductions Are Available: Yes

    Photographic Prints: Yes   **Digital Prints:** Yes

    Digital Images on CD or Electronically: Yes

Books: Yes   **Number of Books in Collection:** 10,000

Description of Books: Regional and local history, city directories, Pacific Northwest, Native Americans

Newspapers: No

Microfilm and Dates: Microfilm at Spokane Public Library

Oral Histories: Yes   **Oral Histories Number:** 950

Oral Histories Description: Interviews of Inland Northwest residents taken from early 1970s to present. Most have been transcribed.

Maps and Drawings: Yes   **Estimated Number of Maps and Drawings:** 250

Description of Maps and Drawings: Architectural drawings, regional maps

Genealogy Sources: No

Special Collections: Yes

    Special Collections Description: Kirtland Cutter drawings, Whitehouse and Price architecture records, W. W. Hyslop architectural records

Indexes: Card files index books and some other items.

    Manuscript Finding Aids: Manuscript finding aids and collection indexes are available in file cabinets in research room.

    Published Guides: *A Guide to the Manuscript Collections in the Eastern Washington Historical Society*, by Edward W. Nolan

    Online Sources: Some of the book holdings are listed on WorldCat. Some photographic images available through the University of Washington Web site

Review of Collections: The research collections consist of materials from throughout eastern Washington and northern Idaho. Materials from the former Museum of Native American Cultures (MONAC) have been incorporated into the collection. There are large collections of architectural records from several large firms involved in many of the historic buildings in eastern Washington. This includes the architectural records of Kirtland Cutter. The MAC collection also includes 400 VHS tapes and 1,200 reel-to-reel films on various topics and news reports.

Museum on Premises: Yes

Museum Is Handicapped Accessible: Yes

Description of Museum: Large, professionally curated museum with rotating displays on Inland Northwest history and art

Parking: Free parking garage on property

Lunch: Cafe on site and short drive to upscale cafes and numerous restaurants

Lodging: http://www.visitspokane.com

Nearest Commercial Airport: Spokane International (GEG) [6 miles]

Subjects

Historical Periods: 1865–1900; 1900–1940; 1940–present

Eras: Fur Trade; WPA; CCC; World War II

Natural Resources: Water; Dams; Irrigation; Fishing; Hunting; Logging

Mining: Gold; Silver; Surface Mining; Tunnel Mining

Transportation: Railroads; Stagecoach/Freight; Aviation

Agriculture: Dairy; Ranching/Livestock; Vegetable/Truck Crops; Grains; Orchards; Dry Land Farming

Business: Banking; Retail; Legal/Medical Services; Hotels/Restaurants; Entertainment/Theaters

Manufacturing: Brewery; Grist/Flour Mills; Creamery; Brick Making; Sawmills; Wood Products

Government: City; Tribal

Organizations: Schools; Hospitals/Medical Facilities; Charities; Nonreligious Organizations; Civic and Fraternal; Women's; Business; Children's; Labor and Union

Ethnic Groups: Native American; African; Japanese

Religious Sites and Organizations: Jewish

Date of Reviewer's Visit: 8/18/2004

Profile Updated by Institution: 11/22/2004

✳✳✳✳

Name: Spokane Public Library

County: Spokane

Mailing Address: 906 W. Main

City: Spokane   **State:** WA   **Postal Code:** 99201-0976

Street Address: 906 W. Main

Institution Email: None

Telephone Number: (509) 444-5300   **Fax Number:** (509) 444-5365

Contact Name: Rayette Sterling   **Contact Email:** rsterling@spokpl.lib.wa.us

Institution Type: Public Library

Affiliation: City of Spokane

Web site URL: http://www.spokanelibrary.org

Hours: M–T 10–8, W–Su 10–6

Staff in Archives: 1f

Archives Are Handicapped Accessible: Yes

Review of Facilities: The Spokane Public Library is located in downtown Spokane in a 1994 building. The library is located on the second and third floors of the building. The main entrance is on the second floor and the Northwest Room is at the back of the building on that floor. The room is large and the center is filled with bookshelves. One wall houses a long row of file cabinets. A row of large research tables are ranged by the windows. Personal items must be left at the desk near the Northwest Room entrance, and only pencil and paper can be carried into the room. The staff desk at the entrance opens into a small workroom and into a vault where the rare books and manuscripts are kept. The room is warm with soft woods and classic décor.

Vertical Files: Yes

Vertical File Description and Subjects: Northwest history

Manuscripts: Yes   **Manuscripts Volume in Cubic Feet:** 40

Manuscript Types: Organizational records, government records

Manuscript Subjects: Sons and Daughters of Pioneers, local organization papers

Photographs: Yes   **Number of Photographs:** 4,000

Storage of Photographs: Photos stored in file cabinets or clamshell boxes, negatives in clamshell boxes

Photograph Subjects: Gilbert collection, Teakle collection housed separately

Photograph Reproductions Are Available: Yes

Photographic Prints: Yes   **Digital Prints:** Yes

Books: Yes   **Number of Books in Collection:** 13,000

Description of Books: Northwest and regional history, city directories, annuals, telephone books

Newspapers: Yes

Newspapers on Microfilm: Yes

Microfilm and Dates: Spokane papers from 1879–1894, microfilm is in periodicals section

Oral Histories: Yes   **Oral Histories Number:** 60

Oral Histories Description: Voices of the pioneers, some still reel-to-reel, all transcribed, searchable in catalog

Maps and Drawings: Yes   **Estimated Number of Maps and Drawings:** 100

Description of Maps and Drawings: Variety of railroad, exploration maps, most not cataloged, Metsker, Sanborn maps

Genealogy Sources: Yes

    Genealogy Sources Description: Full genealogy collection located on third floor of library

Special Collections: Yes

    Special Collections Description: World War I records; index by topic name, mostly clippings, 6 cu. ft., newspaper clippings mounted on cardboard from Spokane area, including draft evasion

Indexes: Books and audiovisual on computer, vertical file has index categories, newspapers have index card file

    Manuscript Finding Aids: Collection-level description

    Online Sources: A large part of the collection is searchable through the library catalog.

Review of Collections: The greatest strengths of the collections of the Northwest Room are in the published materials, but that is not all that is available. The book collection goes back to the early years of the library and has a broad and deep base of information. The vertical files likewise have been collected for many decades, and the contents reflect the history of the collecting. Photographs have never been a main collecting area, although there are thousands of great images. The Edward Curtis Folios; videos of local area events/history, and the oral history collection are significant areas of note. The collection is professionally processed and managed.

Museum on Premises: No

Parking: Parking garage in basement, take elevator to second floor

Lunch: Espresso cart in lobby, skywalk to food court and all types of restaurants

Lodging: http://www.visitspokane.com

Nearest Commercial Airport: Spokane International (GEG) [7 miles]

Subjects

    Historical Periods: Pre-1800; 1800–1865; 1865–1900; 1900–1940; 1940–present

Eras: Fur Trade; Civil War; Indian Wars; Spanish American War; World War I; WPA; CCC; World War II

Natural Resources: Water; Dams; Irrigation; Fishing; Hunting; Shellfish; Logging

Mining: Gold; Silver; Copper; Coal; Placer Mining; Surface Mining; Tunnel Mining

Transportation: Railroads; Stagecoach/Freight; Ships and Shipping; Ferries; Aviation

Agriculture: Dairy; Ranching/Livestock; Vegetable/Truck Crops; Grains; Orchards; Vineyard; Dry Land Farming

Business: Banking; Retail; Legal/Medical Services; Hotels/Restaurants; Entertainment/Theaters

Manufacturing: Cannery; Brewery; Grist/Flour Mills; Creamery; Woolen/Fabric Mills; Brick Making; Boatbuilding/Shipyard; Technology/Computers; Sawmills; Wood Products

Government: City; County; State; Federal

Organizations: Schools; Colleges/Universities; Hospitals/Medical Facilities; Charities; Nonreligious Organizations; Civic and Fraternal; Women's; Business; Children's; Labor and Union

Ethnic Groups: Native American; Latin American; African; Pacific Islander; Chinese

Religious Sites and Organizations: Protestant; Catholic; LDS (Mormon); Jewish; Muslim; Hindu; Buddhist; Mennonite/Amish

Date of Reviewer's Visit: 8/16/2004

Profile Updated by Institution: 11/29/2004

✻✻✻✻

Name: Whitworth College Archives   **County:** Spokane

Mailing Address: Harriet Cheney Cowles Memorial Library, 300 W. Hawthorne Rd., MS 0901

  City: Spokane   **State:** WA   **Postal Code:** 99251-0001

Street Address: 300 W. Hawthorne Rd.

Institution Email: None

Telephone Number: (509) 777-4751   **Fax Number:** (509) 777-3231

Contact Name: Janet Hauck **Contact Email:** jhauck@whitworth.edu

Institution Type: Academic Library

Web site URL: http://www.whitworth.edu/library/archives

Hours: M–F 9–12; 1–4 by appt.

Staff in Archives: 1f, 2v

Archives Are Handicapped Accessible: Yes

Review of Facilities: The Whitworth College Archives is located in the Harriet Cheney Cowles Library, in the center of the Whitworth Campus in north Spokane. This collection is divided into two parts, the College Archives and the Pacific Northwest Protestantism Archives. The collection is open by appointment only. The area for research is a moderate-sized, well-lit room with two large square tables in the center of the room and several study carrels. The locked bookcases that line the wall are not part of the archival collection. The archives are stored in a staff-only area across the hall and up a ramp. There are two large floors of book stacks that are dedicated to the processing and storage of this growing collection. The collections are divided between the Whitworth College Archives and the Pacific Northwest Protestantism Archives. There is also some storage for special collections books that relate to the archives holdings.

Vertical Files: Yes   **Vertical Files in Cubic Feet:** 15

Vertical File Description and Subjects: Faculty and alumni biographical files with photos, clippings, and lists (some copies) of publications

Manuscripts: Yes   **Manuscripts Volume in Cubic Feet:** 450

Manuscript Types: Archives, organizational records, personal papers

Manuscript Subjects: Church records and histories from over 40 churches from primarily Washington and Idaho. Presbyterian, Methodist, Lutheran, Nondenominational Churches, and other Protestant organizations from the 1870s to the present.

Photographs: Yes   **Number of Photographs:** 4,000

Storage of Photographs: Photographs stored in acid-free folders in document boxes

Photograph Subjects: Whitworth College from the earliest years to the present

Photograph Reproductions Are Available: Yes

Photographic Prints: Yes   **Digital Prints:** Yes

Digital Images on CD or Electronically: Yes

Books: Yes   **Number of Books in Collection:** 500

Description of Books: Protestant history of the Pacific Northwest or western region. Some Whitworth College books.

Newspapers: No

Oral Histories: Yes   **Oral Histories Number:** 100

Oral Histories Description: Thirty Protestant history interviews done in the 2000s; 30 Japanese-American interviews regarding life during World War II period in and out of the internment camps done in 2002; 20 interviews of personal experiences in Civilian Conservation Corps (CCC) camps from 2003; 20 interviews with Whitworth College retired faculty and alums (5 from 1960s, remainder from recent years)

Maps and Drawings: No

Genealogy Sources: No

Special Collections: Yes

Special Collections Description: Whitworth Family Diaries—a collection of diaries from 1853 to 1907 from the family of the founder of Whitworth College. Fifty of the diaries are from George Whitworth himself; 20 from his wife, Mary; three from his son Harry and one from his daughter Etta. George Whitworth traveled the Oregon Trail in 1853 as a Presbyterian Missionary, founded at least 20 churches in the Pacific Northwest, worked as superintendent of education in several communities, was president of the fledgling University of Washington, and founded Whitworth College's predecessor, Sumner Academy, in 1884. Some of the diaries have been transcribed for easier reading.

Indexes: Yes

Manuscript Finding Aids: Processed manuscript collections have written finding aids.

Online Sources: Bibliographic records of collections can be found in the online Whitworth Library catalog with future links to finding aids. There are several online exhibits available from the Archives Web page.

Review of Collections: The Pacific Northwest Protestantism Archive Collection was begun in 1999. In the few years since its beginning, the collection has grown tremendously. At the time of review, 40 churches had collections that had been transferred to the Archives. These collections range from .5 cu. ft. to 25 cu. ft. each. All types of church documents, photographs, and histories are included with the collections. Some of the materials date as far back as the 1870s. Collections of materials for other Protestant groups are also being added. A collection of interest is Sunday school newspapers from 1870s to the 1890s. Although Whitworth is a Presbyterian institution, the collection focus is on all Protestant churches. Although Oregon is included in the collecting area, currently all churches were from Washington and Idaho. The Whitworth College Archives houses standard college history, administrative records, and publications. In addition the photograph collection illustrates the life of Whitworth College from the beginning.

Museum on Premises: No

Parking: Parking permit required from Facilities Services

Lunch: Long walk or short drive to wide variety of chain and local restaurants

Lodging: http://www.visitspokane.com

Nearest Commercial Airport: Spokane International (GEG) [14 miles]

Subjects

   Historical Periods: 1865–1900; 1900–1940; 1940–present

   Organizations: Schools; Colleges/Universities

   Religious Sites and Organizations: Protestant

Date of Reviewer's Visit: 7/8/2004

Profile Updated by Institution: 11/12/2004

TACOMA

Name: Pacific Lutheran University Archives and Special Collections

County: Pierce

Mailing Address: Robert A L Mortvedt Library, Park and 121st St. South

   City: Tacoma   **State:** WA   **Postal Code:** 98447-0013

Street Address: Park and 121st St. South

Institution Email: archives@plu.edu

Telephone Number: (253) 535-7500   **Fax Number:** (253) 535-7315

Contact Name: Kerstin Ringdahl   **Contact Email:** ringdak@plu.edu

Institution Type: Academic Library

Web site URL: http://www.plu.edu/~archives

Hours: M–F 10–12 and 1–4

Staff in Archives: 1p

Archives Are Handicapped Accessible: Yes

Review of Facilities: The Pacific Lutheran University Archives and Special Collections are located on the third floor of the Mortvedt Library. The research room is in the center of the archives area with the offices to the back and doors to the collections on each side. The room is designed in a casual manner with easy chairs, a medium sized worktable, and art and photographs on the walls. To the right of the research area is a door leading to a large room housing the university archives and the Evangelical Lutheran Church Archives (ELCA). On the other side is a door leading to the Scandinavian Immigrant Experience Collection.

Vertical Files: Yes   **Vertical Files in Cubic Feet:** 15

   Vertical File Description and Subjects: General information on Scandinavian immigrants, ELCA file of pastors and churches

Manuscripts: Yes   **Manuscripts Volume in Cubic Feet:** 10,000

Manuscript Types: Archives, organizational records, business records, personal papers

Manuscript Subjects: Pacific Lutheran University; Norwegian, Swedish, Finnish, Danish, and Icelandic Americans; Lutheran church history

Photographs: Yes   **Number of Photographs:** 502,200

Storage of Photographs: Photographs are stored in acid-free folders in file cabinets. Arranged by subject or name.

Photograph Subjects: Pacific Lutheran University, Lutheran church, and a few Scandinavian immigrants

Photograph Reproductions Are Available: Yes

Photographic Prints: Yes   **Digital Prints:** Yes

Digital Images on CD or Electronically: Yes

Books: Yes   **Number of Books in Collection:** 10,000

Description of Books: 10,000 monographs in the Scandinavian Immigrant Experience Collection dealing with all aspects of the immigrant experience and including books owned by the immigrants, fiction and nonfiction in all five languages, as well as English. Books are listed in the electronic catalog and searchable through the web page.

Newspapers: No

Oral Histories: Yes   **Oral Histories Number:** 335

Oral Histories Description: 285 in the Scandinavian Immigrant Experience (SIE) collection, some with partial transcriptions, and listed on Web site. 50 on Pacific Lutheran Society (PLU) topics of university history; few have transcriptions.

Maps and Drawings: No

Genealogy Sources: Yes

Genealogy Sources Description: Some local histories from Scandinavia and very limited sources in genealogy

Special Collections: No

Indexes: Yes

Online Sources: Books are searchable through the electronic online catalog of main library.

Review of Collections: There are five distinct parts to the Pacific Lutheran Archives and Special Collections. University Archives—(10, 350 linear ft., 1250 recordings, 500,000 photographic images, all dealing with Pacific Lutheran University, from the earliest day to the present); Evangelical Lutheran Church Archives [ELCA]—(570 linear ft. of manuscripts, 2,000 photographic images, 27 publications, including synod records and records of closed churches in the region); Scandinavian Immigrant

Experience Collection [SIE]—(65 linear ft. of manuscripts, 200 photographic images, 285 oral histories, 10,000 monographs all related to the experience of Scandinavian immigrants in the United States. The Nisqually Plains Collection was started by the history department of the university and consists mainly of student papers on all issues of local history, rather than original documents. Rare Books includes a large number of books on the history of the Lutheran Church from the earliest period.

Museum on Premises: No

Parking: On-street parallel parking (2-hr. limit) or obtain permit from campus safety in Harstad Hall next door to the library

Lunch: University Center Cafeteria and coffee shop several buildings away and a few off-campus ethnic or local eateries within walking distance

Lodging: http://www.traveltacoma.com

Nearest Commercial Airport: Seattle-Tacoma International (SEA) [27 miles]

Subjects

    Historical Periods: 1865–1900; 1900–1940; 1940–present

    Eras: World War II

    Organizations: Colleges/Universities; Civic and Fraternal; Women's

    Ethnic Groups: Native American; Danish; Finnish; Norwegian; Swedish; Icelandic

    Religious Sites and Organizations: Protestant

Date of Reviewer's Visit: 1/14/2004

Profile Updated by Institution: 11/22/2004

Name: Tacoma Public Library Special Collections   **County:** Pierce

Mailing Address: 1102 Tacoma Ave., S.

  City: Tacoma   **State:** WA   **Postal Code:** 98402-0000

Street Address: 1102 Tacoma Ave., S.

Institution Email: nwr@tpl.lib.wa.us

Telephone Number: (253) 591-5666   **Fax Number:** (253) 591-5470

Contact Name: Julie Ciccarelli

Contact Email: jciccarelli@tpl.lib.wa.us

Institution Type: Public Library

Affiliation: City of Tacoma

Web site URL: http://www.tpl.lib.wa.us

Hours: M–Th 9–9, F–Sa 9–6

Staff in Archives: 4f 5 p

Archives Are Handicapped Accessible: Yes

Cost for Researcher—Remote: Fee schedule

Review of Facilities: The Tacoma Public Library Special Collections is located in the beautifully restored old wing of the library. The reference desk is in a circle in the middle of the room, with the research worktables and collections surrounding it. There are numerous large, well lit worktables in this spacious, high-ceilinged room. The room houses both the Northwest Collection and the genealogy collection. Computer stations, paper card indexes, and numerous notebooks of compiled information provide access to the collections. The large vertical file is open to researchers. Photocopies of photographs are arranged in subject binders and available as well. The bulk of the manuscript collections, as well as the original photographs, are stored in the basement of the building in a huge warehouse room.

Vertical Files: Yes   **Vertical Files in Cubic Feet:** 530

> **Vertical File Description and Subjects:** Large collection of Pacific Northwest history topics arranged by subject

Manuscripts: Yes

> **Manuscript Types:** Personal papers, business records
>
> **Manuscript Subjects:** Labor history, railroad history

Photographs: Yes   **Number of Photographs:** 1,500,000

> **Storage of Photographs:** Browsable subject binders with photocopies of photographs in research room. 40,000 images available online. Originals stored in basement in file cabinets by general subject or accession number.
>
> **Photograph Subjects:** One million images from the Richards Studio Collection from the 1930s to the 1970s. Richards Studio did photography for local newspapers, commercial and studio shots. They also have a large collection of aerial photographs and early color photos. Other photographs are from a variety of sources on all subjects on Pacific Northwest history, but with an emphasis on the Tacoma area.
>
> **Photograph Reproductions Are Available:** Yes
>
> > **Photographic Prints:** Yes   **Digital Prints:** Yes
> >
> > **Digital Images on CD or Electronically:** Yes

Books: Yes   **Number of Books in Collection:** 26,000

Description of Books: Northwest history, city directories, and genealogy

Newspapers: Yes

> **Newspapers on Microfilm:** Yes
>
> **Microfilm and Dates:** Tacoma area papers

Oral Histories: Yes

> **Oral Histories Description:** Small bicentennial project of the general history of Tacoma—most have been transcribed

Maps and Drawings: Yes

> **Description of Maps and Drawings:** Large map collection on all aspects of Pacific Northwest history

Genealogy Sources: Yes

> **Genealogy Sources Description:** Full genealogy collection of books, large obituary index on file cards, 36 cu. ft. of vertical file materials

Special Collections: No

Indexes: Northwest Room card files

> **Online Sources:** Photography Archive—40,000 images searchable by keyword. Tacoma and Pierce County Building Index of 37,000 homes built prior to 1940. Washington Place Names—listing of place names online. Tacoma Obituary Index. Murray's People—a selection of essays by Murray Morgan. Magnificent Views and Vistas—photographs, journals, and maps of early climbers.

Review of Collections: The Tacoma Public Library Northwest Room and Special Collections house a variety of materials related to the Pacific Northwest. There are 1.5 million photographs on Tacoma, Pierce County, and beyond for the years 1888 to the present. 40,000 of these images are searchable and available from the Web site. There is a huge vertical file collection of assorted historical subjects. The book collection has about 22,000 books on Pacific Northwest history and related subjects. The genealogy collection likewise is large and well rounded. The manuscript collections are not one of the major collecting focuses but still represent a sizable collection of original documents. Several of the major indexes are being put online.

Museum on Premises: No

Parking: Library pay box lot across the street on Tacoma Ave. Cost is $1 per hr. or $9 per day maximum. On-street metered parking is also available, most for 30 mins.

Lunch: Variety of restaurants within walking distance

Lodging: http://www.traveltacoma.com

Nearest Commercial Airport: Seattle-Tacoma International (SEA) [21 miles]

Subjects

> **Historical Periods:** 1865–1900; 1900–1940; 1940–present
>
> **Transportation:** Railroads
>
> **Government:** City; County; State; Federal
>
> **Organizations:** Charities; Nonreligious Organizations
>
> **Ethnic Groups:** Japanese

Date of Reviewer's Visit: 1/14/2004

Profile Updated by Institution: 12/6/2004

✵✵✵✵✵

Name: Washington State Historical Society Research Center **County:** Pierce

Mailing Address: Special Collections Division, 315 N. Stadium Way

City: Tacoma **State:** WA **Postal Code:** 98403-0000

Street Address: 315 N. Stadium Way

Institution Email: researchcenter@wshs.wa.gov

Telephone Number: (253) 798-5914 **Fax Number:** (253) 597-4186

Contact Name: Joy Werlink or Elaine Miller

Institution Type: Historical Society Archives

Affiliation: Washington State quasi-state agency

Web site URL: http://www.washingtonhistory.org

Hours: Tu–Th 12:30–4:30 by appt.

Staff in Archives: 1f 2p

Archives Are Handicapped Accessible: Yes

Cost for Researcher—Remote: Out-of-state 2-hr. limit (fee schedule)

Review of Facilities: The Research Center of the Washington State Historical Society is housed in the old but refurbished museum building several miles from the current museum. There is a call box outside the entrance to notify the staff of your arrival, as the front door is kept locked at all times. The research room is directly to the left of the main entrance. This is a long narrow room with six small worktables and two large tables. Green shaded lamps are located on each table. Card files and bookcases line two walls of the room. A reference area and map cases line another. Lockers are available with a key obtained at the desk on registration. A coat rack is also available. Laptops can be used (without the case) and power sources are available under each table. Registration is required and only pencils and notes are allowed at the worktables. The large card index to the collections is available to researchers, as is an index to photographs. The general index is kept current, but the photo index has current materials listed on a staff computer. City directories to localities in Washington State fill the bookcases. The majority of the collection including the books is stored elsewhere in the building.

Vertical Files: Yes **Vertical Files in Cubic Feet:** 125

Vertical File Description and Subjects: Vertical files consist of 60 linear ft., while a pamphlet file is another 65 linear ft.

Manuscripts: Yes **Manuscripts Volume in Cubic Feet:** 1,500

Manuscript Types: Business records, personal papers, organizational records 7.5 million items, 450 collections

Manuscript Subjects: Washington State history and life, Seattle General Hospital, Northern Pacific Hospital, banks, ethnic fraternal organizations, furniture unions, carpentry union, hotel and restaurant unions, lumber companies, early Puget Sound residents, environmental activists, gay and lesbian activists, state politicians

Photographs: Yes   **Number of Photographs:** 500,000

Storage of Photographs: Subject notebooks of photographs, about 40 percent of the collection is browsable

Photograph Subjects: Washington State history, Native Americans

Photograph Reproductions Are Available: Yes

Photographic Prints: Yes   **Digital Prints:** No

Digital Images on CD or Electronically: Yes

Books: Yes   **Number of Books in Collection:** 15,000

Description of Books: Regional and local history, city directories

Newspapers: No

Microfilm and Dates: Newspapers available from Washington State Library and University of Washington

Oral Histories: Yes   **Oral Histories Number:** 40

Oral Histories Description: Miscellaneous oral histories

Maps and Drawings: Yes   **Estimated Number of Maps and Drawings:** 3,200

Description of Maps and Drawings: Washington State, Pacific Northwest from all historical periods, and Edward Allen collection of 300 maps of the cartographic history of the Northwest coast, 1512–1865

Genealogy Sources: No

Genealogy Sources Description: Institution does not attempt to be a genealogical resource, although they have some items of genealogical interest.

Special Collections: Yes

Special Collections Description: Asahel Curtis photographs documenting development of Washington, 1898–1938, 60,000 negatives; Chapin Bowen, Tacoma and Pierce County, 1925–1955, 62,000 negatives; Marvin Boland, Tacoma and Pierce County, 1914–1939, 75,000 negatives; Western Ways/ Pomeroy Collection, low-level aerial photographs, mainly of cities and industrial sites (including lumber mills) in Washington, Oregon, California, and Idaho, 1950–1976, 124,000 negatives; a variety of collections documenting Native Americans, Japanese Americans, and other ethnic groups; Pacific Northwest maritime Subjects

Indexes: Card files of the index to collection including ephemera, manuscripts and books. Separate photo index includes most items older than six years.

Manuscript Finding Aids: The newer manuscript collections have finding aids, and about 20 percent of them are available from the Web site.

Online Sources: Online exhibits "Golden Dreams: Quest for the Klondike," Northwest Imagery

Review of Collections: The collections of the Washington State Historical Society focus on all aspects of Washington history from before the territorial period to the present. The holdings strongly represent the areas of western Washington and cover the remainder of the state with less comprehensiveness. The collection is large, and some parts are not easily accessible. The photograph collections are strong, with numerous large donations of historically significant photographs by leading photographers of the region. In addition to sizeable vertical file and pamphlet collections, they also have a printed ephemera file consisting of 12,000 cataloged pieces, but totaling closer to 50,000 items. The collections are large and very significant to Washington State history.

Museum on Premises: No

Parking: Free parking lot to the side of the building with a full flight of stairs up to the entrance. Handicap slots on street accessible to main entrance.

Lunch: Nearby restaurants, deli, 3–5 blocks away

Lodging: http://www.traveltacoma.com

Nearest Commercial Airport: Seattle-Tacoma International (SEA) [23 miles]

Subjects

Historical Periods: 1800–1865; 1865–1900; 1900–1940; 1940–present

Eras: Indian Wars; Spanish American War; World War I; WPA; CCC; World War II

Natural Resources: Dams; Irrigation; Fishing

Mining: Gold; Coal; Tunnel Mining

Transportation: Railroads; Ships and Shipping; Ferries

Agriculture: Vineyard

Business: Banking; Retail; Legal/Medical Services

Manufacturing: Brewery; Grist/Flour Mills; Woolen/Fabric Mills; Boatbuilding/Shipyard; Sawmills; Wood Products

Government: State

Organizations: Hospitals/Medical Facilities; Nonreligious Organizations; Civic and Fraternal; Women's; Business; Children's; Labor and Union

Ethnic Groups: Native American; African; Pacific Islander; Japanese; Chinese; Lao; Vietnamese; German; Norwegian; Swedish

Religious Sites and Organizations: Protestant; Catholic; Jewish

Date of Reviewer's Visit: 1/14/2004

Profile Updated by Institution: 11/12/2004

VANCOUVER

Name: Clark County Historical Museum   **County:** Clark

Mailing Address: 1511 Main St.

   City: Vancouver   **State:** WA   **Postal Code:** 98668-0000

Street Address: 1511 Main St.

Institution Email: cchm@pacifier.com

Telephone Number: (360) 695-4681

Contact Name: Eileen Trestain/Kathie Klingler

Institution Type: Local Museum

Affiliation: Clark County Historical Society

Web site URL: http://www.pacifier.com/~cchm

Hours: Tu–Sa 12:30–4:00, no admission charge

Staff in Archives: 2P, 6V

Archives Are Handicapped Accessible: No

Access Description: Neither the museum or the research area are handicapped accessible. There is a full flight of steep stairs to enter the building.

Cost for Researcher—Remote: $10 hour

Review of Facilities: The Clark County Historical Museum places a great deal of emphasis on their research room and archival collections. The room is on the main floor of the building and is large and spacious feeling. The room is lined by bookshelves holding published books, periodicals, and vertical file–type collections. There are two oversize worktables and a staff desk area in the room. The remaining manuscript collections are housed in the basement of the building in a staff-only area. The area is well lit, and although not fancy, is certainly pleasant and functional.

Vertical Files: Yes   **Vertical Files in Cubic Feet:** 65

   Vertical File Description and Subjects: Clippings, ephemera, and small manuscript collections stored in clamshell boxes and filed on the book shelves by subject alongside the books. Some materials are in small binders also on the shelves.

Manuscripts: Yes

Manuscript Types: Business histories, organizational records, land records

Manuscript Subjects: Clark County business and property surveys; local history

Photographs: Yes   **Number of Photographs:** 3,800

Storage of Photographs: Photocopies of the originals arranged in binders by subject. Originals stored in file cabinets.

Photograph Reproductions Are Available: Yes

   Photographic Prints: No   **Digital Prints:** Yes

   Digital Images on CD or Electronically: Yes

Books: Yes   **Number of Books in Collection:** 3,800

Description of Books: Local and Northwest history, professional collection filed by subject, yearbooks and city directories

Newspapers: No

Oral Histories: Yes

   Oral Histories Description: Local area residents. Transcriptions for all interviews.

Maps and Drawings: Yes   **Estimated Number of Maps and Drawings:** 1,500

Description of Maps and Drawings: Large map collection including land claim, Sanborn maps, 1855 Vancouver Barracks, 1860 Vancouver maps, and 1,000 aerial photo maps of area taken from 1945–1959

Genealogy Sources: Yes

   Genealogy Sources Description: Cemetery records and marriage records for the Clark County area

Special Collections: No

Indexes: No

Review of Collections: The library collections are arranged by subject on the shelves. Vertical file materials are interspersed in either notebooks or clamshell boxes, depending on the amount of material. This is an interesting system, but it seems functional for their purposes. The binders with the browsing photograph copies are nearby. The photograph collection is moderate-sized but easily accessible. One side of the room is devoted to periodicals, both local and professional in nature. The manuscript materials are stored downstairs. The subjects covered by the collection includes all aspects of Clark County historical development. The earliest records date from the mid-nineteenth century.

Museum on Premises: Yes

   Museum Hours: Tu–Sa 12:30–4:00

   Cost of Entry to Museum: Free

   Museum Is Handicapped Accessible: No

Parking: Metered on-street parallel parking

Lunch: Variety of restaurants within a short distance

Lodging: http://www.southwestwashington.com

Nearest Commercial Airport: Portland International (PDX) [12 miles]

Subjects

    Historical Periods: 1800–1865; 1865–1900; 1900–1940; 1940–present

    Eras: World War I; World War II

Date of Reviewer's Visit: 11/7/2003

Profile Updated by Institution: 11/2004

WALLA WALLA

✹✹✹

Name: Fort Walla Walla Museum   **County:** Walla Walla

Mailing Address: 755 Myra Rd.

  City: Walla Walla   **State:** WA   **Postal Code:** 99362-0000

Street Address: 755 Myra Rd.

Institution Email: info@fortwallawallamuseum.org

Telephone Number: (509) 525-7703   **Fax Number:** (509) 525-7798

Contact Name: Administrative Assistant

Institution Type: Historic Site

Web site URL: http://www.fortwallawallamuseum.org

Hours: M–F 9–3:30; 8–4:30 by appt.

Staff in Archives: 1f 3v

Archives Are Handicapped Accessible: Yes

Cost for Researcher—Remote: Fee schedule

Review of Facilities: Fort Walla Walla is a living history museum basically arranged in two tiers. The archives and library are in the modern headquarters building on the upper level of the complex. From April to October the entrance to the research area is the entrance on the lower level. From November to March the entrance is the staff entrance on the upper level. Although the library and archives are available year round, the museum is not open. The library is located on the first floor among the staff offices. The library houses the book collection, vertical files, audiovisual materials, and periodicals. There is a long worktable and smaller table forming a T in the middle of the room. A desk is against one wall. File cabinets and bookshelves surround the room. It is moderate-sized but well lit and arranged. The books are classified in Library of Congress order with a card index. The manuscript and photograph collections are housed in a climate-controlled room elsewhere in the building. Access to the photograph collections and indexing to the manuscripts are on PastPerfect, but there is not a computer in the library.

Vertical Files: Yes   **Vertical Files in Cubic Feet:** 9

Vertical File Description and Subjects: Local area history in a subject arrangement. Small collection of genealogical files of local families (2 cu. ft.).

Manuscripts: Yes   **Manuscripts Volume in Cubic Feet:** 75

Manuscript Types: Organizational records, personal papers

Manuscript Subjects: Walla Walla Valley history, local schools (twentieth century). Variety of local area history, not necessarily relating to Fort Walla Walla. Some small family collections. Most of the collections are grouped by similar types of individual items rather than large or even medium collections. 5,100 individual cataloged items or collections.

Photographs: Yes   **Number of Photographs:** 4,500

Storage of Photographs: The images are stored and indexed on PastPerfect software. The original photographs are housed in file cabinets in acid-free envelopes in a climate controlled room.

Photograph Subjects: Photographs include all subjects of Walla Walla Valley history.

Photograph Reproductions Are Available: Yes

Photographic Prints: Yes   **Digital Prints:** Yes

Books: Yes   **Number of Books in Collection:** 1,200

Description of Books: Agriculture, regional history, city directories, and professional collection make up the bulk of the book collection. Books are classified by Library of Congress classification number and accessible through a card index.

Newspapers: No

Microfilm and Dates: Available at Whitman College nearby

Oral Histories: Yes   **Oral Histories Number:** 20

Oral Histories Description: Collection of videotaped oral histories of area sheep farming history

Maps and Drawings: No

Genealogy Sources: No

Genealogy Sources Description: Refers to local library

Special Collections: No

Indexes: Manuscript collections and photographs are indexed on PastPerfect. Books from the library are indexed by a card file.

Review of Collections: Collections are limited in both scope and size. The photograph collection is the strongest area. The majority of the materials of all formats deals with the general history of the Walla Walla area, and very little with the direct history of Fort Walla Walla. This is a problem they are trying to rectify. Most of the manuscript materials are arranged by type of materials rather than general collections. Most collections are either extremely small or inventoried at an individual level. Over 5,100 separate items are listed in their manuscript collections. The inventory of the collections has been completed, but detailed indexing has not been done.

Museum on Premises: Yes

　Museum Hours: Daily 10–5, Apr 1–Oct 31

　Cost of Entry to Museum: $7

　Museum Is Handicapped Accessible: Yes

Parking: Free paved parking lot on the lower level of the complex, or a gravel lot on the upper level of the complex (off season the upper lot is staff only)

Lunch: Driving distance to numerous restaurants and fast-food chains

Lodging: http://www.wwchamber.com

Nearest Commercial Airport: Walla Walla Regional (ALW); Tri-Cities (Pasco) (PSC) [47 miles]

Subjects

　Historical Periods:1865–1900; 1900–1940; 1940–present

　Eras: World War II

　Mining: Gold

　Transportation: Railroads

　Agriculture: Ranching/Livestock; Grains; Orchards; Vineyard; Dry Land Farming

　Organizations: Schools; Hospitals/Medical Facilities

Date of Reviewer's Visit: 3/23/2004

Profile Updated by Institution: 11/9/2004

Name: Whitman College—Whitman College and Northwest Archives
County: Walla Walla

Mailing Address: Penrose Memorial Library, 345 Boyer Ave.

　City: Walla Walla　　**State:** WA　　　　**Postal Code:** 99362-9982

Street Address: 345 Boyer Ave.

Institution Email: None

Telephone Number: (509) 527-5922   **Fax Number:** (509) 527-5900

Contact Name: Colleen McFarland   **Contact Email:** mcfarlcd@whitman.edu

Institution Type: Academic Library

Web site URL: http://www.whitman.edu/penrose/archives.html

Hours: Tu, W, and Th 1–5; Th 7–10 or by appt

Staff in Archives: 1f

Archives Are Handicapped Accessible: Yes

Access Description: Electronic doors, elevator

Cost for Researcher—Remote: Fee schedule

Review of Facilities: The Whitman College and Northwest Archives are located on the first floor of the Penrose Library. The Library is on the central quad of campus. The Archives are located on the lower level (marked first floor). The Eells Library of Northwest History is available in the main part of the library and consists of a large vertical file, annuals, and books on local and regional history. The formal Archives reading room leads off this area. The Archives reading room has a reference desk and wooden tables for 8–10 researchers. There are vertical files, a manuscript card file, and a reference collection housed in the reading room. The room also has wireless internet connectivity. Appointments are necessary.

Vertical Files: No   **Vertical Files in Cubic Feet:** 100

   Vertical File Description and Subjects: Various Pacific Northwest subjects, clippings and miscellaneous materials, Whitman College subjects and people, Walla Walla people and Subjects

Manuscripts: Yes   **Manuscripts Volume in Cubic Feet:** 3,500

   Manuscript Types: All manuscript types

   Manuscript Subjects: Dorsey Syng Baker Family Papers (1857–1902); bankers; Pacific Northwest Waterways/Inland Empire Waterways Association (1938–1982); business and associations including G.A.R., Carpenters' Union, women's clubs, Chamber of Commerce, Walla Walla Meat and Cold Storage, Baker Loan and Investment; Marissa Whitman journal and correspondence; Henry Spaulding correspondence; Sager family papers; Cushing and Myron Eells papers; missionary records

Photographs: Yes   **Number of Photographs:** 20,000

   Photograph Subjects: Buildings, people, economic activity of Walla Walla Valley. Vitart Sudio Collection, 10,000 images of portraits and businesses in Walla Walla 1929–1983.

   Photograph Reproductions Are Available: Yes

      Photographic Prints: Yes

Books: Yes   **Number of Books in Collection:** 7,500

Description of Books: Regional and local history, annuals, city directories, telephone books, Myron Eells Library of Northwest history

Newspapers: Yes   **Newspapers in Paper Format:** No

Newspapers on Microfilm: Yes

Microfilm and Dates: Available on second floor behind reference desk, *Walla Walla Union, Walla Walla Statesman,* 1865–present; *Oregonian,* 1850–present; *Oregon Spectator,* 1846–1855; *Seattle Post-Intelligencer,* 1876–1919; *Seattle Times,* 1920–present; *Spokesman Review,* 1884–1899 and 1984–present

Oral Histories: Yes   **Oral Histories Number:** 200

Oral Histories Description: Oral history interviews of Whitman College alumni, administrators, staff, and faculty taken late 1980s to early 1990s on audiocassette, some with transcriptions

Maps and Drawings: Yes   **Estimated Number of Maps and Drawings:** 200

Description of Maps and Drawings: Plat maps of Walla Walla region, aerials, Whitman campus, maps on lock and dam construction on Snake River

Genealogy Sources: No

Special Collections: Yes

Special Collections Description: The Teakle Collection is a 79-volume set of transcribed primary sources on Northwest history covering the years 1820s to 1910s, subjects include geology, fur trade, missions, overland migration, pioneer life, military conflicts, and exploration. Legal documents, letters, diaries, newspapers, and magazines are all transcribed in this amazing collection and arranged by subject before they were bound. Exceptional source of copies of early documents.

Indexes: Indexes available for books and manuscript collections

Published Guides: Stephen B. L. Penrose Jr. Papers; Dorsey Syng Baker Family Papers

Review of Collections: The collections at Whitman College contain some significant items of interest in the early settlement period. The photograph collection is sizable, with 80 percent of the 20,000 images dealing with the history of the greater Walla Walla area and the Pacific Northwest. The remainder is on Whitman College itself. The Teakle collection described above is a wonderful full-text index to the early history of the Inland Northwest and beyond. The collection has been built and maintained well over the years and under the auspices of a new archivist, it will continue to be a research stronghold in the area.

Museum on Premises: No

Parking: Free parking lot west of library

Lunch: Espresso with vending machine of assorted cold and microwavable foods on first floor directly adjacent. Cafeteria dining in Reid Campus Center.

Lodging: http://www.wwchamber.com

Nearest Commercial Airport: Walla Walla Regional (ALW); Tri-Cities (Pasco) (PSC) [47 miles]

Subjects

    Historical Periods: 1800–1865; 1865–1900; 1900–1940; 1940–present

    Eras: World War II

    Transportation: Railroads; Ships and Shipping

    Business: Banking; Legal/Medical Services; Entertainment/Theaters

    Organizations: Schools; Colleges/Universities; Nonreligious Organizations; Civic and Fraternal; Women's; Business; Labor and Union

    Ethnic Groups: German; Italian

    Religious Sites and Organizations: Protestant; Catholic; Jewish

Date of Reviewer's Visit: 3/23/2004

Profile Updated by Institution: 11/9/2004

WASHOUGAL

Name: Two Rivers Heritage Museum   **County:** Clark

Mailing Address: PO Box 204

  City: Washougal   **State:** WA   **Postal Code:** 98671-0000

Street Address: 1–16th St.

Institution Email: None

Telephone Number: (360) 835-8742

Contact Name: Betty Ramsey, Director

Institution Type: Local Museum

Affiliation: Camas/Washougal Historical Society

Web site URL: None

Hours: Tu–Sa 11–3, appt. preferred between 11–3

Staff in Archives: 4v

Archives Are Handicapped Accessible: Yes

Access Description: Ramps both outside and inside building. Doorjamb on entering building.

Cost for Researcher—In-house: Museum admission

Cost for Researcher—Remote: Donation

Review of Facilities: The Two Rivers Heritage Museum is located just off Highway 14 in downtown Washougal across from the Pendleton Outlet store. The museum has a small library in a room close to the front of the museum. Bookshelves line one wall and file cabinets another. The room is bright and pleasant. There is a small square worktable in the library along with a photocopy machine. The photo collection is stored in a volunteer office in another part of the museum. The manuscript materials are stored in the basement in a staff-only area and in the director's office.

Vertical Files: Yes   **Vertical Files in Cubic Feet:** 28

   Vertical File Description and Subjects: Family files, clippings, memorabilia, and ephemera on local history topics

Manuscripts: Yes   **Manuscripts Volume in Cubic Feet:** 30

   Manuscript Types: Business records, land records, personal papers

   Manuscript Subjects: Crown Zellerbach Paper Mill papers (unprocessed) from the years 1928–present

Photographs: Yes   **Number of Photographs:** 10,000

   Storage of Photographs: Photographs are stored in plastic sleeves in binders by subject. Some are stored in file cabinets. The binders have some original and some copies.

   Photograph Reproductions Are Available: Yes

      Photographic Prints: Yes   **Digital Prints:** No

      Digital Images on CD or Electronically: Yes

Books: Yes   **Number of Books in Collection:** 150

   Description of Books: Local history, professional collection, old books, school books, children's storybooks

Newspapers: Yes   **Newspapers in Paper Format:** Yes

   Papers and Dates: *Post Record,* 1965–1979, bound.

Oral Histories: Yes   **Oral Histories Number:** 209

   Oral Histories Description: Audiocassettes of interviews done from 1971 to present. Transcriptions are available for most interviews.

Maps and Drawings: Yes   **Estimated Number of Maps and Drawings:** 30

   Description of Maps and Drawings: Local area and donation land claim and homestead maps

Genealogy Sources: Yes

   Genealogy Sources Description: Family files

Special Collections: Yes

Special Collections Description: Eleven large binders of copies of donation land claim and homestead records of Camas/Washougal area. Has a full index by township and settler name. Abstracts of Title are included.

Indexes: Computer listing of photographs on staff computer. Indexes to land records. Indexes to history records.

Review of Collections: Two Rivers Museum has a small but interesting collection. The area covered is the Camas/Washougal area, but there is some information on Clark County and Skamania County as well. The collection is divided into three distinct parts. The library contains the vertical files, which are well maintained. Also in the library there are some beautifully done compilations of local records. There has been a great deal of work put into the land records to compile copies of the records and index and cross-reference the entire set. This has resulted in a user-friendly system of searching the records. Also a compilation of school records has also been started in the same manner. The photograph collection is also in good shape, with the photos being listed and searchable by the photo coordinator on a computer. The bulk of the manuscript materials have not had the care they deserve, however, and are stored in various nooks and crannies in the basement, without a plan or listing of what is housed there. There is an impressive collection of Crown Zellerbach Paper Mill records, some unprocessed, but totaling about 16 cubic ft. of materials.

Museum on Premises: Yes

Museum Hours: Tu–Sa 11–3

Cost of Entry to Museum: $3

Museum Is Handicapped Accessible: Yes

Description of Museum: Small traditional museum illustrating local area history. Has a personal collection of Indian baskets from various areas that belonged to Princess White Wing (died 1911).

Parking: Free on-street parallel parking, or park in the large Pendleton Mill Store lot across the street. Handicap parking near ramp.

Lunch: Variety of eateries within 6–8 blocks in downtown area. Chain restaurants and fast food in neighboring Camas.

Lodging: http://www.southwestwashington.com

Nearest Commercial Airport: Portland International (PDX) [15 miles]

Subjects

Historical Periods: Pre-1800; 1800–1865; 1865–1900; 1900–1940; 1940–present

Eras: Civil War; Indian Wars; Spanish American War; World War I; WPA; CCC; World War II

Natural Resources: Water; Dams; Fishing; Hunting; Logging

Mining: Gold; Silver; Copper; Coal; Tunnel Mining; Gravel; Granite

Transportation: Railroads; Stagecoach/Freight; Ships and Shipping; Ferries; Aviation

Agriculture: Dairy; Ranching/Livestock; Vegetable/Truck Crops; Grains; Orchards; Dry Land Farming

Business: Banking; Retail; Legal/Medical Services; Hotels/Restaurants; Entertainment/Theaters

Manufacturing: Grist/Flour Mills; Creamery; Woolen/Fabric Mills; Technology/Computers; Sawmills; Wood Products

Government: City; County; State; Federal

Organizations: Schools; Charities; Nonreligious Organizations; Civic and Fraternal; Women's; Business; Children's; Labor and Union

Ethnic Groups: Native American; Latin American; African; Pacific Islander; Japanese; Chinese; Danish; Dutch; English; Finnish; French; German; Irish; Italian; Norwegian; Russian; Scottish; Spanish; Swedish

Religious Sites and Organizations: Protestant; Catholic; LDS (Mormon)

Date of Reviewer's Visit: 11/7/2003

Profile Updated by Institution: 11/15/2004

WATERVILLE

Name: Douglas County Museum   **County:** Douglas

Mailing Address: Box 63

   City: Waterville   **State:** WA   **Postal Code:** 98858-0063

Street Address: 124 W. Walnut

Institution Email: None

Telephone Number: (509) 745-8435

Contact Name: Lori Ludeman

Institution Type: Local Museum

Affiliation: Douglas County Historical Society

Web site URL: None

Hours: Tu–Su 11–5, late May–mid-Oct

Staff in Archives: 3p summer only

Archives Are Handicapped Accessible: Yes

Cost for Researcher—In-house: Donation

Cost for Researcher—Remote: Donation

Review of Facilities: The Douglas County Museum is located in the city park, on Highway 2, one block from the downtown area. The museum building is not overly large but feels spacious. The research collections are stored in various parts of the main floor of the museum. There is a large wooden (jury) table in a room to the right of the entrance. A genealogy area is in the corner of a room, to the left of the main entrance. This contains some books of local and regional interest and genealogy materials. Other collections are in various cabinets and cubbyholes throughout the front area. A staff-only closet has file cabinets with photographs, history books, scrapbooks, and a map file. The vertical files are located at the staff service desk in the lobby area. There is a collection of family history boards depicting the history through text and photos of nearly 70 local families.

Vertical Files: Yes   **Vertical Files in Cubic Feet:** 6

   Vertical File Description and Subjects: Vertical files divided by families, towns, and general subject files

Manuscripts: Yes   **Manuscripts Volume in Cubic Feet:** 25

   Manuscript Types: Land records, scrapbooks

   Manuscript Subjects: Scrapbooks on various aspects of Douglas County history, including local organizations and families

Photographs: Yes   **Number of Photographs:** 500

   Storage of Photographs: Photographs are stored in file cabinets by broad subject areas. Some photo collections are stored in scrapbooks.

   Photograph Subjects: Douglas County life and people

   Photograph Reproductions Are Available: Yes

   Photographic Prints: Yes

Books: Yes   **Number of Books in Collection:** 150

   Description of Books: Local history, professional collection, scattered annuals, genealogy

Newspapers: Yes

   Newspapers in Paper Format: Yes

   Papers and Dates: Douglas County papers, 1886 to the present

   Newspapers on Microfilm: No

   Microfilm and Dates: Washington State University has microfilm

Oral Histories: Yes   **Oral Histories Number:** 6

   Oral Histories Description: Interviews of local area residents from 1980s

Maps and Drawings: Yes   **Estimated Number of Maps and Drawings:** 12

   Description of Maps and Drawings: County roads and land ownership or habitation. Two bound books, sections and townships with land owners in 1915

and mid 30s, location of all early schools in county, Indian trails, maps of early surveys

Genealogy Sources: Yes

    Genealogy Sources Description: Obituary files, family files, cemetery records

Special Collections: No

Indexes: No

Review of Collections: The Douglas County collections are smaller than anticipated for a county of its size. The collection is housed in various parts of the building and so lacks a certain amount of cohesion. Their collection of scrapbooks is probably the area in which they have spent the most effort. They have made reproductions of the pages of many of their old scrapbooks and put them in new binders, thus maintaining the integrity of the scrapbooks without having further deterioration. The subject focus is on Douglas County, and it is important to note that the bulk of the collection and history ends before World War II.

Museum on Premises: Yes

    Museum Hours: Tu–Su 11–5, late May–mid-Oct

    Cost of Entry to Museum: Donation

    Museum Is Handicapped Accessible: Yes

    Description of Museum: Local area history museum

Parking: Free paved parking lot adjacent

Lunch: Local restaurants within short walk or drive

Lodging: http://www.wenatcheevalley.org

Nearest Commercial Airport: Pangborn Memorial (East Wenatchee) (EAT) [30 miles]

Subjects

    Historical Periods: 1865–1900; 1900–1940

    Eras: World War I; CCC World War II

    Natural Resources: Dams; Irrigation

    Transportation: Railroads; Stagecoach/Freight; Aviation

    Agriculture: Ranching/Livestock; Grains; Orchards; Dry Land Farming

    Business: Banking; Retail

    Organizations: Schools; Civic and Fraternal; Women's; Children's

    Ethnic Groups: Native American; German; Norwegian; Spanish

    Religious Sites and Organizations: Protestant; Catholic

Date of Reviewer's Visit: 6/30/2004

Profile Updated by Institution: 11/15/2004

WENATCHEE

Name: Wenatchee Valley Museum—Archival Library   **County:** Chelan

Mailing Address: 127 S. Mission

   City: Wenatchee   **State:** WA   **Postal Code:** 98801-3039

Street Address: 127 S. Mission

Institution Email: None

Telephone Number: (509) 664-3340   **Fax Number:** (509) 664-3356

Contact Name: Mark Behler, Curator

Contact Email: m.behler@wenatcheevalleymuseum.com

Institution Type: Regional Museum

Web site URL: http://www.wenatcheevalleymuseum.com/

Hours: Tu, W, and F 10–12 and 1–4

Staff in Archives: 1f

Archives Are Handicapped Accessible: No

Review of Facilities: The Wenatchee Valley Museum and Cultural Center (formerly known as the North Central Washington Museum) is an alliance of historical agencies, art museum, genealogical society, historic preservation agency, historic site, and history museum. The Archival Library of the Wenatchee Valley Museum is located in the museum annex, a separate building next door to the main museum in downtown Wenatchee. The annex contains both the Archival Library and a genealogical library run by the Wenatchee Area Genealogical Society. These two facilities are separately staffed and are open different hours. This institution was not visited recently but the reviewer has researched in this collection in the past.

Vertical Files: Yes   **Vertical Files in Cubic Feet:** 12

   Vertical File Description and Subjects: Vertical file materials are arranged alphabetically by subject. Also have people/biography and town/place files.

Manuscripts: Yes   **Manuscripts Volume in Cubic Feet:** 450

   Manuscript Types: Business records, organizational records, school records, personal papers, family papers, scrapbooks, diaries

   Manuscript Subjects: Wenatchee history, Chelan County, central Washington

Photographs: Yes   **Number of Photographs:** 8,000

   Storage of Photographs: The photographic images are available to researchers through a computer database in the research room. Original photographs are stored in boxes in a storage room nearby.

   Photograph Subjects: North central Washington communities; geography; fruit industry; railroad (Great Northern); mid-Columbia steam boating; Native Americans; aviation (Pangborn/Herndon first trans-Pacific flight); hydroelectric

Photograph Reproductions Are Available: Yes

  Photographic Prints: Yes

Books: Yes   **Number of Books in Collection:** 2,500

  Description of Books: Regional history, local history, annuals (Wenatchee High School), city directories, telephone books

Newspapers: No

Oral Histories: Yes

  Oral Histories Description: Oral history interviews done of local area residents from 1970 to 1990. Some have been transcribed.

Maps and Drawings: No

Genealogy Sources: No

Special Collections: No

Indexes: Indexing to the collection is available on a staff computer.

  Manuscript Finding Aids: Finding aids to the manuscript collections are available on a staff computer.

Review of Collections: The Wenatchee Valley Museum collects the historical documents and photographs from the communities and people of north central Washington. The fruit industry is a strong topic of materials relating to the importance of the industry in the region. Railroading, particularly the Great Northern Railway, steam boating on the mid-Columbia, and hydroelectric power are also strong topics in the collection. The collection also focuses on the individual communities of the area. A moderate-sized collection but good research potential on central Washington topics.

Museum on Premises: Yes

  Museum Hours: Tu–Sa 10–4

  Cost of Entry to Museum: $3

  Description of Museum: The museum has four floors of exhibits showcasing the history, geology, and arts of the region. Permanent collections include one on the history of the apple and its influence in the region.

Parking: 2-hr. on-street parallel parking or pay lots nearby

Lunch: Short distance to a variety of restaurants

Lodging: http://www.wenatcheevalley.org

Nearest Commercial Airport: Pangborn Memorial (East Wenatchee) (EAT) [6 miles]

Subjects

  Historical Periods: 1865–1900; 1900–1940; 1940–present

  Eras: World War I; CCC; World War II

  Natural Resources: Water; Dams; Irrigation; Logging

Transportation: Railroads

Agriculture: Orchards

Manufacturing: Sawmills

Organizations: Nonreligious Organizations; Civic and Fraternal; Women's

Ethnic Groups: Native American

Religious Sites and Organizations: Protestant; Catholic

Date of Reviewer's Visit: Not visited

Profile Updated by Institution: 11/29/2004

WILBUR

Name: Big Bend Historical Society, Inc.   **County:** Lincoln

Mailing Address: PO Box 523

  City: Wilbur   **State:** WA   **Postal Code:** 99185-0000

Street Address: 505 NW Cole St.

Institution Email: None

Telephone Number: (509) 647-5863

Contact Name: Lois McMillan; Virginia Pipe, or Jo Roberton

Institution Type: Local Museum

Affiliation: City of Wilbur

Web site URL: None

Hours: M–Sa 2–4, June–Aug; appt on request

Staff in Archives: 12v

Archives Are Handicapped Accessible: No

Access Description: Not accessible. Stairs on interior and exterior of building.

Review of Facilities: The Big Bend Historical Society is located in an old stone church building. The main entrance is up a flight of stairs. The research collections are not housed in one room of the building but spread out over many. The main door leads into the photograph room, where a majority of the photos in the collection are on display in binders, on display boards, or covering about every square foot of wall. There is a microfilm room where the reader/printer shares space with a railroad display. The genealogy room houses most of the books in the collection, except for the annuals out in the hallway. The vault in the basement houses the remainder of the research collections. There is some workspace in the genealogy room, but it is limited.

Vertical Files: Yes   **Vertical Files in Cubic Feet:** 7

Vertical File Description and Subjects: Vertical files of general subjects and family files

Manuscripts: Yes   **Manuscripts Volume in Cubic Feet:** 15

Manuscript Types: Scrapbooks, business records; organizational records

Manuscript Subjects: Local stores, hotels, Eastern Star, granges, local pageants, festivals

Photographs: Yes

Number of Photographs: 1,500

Storage of Photographs: Photographs are on display on walls in the photo room and throughout the museum. These are mostly originals and some copies. Some photos are in scrapbooks and photo albums. Each is numbered and indexed in a card file.

Photograph Subjects: Local and regional history and people

Photograph Reproductions Are Available: Yes

  Photographic Prints: Yes

Books: Yes   **Number of Books in Collection:** 200

Description of Books: Local history, professional collection, old books, annuals from three towns

Newspapers: Yes

Newspapers in Paper Format: Yes

Papers and Dates: Bound newspapers of local papers

Newspapers on Microfilm: Yes

Microfilm and Dates: *Wilbur Registers,* 1889–present; Almira paper, 1913–1971, and Creston paper, 1901–1941

Oral Histories: Yes   **Oral Histories Number:** 50

Oral Histories Description: Variety of interviews of local area residents. Interviews from 1960s to present. No transcriptions.

Maps and Drawings: No

Genealogy Sources: Yes

Genealogy Sources Description: Family files

Special Collections: No

Indexes: No

Review of Collections: The research collections are in various states of usability. The photograph collection is difficult to use, if the researcher needs a specific subject. Most of the collections are not listed or indexed, so access to them is by luck and by knowledge of the volunteer assisting. Despite that, there are some interesting research items. Significant areas include some of the ledgers from local stores, hotels, and other businesses. There is also a fair amount of information on the granges. Though not large, the collection is interesting nonetheless.

Museum on Premises: Yes

    Museum Hours: M–Sa 2–4, June–August

    Cost of Entry to Museum: Donation

    Museum Is Handicapped Accessible: No

    Description of Museum: Museum in old church displaying the history of the Big Bend country in a variety of museum styles. Several very creative display techniques. Overall fun and a little quirky.

Parking: Off-street diagonal paved and gravel parking

Lunch: Several local cafes and drive-ins within walking or driving distance

Lodging: http://www.grandcouleedam.org   ;   http://www.visitspokane.com (Spokane, 1-hr. drive)

Nearest Commercial Airport: Spokane International (GEG) [60 miles]

Subjects

    Historical Periods: Pre-1800; 1800–1865; 1865–1900; 1900–1940; 1940–present

    Natural Resources: Irrigation

    Transportation: Railroads; Ferries

    Agriculture: Ranching/Livestock; Grains; Orchards; Dry Land Farming

    Business: Retail; Legal/Medical Services; Hotels/Restaurants; Entertainment/Theaters

    Government: County; State

    Ethnic Groups: Native American; Chinese; Danish; English; German; Irish; Scottish

    Religious Sites and Organizations: Protestant; Catholic

Date of Reviewer's Visit: 6/29/2004

Profile Updated by Institution: 11/19/2004

YAKIMA

✹✹✹✹

Name: Yakima Valley Museum   **County:** Yakima

Mailing Address: 2105 Tieton Dr.

    City: Yakima   **State:** WA   **Postal Code:** 98902-3766

Street Address: 2105 Tieton Dr.

Institution Email: info@yakimavalleymuseum.org

Telephone Number: (509) 248-0747   **Fax Number:** (509) 453-4890

Contact Name: Michael Siebol, Curator of Collections

Institution Type: Regional Museum

Web site URL: http://yakimavalleymuseum.org; http://www.wolfenet.com/~museum

Hours: Tu–F 11–5; M 8–5, Tu–F, 8–11, and Sa 8–5 by appt.

Staff in Archives: 1f 10v

Archives Are Handicapped Accessible: Yes

Cost for Researcher—Remote: Donations

Review of Facilities: The Sundquist Research Library is located on the main floor of the Yakima Valley Museum. The research room is long and narrow and consists of three small worktables and some bookcases. There are also the card catalog indexes and a computer station that will eventually supersede the paper card files. A large adjacent room (staff-only) houses about half of the research materials. There are numerous file cabinets with vertical file materials, compact shelving with the large book collections and some manuscript materials, cabinets of photographs, and shelves of bound newspapers. Additional storage on the lower level houses the remainder of the manuscript collection.

Vertical Files: Yes   **Vertical Files in Cubic Feet:** 78

> **Vertical File Description and Subjects:** Twelve file cabinets are filled with general and specific subject files on Yakima Valley history, biographical information and small manuscript and ephemeral materials

Manuscripts: Yes   **Manuscripts Volume in Cubic Feet:** 1,100

> **Manuscript Types:** All manuscript types
>
> **Manuscript Subjects:** Justice William O. Douglas papers, Yakima Valley Transportation Company records, Paddock & Hollinbery architectural records, 4,000 local fruit labels, Yakima Sheep Company records, Mabton Bank records, Clearwater Mining records, school records (several districts), personal and local history subjects, pamphlets, scrapbooks, and ephemera

Photographs: Yes   **Number of Photographs:** 7,600

> **Storage of Photographs:** Many of the photographs are available through the Web site Yakima Memory (see "Online Sources" below for URL). Original photographs are stored in file cabinets in plastic sleeves and arranged by subject.
>
> **Photograph Subjects:** Yakima Valley subjects, agriculture, William O. Douglas collection
>
> **Photograph Reproductions Are Available:** Yes
>
> > **Photographic Prints:** Yes   **Digital Prints:** Yes
> >
> > **Digital Images on CD or Electronically:** Yes

Books: Yes   **Number of Books in Collection:** 6,600

Description of Books: Local and regional history, professional collection, annuals, city directories, old books. Collection is cataloged in Dewey decimal system and listed in a card catalog by author, title, and subject.

Newspapers: Yes

Newspapers in Paper Format: Yes

Papers and Dates: Yakima newspapers in bound volumes, 1889 to 1954

Oral Histories: Yes   **Oral Histories Number:** 245

Oral Histories Description: Local area residents' interviews; about 40 percent have transcriptions. Many interviews done in the late 1980s.

Maps and Drawings: Yes   **Estimated Number of Maps and Drawings:** 1,700

Description of Maps and Drawings: 200 maps of the Yakima Valley; 1,500 architectural drawings of homes and buildings in area, Sanborn and Kroll maps

Genealogy Sources: Yes

Genealogy Sources Description: Large biographical clipping file and family histories

Special Collections: Yes

Special Collections Description: William O Douglas papers, including correspondence, books, photographs, slides, taped speeches, and other ephemera related to the career of the Yakima native and Supreme Court justice.

Indexes: There are several card indexes that are migrating to a local computer system. The photographs can be searched online (see below). Other indexes, including the detailed Local History Index (indexing the manuscript, scrapbook, and ephemera collections), the book catalogs, and complete photograph index are being entered in a Filemaker Pro system.

Online Sources: Yakima Memory, http://www.yakimamemory.org, is a digitization project done jointly with the Yakima Valley Museum and Yakima Valley Regional Library. 9,000 images are available through the internet.

Review of Collections: The collections of the Yakima Valley Museum are large and represent well the geographic area. Subjects cover all aspects of life and history of the Valley. Business records represent many diverse companies and industries. Organizational records include fraternal, religious, social, and political groups. Some of the largest collections are fully processed, while others are in limbo. The photograph collection is available through the Web site. Other indexes are searchable in the research room. The collections are heavily used by researchers.

Museum on Premises: Yes

Museum Hours: Tu–Su 11–5

Cost of Entry to Museum: $3

Museum Is Handicapped Accessible: Yes

Description of Museum: Yakima Valley Museum is a large, modern, and very well executed museum. Special displays include carriages and horse-drawn conveyances, Native American history, agriculture, and a children's history area.

Parking: Free parking lot adjacent to the museum

Lunch: Delightful soda fountain with soup and sandwiches, as a living history exhibit/cafe.

Lodging: http://www.yakima.org

Nearest Commercial Airport: Yakima Air Terminal/McAllister Field (YKM) [2 miles]

Subjects

Historical Periods: 1865–1900; 1900–1940; 1940–present

Natural Resources: Irrigation; Logging

Transportation: Railroads; Stagecoach/Freight

Agriculture: Ranching/Livestock; Vegetable/Truck Crops; Grains; Orchards; Vineyard; Dry Land Farming

Business: Retail; Legal/Medical Services; Hotels/Restaurants; Entertainment/Theaters

Manufacturing: Sawmills

Government: City; County

Organizations: Schools; Colleges/Universities; Hospitals/Medical Facilities; Charities; Nonreligious Organizations

Ethnic Groups: Native American; Latin American; Japanese

Religious Sites and Organizations: Protestant; Catholic

Date of Reviewer's Visit: 3/25/2004

Profile Updated by Institution: 11/24/2004

✤✤✤

Name: Yakima Valley Regional Library **County:** Yakima

Mailing Address: 102 N. Third St.

City: Yakima **State:** WA **Postal Code:** 98901-2705

Street Address: 102 N. Third St.

Institution Email: None

Telephone Number: (509) 452-8541 **Fax Number:** (509) 575-2093

Contact Name: Diane Tufts **Contact Email:** dtufts@yvrl.org

Institution Type: Public Library

Affiliation: Library District

Web site URL: http://www.yvrls.lib.wa.us

Hours: M–W 9–9, Th–F 9–6, Sa 10–6, Su 12–4

Staff in Archives: 1f

Archives Are Handicapped Accessible: Yes

Review of Facilities: The special collections at the Yakima Valley Regional Library are available in the downtown Yakima Library through the reference desk. The local history vertical file materials, microfilmed newspapers, some reference books, and indexes to the collections are available on the main floor. Large work areas, computer search terminals, and corresponding materials are also on the main floor. The Relander Collection is housed in a-staff only area in a locked room in the basement of the library. After selecting materials out of the index and guide to the Relander Collection, the materials are brought upstairs to be used under librarian supervision.

Vertical Files: Yes   **Vertical Files in Cubic Feet:** 36

  Vertical File Description and Subjects: Subject arranged clipping files of local newspaper articles

Manuscripts: Yes   **Manuscripts Volume in Cubic Feet:** 100

  Manuscript Types: Business records, family papers, personal papers

  Manuscript Subjects: Irrigation, Yakama and Wanapum Indians, agriculture, mining, Yakima City, missionary work, railroads

Photographs: Yes   **Number of Photographs:** 2,000

  Storage of Photographs: Photos available through Web site (see below). Originals stored in fire-safe file cabinets with plastic sleeves. Negatives in file boxes.

  Photograph Subjects: Yakima Valley area subjects

  Photograph Reproductions Are Available: Yes

    Photographic Prints: Yes   **Digital Prints:** Yes

    Digital Images on CD or Electronically: Yes

Books: Yes   **Number of Books in Collection:** 4,000

  Description of Books: 4,000 Relander Collection books, local and regional history, city directories

Newspapers: Yes

  Newspapers on Microfilm: Yes

  Microfilm and Dates: Yakima newspapers, 1889–present; index from 1975 to present.

Oral Histories: No

Maps and Drawings: Yes   **Estimated Number of Maps and Drawings:** 15

  Description of Maps and Drawings: Yakima City and County

Genealogy Sources: No

Special Collections: Yes

> **Special Collections Description:** Relander Collection: Personal papers and collections of Click Relander, including Northwest history books, photographs, manuscripts (100-plus cu. ft.) focusing on the Wanapum and Yakama Indian cultures and Yakima Valley history

Indexes: *Relander Collection Guide*

> **Published Guides:** *Relander Collection Guide*

> **Online Sources:** Yakima Memory, http://www.yakimamemory.org, is a digitization project done jointly with the Yakima Valley Museum and Yakima Valley Regional Library. 9,000 images are available through the internet.

Review of Collections: The collections of the Yakima library are divided into several main parts. The photograph collection is rather small for the community size, but the nearby Yakima Valley Museum has the bulk of those collections, as well as most of the manuscripts from the area. The Relander Collection is the most notable item in this institution. A life's collection of Click Relander, it emphasizes the collector's interests, providing thereby a legacy of historical information.

Museum on Premises: No

Parking: On-street free parallel (or diagonal) 2-hr. parking or pay lots

Lunch: Full variety of restaurants within driving distance

Lodging: http://www.yakima.org

Nearest Commercial Airport: Yakima Air Terminal/McAllister Field (YKM) [5 miles]

Subjects

> **Historical Periods:** 1800–1865; 1865–1900; 1900–1940; 1940–present

> **Eras:** Fur Trade; Civil War; Indian Wars; Spanish American War; World War I; WPA; CCC; World War II

> **Natural Resources:** Water; Dams; Irrigation; Fishing; Hunting; Logging

> **Mining:** Gold; Silver; Copper; Coal; Placer Mining; Surface Mining; Tunnel Mining; Petroleum

> **Transportation:** Railroads; Stagecoach/Freight; Ships and Shipping; Aviation

> **Agriculture:** Dairy; Ranching/Livestock; Vegetable/Truck Crops; Grains; Orchards; Vineyard; Dry Land Farming

> **Business:** Banking; Retail; Legal/Medical Services; Hotels/Restaurants; Entertainment/Theaters

> **Manufacturing:** Cannery; Brewery; Grist/Flour Mills; Creamery; Brick Making; Sawmills; Wood Products

> **Government:** City; County; State; Federal

Organizations: Schools; Colleges/Universities; Hospitals/Medical Facilities; Charities; Nonreligious Organizations; Civic and Fraternal; Women's; Business; Children's; Labor and Union

Ethnic Groups: Native American; Latin American; African; Japanese; Filipino; Basque; Dutch; English; French; Italian; Norwegian; Spanish; Swedish

Religious Sites and Organizations: Protestant; Catholic; LDS (Mormon); Buddhist

Date of Reviewer's Visit: 3/25/2004

Profile Updated by Institution: 11/22/2004

7

Digital Sources of Pacific Northwest History

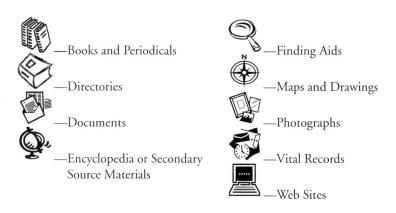

—Books and Periodicals

—Directories

—Documents

—Encyclopedia or Secondary
Source Materials

—Finding Aids

—Maps and Drawings

—Photographs

—Vital Records

—Web Sites

PACIFIC NORTHWEST HISTORY SOURCES

General Regional Sources

AAAHRP—Association for African American Historical Research and Preservation

This organizational Web site provides access to genealogical and historical information on African Americans in the Pacific Northwest. Currently, they have a list of Washington State obituaries from 1850 to present and hope to add additional states. Arrival lists for African American in the Pacific Northwest are also tracked for the nineteenth century.

http://www.aaahrp.org/
Source: AAAHRP

Center for Columbia River History

The center is a regional partnership of historical and cultural institutions to promote the study of Columbia River Basin history. Projects include a Columbia Communities project, which contains virtual exhibits on selected communities; an oral history project; curriculum projects, and social history events.

http://www.ccrh.org/

Source: Center for Columbia River History

Columbia River Basin Ethnic History Archives

This project is a collaboration of WSU-Vancouver along with WSU-Pullman, and the state historical societies of Washington, Oregon, and Idaho. The focus is on the diverse populations of the region that have been under-represented. Currently they have materials on German, African, Jewish, Basque, Italian, Mexican, Chinese, Japanese, and Russian Americans. The section on Native Americans links to other resources. The collection includes text, photographs, oral histories, ephemera, and artifacts. These are original scanned documents and photographs of original objects.

http://www.vancouver.wsu.edu/crbeha/home.htm

Source: Washington State University, State Historical Societies

Northwest Digital Archives

The Northwest Digital Archive encompasses Washington, Oregon, Idaho, and Montana. Fifteen major repositories in the four states are anchoring this database of finding aids of significant collections of regional interest. The project hopes to expand to additional institutions. The beginning phase of the project is for finding aids only and is fully searchable.

http://nwda.wsulibs.wsu.edu/

Source: Northwest Digital Archives

Northwest History Database

The Wallis and Marilyn Kimble Northwest History Database contains scanned images from 20,000 newspaper clippings from Spokane, Portland, and Seattle newspapers from the early twentieth century. Begun as a WPA project, the undertaking has been expanded to encompass far more than the original paper file. It also includes such primary sources as government reports, maps, and legal documents dealing with the settlement of the Pacific Northwest. There is an online index to the collection.

http://content.wsulibs.wsu.edu/pncc/pncc.htm
Source: Washington State University

Pacific Northwest History

This site provides a listing of Web sites on Pacific Northwest History, some of which contain original documents, photographs, books, or online exhibits. Also provides links to selected national sites.

http://www.lib.washington.edu/subject/history/tm/pnw.html
Source: Theresa Mudrock, University of Washington

Regional African American Research and the Availability of Primary Sources

This Web site connects to various resources and online collections dealing with African American research, particularly on Pacific Northwest people and topics. Links to institutions, associations, collections, and statistics.

http://lib.washington.edu/mcnews/afroamerican_primarysources/
Source: University of Washington

Tacoma Public Library—Northwest Room

This online collection has a number of significant sources. The Photography Archives is keyword searchable and has over 40,000 images. The Pierce County Building Index and Tacoma Obituary Index provide keyword searchable information based on the paper indexes at the library. The Ships and Shipping Database indexes 13,000 ships and provides full-text descriptions for 1,000 ships built on the Pacific coast or having a connection to the Pacific Northwest.

http://www.tpl.lib.wa.us/v2/nwroom/nwroom.htm
Source: Tacoma Public Library

University of Washington Libraries Digital Collections

The digital collections at University of Washington represent a cross-section of the best materials housed at that facility. These collections encompass most areas of Pacific Northwest history. Eighty percent of the collection's digitized content are photographs or other images. Significant text collections include the Washington State Pioneer Life Database and the American Indians of the Pacific Northwest. Each collection can be searched separately, or one can search across all collections. This is the largest digital archive in the Pacific Northwest and one of the largest in the United States.

http://content.lib.washington.edu/
Source: University of Washington

Washington State University Libraries Digital Collection

The digital collections at Washington State University consist of photographs, text, oral histories, and films. Significant topics are African-American Oral Histories, Frank S. Matsura images, and the Northwest History Database (see entry).

http://www.wsulibs.wsu.edu/holland/masc/imagedatabases.htm
Source: Washington State University

Works Projects Administration in the Pacific Northwest: A Guide to Archival Records in the Pacific Northwest

A listing of facilities that have records of projects from the Work Projects Administration (WPA) or its predecessor agencies—the Civil Works Administration, the Federal Relief Administration, and the Works Progress Administration—in the Pacific Northwest. Repositories in Idaho, Washington, and Oregon are listed as well as the National Archives and Records Administration (NARA) Pacific Alaska Region (Seattle, WA)

http://www.ci.seattle.wa.us/cityarchives/Resources/WPA2_files/WPAGuide.htm

Source: Valoise Armstrong, National Archives and Records Administration, Pacific Alaska Region.

Idaho Online History Sources

Idaho—History Genealogy

Although this Idaho version of "A Place Called Oregon" (profiled below) has far less content than the Oregon counterpart, it still remains important because of the scarcity of online resources on Idaho history. Secondary history, transcribed documents, and a postcard collection make up the bulk of the resources available.

http://gesswhoto.com/idaho

Source: R. Gess Smith at Gesswhoto.com

Idaho State Historical Society—Reference Series

Site provides links to a variety of sources on Idaho history, including primary and secondary source materials, information, and historical statistics. Files are in Microsoft Word.

http://www.idahohistory.net/reference_series.html

Source: Idaho State Historical Society

Kate and Sue McBeth: Missionary Teachers to the Nez Perce

Online collection of documents and images dealing with the McBeth sisters' life and experiences with the Nez Perce people during the late nineteenth century. Letters, journals, diaries, and government documents are transcribed and provided in full-text form. The site provides multiple points of view but does not interpret the materials.

http://www.lib.uidaho.edu/mcbeth/

Source: University of Idaho Library

Oregon Online History Sources

A Place Called Oregon

A guide to the people, places, and events that shaped Oregon from the earliest recorded history. Primarily consisting of transcribed history, secondary sources, and links to statewide subject resources, this database is an interesting collection of information and links. This site also contains some photograph and postcard collections.

http://gesswhoto.com/

Source: R. Gess Smith at Gesswhoto.com

Oregon Historical County Records Guide

The Records Guide is a comprehensive inventory of selected records for all 36 Oregon counties. Lists records held by the counties and the Oregon State Archives, but also other repositories in the state. Includes brief histories of each county in Oregon.

http://arcweb.sos.state.or.us/county/cphome.html

Source: Oregon State Archives

Oregon Historic Photograph Collections

Access to thousands of photographs of Oregon history from the collections at Salem Public Library and some other state collections. Dating from the mid-1800s, these photos are digitized and searchable. Focuses mainly on the Salem area but includes other Oregon scenes as well.

http://photos.salemhistory.org
Source: Salem Public Library, Salem History Project

Oregon History Project

The history project includes a narrative overview of Oregon's history, a Historical Records section, and a Learning Center (K–12 resources). The historical records include digitized copies of ephemera, maps, documents, periodicals, and some photographs.

http://www.ohs.org/education/oregonhistory/
Source: Oregon Historical Society

Southern Oregon Digital Archives

Divided into two distinct collections, the Southern Oregon Digital Archives is digitizing collections of federal, state, and county publications. The first collection is on the Southern Oregon Bioregion. The second is the First Nations/Tribal collection. The First Nations collection has documents, books, and articles related to the tribes of southwestern Oregon, but many of the documents would apply to other Pacific Northwest First Nations as well.

http://soda.sou.edu
Source: Southern Oregon University

Washington Online History Sources

Association of King County Historical Organizations (AKCHO)

This site consists of a directory of 180-plus historical organizations in King County, with contact information, Web sites, and other information. Entries vary in length from one line to one-half page.

http://www.akcho.org

Source: Association of King County Historical Organizations

Early Washington Maps: A Digital Collection

A collection of nearly 1,000 maps of early settlement drawn from the collections of Washington State University and University of Washington. Encompassing 300 years, the collection includes maps from sea and land exploration through town building and beyond. Maps are searchable by keyword. This is a significant collection for the entire Pacific Northwest and beyond.

http://www.wsulibs.wsu.edu/holland/masc/xmaps.html

Source: Washington State University

History Link.org

An online encyclopedia of Seattle, King County, and Washington State history, this site provides secondary source material and photographs; each entry has a comprehensive bibliography.

http://www.historylink.org/

Source: History Ink

King County Snapshots

A photographic archive on King County and the greater Seattle metropolitan area. Photos are from the collections of 12 different historical organizations in the county. The collection of over 12,000 images can be browsed or searched by keyword as a group or through the individual organization providing the photographs.

http://content.lib.washington.edu/imls/kcsnapshots/
Source: King Country Snapshots

Seattle Municipal Archives

Extensive online resources including finding aids of municipal record groups, special collections, and 48,000 photograph images of the city of Seattle
http://www.cityofseattle.net/CityArchives/
Source: City of Seattle: Office of the City Clerk Legislative Department

Washington History

Washington History is a joint effort by two state government agencies. The site provides access to state archival records, search engines, and the state library catalog. In addition it provides digitized historical maps, a large group of classic books on Washington history, and a copy of the Washington State constitution. Some secondary source histories are also available.

http://www.secstate.wa.gov/history/
Source: Washington State Library and State Archives

Washington Place Names Database

This database written, by Gary Fuller Reese at Tacoma Public Library over a 25- year period, lists Washington place names with notes to sources of information and usage.
http://search.tpl.lib.wa.us/wanames/placabout.asp
Source: Tacoma Public Library

Washington State Digital Archives

Web site of the Washington State Digital Archives collections. Digitized state, county, and local government records from throughout the state of Washington. (See also listing in chapter 6.)
http://www.digitalarchives.wa.gov
Source: Washington State Archives

Washington State Digital Collections

This source provides a listing of Web sites with links to digital collections from throughout Washington State. Many but not all of the collections listed are profiled in this chapter.
http://digitalwa.statelib.wa.gov/wscollections.htm
Source: Washington State Library

Yakima Memory

The Yakima Memory Project digitized 9,000 photographs to provide access via the internet. The photographs are primarily from the collections of Yakima Valley Museum and Yakima Valley Regional Library. Photographs are mainly of Yakima Valley, with transportation, irrigation and agriculture being strong subjects.

http://www.yakimamemory.org
Source: Yakima Valley Regional Library and Yakima Valley Museum

NATIONAL SOURCES OF REGIONAL INTEREST

American Local History Network

The American Local History Network is a starting point resource to finding independent historical and genealogical Web sites on the internet. Pages can be located either regionally (by state, county, and city) or topically. It is an access point for historical documents as well as genealogy resources.

http://www.alhn.org
Source: American Local History Network

American Memory: Historical Collections for the National Digital Library

American Memory provides a gateway to primary source materials available online relating to the history and culture of the United States. The site provides links and search capabilities to collections of photographs, documents, ephemera, oral history transcripts, sheet music, maps, audio and video files of music, advertising, and history subjects. Collections from throughout the United States are listed and searchable through this site.

http://memory.loc.gov/
Source: Library of Congress

Early Canadiana Online

Early Canadiana Online is a digital library of documents and printed material from the era of early exploration to the present. Focusing on the history of

Canada, it includes documents pertaining to the exploration, settlement, and development of the Pacific Northwest on the United States side as well. Hudson's Bay, Native American studies, Jesuit relations, and early governmental publications are some applicable areas.

http://www.canadiana.org/eco/english/

Source: Canadian Institute for Historical Microreproductions

Geostat Center: Historical Census Browser

Geostat Historical Census Browser provides access to the raw statistical data contained in the U.S. census from the years 1790 to 1960. The site allows you to select the type of data by national, state, or county level. As it is a statistical analysis site, it may be confusing at first, but the results are well worth it. Note: this does not contain census data on individuals, but on population and housing units. Some statistics are available only for certain years, as the methodology of the census has changed through the centuries.

http://fisher.lib.virginia.edu/collections/stats/histcensus/

Source: University of Virginia Library

Historical Map and Chart Project

The Historical Map and Chart Projects makes available 20,000 maps and charts from the late 1700s to the present day. The collection includes nautical maps, aeronautical maps, topographical maps, and some old cartographic maps of the Pacific coast and the Pacific Northwest region. Searchable by keyword, type, year, and region.

http://historicals.ncd.noaa.gov/historicals/histmap.asp

Source: Office of Coast Survey—National Oceanic and Atmospheric Association

History of the American West

Photoswest.org is a collection of 95,000 digitized photographs from the collection of the Denver Public Library Western History Department. Most photos were taken between 1860 and 1950. Although most are centered in Colorado and neighboring western states, there are some images of Pacific Northwest locales, including many William Henry Jackson photographs. There are photos of most of the locomotives that ran on rail lines through the Pacific Northwest, and portraits (1890–1900) of many Pacific Northwest tribes as well. A limited collection of 30,000 photos is available from the American Memory site, which has a better search feature, at http://lcweb2. loc.gov/ammem/award97/codhtml/hawphome.html

http://www.photoswest.org
Source: Denver Public Library

Japanese American Relocation Digital Archives

This digital archive features 10,000 photographs, drawings, and pieces of artwork and 20,000 pages of text documentation. This includes oral histories, letters, government documents, publications, and reports. In addition, finding aids of materials on the subject are included. Site allows searching or browsing of content.

http://jarda.cdlib.org/
Source: Regents of the University of California

Library of Western Fur Trade Historical Source Documents: Diaries, Narratives, and Letters of the Mountain Men

This digital archive includes accounts of the Rocky Mountain fur trade during the first half of the nineteenth century. Most are primary or secondary historical sources. Diaries, reminiscences, journals, and personal narratives make up the bulk of the collection. Note: these have been transcribed rather than being facsimiles.

http://roxen.xmission.com/~drudy/amm.html
Source: Volunteers of American Mountain Men

Making of America—Cornell

Making of America—Cornell is a collaborative project to make available primary source documents electronically. This version has access to 267 monograph volumes and 22 journal titles (100,000 articles) with imprints between 1840–1900. All issues and volumes are searchable full-text and available in scanned image format. Sister site to the Michigan Making of America project (see entry), but each has digitized different materials.

> http://moa.cit.cornell.edu/moa
> Source: Cornell University

Making of America—Michigan

A digital library of primary source materials, Making of America at Michigan, like its Cornell counterpart (see entry), provides full-text access to 8,500 books and 50,000 journal articles with nineteenth-century imprints. The full text of the articles and books are keyword searchable, including the back matter/ads of the old journals. The project focuses on social history and includes numerous sources with references to the Pacific Northwest region.

> http://www.hti.umich.edu/m/moagrp/
> Source: University of Michigan

National Park Service: Links to the Past

The National Park Service Cultural Resources Web site provides links to a wealth of content from across the country. Much of the content in is the form of online historical exhibits; but it also links to a sizeable online collection of books and documents on National Park Service history and issues. Links to resources are provided for historical sites within the National Park Service and other federal agencies.

> http://www.cr.nps.gov
> Source: National Park Service

National Register of Historic Places

Online access is provided to the National Register of Historic Places database. The site also provides access to educational resources for teaching about the importance of place. Although not primary sources, the National Register Travel Itineraries includes three collections from the Pacific Northwest: Seattle; Ashland, Oregon; and the Lewis and Clark Expedition.

http://www.cr.nps.gov/places.htm
Source: National Register of Historic Places—National Park Service

National Archives and Records Administration (NARA) Access to Archival Databases

National Archives and Records Administration Access to Archival Documents provides online access to electronic records (50 million) created by 20 federal agencies on a wide range of topics. Read the "Getting Started" section to understand the arrangement and complexities of this database.

http://www.archives.gov/aad
Source: National Archives and Records Administration

Online Books Page

This archive connects users to online full-text books in facsimile or transcribed versions available freely through the internet. There are a number of books of the early history of the Pacific Northwest, including writings of exploration, settlement and history.

http://digital.library.upenn.edu/books/
Source: University of Pennsylvania

Repositories of Primary Sources

Listing of 5,500 Web sites worldwide that have primary sources available
for the historical scholar.
   http://www.uidaho.edu/special-collections/Other.Repositories.html
   Source: Terry Abraham, University of Idaho

US Gen Web Archives

The US Gen Web Archives provides transcriptions of public domain
documents. The database is a cooperative effort of volunteers nationwide
who coordinate the digitalization of census records, marriage documents, and
other public documents.
   http://www.rootsweb.com/~usgenweb/
   Source: RootsWeb

Water in the West: Western Waters Digital Library

The Western Waters Digital Library is a collection of resources from various research institutions on a myriad of issues dealing with water in the West.
The database allows you to search all collections or browse by the subjects.
   http://www.westernwater.org
   Source: Greater Western Library Alliance

GENEALOGY SOURCES OF PACIFIC NORTHWEST HISTORY

Family Search

The Family Search database provides links to the online genealogical
resources of the Mormon Church. The ancestor search function can link to

seven separate databases that provide vital records, including the U.S. census and the U.S. Social Security Death Index. Search features allow queries by name, state, and record type. Web sites of other resources for genealogical research are also listed. The Family History Centers that are located worldwide can be identified by a regional or local search from this Web site.

http://www.familysearch.org

Source: The Church of Jesus Christ of Latter-Day Saints

Kindred Trails

Genealogy site with access to county information worldwide but headquartered in Idaho. Links to census, vital statistics, and local and regional sources.

http://www.kindredtrails.com

Source: Kindred Trails Worldwide Genealogy Resources

RootsWeb.com

RootsWeb is a free online directory of genealogical sources. Sponsored by the commercial genealogical publisher Ancestory.com, this free site provides links to thousands of resources collected by volunteer contributors throughout the country. Because much of the information is gathered and posted by volunteers at a local level there is a great discrepancy between what types of records are available for what counties. Most sources are transcriptions (subject to error) or original documents of vital records.

http://www.rootsweb.com

Source: RootsWeb sponsored by Ancestory.com

Western States Historical Marriage Record Index

Marriage records from throughout the western United States have been extracted from individual county records and incorporated into a database that is available online. Marriages from the pre-1900 period are included, and some regions have marriages listed up through the 1930s and beyond. The database is searchable by bride or groom and by county.

http://abish.byui.edu/specialCollections/fhc/gbsearch.htm

Source: Brigham Young University–Idaho

Statewide Genealogical Societies in the Pacific Northwest

Idaho Genealogical Society http://www.lili.org/idahogenealogy

Genealogical Forum of Oregon http://www.gfo.org

Oregon Genealogical Society http://www.rootsweb.com/~orlncogs/ogsinfo.htm

Washington State Genealogical Society http://www.rootsweb.com/~wasgs

8

⌐⌐

Travel Sources

VISITING THE PACIFIC NORTHWEST

Traveling through the three-state region can be an uplifting experience. The geographic diversity of the area is unparallel in the country. From the Rocky Mountains to the beaches of Oregon, from the arid plains to the rain forest, the scenery is magnificent. Many of the institutions profiled in this book are in small and/or remote locations in the three states.

There are many tourism sites that can aid a traveler in planning a journey to the area. I am including only a few of those here. The state tourism sites listed are all sponsored by their respective states. There are dozens of other sites sponsored by chambers of commerce and visitors' information bureaus that provide good information on the many options for lodging, activities, and scenic areas. Some of these sites are listed under the lodging category on specific institutional entries.

State departments of transportation sites have also been listed. Each state provides slightly different information on their transportation sites. Road reports, weather, and basic information are available on all three state sites. Locating road construction and traffic delays before the trip can be extremely helpful and time-saving.

Airports with commercial flights are listed on the specific profiles, but many small towns have private airports nearby. The site provided is primarily one for pilots, providing information on lengths of runway and so on, but it also offers the availability to search for specific airports and provides links to their individual homepages. Airport Web sites will often list the names of the carriers that provide commercial flights into their facilities.

As with everything in this book, this chapter provides a starting place and not an end to research. As you travel to engage in your historical research, take the time to enjoy the beauty and grandeur of Idaho, Oregon, and Washington. The history of the Pacific Northwest was shaped as much by its geography as it was by the individuals who lived and died here.

STATE TOURISM SITES

Visit Idaho

State-sponsored tourism site that provides access to local attractions, lodging, links to local area tourism boards, and chambers of commerce.
http://www.visitid.org/
Source: Idaho Department of Commerce

Travel Oregon

State-sponsored tourism site that provides access to local attractions, lodging, links to local area tourism boards, and chambers of commerce.
http://www.traveloregon.com/
Source: Oregon State Tourism Commerce

Experience Washington

State-sponsored tourism site that provides access to local attractions, lodging, links to local area tourism boards, and chambers of commerce.
http://www.experiencewashington.com/
Source: Washington State Tourism

STATE TRANSPORTATION SITES

Idaho Transportation Department

http://www.itd.idaho.gov
Road reports, travel conditions, road cameras, and weather.

Trip Check—Oregon Department of Transportation

http://tripcheck.com
Road reports, travel conditions, mileage calculator, road cameras, and bus, rail, and local transportation links.

Travel Information—Washington State Department of Transportation

http://www.wsdot.wa.gov/traffic

Maps, road reports, weather, travel conditions, road cameras, ferries, and air, rail, and local transportation links.

AIR TRAVEL

Air Nav.com—Airport Information

http://www.airnav.com/airports/

Web site designed for pilots with airport information useful for locating airports. Enter city and state or airport code to identify specific airports. Near the bottom of each page are links to local airport information.

Glossary

Archives—A collection of documents or records on organizations or individuals that is retained permanently for future use or research. Archives are often defined as the official documents of an organization. An archive may also be the location in which those documents are housed.

Circulating—Items in a library that are available for check-out or removal from the institution by an individual or other library. Most institutions will not circulate items from their archives or special collections.

Interlibrary Loan (ILL)—Interlibrary Loan is the process of borrowing items from one library for the use of patrons at another library.

Manuscripts—Originally referring to handwritten documents, manuscripts have come to be defined in broader terms. Currently the term *manuscript* may refer to any type or group of original primary source materials that were collected and maintained for historical purposes. The collection may be in an original or artificial arrangement. In formal archives the term *manuscripts* may be used to differentiate the materials from the official archival records of the institution.

Primary Sources—Primary sources consist of original materials that demonstrate the past or present. Materials must be contemporary to the time being examined. Such sources may include diaries, correspondence, minutes, official documents, speeches, newspapers, photographs, drawings, and maps. Primary sources may be published or edited but give the words or impressions of an individual or group as they were experiencing them firsthand.

Secondary Sources—Secondary sources provide a level of synthesis and analysis to the primary source information. Most published sources are secondary in nature.

Universal Borrowing—Universal borrowing is a system allowing patrons of one library to borrow books directly from another library in a consortium.

WorldCat—WorldCat is a large electronic database that lists the holdings of thousands of libraries in the United States and elsewhere in the world. This database is only available through libraries but provides the best source to locate published materials. Many institutions are also using WorldCat to list their manuscript and special collections holdings.

Appendix

**COMMON RULES AND PROCEDURES OF
ARCHIVES AND SPECIAL COLLECTIONS**

1. All researchers must make an appointment.
2. All researchers are required to register and provide picture identification.
3. Personal items including briefcases, backpacks, purses, coats, and laptop cases must be surrendered before entering the research room. Lockers may or may not be provided.
4. Food, drink, or tobacco products are never allowed in the research room. (Water bottles are banned as well.)
5. Only paper and pencil (sometimes laptops without cases) may be taken into the research room.
6. Use finding aids, indexes, or online resources to identify the materials desired for research.
7. Request research items from staff; they will bring them to you.
8. Paper and pencil only allowed on the table with research materials.
9. Only one box of research materials may be used at a time.
10. Preserve the original order of all materials within the folders as well as boxes.
11. Great care should be exercised when handling materials. Do not lean on them, write on them, fold them, or attach adhesive notes or stickers to them.
12. Cotton gloves should be worn when handling photographs and fragile materials.
13. Materials do not leave the room for any reason.
14. Materials may be photocopied by special permission only and may have to be photocopied by staff only. Limitations may be placed on photocopying items because of copyright, condition of materials, or restrictions placed by donors.

15. Institutions may reserve the right to refuse access to archival materials to anyone who does not abide by the rules.
16. Researchers agree to give proper credit to the institution for use of any materials in their subsequent publications or presentations. Citation should be done in accordance to the institution's standard.

Digital Sources Alphabetical List

Alphabetical by Name of Institution

County Index

Collection Material Dates

Institutions reported having primary source materials covering the selected time periods.

Pre-1800

Anacortes Museum, 227
Big Bend Historical Society, 445
Center for Pacific Northwest Studies, 239
Council Valley Museum, 38
Eastside Heritage Center, 234
Harney County Historical Museum, 131
Lewis and Clark College, 179
Lewis and Clark National Historical Park, 113
Linn County Historical Museum, 128
Lopez Island Historical Museum, 316
Makah Cultural and Research Center, 323
Maryhill Museum of Art, 290
Multnomah County Library,181
National Archives and Records Admin., 377
Nez Perce National Historic Park, 93
Orcas Island Historical Society, 271
Oregon Historical Society, 186
Pacific County Historical Society, 406
Polk County Museum, 198
Puget Sound Maritime Historical Society, 385
Seaside Museum, 213
Sherman County Historical Society, 164
Spokane Public Library, 416
Two Rivers Heritage Museum, 437
University of Washington, 394
Washington County Historical Society, 193
Washington State Archives, Central, 279
Washington State University, 350

1800-1865

Anacortes Museum, 227
Bandon's Coquille River Museum, 121
Benton County Historical Museum, 176
Big Bend Historical Society, 445
Bonner County Historical Society, 91
Brownsville Community Library, 126
Cassia County Historical Society, 31
Center for Pacific Northwest Studies, 239
Clark County Historical Museum, 430
Clearwater Historical Museum, 75
Columbia Gorge Discovery Center, 215
Community Library Association, 61
Council Valley Museum, 38
Cowlitz County Historical Museum, 300
Deschutes County Historical Society, 124
Douglas County Museum (OR), 201
East Benton County Historical Society, 303
Eastern Washington University, 256
Eastside Heritage Center, 234
Ellensburg Public Library, 276
Heritage Museum / Clatsop County, 110
Hood River County Historical Museum, 150
Idaho State Historical Society, 28
Island County Historical Society, 266
Jefferson County Historical Society, 347
Jerome County Historical Society, 54
Keller Heritage Center, 263
Kitsap County Historical Society, 246
Klickitat County Historical Society, 288
Lacey Museum, 311
Lane County Historical Museum, 142
Lemhi County Historical Society, 89

1865–1900

1940–present

Ethnicity and Religion Index

Ethnic Groups and Religions are listed under general terms and were provided by the institutions. It is understood that the ethnic backgrounds may include both first and successive generations from a specific group. Types of materials and volume of material varies greatly by facility.

African: Bannock County Historical Museum, 78; Black Heritage Society of Washington State, 365; Eastern Washington University, 256; Ellensburg Public Library, 276; Franklin County Historical Museum, 338; Greater Kent Historical Society, 306; Heritage Museum / Clatsop County, 110; Kitsap County Historical Society, 246; Northwest Museum of Arts and Culture, 414; Oregon Historical Society, 186; Pacific County Historical Society, 406; Polk County Museum, 198; Renton Historical Museum, 355; Southern Oregon Historical Society, 161; Spokane Public Library, 416; Two Rivers Heritage Museum, 437; Washington State Historical Society, 427; Yakima Valley Regional Library, 450

Armenian: Washington County Historical Society, 193

Austrian: Community Library Association, 61

Basque: Basque Museum and Cultural Center, 21; Community Library Association, 61; Deschutes County Historical Society, 124; Harney County Historical Museum, 131; Idaho State Historical Society, 28; Malheur

Historical Project, 221; Oregon Historical Society, 186; Oregon State University Archives, 136; South Bannock County Historical Center, 63; Twin Falls Public Library, 96; Valley County Museum, 43; Yakima Valley Regional Library, 450

Belgian: Baker County Public Library, 116; Jesuit Oregon Province Archives, 411

Buddhist: Greater Kent Historical Society, 306; Heritage Museum / Clatsop County, 110; Kam Wah Chung & Co. Museum, 152; Oregon Historical Society, 186; Spokane Public Library, 416; White River Valley Museum, 230; Wing Luke Asian Museum, 399; Yakima Valley Regional Library, 450

Catholic: Anacortes Museum, 227; Bainbridge Island Historical Museum, 232; Baker County Public Library, 116; Bannock County Historical Museum, 78; Basque Museum and Cultural Center, 21; Big Bend Historical Society, 445; Black Heritage Society of Washington State, 365; Columbia Gorge Discovery Center, 215; Community Library Association, 61; Cowlitz County Historical Museum, 300; Deschutes County Historical Society, 124; Douglas County Museum (OR), 201; Douglas County Museum (WA), 440; East Benton County Historical Society, 303; Ellensburg Public Library, 276; Franklin County Historical Museum, 338; Garfield County Historical Association, 340; Greater Kent Historical Society, 306; Harney County

Subject Index

Subject headings were provided by the institution. Type and volume of materials on the subject will vary by facility. This is a starting point only. Some institutions provided detailed subjects while others stayed very general.

Agriculture: Anacortes Museum, 227; Bainbridge Island Historical Museum, 232; Bannock County Historical Museum, 78; Benton County Historical Museum, 176; Big Bend Historical Society, 445; Bonner County Historical Society, 91; Cassia County Historical Society, 31; Clark County Historical Museum, 430; Council Valley Museum, 38; Crook County Historical Society, 196; Deschutes County Historical Society, 124; Douglas County Museum (OR), 201; Douglas County Museum (WA), 440; East Benton County Historical Society, 303; Eastern Washington University, 256; Eastside Heritage Center, 234; Fort Walla Walla Museum, 432; Franklin County Historical Museum, 338; Garfield County Historical Association, 340; Gem County Historical Society, 45; Gig Harbor Peninsula Historical Society, 285; Gilman Town Hall Museum, 298; Grant County Historical Museum, 133; Greater Kent Historical Society, 306; Hagerman Valley Historical Society, 47; Harney County Historical Museum, 131; Heritage Museum / Clatsop County, 110; Heritage Station Museum, 172; Hood River County Historical Museum, 150; Idaho State Historical Society, 28; Idaho State University, 80; Ilo-Vollmer Historical Society, 41; Island County Historical Society, 266; Jerome County Historical Society, 54; Josephine County Historical Society, 147; Keller Heritage Center, 263; Kitsap County Historical Society, 246; Klamath County Museum, 157; Lacey Museum, 311; Lake Chelan Historical Society, 254; Lake Roosevelt Nat'l Recreation Area, 269; Lane County Historical Museum, 142; Latah County Historical Society, 70; Lemhi County Historical Society, 89; Linn County Historical Museum, 128; Lopez Island Historical Museum, 316; Lynden Pioneer Museum, 318; Malheur Historical Project, 221; Marion County Historical Society, 204; Minidoka County Historical Society, 86; Museum of Clallam County, 342; Museum of Idaho, 51; Museum of North Idaho, 34; Museum of Snohomish County History, 283; Museum of the Oregon Territory, 169; National Archives and Records Admin., 377; Nez Perce County Museum, 66; Nez Perce National Historic Park, 93; North Cascades National Park, 321; Okanogan County Historical Society, 328; Orcas Island Historical Society, 271; Oregon Coast History Center, 166; Oregon Historical Society, 186; Oregon Jewish Museum, 189; Oregon State Archives, 207; Oregon State University Archives, 136; Pacific County Historical Society, 406; Pend Oreille County Historical Society, 325; Polk County Museum, 198; Renton Historical Museum, 355; Ritzville Li-

About the Author

NANCY A. BUNKER is Associate Professor and Coordinator of Reference Services at the Whitworth College Library, Spokane, Washington.